A Little Parliament

A Little Parliament

The Virginia General Assembly in the Seventeenth Century

BY WARREN M. BILLINGS

The Library of Virginia, in partnership with
Jamestown 2007/Jamestown-Yorktown Foundation
Richmond • 2004

Library of Congress Catalog Card Number: 2003114675
Standard Book Number: 0-88490-202-1 casebound

Library of Virginia, Richmond, Virginia.
© 2004 by The Library of Virginia.
All rights reserved.
Printed in the United States of America.

This book is printed on acid-free paper meeting requirements of the
American Standard for Permanence of Paper for Printed Library Materials.

This book has been published in partnership with Jamestown 2007/Jamestown-Yorktown
Foundation, in commemoration of the 400th Anniversary of Jamestown, the first permanent
English settlement in the Americas.

Dedicated to the memory

of

George J. Dunlap (1917–1994)

&

N. Cleo Baker Dunlap (1919–2000)

The best in-laws

Contents

Preface

From boyhood I have always been fascinated by how things work. It was my late father who first molded my curiosity to purposeful ends. He taught me the use of fine tools, the ways of craftsmanship, and the skill to make or fix almost anything. We spent innumerable, happy hours together in his workshop, where I mastered the fashioning of sailing ship models, furniture, houses—even automobiles. My father was also my first instructor of history. Because he loved history, he always insisted on teaching me the origins of things we built, their importance, and the ways they changed or were changed by the people who depended on them. He continually directed me to his library, which he stocked with a huge, eclectic accumulation of books that ranged across an immense variety of subjects. Birthdays, Christmases, or special occasions were likewise incidents when he gave me books for my own, and they were invariably about Virginia and its history. We also toured the commonwealth and the East Coast to visit art galleries, museums, churches, houses, and public buildings, as well as historic sites so that I might observe firsthand examples of particular things that he treasured. It was his hope that such experiences would beckon me to his path and a career in architecture, but I answered a different call. My choice disappointed him somewhat, though he gracefully accepted what he could not alter, and at length he took considerable pleasure in seeing me well established as a historian. His delight increased when I asked him to illustrate my first book (*The Old Dominion in the Seventeenth Century: A Documentary History of Virginia, 1606–1689* [Chapel Hill, 1975]), a copy of which he never tired of showing visitors to his home.

Links between these formative experiences and this book are palpable. Part political history, part social history, part institutional history, and part legal history, the volume responds to a single, plain question. How did the General Assembly work throughout the seventeenth century?

My first systematic attempt at an answer began in response to a telephone call I received one October afternoon in 1993. Joseph Gutierrez, Director of Education for the Jamestown-Yorktown Foundation, asked if I might be willing to open a lecture series that he was organizing to commemorate the three-hundred-seventy-fifth anniversary of the beginning of the General Assembly and the arrival of the first African Virginians. I agreed to speak about how the assembly started and took shape after 1619, and in due season I made my presentation to a receptive audience on a cold January evening at the Yorktown Victory Center. In the ensuing question time, someone asked me where he might find a copy of my book. Puzzled, I responded, "What book?" Came the retort, "Why, the one on which you based your talk." There was no such book, I admitted, though I hastened to add that it would be a good one for someone to write. The idea stuck with me, and the following pages are the result.

Acknowledgments

Along the way in crafting this book, I benefited from the assistance of the following friends, all of whom were uncommonly kind and unfailingly helpful to me. My colleagues at the University of New Orleans, as they always have, favored me with flexible teaching schedules, research aid, and time to write. I am most grateful for that support. Daphne S. Gentry assisted in tracking down various sources and other information. Mark F. Fernandez offered encouragement and useful advice at an early stage in the composition. Sara B. Bearss, Carol Dunlap Billings, Emory G. Evans, Mark F. Fernandez, Kevin R. Hardwick, Spotswood Hunnicut Jones, David W. Jordan, William M. Kelso, John T. Kneebone, John Ruston Pagan, William S. Price, Jr., Emily J. Salmon, Judith Kelleher Schafer, Brent Tarter, Thad W. Tate, Sandra Gioia Treadway, and Camille Wells read the manuscript in whole or in part. Their comments made this a better book. From the Library of Virginia, I also thank Gregg D. Kimball, director of Publications and Educational Services, John G. Deal, Donald W. Gunter, Marianne E. Julienne, and Patricia A. Kloke for their assistance with preparing my manuscript for publication, as well as Amy Winegardner, the Library's graphic designer, for creating the dust jacket. From the Office of Graphic Communications, I am grateful to Paris Ashton, director, and Calvin Smith for the design of *A Little Parliament*. I am also indebted to Jamestown 2007/Jamestown-Yorktown Foundation for their financial support of this publication.

I must also recognize a substantial intellectual debt to Jon Kukla, a friend of long-standing. His published writings, our correspondence, and our many conversations all significantly informed my understanding of early Virginia politics on the whole and the General Assembly in particular.

Those to whom I dedicate this volume received me into their family for a son-in-law, giving me friendship and love. My thanks to them is beyond measure. I am saddened that neither lived to receive this token of my affection for them.

A Note on Dates and Documentation

Dates in this book accord with the Julian calendar, a mode of reckoning the English used until 1752, when they replaced it with one designed by Pope Gregory XIII. Continental Europeans had adopted the Gregorian calendar two centuries earlier, and when they did, the change necessitated advancing dates by ten days. Thus 5 October 1582 became 15 October. To confuse matters a bit more, seventeenth-century Britons also began their year on 25 March, though they customarily wrote both years, that is 1 January 1600/01, in the interval between 1 January and 24 March. That habit is followed throughout this book, too.

Direct quotations from manuscript sources are rendered according to the prescripts of modern documentary editing. Archaic usages are regularized only to the extent that modern spelling is imposed on proper names. Antique abbreviations or symbols are expanded, and sentences begin with capital letters and end in appropriate terminal punctuation. Citations to sixteenth-, seventeenth-, and eighteenth-century legal treatises, statutory abridgments, law dictionaries, and procedural manuals, unless noted otherwise, are to the editions in my personal library.

Foreword

Cast and recast many times over, the tale of the General Assembly of Virginia in the seventeenth century has a familiar ring to it.[1] Consequently, the challenge for someone wishing to explain the assembly's workings anew is twofold: find novel twists for an old yarn, and write around massive holes in the evidence. Governor Sir William Berkeley deserves the credit for showing me a way. I discovered it among his extant papers while editing them for publication.

In a letter written in 1670, the English Privy Council sought the governor's advice about informing King Charles II "on the care and management of … his Plantations," and to that end, the councillors sent Berkeley specific interrogatories about conditions in Virginia. One of the questions demanded "what Councills, Assemblies, and Courts of Judicature are within your Government, and of what nature and kind?"[2] The query was well directed because few Virginians of that day knew better answers than the governor, and fewer still were those among his contemporaries who had done as much as had he to shape the General Assembly. Nevertheless, Berkeley forbore a detailed response, preferring instead to provide this terse reply. "There is," he averred, "a Governor and Sixteene Counsellors, who have from his Sacred Majesty a Commission of oyer and Terminer, who judge and determine all Causes that are above 15 li. Sterling. For what is under there are particular Courts in every County which are Twenty in number. Every yeare at least," he concluded, "the Assembly is Called, before whome Lye Appeales, And This Assembly is Composed of Two Burgesses out of every County. These lay the necessary taxes, as the necessity of the Warre with the Indians, or other exigencies require."[3] Seven years after penning these lines, Berkeley left Virginia, disgraced by his mishandling of Bacon's Rebellion. His departure abruptly shifted Anglo-Virginia politics, and that volte-face forever affected the way the colonial General Assembly did business.

Filling in the spaces that Berkeley left unfilled and detailing the changes that followed in the wake of his leave-taking afforded a means of analyzing the structure of the assembly and the nature of its business in a way that is consistent with the extant documentary record.[4] Such a detailing also dictated the design of this book as well as its argument, both of which may be summarized as follows.

Over the course of the seventeenth century the members of the General Assembly strove to create laws and political institutions appropriate for Virginia. That propensity was natural enough, because the assemblymen had settled in an uncivilized place.

A Little Parliament

For their colony to become orderly it needed recognizable rules and structures to govern those who inhabited it. Seeking models, they rummaged their cultural heritage for examples to emulate.

Ideas of governance—that is, who ruled, by what warrant and means—ran to the deepest core of English political thought. Britons accepted government as a condition of society because, in the words of Sir Thomas Elyot, "where governours be not, the people shall falle into ruyne."[5] Fundamentally, they believed that "governours," whether monarchs or Parliaments, manor lords or local magistrates, churchmen or parents, were instituted of God to cherish good subjects and to chastise bad ones. They likewise acknowledged the necessity of rules and institutions that differentiated the powerful from the powerless and that existed to maintain a peaceable kingdom. Michael Dalton, author of a widely regarded treatise, *The Countrey Justice, Containing the Practice of the Justices of the Peace Out of their Sessions*, first published in 1618, captured those presumptions this way. "The Common Laws of this Realm," he wrote, "even from their beginning, have continued a special care for the Conservation of the Peace of this Land." Contests over who ultimately made the rules and who kept the "Amity, Confidence, and Quiet that is between men" led king and literate commoner alike to plumb the nature of English polity throughout the seventeenth century.[6]

Those understandings arrived in Virginia with the intellectual baggage and other belongings the colonists brought with them. They animated the members who sat in every General Assembly after 1619 but were by no means the sole sources of inspiration or even the preponderant ones. An ocean between Jamestown and London, the desire to find private gain in a place largely innocent of European restraints, the need for ways to raise revenue, to improve courts, to delineate parishes, to establish property rights, to settle debts, to correct miscreants, to define matters of race and gender, or to defend the colony—all these, too, afforded an ample atmosphere for experimenting with the forms of governance and the uses of power. Even so, the actual beginning of the General Assembly was an unintended consequence of colonizing Virginia. None of the investors who financed the settlement foresaw that such an entity, and all that it might imply, would arise on the banks of the James River. Moreover, inexperience and inattention kept Crown and Parliament from framing consistent administrative policies for fifty years after the Virginia Company of London went bankrupt. Left unfettered and unadvised, the colonists, sometimes eagerly, sometimes not, did largely as they chose.

Foreword

In a sense, then, the General Assembly merely happened. Hewing to no grand design, a succession of governors, councillors, and burgesses schooled themselves in the arts and mysteries of ruling others. Bit by bit, they modified the assembly and augmented its prerogatives as contingencies arose and solutions of the moment translated into fixed customs and presumed rights. Qualities of happenstance gave particular patterns of growth to the workings of the General Assembly over the eight decades between its first and last sessions of the seventeenth century. First came a time of beginnings, which lasted until 1642. Provisions for an assembly of colonists were among the steps the managers of the Virginia Company employed to save their colonial venture. The salvage plan proved overly ambitious, the company failed, and in 1624 Virginia passed under royal control. Dissolution of the Virginia Company jeopardized the General Assembly because the Crown neglected to stipulate that it continue. The mistake threw the assembly into constitutional limbo; successive governors, however, regularly summoned it throughout the 1620s and 1630s. Routine meetings abetted the belief that certain colonial men were entitled to share in the government of Virginia and strengthened the view that the General Assembly was an appropriate mechanism through which to govern. Regular sessions, in turn, added to the assembly's definition and reinforced the members' control of their proceedings as well as their legislative reach. Persistence eventually bore fruit when King Charles I confirmed the assembly in 1639 and gave orders for it to sit annually thereafter.

These accidents spurred a second cycle of growth, which extended from 1642 to 1677. Foremost among the advancements was the creation of a House of Burgesses that sat separately from the governor and the Council of State. That modification was one in a series that Sir William Berkeley promoted during his long tenure as he made common cause with the colony's emerging great planter elite. Those changes led toward bicameralism and decentralized political authority. The English Civil War, the overthrow of the monarchy, and the subsequent Interregnum merely enhanced those proclivities, and by the time of the Restoration in 1660, the General Assembly had become a little parliament, replete with prerogatives that often exceeded those of the Parliament at Westminster.

The General Assembly was far from omnipotent or omnicompetent. It lacked the imprimatur of royal sanction because the enlargement escaped notice in London before 1676. Its prerogatives therefore rested on constitutional footings no surer than customary colonial usage or gubernatorial sufferance. Crown reaction to Bacon's Rebellion proved that those were thin pillars on which to stand.

A Little Parliament

Nathaniel Bacon not only ruined Berkeley, but he also compelled the later Stuart monarchs to intervene in the General Assembly's affairs as never before. Royal interference took the form of direct assaults on what Crown bureaucrats saw as the assembly's independence, and practices deemed inconsistent with English parliamentary habits came under attack. As a result, the full body lost "antient rights of Assemblies" such as the privilege of annual sessions and the liberty to sit as a court of last resort, and the burgesses surrendered their free choice of their clerk. Consequently, the assembly passed through a time of readjustment and redefinition that ushered in an era of dominance by the Council of State. That permutation shifted the focus of lawmaking and politics away from local issues toward provincial and imperial concerns, especially as generational changes altered membership in both House and Council and as the colony's ruling elite matured. The ultimate outcome of these adjustments was a General Assembly shorn of power whose members wrestled for the remainder of the colonial era to regain the degrees of autonomy their predecessors had once enjoyed.

To know the membership is to understand the governors, councillors, burgesses, clerks, and Speakers who shaped and embellished the General Assembly. Typically, the chief executives sprang from the upper echelons of English society. Some put Virginia first, whereas others set the interests of empire ahead of those of the Old Dominion, and that attitude fostered an adversarial style of politics, especially during the concluding decades of the century. All influenced the evolution of the legislature in some fashion, though Sir William Berkeley, who stood center stage in Anglo-Virginia politics for the better part of three and a half decades, stamped the deepest impression on the assembly and the office of governor.

By contrast, the men who became councillors, burgesses, clerks, and Speakers arose from that much-studied stock of middling immigrants who streamed into Virginia in ever-increasing numbers after 1619. Some were of genteel origin, to be sure, though the predominant background was mercantile. On the whole, they were a rapacious lot at first who sought to exchange the intricate legalities of England for the opportunities to stalk personal gain in nearly untrammeled freedom. Their aggressiveness abated once they gained acceptance by those they presumed to lead, and they acquired the habits of a ruling establishment.

However much outlook or abilities may have differentiated individual assembly members one from another, a common attribute bound them all. Few, governors included, had ever sat in Parliament or held any local office or trained for the law before they left England for Virginia. So obvious is this characteristic that its significance is easily missed. Plainly stated, it meant that the General Assembly and colonial statutes were the creatures of novices. That trait raises fascinating questions. What did these neophytes know of law, politics, and government? How came they by their understanding? What qualities situated them to assume their role? What links, if any, connected their social origins to their making of the assembly?

Lack of political experience did not equate with political ignorance. To be an Englishman was to know that regulation of the realm proceeded from the monarch, Parliament, the courts, the church, the family, the law, the army, or any other mechanism that constrained Britons into society. Virginia lawmakers accepted that knowledge; it was as natural to them as breathing. Its application in a colonial setting required no more than a compulsion to act, and that was an impulse these particular novices keenly felt. How they bent their lay understanding of statecraft shows up in their perfection of the General Assembly. Legislative sessions provided regular forums for sorting out prerogatives, lines of authority, internal organization, procedural rules, and even where to assemble. Beyond that, sittings were for the main business of legislatures—making statute law.

From the start, the General Assembly enjoyed the power to "ordeine & enact such generall Lawes & orders for the behoof of the said Colony and the good government thereof as shall time to time appeare necessarie or requisite."[7] That authority increased, and by the end of the seventeenth century there were few facets of life in the Old Dominion over which members were reluctant to legislate. Thus, the accumulation of statutes down to 1700 is not only a testament to the re-creation and adaptation of English law in a Virginia setting, but it also is a reflection of the assemblymen's transit from novices to sophisticated lawmakers who had a firm awareness of power and the uses to which it might be put. Results of that appreciation, like chattel slavery, could be perversely clever variations whose malign effects lasted for centuries, whereas others wound distinctive cords into the fabric of American political culture that are hallowed to this day.

The foregoing assumptions stand opposite those I advanced in my previous writings on Virginia politics. When I crafted those studies, I argued for a more chaotic brand of politics than I depict here, and I took the position that the General Assembly remained an amorphous, undeveloped entity that did not become bicameral until the 1680s. My stance rested unquestioningly on the prevailing wisdom of Philip Alexander Bruce, Charles M. Andrews, Wesley Frank Craven, Richard Lee Morton, Bernard Bailyn, and Jack P. Greene, among others, as well my own lack of interest in the assembly, per se. That body intrigued me far less at the time than did the county courts, which were then at the center of my research.[8] Then too, my early work preceded the pioneering investigation by Jon Kukla, who convincingly demonstrated how during the 1640s bicameralism became an established feature of the assembly.[9] Findings of Chesapeake social historians refocused my thinking about the milieu in which colonial politicians flourished, especially as I delved deeper into the backgrounds of councillors, burgesses, and county officeholders who served between 1619 and the end of the century.[10] Exploring the origins of colonial law and the gubernatorial careers of Sir William Berkeley and Francis Howard, fifth baron Howard of Effingham, ushered me into the realm of legislative and provincial politics. Deepening knowledge led me to reject my earlier interpretation in favor of the one I set forth here.

Some readers will undoubtedly decry the lack of comparisons between the General Assembly and its companions in other English colonies. The omission was deliberate. Much as I regard comparative analysis as a useful tool, it was not particularly so in this instance. One might assume otherwise on first thought, given that Virginia and Maryland had much in common socially and economically. And yet nothing in the extant record revealed Virginia assemblymen as seeking inspiration from north of the Potomac or elsewhere other than England. Conversely, George Calvert, first baron Baltimore, who knew Virginia firsthand, did not look south when he molded the General Assembly of Maryland. Nor did Marylanders deliberately imitate their Virginia cousins as they gave shape and purpose to their legislature.[11] Others may wonder that I did not cast some portion of the volume as a meditation on how the General Assembly related to the rise of popular government in English North America. To have done so would have taken the book in a direction I did not wish it to go, and as much has been written on that account already, I concluded that I could add little except by way of implication. Besides, understanding the effects of personality on early Virginia politics and procedures in the assembly interested me more because that relationship has garnered less scrutiny heretofore. Hence the emphasis on Sir William Berkeley, Francis Howard, fifth baron Howard of Effingham, and whenever possible individual burgesses, councillors, Speakers, and clerks. Theirs are

Foreword

voices and actions that need to be heard clearly if one is to comprehend how the workings of their General Assembly fed into the traditions of American self-government. It is through their actions that the founding and growth of the assembly can best be understood. Often, theirs are the only records that have survived to allow us to trace their footsteps through history. The unfortunate loss of a large portion of the assembly's archives and working papers requires displacing the usual narrative of institutional history with an examination of how and why the leading actors on this stage of history molded their creation, even without planning to, into a little parliament.

A Little Parliament

PART I

Patterns of Growth

The other Counsell, more generall, to bee called by the Governor, and yeerly, of course, & no oftner but for very extreordinarie & important occasions, shall consist for the present of the said Counsell of State and of tow burgesses out of every towne, hunder [hundred] and other particuler plantation to bee respetially chosen by the inhabitants. Which Counsell shallbee called the Generall Assemblie.

—An Ordinance and Constitution for a
Council and Assembly in Virginia, 1621

Desperate to revive its failing colony, the Virginia Company of London completely revised the government of Virginia. Among its projected changes was a provision for a general assembly. When the orders to convene the first assembly went out in 1618, no one anticipated how it would grow from an administrative appendage into a representative legislature.

Chapter I

Beginnings

Ten years had passed since the Virginia Company of London sent its first expedition of settlers to America. Backer and adventurer alike held high hopes in 1606 of founding a prosperous settlement, but nothing about Jamestown went according to expectation. There were neither gold mines nor passages to the Indies nor even desirable staples on which to found a prospering commerce. Relations with the natives, troublesome from the first days, continued edgy. The expense of keeping the colony buoyant beggared the imagination. Death summoned colonists with appalling frequency. Survivors consumed more than they contributed, and no amount of prodding from London, not even the imposition of the stern discipline of martial law, made them flourish. Two reorganizations of the company, as well as proceeds from a lottery, failed to ensure solvency.

As Virginia approached its tenth anniversary, it still had life, but only just. Near collapse corroded energies and sapped confidence as it set investor against investor. No one considered quitting, though. Too much was at stake to give up. Demands for a thorough audit of company books prompted an inquiry that soon turned into a cranky debate over the future of the entire enterprise itself and how the colony might be rendered profitable. In the end, Sir Edwin Sandys replaced his rival, the embattled company treasurer, Sir Thomas Smith.

One of Smith's more persistent critics, Sandys had long contended for a top-to-bottom revamping of the colony. He imagined that the key to salvaging Virginia was a workforce producing a variety of commodities that had ready buyers in England. Making such produce depended on a manifest ingredient, colonists with agricultural skills. That sort of settler had always avoided Virginia in appreciable numbers because of a reluctance to live as company employees in a largely male outpost on the far side of the world. Sandys knew all that. The cure, as he saw it, lay in exchanging the martial plan of settlement that had been in use since 1607 for a scheme more attuned to traditional English social patterns.

As treasurer, Sandys embodied his proposed remedies in a series of papers, which the company promulgated in 1618. One, the so-called "Great Charter," restructured the colony. Private land tenure supplanted company ownership; anyone who paid his passage was entitled to fifty acres and an additional fifty for every other person he transported at his expense. Promises of political authority and generous tracts of real estate served to entice hardened settlers to become subsidiary developers of so-called particular plantations. Regulations that looked remarkably like English local law substituted for the hated *Lawes Divine, Morall and Martiall.* Four boroughs—the Corporations of James City, Charles City, Kicoughtan (later Elizabeth City), and Henrico—consolidated existing settlements in the James River basin. A second document directed to a governor-general and an overhauled council of state charged them with powers of overall administration. Another commission authorized the governor periodically to convene a general assembly with "free power to treat, consult & conclude … all emergent occasions concerning the pupliqe weale of the said Colony and evrie parte therof." In a word, the Great Charter and its companion papers empowered the settlers to bear a greater responsibility for decisions that affected them on a day-to-day basis or in emergencies. Thus was born the General Assembly of Virginia.[1]

Providing the colony with such a body in no way diminished the company because the assembly was an appendage of the company, and the company retained ultimate control. Its treasurer and council still guided routine operations, and the investors still met quarterly as a general court to set strategic directives, enact ordinances, and elect officers for company and colony alike.

Sandys cut his pattern for the Virginia assembly to fit the design of the company's corporate structure, not to resemble Parliament. He had no wish, contrary to myth, to see representative government transplanted to America. Instead, his rationale sprang from his twin desires to improve the management of a distant plantation and to avoid the missteps of the past. Neither he nor many other company officials or stockholders ever went to the New World. The greater part therefore knew nothing of Virginia from firsthand encounters, which made them only vaguely aware or even ignorant of its peculiarities and possibilities. Nevertheless, they collectively appointed leaders, gave orders, and issued instructions about how to run the colony, all of which the settlers were obliged to obey. Experience repeatedly revealed how directions that seemed prudent in London usually proved foolhardy when applied to the actual conditions in Virginia. Consequently, tensions between the desirable and the possible perpetuated a continual dissonance that hampered success. New charters in 1609 and 1612 had aimed at relieving the stresses by assigning more local control to a governor and an advisory council, both of whom took fewer orders from London. The late unhappy administration of Governor Samuel Argall (1617–1619), however, showed Sandys the folly of allowing one man too much power.[2] Adding an assembly—made up of governor, councillors, and colonists—diffused control without unduly sacrificing unified leadership. Putting more authority into the settlers' hands not only eased the strains of rule from afar, but it also contented the colonists by giving them greater say in the ordering of their affairs. Beyond that, the existence of an assembly could serve as a further inducement to attract settlers who balked at living under martial law.

To George Yeardley fell the assignment of putting Sandys's schemes into play. A onetime soldier in the Netherlands and a company investor, Yeardley first went to Virginia in 1609 with Sir Thomas Gates. He served there in various capacities, including a stint as deputy governor, before returning to England. Picked to succeed Argall in September 1618, he was confirmed by the company at a quarterly court on 18 November. Six days later, James I tapped him for a knight, "to grace him the more."[3] The freshly minted Sir George Yeardley then married Temperance Flowerdieu, whose cousin John Pory had just been appointed secretary of the colony, and the couple sailed for America early in the new year.[4] After a rough passage they landed safely at Jamestown in April. Sometime about 25 June 1619, Governor Yeardley issued writs to the "freemen and Tenants," ordering them "by pluralitie of voices to make ellection of two sufficient men" to meet with him and the Council of State as a "generall Assemblie." Yeardley, six councillors, and twenty-two burgesses gathered at Jamestown on 30 July 1619.[5]

After organizing itself, the General Assembly took up its principal business. The members proposed several amendments to the Great Charter; they legislated on such concerns as tobacco prices, servant contracts, and Indian affairs; and they petitioned the company for the right to accept or reject orders from London. They then adjudicated several criminal cases. Those had barely concluded before summer heat and sickness intervened, compelling Yeardley on 4 August to prorogue the assembly to the following March.

John Pory maintained a journal of the assembly's deliberations. Had he done no more than that, he would still command notice. His "reporte of the manner of proceeding in the General assembly" is the sole account of what happened, but, more important, he also shaped how the first assembly did its business.[6] Alone among his colleagues Pory brought experience of legislatures to the tasks at hand. Having sat in the House of Commons between 1605 and 1611, he possessed a practical understanding of legislative organization and procedures that he could teach others to use in the fledgling assembly. Indeed, to read his "reporte" closely is to gain an abiding appreciation for how his tailoring of parliamentary practices dictated the body's workings long after he had passed from the scene.[7]

"The most convenient place we could finde to sitt in," Pory wrote, "was the Quire of the churche." What happened next bears the first testimony to his influence. When all had congregated, Yeardley chose Pory as Speaker before naming John Twine clerk and Thomas Pierse sergeant-at-arms. Next, the Reverend Richard Bucke prayed, imploring divine guidance and sanctification for the deliberations that were about to occur. Prayers done, the burgesses withdrew to "the body of the Churche," where they each swore oaths of supremacy and allegiance to James I and stood by until their formal entry into the assembly.[8]

Each of these occurrences reflected parallels in contemporary parliamentary practice, albeit with noticeable differences. Swearing the oaths was common for members of Parliament, or anyone else who held a public trust, so administering them to the assemblymen marked no departure from custom. Bucke merely prayed, but at the opening of Parliament some "discreet and eloquent" divine preached a sermon. Parliament had not one but several clerks, plus a small legion of lesser officials. Yeardley chose Pory Speaker before the assembly had organized itself, which meant that the burgesses had nothing to do with the secretary's selection, and that was contrary to the example of the House of Commons. Moreover, it was customary for the Speaker to deliver an address wherein he begged the monarch to grant members the privileges of royal access, liberty of speech, and freedom from arrest for the duration of the sitting. Pory made no such speech. Furthermore, he sat in the Council of State, not among the burgesses, which also made his choice inconsistent with parliamentary norms.[9]

An explanation for these variations is plain enough. Nothing in the company's instructions for the assembly implied that it should become bicameral or that it should be patterned on Parliament. The intentional model was the general court of the company. Accordingly, Yeardley, his councillors, and the burgesses all met together as one. Hence, there was no need for someone to act the role of spokesman—Speaker—for the assembly in addressing the throne, which was a principal duty of the Speaker in Parliament. Nothing in Pory's journal indicates that he acted as the burgesses' advocate. Instead, it emphatically reveals how he spent his time doing secretarial and clerical tasks. He prepared the legislative agenda, organized Yeardley's paperwork, drafted bills, wrote orders, supervised minute-taking, and read acts aloud before they became law.[10]

For all of its insight into the assembly's work, the "reporte" does not indicate why Pory was styled Speaker. Perhaps it was a courtesy title that Yeardley and the others conferred out of respect for his knowledge of parliamentary affairs, or perhaps it was a rank Pory arrogated for himself. Whatever the reason, calling Pory Speaker fostered an impression that the General Assembly took life as a bicameral legislature modeled after Parliament—a mistake that has bewitched or misled several generations of Virginians and scholars alike.[11]

A second example of Pory's influence occurred during the reading of the names of the burgesses as each was admitted into the assembly. When Clerk Twine came to that of Captain John Ward, "Exception was taken" because he had "planted here in Virginia without any authority or commission from the Tresurer, Counsell and Company in Englande." Someone offered two pointed observations in the ensuing debate: Ward had long been a useful colonist who paid his own way; but, more tellingly, the election writ placed no "restrainte or exception" on the choice of burgesses. Those arguments persuaded the assembly to allow Ward and his lieutenant "into their society," providing the captain obtained the company's "commission lawfully to establishe & plant himselfe ... as the Chieffs of other plantations have done."[12]

Governor Yeardley then objected to the burgesses from Martin's Hundred, citing a clause in the patent of the proprietor, John Martin, that not only exempted Martin from uniform laws, "which the great charter saith, are to extende over the whole Colony," but also from any acts of assembly as well. The members pondered the objection and then called Martin in and tried to convince him to forswear his immunity. He declined, whereupon his burgesses were refused their seats. In the end, the assembly members not only denied Martin but also directed that the "Speaker in their names should ... Demaunde of the Treasurer, Counsell, and Company an exposition" of Martin's rights.[13]

No one in London anticipated the issues raised by Ward and Martin, and neither had Yeardley; consequently the assembly lacked written guidance on what it should do. Obviously, the session could not go forward until someone decided whether Ward or the Martin's Hundred burgesses were entitled to membership. Pory showed his colleagues a way to resolution. They could act as Parliament might and decide for themselves who was qualified to sit in their company. Lest it seem that the assembly appeared to overstep its authority, it covered itself by appealing to the company for clarification of the disputed credentials. In ruling as they did, the members laid down a precedent that later General Assemblies translated into an exclusive right, much as the Commons had done in the 1580s.[14]

The issue of qualifications settled, the assembly turned to its main purpose, legislating. How it proceeded reveals Pory's hand in directing the dispatch of business. He set the agenda. First, he "delivered in briefe ... the occasions of their meeting," as he laid out the assembly's prescribed duties. Second, he took up the Great Charter, which he read aloud to the whole company. Third, he separated the legislative work into four parts: perusing the Great Charter to determine which sections required modification, adopting particular company instructions as law, proposing new regulations, and preparing petitions to London. Two committees, consisting of eight burgesses each, examined the Great Charter with an eye toward suggesting revisions. (Who appointed the committees is unclear, though their use mirrored a practice that came into being during Pory's time in the House of Commons.) One other parliamentary habit Pory seems to have appropriated was the custom of giving each proposed act three readings before final passage.[15]

Scattering from the churchyard on 4 August, their work complete, Pory, Yeardley, the councillors, and the burgesses had reason to be pleased with what they had done. A mere five days' work had ushered in a new era of colonial government. Now they and their fellow colonists had a device with which they might define their interests and direct their affairs as never before. The assembly also strengthened popular regard for the company and its designs. With luck, the renewal of Virginia might actually come to pass.

For a time it seemed as though Sandys had drawn winning cards. Persistent recruitment of settlers, especially women, children, and families, expanded the population. Agricultural production increased. The General Assembly gained in favor with leading colonists as other familiar legal, social, and political usages were imported and began a gradual flowering in their new environment. Heartening as those signs were, they failed to generate the profits that could resuscitate the ailing company. Sandys and his allies refused to see opportunity in cultivating tobacco, which was hugely popular in the colony as a cash crop because of its ready demand in England. Instead, they continued to press settlers to develop a diversified economy based on silk, wine grapes, and other exotic staples. Their insistence provoked festering controversies that would not go away. Sandys remained a convenient target for his enemies, and not even his removal from the treasurer's seat quelled the sniping. The bickering eventually caused an annoyed James I to revoke the lottery, which cut off the company's single source of dependable capital.

Things got worse in the spring of 1622. The Indian leader Opechancanough launched a surprise attack on the settlements that killed about a third of the colonists within a matter of hours and plunged survivors and natives into a protracted conflict of attrition. The company suddenly had to prosecute a war amid all its other troubles. That exigency finally broke the will of the investors, who grew ever more quarrelsome. Sandys and his supporters again came under attack, and they were by no means impeccable. Their extravagant promotions plus the rapid influx of new settlers had sorely stressed a warring colony and very likely had encouraged the Indians to mount the assault. Lacking assistance from London, the colonists fumed at the company's inability to assist them in fighting their foe. Most destructive of all, none of Sandys's efforts resulted in the one thing he had promised most—profit—and the company lurched ever closer to bankruptcy. The uproar led the Crown to intervene in hopes of staving off disaster, but the intercession had no effect. James I elected a more radical measure, revocation of the company charter. To that end, he commanded Attorney General Sir Thomas Coventry to sue for recovery of the charter. Coventry filed a writ of quo warranto in the Court of King's Bench on 4 November 1623, which compelled the patentees to show cause why they should not surrender their rights to Virginia. The outcome was never in doubt. Within six months the court found for the king, the charter was vacated, and the Virginia Company of London was no more.

James I intended to put the colony under the management of a reorganized corporate entity that more directly answered to him. For advice about how to arrive at that goal he turned to a commission headed by Henry Montagu, viscount Mandeville, president of his Privy Council. Mandeville's work was cut short by the sudden death of the king on 27 March 1625. What to do with Virginia now became the province of the new monarch. Barely seven weeks into his reign, Charles I promulgated *A Proclamation for setling the Plantation of Virginia*, which made the colony a royal dominion.[16]

A Little Parliament

Declaring himself "bound by Our Regal office, to protect, maintaine, and support [Virginia], and are so resolved to doe, as any other part of Our Dominions," Charles set forth his plans for the colony's foreseeable future. The Virginia government would "immediately depend upon Our Selfe, and not be committed to any Company or Corporation, to whom it may be proper to trust matters of Trade and Commerce, but cannot bee fit or safe to communicate the ordering of State-affaires, be they of never so meane consequence." The king promised to honor company land grants and to maintain "at Our owne charge" all "publique Officers and Ministers ... as shall be fit and necessary for the defence of that Plantation." He then concluded by pronouncing some provisions regarding the burgeoning tobacco trade, saying, "We are resolved to take the same into Our owne hands."[17]

The proclamation was as remarkable for things it left undone as it was for things it did. Most notably, the king neglected to make any allowance for the continuance of the General Assembly. That oversight proceeded more from his ignorance than from any incipient animus toward representative government. Charles was fresh to his throne and his duties as sovereign. While a prince he had little involved himself in Virginia matters, so the concept of an assembly of obscure colonists in a faraway place as a useful instrument of colonial administration was quite lost on him as king. To the extent that he had had any opportunity for reflection, his inclination seemed to be that of his father's, meaning he would prefer a reconstituted company to run the colony. His thoughts surely drifted elsewhere as he signed the proclamation. England was at war with France and Spain, and he was about to marry the woman who would be his queen, Henrietta Maria, of France.[18]

As for the General Assembly, the fall of the Virginia Company had two immediate effects, and their repercussions gradually transformed the assembly from a corporate appendage into a miniature parliament. The company's reforms of 1618 composed a constitution of sorts for Virginia's governance, and they gave the assembly its right to existence. After 1625, the royal proclamation and the king's commission to his governors-general served as the constitutional basis of authority in the colony. The silence of those documents regarding the continuation of the assembly, while not necessarily abolishing it, certainly cast doubt on its legitimacy and future.

In creating the General Assembly, the company, for all of its many flaws, had hit on a useful mechanism of colonial administration. The assembly became the principal conduit through which the company funneled its executive directives. The connection afforded an effective means of exercising government from the center. As events proved, that part of Sandys's plans worked better than just about anything else. Dissolution destroyed the link, and in its place stood naught but vague promises from an untried king. Unless and until the Crown provided more explicit direction, the colonists had to rely on their own devices.

Regulation from London was long in coming. The new king's appetite for learning and the arts, his need for a foreign policy in the face of the Thirty Years' War, and his troubles with his Puritan antagonists all shouldered aside his concern for Virginia. Consequently, except for naming governors and councillors or maintaining an infrequent correspondence, the Crown soon left Virginia mostly to Virginians. Royal inattention and exigencies born of English domestic politics thus assured Virginians several decades of inconsistent and generally lax central administration. The effect was an attenuation of political bonds between Crown and colony at a crucial time for the development of the General Assembly. The Crown had inadvertently let slip an early chance to fashion that growth according to its dictates. To expect that Charles and his advisers should have acted other than they did, though, is to credit them with a knowledge and foresight that was beyond their command.

Virginians were of divided minds about the breakup of the company. Many feared for the validity of their land titles, which were in doubt until the king pronounced otherwise. Some shared Charles's expectation that a revived corporation held the best promise for the colony's future and waited hopefully for its prompt restoration. Others welcomed the dissolution and became vehement opponents of any efforts at reconstituting the company. All seemed to agree that the assembly assured a modicum of continuity in uncertain times, and because it served everyone's interest, all determined to save it.

Rescue operations moved along two fronts. Governors continued to call regular assembly sessions, sustaining the precedent of 1619. Precedents were of little value without royal sanction, so members and other colonists lobbied the king to legitimate the General Assembly. Their maneuvering consumed fifteen years of effort before it finally succeeded, and in the interval the assembly inevitably took on certain attributes of a representative legislature.[19]

Sir Francis Wyatt, the company's last governor and the Crown's first, summoned the General Assembly of 1624 partly in response to news of Attorney General Coventry's suit against the company charter in England. Governor, councillors, and the burgesses all gathered at Jamestown in February, aware that the litigation threatened their future as an assembly, and they resolved to meet the challenge. They named Councillor John Pountis their agent "to solicite the general cause of the country to his majesty and the counsell," they voted funds for Pountis's expenses, and they armed him with four papers that phrased the views they wanted vented at court. Two of the documents were close, point-by-point rejoinders to London Alderman Robert Johnson and Nathaniel Butler, who were adherents of former company treasurer Sir Thomas Smith. Each had recently leveled caustic indictments against Sandys, and those charges jeopardized the assembly because by implication the allegations reflected badly on it. Pountis's other papers were petitions to James I and to the Privy Council. The one to the king expressed the assembly's "great Comfort" at knowing he had taken Virginia matters into "your more neere and especiall care" and begged him not to "suffer your poore Subjectes to fall into the handes of Sir Tho. Smith or his Confidents, who have lately abused your Sacred cares with wrong Informations." The petition went on to ask the king to confine the tobacco trade to Virginia and Bermuda and to send over "Souldiers." It closed with an expression of hope that James would give the assembly "voyce" because no one in England "by reason of accidents and emergent occasions" could govern Virginia "so advantagiously as our presence and experience." The plea to the Privy Council was similarly pitched, though its entreaty for the assembly's continuance was the more emphatic. "But above all," it concluded, "we humblie intreat your Lordships that we may retaine the libertie of our generall Assemblie, then which nothing can more conduce to our satisfaction or the publique utilitie."[20]

When James named Wyatt royal governor, he chose not to sanction the assembly, though he did assign Sir Francis "full power and authoritie to performe and execute the places powers and authorities incident to a governour." That warrant provided the basis for Wyatt's issuing election writs on 25 April 1625 for an assembly to convene "at James Cyttie the 10th of Maye next ensuinge." Fragmentary records suggest that the principal action of the session turned on opposition to rumored changes in the government and a tobacco monopoly that members feared would ruin the colony. There were also apprehensions about the papers that the General Assembly of 1624 had entrusted to John Pountis because he had perished at sea. Those forebodings prompted the appointment of another agent, Sir George Yeardley, who sailed for London carrying fresh copies of the Pountis documents together with a new petition to the king and another set of "propositions" for the Privy Council. One of the latter trenchantly urged the council to "avoide the oppression of Governours" by continuing and confirming "the liberty of Generall Assemblyes" so the colonists might "have a voice in election of officers, as in other Corporations."[21]

Wyatt left office in 1626, but before he did, he presided over one more assembly. When he circulated writs for the elections of burgesses and when the meeting convened are unknown because there are no minutes of the deliberations. A series of orders-in-council, dated 7 and 8 August 1626, summarize the content of the legislation that was adopted. One act required that "there be an uniformitie in our Church kept as neere as may be to the Canons of Englande," and another established monthly courts in various locations to dispense with petty civil and criminal matters. Still others provided for regular quarterly meetings of the Council as a court and for strengthening defenses against the natives.[22]

Yeardley, Wyatt's successor, seems not to have summoned an assembly during his fifteen-month stint in office. No laws or other papers that would verify a sitting during 1627 have ever come to light. On the other hand, though, the Council minutes for the period of Yeardley's second administration are fairly complete. These contain no indication that he ever contemplated calling an assembly or hint at any emergency that could have justified a summons. Lacking such excuses, he was perhaps reluctant to be as venturesome as Wyatt, especially in light of his recent failure at lobbying the Crown to legitimate the assembly.[23]

Ironically, it was the Crown itself that inched legitimacy forward a step or two. In 1627, the king sent a letter to Virginia, setting forth his scheme for another tobacco monopoly and commanding the General Assembly to conclude the bargain for the colony. By the time those orders reached Jamestown, Yeardley had been dead for three months, so their implementation fell to acting-governor Francis West.[24] Writs went out on 27 February 1627/28, and within two weeks newly elected burgesses joined West and the Council to act on the king's wishes. That session was also significant in that it marked the beginning of annual meetings that, with the possible exception of the year 1636, continued unbroken for half a century.[25]

Despite this all-but-formal recognition of the General Assembly, Charles I temporized at taking the final step. He still favored governing through a reconstituted company, though it was not until 1631 that he at last named a commission to advise him on the problem. The queen's lord chamberlain, Edward Sackville, fourth earl of

Dorset, chaired the commission. Consisting of twenty-three members, it included, among others, Henry Danvers, first earl of Danby, Secretary of State Sir John Coke, Attorney General Sir Robert Heath, Sir Thomas Roe, Nicholas Ferrar and John Ferrar, Sir John Wolstenholme, and former governor Wyatt, all of whom brought a broad fund of colonizing experience and political influence to their assignment.

The Dorset Commission met for several months before it reported a scheme that accorded with the king's proclivity, but the combination of an irresolute monarch and hostile colonials effectively scuttled the recommendation. Charles subsequently directed a privy council subcommittee to explore other ideas. It soon received a petition from the General Assembly of February 1632 that pleaded for "confirmation of all our lands and dividents" and asked that the assembly receive the royal sanction. The subcommittee's work came to a precipitate stop when the Crown had to placate the Virginians after they overthrew Governor Sir John Harvey in 1635. Harvey's ouster led to the reappointment of Wyatt. When Sir Francis sailed for Virginia in January 1639, he carried instructions that he likely had a hand in drafting, given their tenor and his understanding of Virginia. The instructions commanded that Wyatt and "the Councellors as formerly once a year or oftner if urgent occasion shall require, Do Summon the Burgesses of all and Singular the Plantations there which together with the Governor and Councill makes the Grand Assembly, and shall have Power to make Acts and laws for the Government of that Plantation, correspondent as near as may be to the laws of England." That order gave constitutional sanction to the assembly, although the Crown retained an implicit right to interfere at any time it chose.[26]

Wyatt faced a general assembly much altered from the one he met in earlier days because the body had gone a considerable distance in its passage from corporate appendage to little parliament by the time he returned. Certain Virginians by 1639 presumed a share in ruling the colony and regarded the assembly as the appropriate mechanism through which to exercise that entitlement. Three significant consequences followed from that presumption. Together governors, councillors, and burgesses assumed ever-broadening powers of legislation, they arrogated additional parliamentary privileges to themselves, and they enhanced their role as a high court of judicature.

To peruse the laws enacted up to 1639, even casually, is to appreciate how much the assembly's legislative reach had grown in the span of two decades. Acts regulated everything from the church, Indian policy, and landowning to local government, tobacco pricing, servant relations, and urban growth. The accumulation of laws eventually became "in some cases defective and inconvenient," which caused the General Assembly of September 1632 to declare existing laws "voyd and of none effect." In their place, that legislature substituted a thoroughgoing statutory revision that stood as an example for later assemblies.[27]

Nearly total destruction of legislative journals or other working papers from the period of the 1620s and 1630s hides the augmenting of privileges. Fragments here, scraps there—these are the remnants from which to trace the enlargement. The snippets are sometimes helpful for establishing precisely when a particular power or custom was arrogated. Several examples make the point.

How and why the assembly first asserted its right to impose qualifications on the burgesses can be pinpointed exactly. Its assumption of a fundamental privilege passed unchallenged after 1619 and remained good precedent for the duration of the colonial era. The General Assembly of 1624 exempted future burgesses from being "arrested during the time of the assembly, a week before and a week after." It also established a right to erect local subdivisions by creating monthly courts and parish churches, just as it presumed to limit the governor's power to levy taxes or "ymposistions." Later assemblies reinforced and extended these claims. The meeting in February 1632 produced extensive elaborations of the laws relating to the church. Two years later, the monthly courts were replaced by county courts, a move that opened the way to an articulation of local administration that took decades to effect. Members who attended the session of 1629 were the first to specify detailed dispositions of public revenues. That was a step in the direction of a right of taxation, which the General Assembly claimed in September 1632. Finally, the Anglo-Powhatan War of 1622–1632 compelled members to make defensive preparations; indeed assemblies in whole or in part frequently sought the means of carrying the fight to the enemy.[28]

These illustrations clearly document when the General Assembly acquired various prerogatives or adopted new procedures. Unfortunately, they reveal few insights into the specific contingencies that led to such innovations, let alone the political considerations that drove the decisions. A good case in point related to the bases of membership in the assembly, that is, who could be burgesses, who elected them, and what constituencies they represented.

A Little Parliament

The manner of picking burgesses throughout the seventeenth century bears no relation to modern ways. Aspirants for office did not raise huge sums of cash in order to campaign out of loyalty to a political party. The very idea of elections contested by organized political parties was completely foreign. No candidates ran on issues, and there were no platforms, consultants, rallies, campaign speeches, or stifling media coverage.

Being English, the colonists knew something of electoral politics in Britain. The only popular elections were for seats in the House of Commons, which were unevenly distributed among a patchwork of counties and boroughs, but a member did not have to live in the place that elected him. Elections were erratic. No law required regular meetings of Parliament, at least not until the end of the century, when the Triennial Act compelled the monarch to call it at least once every three years.[29] Until then, Parliament sat only when the Crown chose to summon it to Westminster. Women cast no votes, and only those adult males who owned or rented land worth forty shillings or more enjoyed the liberty of the franchise. A right to vote did not automatically enable any freeholder to stand for election; that opportunity was reserved for highly placed English men. Polling days were at the Crown's discretion, although election writs circulated forty days before the poll. Local sheriffs conducted the elections, and voters declared their choices orally.

As with the House of Commons in England, a place among the burgesses would be the only elective office in Virginia until after the Revolution. Yeardley allowed about a month's interval between his call for elections and the opening of the first General Assembly. Other governors opted for a smaller lapse of time. In 1624 Wyatt set the meeting date two weeks after he promulgated his writ, and in 1628 acting-governor Francis West instructed the General Assembly to convene within thirteen days. Whether Wyatt and West acted typically is unknown because these are the sole examples from the period for which it is possible to establish both a date when the writ was issued and a date when the session commenced.[30]

Yeardley also established voter qualifications. When he called the election in 1619, he enjoined every free man and company tenant to vote without regard to landholding. That automatically enfranchised all the adult male colonists, making the right to vote more generous than in England. Yeardley's rule apparently remained the standard into the 1630s, for there are no clues to suggest that the General Assembly attempted to modify it.

The burgesses all fit the same pattern. They were to a man seasoned colonists. Gentility, it seems, counted less than demonstrated capacities for prospering in

Virginia. Beyond those characteristics, there is little indication of why voters favored one man instead of another. Nor is there any suggestion that down to 1639 the assembly actually contemplated explicit criteria for holding office.

Voters first elected two burgesses from each of the four corporations and the various particular plantations that made up the colony. The corporations never fulfilled their intended purpose, and they were slowly abandoned as electoral units. As time passed, burgesses tended to come from smaller areas within old corporate limits or from newer settlements. Particular plantations were also absorbed once immigration resumed after the mid-1620s. When these changes accounted for increased numbers of burgesses turning up at Jamestown, things began to get out of hand. The makeup of the General Assembly of 1633 illustrates the problem. Thirty-two burgesses, who represented twenty-one different settlements, attended the meeting. As few as one man or as many as four might represent a constituency, though there was little rhyme or reason to the areas or groups of colonists they represented. Even so, the General Assembly displayed little disposition to regulate the situation. It actually complicated matters further when it divided Virginia into counties. Thereafter, some burgesses represented counties while others continued to serve the older constituencies.[31]

The assembly's role as a high court of judicature began when the General Assembly of 1619 acted in a judicial capacity in order to dispose of four items on its agenda. Three were civil matters that the complainants moved by petition, and they were readily resolved. The fourth was a criminal case that turned on allegations of treason against one of the colony's interpreters, Henry Spelman. In the end, the assembly decided that proofs were insufficient to convict Spelman, so he escaped execution.[32]

Later assemblies also performed as a court but records are sparse. For certain, they did not sit on criminal causes much after 1619, if at all. Disposal of petty offenses devolved first to the monthly courts and then to the county benches. Trials of felonies—crimes for which the punishment was either death or loss of limb—became the exclusive jurisdiction of the governor and Council, who composed the Quarter Court.[33] It seems, therefore, that by the time of Wyatt's return, the General Assembly occasionally acted as a court of last resort that received appeals in civil matters from both the Quarter and the local courts. No records of that activity are extant before the 1650s, and that loss precludes any account of the assembly's appellate work before midcentury.[34]

A Little Parliament

In spite of the accretions of privileges and other modifications, the structure of the General Assembly remained the unicameral body of its first session. Whether it handled its legislative work through committees, or whether any man who came after John Pory served as Speaker, is uncertain. The extant records are silent on these and other organizational matters.[35]

There was little inclination after 1619, and even less need, for anyone to contemplate another arrangement. Opposition to reviving the company, concerns about the future of the tobacco economy and the Indian war, as well as the drive to confirm land titles and to preserve the assembly encouraged all the members to act with one accord. As long as the population stayed relatively small and confined mainly to the James River basin, the interests of the voting colonists did not much differ.

One way or another, those impulses toward unity of purpose diminished during the 1630s. The population rose from 1,210 in 1625 to 4,914 a decade later and by 1639 surpassed 10,000.[36] New arrivals scattered northward along the Peninsula to the York River and over the Chesapeake Bay to the Eastern Shore. They distanced themselves from Jamestown and the older settlements and added to the areas under tobacco cultivation. Tobacco's growing importance as the mainstay of the Virginia economy also tended to wedge the colonists apart as each sought to arrange the most advantageous outlet for his product whose value declined as its quantity mushroomed. Competing economic interests spilled over into politics, creating several blocs among both burgesses and councillors. A dominant faction of merchant-planters coalesced around Councillors Samuel Mathews and William Claiborne. They and their followers aimed to control the tobacco trade, but they were temporarily deflected by the contretemps that ousted Sir John Harvey.

Harvey became governor in 1628. Almost from the moment he stepped onto the Jamestown docks two years later, he and his councillors stood at swords' points. Rash and prickly, he contested their claims to bind him by majority will. He went against the advice of Councillor John Pott and others and struck the deal that finally ended the Indian war. His support of the Maryland colony opened him to the suspicion that he inclined toward the hated Catholics, a mistrust that grew once it was known that he had sent supplies and other assistance to the Marylanders. Worst of all, he sustained Cecilius Calvert, second baron Baltimore, in his claims to the whole of the northern reaches of Chesapeake Bay. Doing that not only undercut Virginia's title to the region, but it also jeopardized Claiborne's trading interests in the area.[37]

Beginnings

A meeting of disgruntled colonists in April 1635 kindled the events that led to Harvey's overthrow. The participants voiced their displeasure at his highhanded behavior and expressed fears that his Indian policy would lead to renewed conflict. Hearing of the gathering, the governor ordered the malcontents detained for trial at martial law in the Council of State. Some councillors rose to the defense of the dissidents, which enraged Harvey. He insisted that each councillor indicate his views on what should be done with the accused. They balked, and after an exchange of hot words they adjourned without settling anything. Debate continued at the next meeting, but this time it centered on the councillors' dissatisfaction with Harvey's government. The bone of contention was his refusal to forward letters from the General Assembly to London. Infuriated, Harvey sprang from his seat and arrested George Menefie for speaking treasonable words, whereupon Mathews and John Utie grabbed the governor. They and their confederates kept him prisoner until he promised to return to England to answer their charges, and as if to reinforce their point, Pott beckoned a troop of militia into the Council chamber. High cards in hand, the Council put one of their number, John West, in Harvey's place and called the assembly to hear their complaints. Days of anxious bargaining passed before Sir John sailed away to London.

Once there, he appeared before the Privy Council. He contended that the allegations laid against him were baseless but that Mathews, Claiborne, Utie, and the rest wished him gone for purely personal reasons. The arguments won over the king, who gave his governor a new commission and warrants to arrest the mutineers and ship them back to England for a proper trial. A triumphant Harvey landed at Jamestown in 1637 and soon apprehended his adversaries. Sending them abroad backfired, because instead of standing trial, they used their connections at court to unhorse Harvey. Their lobbying partly contributed to Wyatt's replacing him.[38]

Although the Mathews-Claiborne faction on the Council of State characterized popular opposition to Harvey's misgovernment as the reason, his overthrow had little to do with an expression of the colonists' general will. His troubles arose because he struggled with grasping settlers who expected a large measure of control in Virginia politics. His downfall widened the door to the emergence of the colony's ruling class of great planters, and it served as a cautionary tale to his successors.

It also further polarized those councillors and burgesses who were less critical of Harvey but who cast hostile eyes at Mathews and his ilk. That stance mirrored the sentiments of the people for whom they spoke. Lesser planters, for the most part, their constituents looked to Dutch traders as providing the most lucrative markets for their tobacco. Accordingly, their unfriendliness to the Mathews-Claiborne faction grew out of an animus toward its attempt at monopolizing the tobacco trade and reconstituting the Virginia Company.[39]

Wyatt immediately grasped the dynamics of the situation. He treated the Mathews crowd deferentially, though he was also at pains not to appear overly partial to them. That approach quieted lingering hostilities, but it did not dissolve all bitterness. Secretary of the Colony Richard Kemp, who proved especially nettlesome, did not let bygones be bygones. A nominal Harveyite and no friend to Mathews or Claiborne, he put Wyatt in an awkward spot in 1640 after Claiborne revealed that he had solicited royal approval for the creation of a signet office for the purpose of validating public records. The king approved of the idea in principal, but he left the decision to the governor and Council. Kemp "was ... required to attend the answering thereof yet did notwithstanding presently depart the colony." Angered by Wyatt's failure to end some festering litigation in his favor, Kemp slipped away to London, without notice or permission, to work against the governor. Indeed, his friend Thomas Stegge was fined and imprisoned for assisting him "with money in England because it endangered the records some of which [Kemp] had carried with him."[40]

Wyatt and the rest of the Council adopted Claiborne's idea, which had the effect of diminishing the office of secretary because the great seal of Virginia and its attendant fees were transferred to the newly created signet office. The Council also "thought fit that the said Mr Claiborne shall be admitted to the said office." Creation of the signet office was of a piece with reforms that Wyatt initiated on his own. His main concern was fashioning local government into an institutional device more able to meet the demands of a fast-growing colony. The General Assembly had already created the basic instrument in Harvey's time, so it was merely a matter of assigning the county courts additional responsibilities, and to that end, Wyatt called assemblies in 1640, 1641, and 1642 to enact the necessary legislation.[41]

Wyatt's work came to an abrupt halt on 8 March 1641/42, the day he surrendered his office to his replacement. Six months before, Charles I had signed "A Commission nominatinge and appointinge Sir William Barkley Kt. to be Governor of Virginia." That appointment set Wyatt's retirement in motion, and it had wide-ranging consequences for the Crown and Virginia. In the context of the moment, however, the timing of the change was odd. So was Charles's preference to succeed Wyatt.[42]

No outward appearances hint at the reasons for the change of governors. Barely two years had passed since Wyatt returned to his former post. Virginians liked him, he performed well, and, except for Secretary Kemp, no one clamored for his removal. All that being so, why did the king turn him out? Sir William Berkeley seemed an unusual choice for a replacement. He was a minor court personality without practical experience of colonizing or governing. And why should he seek to exchange the comforts of court for a life in America? The explanation had more to do with personal desires than royal displeasure or carefully crafted administrative policy. Berkeley, frustrated by his failures in England, sought a place of fresh beginnings where he might prosper as he could not as a courtier. Ties of kin and friendship enabled him to buy the office from Wyatt and to convince the king to put him in Wyatt's stead.[43]

The bargain they struck was embodied in a contract that Berkeley and Wyatt's agent, William Claiborne, signed on 4 September 1641. By it, Wyatt retained his seat on the Council of State, and Berkeley agreed not to assume office before 14 January 1641/42. That stipulation enabled Wyatt to receive a full year's income as governor. Berkeley also paid him £300 and promised to purchase Wyatt's "dwelling house in James Cittie at the rate hee paid Mr. Kemp for it, with further allowance for what hee hath expended thereuppon." Berkeley also consented to cure a flaw in his commission by restoring "the old Councellors that are left out ... & rank them in their places, which are, Captaine William Claiborne, Captaine William Tucker & Mr. Ralph Wyatt."[44]

Berkeley's assumption of office marked both an end and a beginning for the General Assembly. No longer was the assembly a mere adjunct to a distant corporate authority; it held legislative and political authority on its own. To be sure, those powers still lacked ample definition, just as the assembly itself could hardly be described as fully formed, but in 1642 it stood at the verge of being a little parliament. In the decades to come, Sir William Berkeley and the men who joined him as councillors and burgesses completed that transition.

Chapter 2

Little Parliament

E agerness for fresh beginnings landed Sir William Berkeley half a world away from his accustomed comforts and the conversation of court and plunged him into a wholly new life. He caught panoramic glimpses of the Virginia countryside from the deck of the ship that bore him up the broad, brown waters of the James River to his destination, and as the seamen smartly worked it to a berth at the town wharf he beheld "James Cittie" for the first time. Little of what he saw had a familiar look, for Jamestown barely surpassed a rural English hamlet in size or amenity. His gaze caught few trappings of a city worthy of being a capital or fitting his new dignity as the king's vice-regent. If, for an instant, he pondered his responsibilities anew, then he grasped how much greater they were than any he had shouldered heretofore. Perhaps, too, he reflected on his taking them up in trying times.[1]

Berkeley arrived at Jamestown in February 1641/42 during a meeting of the General Assembly. Undeterred by the impending change in administrations, Governor Wyatt had ordered the session to complete reforms started three years earlier, but out of deference to his successor he recessed the legislators until April. Secretary Richard Kemp administered the oaths of office to Berkeley and swore in the councillors on 8 March. The new chief executive soon turned his thoughts to the assembly. Wyatt's work remained incomplete. There was news to report on the situation in England. Most of all, Berkeley wanted to present himself to colonial politicians to establish himself as their leader. These were obvious reasons for meeting with the assembly, and they presented him with the first test of his acumen: whether to circulate writs for new elections or merely to reconvene the assembly that Wyatt had summoned. He chose the latter course.[2]

Governor and Captain General Sir William Berkeley and the General Assembly of Virginia formally encountered one another for the first time on April Fools' Day 1642. If the comedic playwright in Berkeley inspired him to spin word games when he greeted his colleagues, his puns are lost. So, too, are all but one record from the session itself. That singular item, "The Declaration Against the Company," reveals a high priority on the governor's agenda: stopping the Long Parliament from resurrecting the Virginia Company.

Berkeley was no stranger to the revival issue. He left London knowing that George Sandys, "appointed agent for the colony by an Assembly 1639," had just presented a petition to the House of Commons wherein the colonists were made to appear to support the company's recharter. Berkeley understood that many in Virginia had for years adamantly opposed reviving the company in any form. Thus, he engineered passage of the Declaration expressly to knock down any impression that Virginians had undergone a change of heart.[3]

Addressed to Charles I, the Declaration[4] disowned Sandys, baldly asserting that he had mistaken "his Advice and Instructions from the ... Assembly for his so doing it being neither the meaning nor Intent of the ... Assembly or Inhabitants here for to give way for the Introducing of the said Company or any other." The balance of the Declaration mounted a zestfully worded attack on the concept of management by company and set forth an equally energetic defense of the status quo in Virginia. Avowing "a most faithful and loyal Obedience to his Sacred Majesty our dread Sovereign," the petitioners ended on a threatening note. Anyone who attempted "by any way or means Either directly or indirectly to sue for Advice Assist abet Countenance or Contrive the reducing of this Colony to a Company or Corporation or introducing a Contract or Monopoly upon our Persons Lands or Comodites" faced the forfeiture of his entire estate.[5]

An addendum postponed further legislative deliberations until 2 June. At that time, the assembly would again gather "to determine and finish all such matters as shall be found necessary to be concluded and Enacted whether in matters already begun or any Business that shall then begin or be proposed." This postscript suggests that cobbling together the Declaration took so long that no other legislation was possible without a break to smooth ruffled feathers. That implication is hardly surprising because Samuel Mathews, Richard Bennett, and Thomas Dew, among other legislators, favored revival and likely used their influence to forestall the Declaration while they probed Berkeley for his weaknesses. Berkeley's embrace of the document was the first signal of his gravitation toward leading planters opposed to the Mathews-Claiborne faction. In the end, the passage of the Declaration in its final form testifies to Berkeley's newfound skill at besting those who stood against him.[6]

Further evidence of his success at checking the Mathews-Claiborne coalition comes from the June legislative session. Berkeley sanctioned all of Wyatt's improvements in local government and the legal structure, which drew both nearer "to the law and customs of England in proceedings of the court and trials of causes." He also approved changes that clarified parish boundaries and refined the resolution of cases of disputed land titles. His espousal of these and other reforms kept faith with his instructions, but he also signaled something more trenchant: his willingness to accept Virginia's institutional order as he found it. More overtly, he bid for popular support by signing a repeal of a head tax whose proceeds had been paid into the governor's pocket. The assembly returned favor for favor, giving him an orchard and two rental properties in Jamestown that offset the loss of income.[7]

Berkeley displayed his deft touch again several months later when he met the General Assembly of March 1642/43. Confident of the outcome, he called an election beforehand that assured him of a crop of friendly burgesses, and he quickly turned his advantage to good effect. He not only encouraged the assembly to proceed with a comprehensive revision of the colony's laws in force, but he also urged the burgesses to sit apart from the Council of State and become a separate House of Burgesses. They accepted the suggestion, and so the assembly became bicameral.

In pressing his ideas, Berkeley had evidently been careful to elicit the cooperation of the Mathews-Claiborne group. How else to explain the otherwise curious course of faction member Councillor Thomas Stegge? He resigned his Council seat, won a place as burgess for Charles City County, and became the first Speaker since John Pory. None of that could have happened without the consent of Claiborne and Mathews.[8]

Berkeley need not have pushed the assembly to divide, but once he took that step, he could also have tried to defeat Stegge's candidacy for burgess and Speaker. That he did not reveals his intent to woo his opponents. A possibility of gaining Claiborne's support presented itself when death vacated that most lucrative provincial office, the secretary's post, and Berkeley chose Claiborne as successor to Roger Wingate. Claiborne accepted, though he never became the governor's intimate.[9]

A bicameral General Assembly provided Berkeley additional means to win over colonial politicians who were not part of any conciliar faction. Revising the laws soothed local magistrates by strengthening the county courts in ways that enhanced the reach and prestige of the justices of the peace. Doing these things had three results that altered the political landscape for years to come. Adding to the power of the county courts incrementally decentralized authority and invested county elites with nearly unchecked control of local affairs. In return, Berkeley gained relative freedom to promote his own ideas about the colony's future and to keep Virginia clear of the English Civil War. Dividing the General Assembly gave it the parliamentary form it had lacked since 1619. Division also enabled the members to acquire more of the habits of a representative legislature, especially as they grappled with the events that drove the politics of Berkeley's first administration.[10]

Economic diversification, one of the governor's lifelong goals, neatly dovetailed with the desires of those colonists who favored commerce with the Dutch and had no alliances with London merchants. A free trader in the sense that he opposed restricting the privilege of marketing to a privileged few vendors, whether Londoners, Virginians, or Dutchmen, Berkeley favored selling colonial goods wherever there was call for them. To that end, he secured the assembly's passage of "sundry solemne Acts & ... declarations therupon to invite & encourage the Dutch nation to a Trade & Commerce" even as Parliament and the Mathews-Claiborne faction headed in the opposite direction.[11]

An unexpected boost to Berkeley's leadership came in the wake of renewed war with the Indians. Threatened by the influx of new colonists and the spread of their plantations, the paramount leader of the Powhatans, Opechancanough, laid plans as he had done in 1622 for a swift, surprise stroke to drive the English from his homeland. He attacked on Holy Thursday 1644. His blow cost individual colonists dearly. Nearly five hundred died that April day. Virginia itself was in no danger of destruction, but the attack gave Berkeley the chance to prove his mettle as a warrior. He hurriedly called the General Assembly into session, which sent him back to England for arms and ammunition. He made the new secretary of the colony, Richard Kemp, acting-governor and gave temporary command of the militia to William Claiborne before boarding ship late in June 1644.[12]

Once he arrived in England, Berkeley soon grasped the folly of his mission. Virginia could expect no help from the king or Parliament, each of whom needed weaponry to carry the fight to the other. Seeing disadvantage in lingering, Berkeley planned a speedy exit for the colony, but he joined a campaign with the king, which detained him for months before he sailed on a Virginia-bound vessel in the spring of 1645.[13]

Back in Jamestown by June 1645, he discovered that in his absence the conflict with Opechancanough had gone badly. Claiborne was an indifferent general, more interested in settling a personal vendetta with the Maryland government than in defeating the Indians. Berkeley supplanted him and took the field himself. He sprang a trap on the natives that resulted in capture or death for a number of leaders, although Opechancanough eluded him; then he pillaged the Indians' cornfields and torched their villages until the onset of winter weather stilled his campaign. In the spring of 1646 Berkeley met with the General Assembly, and together they perfected a plan that ended the war. They created a special force of militia for the express purpose of taking Opechancanough. Rangers tracked their quarry and sent a messenger to the governor, who then caught the old chief. Berkeley took his captive to Jamestown, intending to send him to England, but a militiaman stabbed Opechancanough dead as he lay incarcerated in the town jail. Necotowance, the new chief, then sued for peace. The governor assisted in drafting the treaty, which he presented to the General Assembly for ratification in October 1646.[14]

Popularity and sure-handedness sustained Berkeley at times when he underestimated his constituents. His most serious misstep was to launch a policy of strict conformity to the Church of England. Such a measure complied with his instructions from the king, but that compliance jeopardized his hold on office. For one thing, he opened himself to a too close identification with the king's religious views, thereby giving his detractors in England and Virginia a cudgel with which to club him. For another, Virginia Anglicans showed little taste for punishing their nonconformist neighbors, especially because they were themselves rather lax in their own faithfulness to the royal view of church discipline. Few colonists actually wished for Virginia a replication of the English strife that set Anglican against Puritan. Especially not Berkeley. A devout son of the Church who brooked little dissent from its teachings, he rejected the theological rigidities of Archbishop William Laud and the king. His experiences in the Bishops' Wars against the Scots had taught him the disastrous consequences of trying to drive people of faith too hard in directions they balked at taking. Once he recognized similar political liabilities in his religious policy, he drew back and avoided lasting damage to his credibility.[15]

The beheading of Charles I and the ascendancy of the Parliamentarians put Berkeley and Virginia in a precarious spot. News of the king's overthrow reached Virginia a few months after the execution, and the governor acted swiftly to hold the colony loyal. Proclaiming Charles II Virginia's rightful ruler, he dispatched a defiant remonstrance to Whitehall wherein he damned Parliament for overturning the monarchy. Berkeley used his royalist contacts to communicate with the young king and to urge Cavaliers with military training to come to him and use Virginia as a base from which to make war on Oliver Cromwell. At his insistence the General Assembly enacted legislation making treasonable any words that questioned the succession of Charles II or justified regicide.[16]

On receiving Berkeley's remonstrance, the parliamentary Council of State referred the document to its committee of the admiralty "to take into their Consideration how the Government of that Plantation may bee altered." The result was an order in council of 14 August 1650 that interdicted English commerce with the colony. Parliament followed up with a statute that also prevented foreigners from trading to Virginia.[17]

Now it was the governor's turn to retaliate. Scarcely had Berkeley scanned the text of Parliament's law than he summoned the General Assembly for a daylong meeting on 17 March 1650/51. He opened it with a speech that was vintage Sir William the wordsmith. When he finished, "the pretended Act of Parliament was publiquely read in the Assembly," and the members of both houses unanimously condemned it in a joint resolution of their own. Berkeley then sent copies of the resolution and his speech to friends at The Hague who printed them for distribution throughout the Netherlands and England.[18]

Virginia was too important a colony and Berkeley was too much of a lightning bolt for the parliamentarians not to reduce the one and ground the other. Nevertheless, gaining control of the home islands and combating attempts by Charles II to regain his throne commanded higher priority than bringing the faraway colony to heel. Oliver Cromwell crushed royalist hopes when he routed the would-be king and his army from the field at Worcester on 3 September 1650. The threat removed, Parliament acted to square its Virginia account.

Benjamin Worsley, a functionary closely allied to key members of the Commons, argued in general terms that Parliament would never control the colony so long as Berkeley retained office, nor would Virginia benefit England until the Dutch were eliminated as the colonists' trading partners. Building on those points, he suggested a means of conquering Virginia. The Council of State should appoint a commission to lead troops to America. In Worsley's opinion, the commissioners must be Virginians whose loyalties were to Parliament, and they should resort to force only if they failed to negotiate Berkeley's peaceful surrender. Worsley also recommended legislation banning the Dutch from Virginia waters.[19]

Little Parliament

Parliament translated Worsley's advice into action almost to the letter. On 26 September 1651, the Council of State named Richard Bennett, William Claiborne, Robert Dennis, and Thomas Stegge as a commission with orders for "the Reduceing of Virginia and the inhabitants thereof to their due obedience to the Commonwealth of England," gave them forces for that purpose, and sent them on their way. Two weeks later, the Navigation Act of 1651, which interdicted colonial trade with the Netherlands, passed into law.[20]

Dennis and Stegge died at sea, but the convoy made its landfall in January 1652 and took up station at an anchorage in the lower James River, near present-day Newport News. Bennett and Claiborne dispatched messengers to the governor seeking his surrender. When he refused them an answer, they sailed to Jamestown. Ever the dramatist, Berkeley prepared a spirited show for them. He called out a thousand militiamen and placed them strategically about the little capital and its approaches, as if he would contest the invaders. A tense standoff lasted several days before he signed articles of capitulation on 12 March 1651/52.[21]

Berkeley hoped for two results from his display of arms. One was to maintain credibility with his Virginia allies and the putative king. The other was to extract concessions that preserved the colony's political establishment and left Virginians as free as possible from meddlesome outsiders. His ploy succeeded because the commissioners' main goal was gaining Virginia for Parliament. Bennett and Claiborne, in particular, shared with Berkeley a distaste for interference from England. Both men sided with the parliamentarians more for practical considerations than from religious convictions. Each had long campaigned for the monopolization of Virginia commerce by London merchants and for interdiction of the Dutch trade, which was why they allied with those in England who favored their views. Once Parliament codified their goals in the Navigation Act of 1651, they were content that Virginia's political order should remain otherwise intact, which explains the success of Berkeley's tactic. As for the governor, he was spared the indignity of swearing fealty to Parliament. Bennett and Claiborne even allowed Berkeley to send an explanation of the surrender to Charles II, which he dispatched to Holland via a personal courier. The two commissioners gave Berkeley a year in which to liquidate his assets and join the royalists abroad. In the end, however, Berkeley simply retired to private life at his country seat, Green Spring House.[22]

In the eyes of colonial politicians, the participation of the General Assembly in each of the foregoing episodes fixed it as Virginia's equivalent of Parliament. Dividing the assembly into two houses adorned it with a parliamentary character and ornament it had lacked as a unitary body. The growth of its rights took form gradually as governor, councillors, and burgesses sorted out how they related to one another as politicians and in the General Assembly. They had much to learn about the intricacies of legislative procedures, and, as novices are wont to do, they worked tentatively after 1643, venturing beyond the comfortable bounds of the familiar only in the most unusual of circumstances. Distinctions as to which prerogatives resided in which house, and which ones were shared powers, emerged haltingly.[23]

The evolution of the Council of State provides a good example. Division implied that it would fill a place parallel to the House of Lords, even though there were few similarities between the two. Lords sat in their chamber by right of heredity or ecclesiastical office. Elaborate ceremonies ordered their goings and comings whenever they assembled in Westminster. The lord chancellor, bound by finely tuned rules of procedure, presided at their deliberations. As a body the Lords decided questions of privilege, moved legislation, tried capitally accused peers, reversed errors committed by Parliament or in the Court of King's Bench, settled suits that languished elsewhere, and counseled their sovereign on urgent matters of state. Aided by a corps of clerks and lesser functionaries, committees discharged much of the work, though if necessity required it, the Lords took advice from the justices of the central courts at Westminster or the Crown's attorney general.[24]

Virginia's Council of State, by contrast, was not a hereditary house, and it included no bishops. There were few rituals surrounding its convening, other than what attended the start of the General Assembly itself. Berkeley chaired meetings, but there was no provincial officer of state equated with the lord chancellor, and in the governor's absence his lieutenant or the senior member presided. A clerk, and perhaps a deputy or two, assisted in expediting the paperwork, but it is unlikely that the councillors employed committees. At most, the Council comprised only eighteen men, besides the governor, not all of whom showed up at every assembly. Virginia did without an attorney general until the 1640s, and, apart from the Council itself, there were no high courts to which Council members might turn for legal advice. No matters of precedence fell within Council purview either.[25]

The assembly's shifting of routine judicial and administrative responsibilities from the Council to the county courts relieved councillors of burdensome mundane duties and allowed for some redefinition of their authority as advisers, judges, and legislators. Councillors tried all felonies and heard all civil appeals from the county courts, though their judgments in the latter species of litigation were subject to review by the assembly. They advised Berkeley, in the words of the historian Robert Beverley, "in all Important Matters of Government," and they could restrain him "by having each of them an equal Vote with the Governor." Substantial losses of records hide how the councillors developed their legislative abilities. Presumably they joined the burgesses to draft some bills, as was the habit by the 1650s, and they introduced bills, too. Certainly, their assent was necessary before any act passed into law.[26]

Little direct testimony remains for reconstructing the organization and procedures of the House of Burgesses before the mid-1650s. The precedents provided by John Pory and the privileges assumed during the 1620s and 1630s secured ground on which to build, but to what extent is far from clear. How the House chose Speakers and clerks remains hazy, too. Equally murky is Berkeley's role in the selection process, except to say that although the burgesses consulted with him, he seems to have given the House free rein in making its choices.[27]

More apparent was the way the burgesses grew in awareness of their importance as the voters' representatives in a maturing polity. As early as the General Assembly of March 1642/43, they freed themselves from arrest "from the time of ... Election until ten days after dissolution of the Assembly" and declared the supremacy of statutes over court orders or gubernatorial proclamations. Another law required assessment of "the inhabitants of the several counties and precincts ... [for] the defraying of the Burgesses charges" incurred for attending to public business, though it failed to establish a rate of compensation. In 1645, an act passed that limited the number of burgesses from any county to four, excepting James City County, where voters could pick five and those in Jamestown one. For the first time written law also implicitly authorized sheriffs to conduct elections as well as to give the "several inhabitants" at least six-days' notice of the time and place of the elections. In effect, these stipulations pointed toward the eventual monopolization of House membership by the county courts and to the counties becoming the basis of representation.[28]

Internally, the House strengthened its grip on the membership and members' qualifications. It ordered new elections in counties where burgesses had become sheriffs, and it ousted Robert Bracewell, a clergyman whom it deemed "not in a capacity of serving as a Burgess, since it is unpresidentiall, and may produce bad consequences." Similarly, the House also presumed to intervene in extramural disagreements between members and to settle electoral disputes. On at least three occasions before 1660 the House expelled a duly elected burgess that it deemed unqualified. Christopher Burroughs, who sat for Lower Norfolk County, was not only dismissed, but he was also forced to acknowledge an unspecified offense "upon his Knees, before this grand Assembly" and to forebear "any publique office, eyther in Church or Commonwealth, for seaven yeares after yett to come." John Hammond and James Pyland, burgesses for Isle of Wight County, lost their seats because their colleagues judged them "scandalous" and "frequent disturbers of the peace of the country."[29] The House of Burgesses had become keenly conscious of its dignity and reputation.

Berkeley's persuasive and assiduous cultivation of the burgesses likewise imbued them with a keener comprehension of their potential for augmenting the privileges of their House. That feeling intensified to an even greater degree during the Interregnum when the assembly, or more properly the House of Burgesses, ruled supreme. The extinction of royal authority and the capitulation to Parliament upset Virginia's prevailing constitution and forced the House to decide who had power to do what. In the weeks that followed the surrender, William Claiborne, Richard Bennett, and other councillors initiated a process of putting things right. They temporarily assumed executive responsibilities with two ends in mind. First, they authorized incumbent local magistrates "to doe & act in all things in as full & ample manner as [they] have here tofore done ... untill further order." Their mandate assured a degree of continuity in the counties until the next step, a legislative session, played out. To that end, on or about 15 April 1652, the Council proclaimed writs for a general election of burgesses and set the thirtieth as the date for the meeting.[30]

That assembly revised colonial law to accord with the new political reality, and it codified changes at all levels of government. References to the Crown were eradicated from the statutes, as well as from commissions, oaths of office, legal papers, and court procedures, though no acts sequestered royalist estates or replaced local magistrates, and property law remained as in the past. The effect of these revisions proved more cosmetic than substantive because legislators took considerable care not to disturb the colony's fundamental institutions or the way those bodies had operated before March 1652. Constancy, insofar as they were concerned, was the watchword in the transition from monarchy to parliamentary control.[31]

Even so, the changeover altered the assembly. The House of Burgesses found itself the font of political authority in Virginia. Unlike the House of Commons, which abolished the House of Lords as well as the monarchy, the burgesses decided to retain the governor and the Council. The burgesses elected them and elected the secretary of the colony, too. As a result, all three offices became adjuncts of the House, even to the point of requiring the incumbents to swear "the oath Burgesses take." Neither the General Assembly of April 1652 nor any of its Interregnum successors attempted a precise definition of the relationship between its constituent elements, however, largely, one suspects, because imprecision worked to the burgesses' advantage.[32]

Interregnum governors represented a regime that never won the complete loyalty of the burgesses or the planters they represented. Many among the burgesses held steadfast in their belief in monarchy as the organizing basis of society, just as others despised Parliament's commercial policies. Governing in such circumstances demanded finesse and dexterity, qualities seldom seen in the parliamentary chief executives.

Richard Bennett, the first of the three, who served until 1655, lost all credibility with the House before it turned him out. At the outset, his approval of the Navigation Act of 1651 put him in singularly bad odor because its restrictions on trade with the Netherlands provoked the First Anglo-Dutch War (1652–1654) and interrupted commerce with Holland. His interference with the election of a Berkeley ally, Walter Chiles, as Speaker of the House further undermined him. No one missed Bennett after he gave place to Edward Digges. A capable man of no strong allegiance to the parliamentary cause, Digges owed his election to a combination of anti-Bennett and royalist burgesses. His tenure was short, because he soon departed for London on colony business, and he and the House developed little more than a superficial relationship. The same cannot be said of his successor, the second Samuel Mathews.[33]

Eldest son of Councillor Samuel Mathews, the third Interregnum governor took office in December 1656. The curious thing about his election was why the burgesses considered him a worthy candidate in the first place. Barely into his twenties, he had modest experience of politics and bore the stigma of his late father's unpopularity. His age suggests that certain burgesses saw an untried youth as preferable to a more seasoned candidate such as William Claiborne, but members of the Council may have advanced Mathews's candidacy thinking to make a callow boy their malleable pawn. Whatever the calculus, it proved grievously mistaken. Mathews impetuously breached the limits of his authority, and his transgression plunged him into costly controversies with the burgesses.

An early shadow of trouble was his refusal to convene the General Assembly in the spring following his election. Why Mathews put aside the members' request is unclear, although some hinted after the fact that he had acted on bad advice from unnamed councillors. Whatever Mathews's reasoning, its consequence was a barbed confrontation that surfaced in the General Assembly of March 1657/58.[34]

That assembly met primarily to undertake yet another revision of the laws in force. Bills cleared the House, only to be rejected by Mathews and the Council. In particular, drafts restricting attorneys' fees, repealing several conciliar perquisites, and retaining the current size of delegations in the House so angered Mathews that, with the Council's backing, he dissolved the burgesses. The House instantly retaliated. By a unanimous vote, it declared that the dissolution was "not presidentiall neither legall according to the lawes, now in force." It ordered every one of its members to remain in town under penalty of censure to "act in all things and to all intents and purposes as a whole and entire house." Deliberations thereafter proceeded in secret, and the Speaker, John Smith (alias Francis Dade), was charged to "signe nothing without the consent of the major part of the house." Caught far out on a slender limb, Mathews retreated, and as a compromise he offered to revoke his dissolution order if the House would let Oliver Cromwell settle the question of his authority to send it packing. His offer failed to mollify the burgesses, who immediately named a committee to compose a "manifestation and vindication" of their prerogatives as well as to recommend a means of settling the issue on House terms. The committee studied the precedents and concluded that the "present power of government" rested with the burgesses, who were not "dissolvable by any power now extant in Virginia, but by the House of Burgesses." It also recommended the reelection of Mathews and the members of the Council "for two yeares ensueinge." The House accepted the committee's report, and it passed three additional measures that reinforced its preeminence. It required the sergeant at arms to execute only those precepts signed by the Speaker, it ordered Secretary Claiborne to surrender the public records to Speaker Smith, and it compelled Claiborne, Mathews, and the councillors to appear before the House to swear new oaths of office. Mathews and the Council had no choice but to give way.[35]

That the burgesses bested their adversaries speaks not only to their self-consciousness, but it also attests to how much the House had grown as a legislative institution since 1643. Its standing rules of order and committee structure are other signs of that maturity. Rules of order are to legislatures what due process is to courts of law in that each dictates the flow of legislation and cases respectively. By definition, then, rules of order regulate all matters that ensure an expeditious dispatch of business. Historically speaking, they incorporate habits, manners, privileges, and precedents of immemorial usage, statutory enactment, or constitutional warrant. Procedures that governed debate in the House of Commons as of the 1640s represented precedential refinements that had ripened during the preceding century. They were readily accessible in handy form to any literate Englishman via a variety of procedural handbooks that circulated on both sides of the Atlantic.[36]

For so long as the General Assembly remained unicameral there was little purpose in elaborating the rules that John Pory introduced in 1619. Those prescriptions standardized the movement of bills and courtesies for controlling debate but not much more. Once there was a House of Burgesses, with its own officers and responsibilities, and as the number of members increased, the need for more precise regulations assumed greater significance. The earliest-known such mandate, establishing proper conduct, dates to the time of the parliamentary takeover; presumably, it was part of a larger restatement that the burgesses enacted when they revised the statutes in 1652. Adopted by "the unanimous consent of the whole house," this rule controlled floor debate. (It survived into modern times only because Thomas Jefferson, who had an abiding interest in legislative procedures, copied it out of records that later burned in 1865.) Subsequently, the rule was incorporated in a set adopted by the General Assembly of March 1658/59.[37]

In tone and substance, those rules bore marked resemblance to orders then in force in the House of Commons. Burgesses were to attend whenever the House sat; those who absented themselves without permission stood liable to arrest and fines. While on the floor, they were to be mindful of the business before them and were supposed to refrain from becoming "disguised" with alcohol. When one wished to debate, he addressed "himselfe to Mr. Speaker in a decent manner"; otherwise, he was not to "entertaine any private discourse" when a colleague held forth. Everyone was forbidden to indulge in intemperate language while speaking, just as all were expected to treat the presiding officer with singular courtesy. As in the House of Commons, whenever there was discussion of "any thing proposed by the Speaker, The party that speaketh shall rise from his seate and be uncovered [i.e., hatless] dureing the time he speaketh, wherein no interruption shall be made untill he have finished his discourse." Transgressors of this rule faced fine and rebuke.[38]

As William Hatcher learned, even nonmembers who aspersed the dignity of the House or its officers suffered speedy censure. The troubles began in October 1654, when Hatcher, a former burgess for Henrico County, accused Edward Hill of blasphemy and atheism. Serious allegations under any circumstances, Hatcher's assumed larger proportions because of Hill's prominence as a senior militia officer and a former Speaker. Hatcher could not sustain his charges in the Quarter Court, which dismissed them. The matter should have ended once the court "cleered the said Coll. Edward Hill," but Hatcher was foolhardy. When the General Assembly convened in November, Hill's colleagues again elected him Speaker, and Hatcher laid his slurs before the House. This time, though, he compounded the insinuations by asserting that "the mouth of this house was a Devil." Affronted by such contempt for their Speaker, the members haled Hatcher before the bar of the House and forced him on bended knee to acknowledge "his offence unto the said Coll. Edward Hill and Burgesses of this Assembly; which accordingly was performed and then he the said Hatcher dismist paying his fees."[39]

The burgesses' treatment of Hatcher mirrored the practice in the House of Commons. As such it affords an additional, precise bit of evidence to sustain the conclusion that by the 1650s the burgesses were consciously modeling their procedures on Parliament. But did the Hatcher episode mark an exact instant at which the burgesses took another parliamentary prerogative for their own? An answer to that question is at best speculative because the incident is the sole example of its kind among the extant assembly records of the period. All that can be said with assurance is this. Hatcher's case illustrates the burgesses' appropriation of a power to punish anyone who held them up to ridicule, although the precept was not then incorporated into the standing rules of order in the House.[40]

Committees originated in 1619, but their development accelerated after the General Assembly became bicameral, and they grew ever more vital to the progress of virtually all matters through the House of Burgesses. Unfortunately, few records survive to reveal anything more than the bare outlines of how House committees worked. Scattered details furnish fleeting glimpses of the how and who of their composition. At least three committees were permanent fixtures by the middle 1650s. One, the Committee for Private Causes, acted more judicially than legislatively. Its primary duty lay in determining which civil appeals from the Quarter Court merited adjudication by the full General Assembly in its capacity as the court of last resort. Any legislation that modified statutory law, or proposed new ones, was given a first reading on the House floor and then routed through the Committee for the Review of the Acts, later known as the Committee for Propositions and Grievances. Its members vetted bills before sending them back to the full House for additional debate and final disposition. Revenue measures originated in the Committee on the Public Levy, which navigated passage of the provincial budget through the assembly. As part of its work, that committee also oversaw the apportionment and collection of taxes throughout the colony, and it enjoyed considerable say in the disbursements of public funds.

Ad hoc committees served the House in special ways. Conference committees routinely met with the governor or the Council of State to reconcile differences in the wording of legislation. Other committees handled matters of the moment such as resolving election disputes or formally communicating with the governor and Council. Some committees were constituted to deal with extraordinary issues, such as the one Speaker Smith appointed in 1658 to compose the dispute with Governor Mathews.[41]

Because standing committees were essential to the timely disposal of business, they were named soon after the House went into session; the rest were chosen according to need. The gift of appointment belonged to the Speaker, who exercised it without apparent gubernatorial meddling, though he sought the governor's pro forma acceptance of his choices. The Speaker also requested the governor to designate councillors as assistants to all committees, a practice that seems to have been a throwback to earlier times and to Parliament itself. As might be imagined, seasoned members of both houses won the appointments as assistants and committee members.[42]

There is even less to tell about the committees and their work. Occasionally chairmen are identifiable by name. Senior burgesses in point of House service customarily appear to have chaired all committees, but it is unclear whether they were elected or appointed. One or more clerks worked with each committee, but who chose them is a mystery, too. Known clerks were drawn from obvious sources: nearby county courts, parish vestries, and clerical deputies in the assembly itself.

The end result of these and other refinements by the late 1650s was a secure House of Burgesses. Jealous of its stature and possessive of its rights, it stood confident as the wellspring of sovereignty in Virginia. As such, the House was strategically positioned to dictate the terms that returned the colony to its former loyalty.[43]

The road to that restoration began in 1659. Shortly after the General Assembly of March 1658/59 convened, Governor Mathews shared with the burgesses the contents of a letter he had recently received from the Council of State in Whitehall.

Council president Henry Lawrence wrote to say how it had "pleased the Lord" to take Oliver Cromwell "out of this world," leaving his son Richard to succeed him. In light of that sad event, Lawrence ordered Mathews to proclaim "his said highnesse Richard, Lord Protector" throughout Virginia. And he commanded "the present Governour and Councill" to apply themselves "with all seriousness, faithfullnesse, and circumspection to the peaceable and orderly management of the affaires of that collony."[44]

Lawrence's words touched off a long debate in the House. Discussion centered on whether the letter required colonial obedience to the younger Cromwell as Lord Protector and whether to accept the letter as "an authentique manifestation" of Parliament's intentions for the Virginia government. The burgesses answered both questions affirmatively, but to protect their own authority they extracted an acknowledgment from Mathews that "the supream power of electing officers to be by the present lawes resident in the Grand Assembly." Moreover, they compelled Mathews to "joyne his best assistance" with them in petitioning Cromwell "for confirmation of their present priviledges."[45]

"Tumbledown Dick" Cromwell was no Oliver, and he soon abdicated, which left a dying parliamentary cause weaker still. Signs in England pointed to the return of the monarchy, but there was no telling when that might happen. Just as no one in Virginia could foresee when Charles II would reclaim the throne of his father, so no one could predict how long the parliamentary regime might last in the colony. Apprehensions about who controlled Britain weakened a government that never enjoyed widespread support among the colonists and minimized Mathews, whose credibility was already sapped by his earlier scrapes with the burgesses.[46]

The issue of what to do unexpectedly came to a head when Mathews died in January 1660.[47] His death immediately exposed troubling fissures in the colony's prevailing constitution. There was no lieutenant governor, as is now the case, who automatically rose to Mathews's chair. Furthermore, neither the Speaker of the House of Burgesses nor the secretary of the colony had constitutional rights to executive power, even on an interim basis. More disquieting was the absence of an explicit procedure for appointing an acting governor, as had once been the case. While Virginia was a royal colony, councillors of state had a royal warrant to fill gubernatorial vacancies with one of their number. Their license ceased to be good law after 1652, but Interregnum General Assemblies neglected to provide a substitute procedure.[48]

That failure contributed to yet another obstacle. None of the prevailing statutes anticipated a situation like the one caused by Mathews's demise. Those laws did no more than set gubernatorial elections for regular meetings of the General Assembly. Assemblies, however, sat at the call of the governor. Mathews died at a time when the assembly stood in recess, leaving it bereft of the one person who could legally recall the burgesses to elect a new governor. Thus the conundrum in finding a replacement.[49]

The trail of events that led to the selection of Mathews's successor is obscure, though former governor Berkeley quickly emerged as the likeliest prospect. Secretary Claiborne and his Council colleagues persuaded Berkeley to become governor pro tempore, providing he agreed to reconvene the General Assembly, at which the burgesses would either confirm him or elect someone else. Of dubious legality, this solution nonetheless offered an elegantly pragmatic means of circumventing the constitutional difficulties.

About the middle of February, Berkeley temporarily resumed his old place. He issued his writ of summons to the General Assembly, which went into session on 13 March. Electing Theodorick Bland Speaker, the burgesses immediately turned to the matter of finding a new governor. As if by prearrangement, Berkeley seems to have been the only name on their list of prospects, and so began the negotiation of terms for his election. Bland appointed a committee, which insisted on Berkeley's recognition of the supremacy of the burgesses for as long as the political situation in England continued uncertain. The committee expected Berkeley to govern in accord with English law and "the established lawes" of Virginia. It also admonished him to call an assembly at least every two years, although it would not permit him to dissolve the burgesses without their consent. Finally, it authorized him to choose his own councillors and secretary, although his choices were subject to the burgesses' approval. These conditions did not sit entirely well with Berkeley, but the House remained resolute, he yielded, and on 19 March 1659/60 he agreed in writing to all terms. That done, governor and assembly took up regular business before deciding to adjourn until 20 March 1660/61 unless Berkeley found an "occasion by the importance of affaires to convene it sooner."[50]

For the time being, the colony had a governor who satisfied those Virginians whose opinions in politics mattered most. Just how long Berkeley and the House of Burgesses could sustain the arrangements that returned him to power depended entirely on events across the ocean. Charles II reclaimed his throne in May 1660, but reports of the king's restoration, plus a royal commission reappointing Berkeley to his office of royal governor and captain general, did not reach Jamestown until that fall.[51]

A Little Parliament

Berkeley reacted swiftly to the news once it reached him. On 20 September 1660 he issued two proclamations, which he ordered read in every parish church and county court in Virginia. One announced the king's return to the throne, declared Charles II the rightful ruler of Virginia, and commanded all colonists immediately to acknowledge their allegiance to the Crown. The other legitimated existing officeholders, commanding all magistrates "whatsoever within this Countrey" to remain in place for the time being.[52]

There was more to restoring royal government than merely issuing proclamations, as Berkeley knew full well. The colony's constitution needed redefinition, meaning that the settlement of 1652 had to be reversed. That reversal required action by the General Assembly, which imposed an exquisite political decision on the governor. Should he honor his engagements with the burgesses? If so, he should then recall the burgesses, persuade them to enact the necessary changes, and hope to justify his action to Charles II. Or should he break his promises, dissolve the House of Burgesses, and issue writs for a general election? A man of his word, he summoned the existing assembly to a meeting on 11 October 1660.

Texts of Berkeley's opening address and the legislative journals have vanished, but much of what occurred can be reconstructed from the session laws. Everyone accepted the return of the Old Dominion to its former loyalty and dependence on the monarchy, some exuberantly so. All were equally determined to protect the integrity of the colony's political establishment by keeping the Crown at arm's length, much as their predecessors had done with Parliament eight years before. At the outset, though, several burgesses questioned the legitimacy of the session because Berkeley had called it "with out a new election." Declaring itself valid to "all intents & purposes," the assembly overrode the objection, observing how a poll of the voters would have delayed resolution of "the Immergent occasions of the Countrey." Turning to constitutional matters, the assembly asked Berkeley to solicit Charles II for a general pardon of the colonists for their "past revolt and disobedience." Embracing "the Kinges most excellent majestie" as the source of authority in Virginia, it repealed various Interregnum statutes that conflicted with royal government. All remaining laws would "Continnue and bee in force." The assembly designated Governor Berkeley, Speaker Bland, and several burgesses a special committee to petition the king for his recognition of its prerogatives and for confirmation of "all such Concessions as were grannted" by Charles's father and grandfather. All that done, the assembly enacted several revenue measures and dispatched a few other routine items before it adjourned. That assembly never sat again.[53]

Early in the new year Berkeley circulated writs for a general election. The ensuing poll returned some holdovers from the October session, but most of the burgesses were friends and allies of the governor. Together with a revamped Council, they sat through seventeen consecutive sessions before their dissolution, which made the General Assembly of March 1660/61–May 1676 the longest of any in the history of Virginia.[54] Berkeley never accounted for why he retained the body some historians later dubbed the "Long Assembly,"[55] though several explanations seem plausible. Regular elections and rotation in office were novel ideas in the seventeenth century, so they found little resonance in Berkeley, the members, or Virginia voters. From a purely expedient standpoint, however, continuing the assembly fulfilled practical purposes of governance until well into the 1670s. Among others, it deepened the loyalties of those who depended on the governor for patronage, it augmented the stature of the House of Burgesses, and it greased passage of important legislation. Not least of all, it bespoke an arrangement between the governor and the planter elite. Berkeley shared power with those he regarded as dependable partners, which ensured them nearly unmitigated dominance in local politics. In return, he gained great latitude in determining the course of public policies such as the colony's economy and its external affairs. This tacit quid pro quo not only drove politics after 1661, but it also raised the assembly institutionally as well.[56]

For instance, when the new General Assembly first convened, it immediately authorized Berkeley to go to London and "oppose the invaders of our freedomes and truly to represent our condition to his sacred majestie." That action foretold the assembly's long-term commitments to the governor's vision for Virginia, just as it portended the ease with which Berkeley would usually have his way with the members. On the other hand, reforms of the county courts and the House of Burgesses as well as plans for a comprehensive overhaul of the laws presaged the assembly's further expansion of its prerogatives.[57]

Regarding the courts, the assembly for the first time since 1634 limited the number of county court justices. An act for the "Regulation of commissioners"[58] rationalized the modification on grounds that the "great number" of justices "hath rendered the place contemptible and raysed factions among themselves rather then preserving the peace." It therefore restricted the total to eight magistrates per court.

Thereafter, Berkeley selected the eight from among the senior members of each bench unless a "knowne defect" or "neere relation" to another judge rendered someone incapable. Other requirements specified that sheriffs be drawn from the benches, too, and that the office "be conferred on the first in commission, and so devolve to every commissioner in course."[59]

Much about this statute restricted executive rights. Constitutionally, the power to appoint subordinate officers belonged to the governor by virtue of his being the king's vice-regent; his commission explicitly said as much. That Berkeley readily consented to the intrusion indicates his style of leadership. The law benefited him politically because it gave him protective covering to rid county benches of vociferous parliamentarians. It also consolidated local control in fewer hands, which was something that contented the great men, and so he deferred to them once more.

Similar dynamics inspired reforms in the House. Existing rules enabled the House to dismiss recalcitrant members, which was why it easily removed John Bond, an Isle of Wight burgess, for his "factious and schismaticall demeanors." Nevertheless, the members took steps to prevent nonconformists or truculent candidates from being elected ever again. To ensure timely elections, an act enjoined the secretary of the colony to exercise greater care in delivering the writs to the sheriffs. Another law, defining members' entitlements, prohibited vote buying, which rendered the office of burgess "mercenary and contemptible." More fundamentally, the House standardized its delegations in two important ways. It designated the counties as the colony's sole electoral districts, which eliminated church parishes as bases of representation, thereby displacing a "great number of Burgesses." The second provision reduced the number of burgesses voters could elect to two per county. There were exceptions for Jamestown, "the metropolis of the country," and for any county that laid out a one-hundred-acre tract of land and populated it with at least "one hundred tithables persons."[60]

As for statutory revision, the assembly named Francis Moryson and Henry Randolph a committee to examine the laws in force. Their task well suited the two men, given their experience and position. A former Speaker, Moryson had recently risen to the Council, and he was about to become deputy governor for the duration of Berkeley's agency at Whitehall. Randolph knew Virginia law intimately. As the incumbent clerk of the House since 1656, he had not only prepared the engrossed texts (the authoritative versions) of all statutes, but he had also composed the bills from which many of the laws originated. After their review was complete, Moryson and Randolph drew up a draft "with such alterations and marked amendments" as they found necessary and presented their report to the next legislative session, which adopted it.[61]

Ostensibly, the new compilation[62] tidied up the return of royal government, but its redactors and their colleagues in the General Assembly had other objects in mind as well. Detailed provisions in the revised statutes underscored the assembly's authority over the colony's ecclesiastical establishment, its courts, its officers of state, and its revenues, and others spoke to the House's mastery of its internal affairs or its place in setting the legislative agenda. Certain laws took the General Assembly beyond the prerogatives of its counterpart at Westminster. Those that empowered the assembly to erect parish churches or to fix the duties of parish vestries are obvious examples; so was the power to create counties and towns and the law that allowed the assembly to "receive the presentments of the grand jury, and inquire into the remisnesse of juries and courts and how the lawes have bin put in execution." Yet another illustration is this quite bold claim of legislative supremacy: "noe act of court or proclamation shall upon any pretence whatsoever enjoyne obedience thereunto contrary to any act of assembly." That law was an especially remarkable enlargement because it invaded an executive power that derived from the Crown. But it was a limitation that Berkeley found acceptable. There is no record of his circumventing it or attempting to overturn it. In sum, much of the revisal anchored the preeminence of the General Assembly securely in written law.[63]

Even as the assembly grew toward its zenith as a little parliament, it remained in the constitutional marshes.[64] None of its prerogatives stood on the sturdy groundings of English precedents or contemporary British practices. They rested instead on undergirders of royal neglect, Berkeley's sufferance, and colonial usage. The buffets of events that culminated in Bacon's Rebellion eroded the assembly's foundations and led to its eventual diminution.

Although the Stuart monarchs' attitude of indifference had long fostered the assembly, that very nonchalance hurt Virginia sorely throughout the 1660s and 1670s. Charles II affirmed Berkeley's schemes for diversified economic growth, although neither he nor his advisers warmed to diversification, predicated as it was on free trade with the Dutch, reduction of tobacco crops, and financial support from the royal coffers. The king's countenancing of the navigation system effectively eviscerated the governor's program and plunged tobacco prices deep into depression. During the Second (1665–1667) and Third (1672–1674) Anglo-Dutch Wars, Charles II embarrassed Berkeley with commands to erect worthless fortifications at the mouth of the James River, which cost Virginia taxpayers dearly. The king compounded that humiliation by giving away the Northern Neck and then by granting the entire colony to Henry Bennet, first earl of Arlington, and Thomas Culpeper, second baron Culpeper of Thoresway. Berkeley's attempts at fending off both grants drove the per capita rates for provincial taxes to usurious heights.[65]

Berkeley lost the confidence of the planters as it became ever more apparent that his grand vision for Virginia's future could not succeed and he seemed able only to worsen the present. The great planters debased his political capital, too. His offering them a loose lead had not inspired the habits and sensibilities of a coherent ruling class collectively. If anything, the opposite was true; they abused their less privileged neighbors, and their callousness bred social discontents that Berkeley failed to grasp, let alone mitigate. Death or retirement took off his guardians at court and narrowed his circle of trusted intimates on the Virginia Council of State and in the House of Burgesses. Declining health and advancing years diminished him as well. Deafness turned him more crotchety and distrustful of all but a few remaining confidants, and his wits dulled to mood changes between royal officials and the Virginians. Such was the deterioration that when the challenges to his leadership came throughout the fall and winter of 1675–1676, a tired, sick, befuddled old man could not comprehend the precariousness of his situation. His failure ignited Bacon's Rebellion.[66]

An Indian raid in July 1675 began a series of killing blows and counterblows that sparked the revolt. Berkeley missed the gravity of the situation, which seemed to him little different from attacks that had occurred intermittently along the Virginia frontier ever since the conclusion of the Anglo-Powhatan War of 1644–1646. Slow to act, he let control of the situation slip through his fingers. He damaged himself even further when he summoned the assembly in March 1676. It committed the province's military establishment to defensive war, it left the strategic decisions to him, and it voted additional taxes to pay the costs of the fight. Little about these measures comforted panicky colonists or allayed growing doubts about Berkeley's abilities.[67]

Quite the contrary, the governor seemed all the more indecisive and cowardly, which emboldened Nathaniel Bacon to tout himself as someone eager to carry the fight to the Indians. Bacon took command of an illegal force of volunteer Indian fighters, despite Berkeley's admonition that leading them constituted mutiny. Angered by Bacon's indifference to his warning, Berkeley raised a force of men, but Bacon gave him the slip, and the governor returned to Jamestown still in a fury. For the first time he realized the precariousness of his position and tried to reclaim it. First, he proclaimed Bacon a rebel and suspended him from his seat on the Council of State. Next, he dissolved the General Assembly and called for the first general election of burgesses in fifteen years. Finally, he circulated a remonstrance to explain his reasons for his dealings with Bacon and vowed redress for whatever grievances the voters had with him. Even so he seemed to doubt his faculties for controlling events because just two days before the new assembly convened, he asked his superiors to replace him.[68]

A supercharged political climate and the first colonywide poll in more than a decade produced the General Assembly that convened on 5 June 1676 and lasted the customary four weeks. It was unruly, it was combative, and it was decidedly unlike any that Berkeley had ever seen before. Many, perhaps most, of the burgesses shared Bacon's view that an Indian was an Indian and the only good one was a dead one. All were, as Berkeley said in characteristically dramatic fashion, full of "ill Humours," but little about the known members sustains the argument that they were bent on revolutionizing Virginia. Neither were they necessarily hostile to Berkeley; nor was he inimical to them. After all, they actually adopted a resolution begging him "still to continue our Governor," and he showed his customary deference by allowing them to have Thomas Godwin for their Speaker.[69] Moreover, Bacon, whom Berkeley pardoned and restored to the Council, skipped most of the session. He returned at the head of five hundred armed men just as the assembly finished its business and extorted from the terrified legislators a general's commission to war on the Indians. Thereafter, Berkeley and Bacon dueled for control of Virginia. Berkeley lost Jamestown, recaptured it, and lost it again to Bacon, who burned it. The governor gained the whip hand after Bacon suddenly died, and by the first weeks of 1677, he had suppressed the last of the insurrectionaries.[70]

Bacon's Rebellion destroyed Sir William Berkeley and more. Compelled to squelch the uprising, royal officials intervened in Virginia affairs as they had not since the 1620s. First they attended to the rebellion; then they took dead aim at the General Assembly.

Chapter 3

New Realities

ews of Bacon's Rebellion pushed Berkeley's superiors in London to react with remarkable speed. Within a matter of months they dispatched a thousand redcoats and a fleet of ships to suppress the rebels and a three-man commission to investigate the reasons behind the uprising. From the outset, however, Charles II and his advisers had much more in mind than merely smashing Bacon or ridding themselves of their aged, discredited governor. Virginia's troubles were in reality an opportunity for them to draw the colony closer to their design of an orderly empire. Attaining that goal, in their estimation, required regaining colonial loyalties, recasting the office of governor-general, and lessening the place of the General Assembly, ends that could be reached by vigorous applications of royal power.[1]

One of the commissioners, Herbert Jeffreys, carried orders to supplant Berkeley. Jeffreys and his colleagues, Sir John Berry and Francis Moryson, immediately jousted with Berkeley over questions of authority. They faulted his brutal treatment of the former rebels and his refusal to follow royal orders to the exact letter. Berkeley bitterly resented their second-guessing of his actions as well as their blaming him and his adherents for the revolt; then, too, he would not surrender his office until Jeffreys seemed likely to pack him off to England in chains. In May 1677 Sir William Berkeley sailed across the ocean one last time. Sick unto death, he desperately sought an audience with Charles II so that he might justify himself, but that was not to be. He died within six weeks of his landing in London, alone, unmourned, and far from the place he called home.[2]

Berkeley's passing clearly marked the dawn of a new day for the Old Dominion. Harbingers of things to come had been evident from the moment the redcoats and the commissioners landed in Virginia. Although the army did little, the troops remained, billeted at colonial expense, well into the 1680s, and their continued presence served as an irritant as well as a tangible reminder of royal intentions.

As for the commissioners, they proceeded to their business with some dispatch. They issued the king's pardon to all but the rebel ringleaders, despite Berkeley's objections and foot-dragging, and they announced Charles's proclamation abrogating the acts of the June Assembly.[3] Exhorting the General Assembly of February 1676/77 to focus its deliberations on "the Glory of God, the Honour of his most Sacred Majestie, and the happy Restauration [of] Publique Good and long-lasting Welfare and Resettlement of this so miserably shatter'd and Lacerated Colony," the commissioners likewise challenged it to become "the healing assembly," but their admonitions fell on the unhearing ears of members.[4] The commissioners solicited the grievances of ordinary Virginians, written complaints providing grist for the final report they sent to the king. At the root of the discontents, the commissioners reported, was an overly independent General Assembly whose frequent meetings and excessive costs had driven the lesser planters to rebellion.[5]

In Jeffreys, the Virginians now had a chief executive like none in living memory. He scorned them, especially any who esteemed "the Power and lawes of A few Ignorant Planters mett in An Assembly for this Government" above the will of Charles II.[6] "A few Ignorant Planters" proved more formidable than Jeffreys had first imagined. The assembly members were not amused by his open disdain of them, nor were they prepared to accept sole responsibility for Bacon's misadventure, and from the day Jeffreys displaced Berkeley until his death in December 1678, they gave him no peace. He answered by driving the more boisterous of them from their places on the Council of State and in the House of Burgesses. That retaliation, far from cowering anyone, merely stiffened the colonials' obduracy.

Such stubbornness bespoke a realignment of politics that began as Berkeley departed. Jeffreys's enemies readily understood that the contours of their political landscape had shifted. For the first time in a third of a century they were without a governor who was like them. Bacon's revolt also awakened them to the lesser planters' discontents and the need to ensure that such rancor would never again burst into rebellion. All acknowledged an intrusive Crown for what it was, a threat to the General Assembly and the great planters' dominance of it. The leaders had to guard themselves against their fellow Virginians and against meddlesome imperialists.

Staving off future Bacons was the easy part. That merely required a more openly deferential attitude toward the interests of lesser planters, and such shows of consideration soon grew commonplace. The change signaled an alteration in the relationship between the leaders and the led, especially as politicians came to rely on greater popular backing in their struggles against imperial policy.[7] Crafting a response to the Crown's challenge was more galling because accommodation was really the only alternative. Therein lay the chafe. Accommodating to imperial authorities raised the irksome issue of how much. On that account Jeffreys's antagonists were of deeply divided counsel, and they quickly split into three factions.

One resisted any form of acquiescence nearly to the last man, or woman. This was the group Moryson, Jeffreys, and Berry denominated "the Green Spring faction" in their correspondence to London and in their final report. Chief among the irreconcilables were Thomas and Philip Ludwell, secretary and deputy secretary of the colony, respectively; Robert Beverley, clerk of the House of Burgesses; and Council members Thomas Swann, Thomas Ballard, and James Bray; burgesses Thomas Milner, Arthur Allen, and William Kendall; and last, but not least, Dame Frances Berkeley, the old governor's widow. They had been among Berkeley's most-trusted intimates and closest advisers. All had lived long in the Old Dominion and, except for Dame Frances, all had enjoyed extensive, lucrative careers at every level of the colony's government. Theirs was a plain scheme. They would obstruct the Crown at every juncture and wear it down, hoping it would tire of trying to impose its will on the colonists and leave them be. Uncomplicated though the strategy was, it carried risks. Beverley, Philip Ludwell, Swann, Ballard, and Bray lost their offices for a time, and their obstinacy raised the possibility that Jeffreys or others might turn to more extreme measures. Even so, irreconcilables dominated every General Assembly until the late 1680s.

The irreconcilables' stance spawned an opposing faction of trimmers who yielded little by way of political experience to the irreconcilables. A few, namely Francis Moryson and Nicholas Spencer, were ostensible Berkeleyites, whereas younger trimmers such as Isaac Allerton, John Armistead, and Matthew Kemp stood at the margins of Berkeley's circle. Others had no connection to the old governor beyond owing him the offices that they occupied in 1677. Collectively, all trimmers lacked the deep commitment to him, his policies, or his world view that typified the irreconcilables. In fact, well before Bacon's Rebellion, various of them had followed the example of Moryson. Having lived in England since the mid-1660s as agent for the Old Dominion, Moryson gradually assimilated the convictions of Stuart policy makers into his own thinking and turned toward London for patronage even as he continued to curry Berkeley's favor. The trimmers, therefore, easily tailored their politics to the changed circumstances. By their lights, the connection between colony and mother country differed in the postrebellion era from that of earlier times. An imperial order centered on Whitehall was a ripe idea, and there were benefits to Virginia in its acceptance. It offered the security and economic gain that Berkeley had failed to deliver, and those who backed it would not only hold their offices but also reap additional royal preferment. Self-interest made the trimmers more than eager to relinquish some of Virginia's autonomy for the sake of their political position. Trimmers turned up in every House of Burgesses after 1677, though they never gained control there. While the Council of State was their stronghold, even there they were in the minority.

Situated between these opposite factions was a group of moderates. A versatile lot, they possessed singular gifts for adjusting to political alterations seemingly without sacrifice to their commitments or their places. Their political pedigrees were as flawless as any others in the Old Dominion, and they were entrenched members of its ruling establishment. Foremost among their leaders were Nathaniel Bacon Sr.— cousin to the rebel—William Byrd, and Augustine Warner. Bacon, in a career that crossed four decades, outlasted parliamentary rule, Berkeley, and the later Stuarts. His junior colleagues proved just as agile; Byrd and Warner, for example, put aside their intense aversion to one another for a greater political goal. Typically, moderates had more of the irreconcilable than the trimmer in them for they wanted no part in any subtraction of their power, let alone any decrease in the authority of the General Assembly. The uncompromising stance of their irreconcilable brethren alarmed them, but they also suspected the trimmers for their too-agreeable embrace of Crown policies. They were astute enough to accede to a recalibration of the relationship of Virginia to Whitehall, but their objective lay in minimizing the degree of the adjustment. Accordingly, the moderates drew the line at open clashes with the governors-general, and they looked for openings to stymie the governors-general even as they made showy gestures of support. That tactic kept them in their offices and largely above royal suspicion. Because they commanded large blocs of followers on the Council of State, in the House of Burgesses, and among the local magistrates, the moderates held the key to politics after 1677.

Had the imperialists recognized these hues among the Virginians for what they were, things might have turned out differently. In truth, however, little about those shadings actually registered with Jeffreys, his replacements, or anyone else in London. The one imperialist who knew Virginia politics better than most, Francis Moryson, departed for England just as the factions started to coalesce. He had the potential for counseling the home government where to strike his former assembly colleagues at their most vulnerable points, but death removed him from the scene within three years of his return to England. Aside from Moryson, few in London troubled themselves to learn the contrasts among Virginians or the circumstances that had spawned the colony's political configuration. Far-off imperialists tended to see the Virginia terrain in stark colors: the colonists were either the king's friends or they were not. Then, too, postrebellion governors came from backgrounds that counteracted any tendency toward indulgence. Well situated in Stuart society, they all scorned the Virginians as subordinate upstarts, and they had neither the need nor the wish to cultivate such rabble, let alone to identify with them, as Berkeley had done. More than that, they were creatures of the Stuarts, committed to refashioning Virginia according to the dictates of their royal masters.[8]

The politics of confrontation became the order of the day, as did clashes between the chief executive and the General Assembly after 1677. Invariably, those battles arose when the governors, acting under royal instruction, attacked long-held assembly prerogatives. Just as invariably, the Virginians retreated. Five of those skirmishes plainly illustrate the interplay that at length forced members of the assembly to accept bridles on their legislative independence.

First to go was a privilege that had existed for half a century, the right to annual sessions. Charles II laid the ground for its elimination when he instructed Berkeley in October 1676, "you shall bee noe more obliged to call an Assembly once every yeare, but only once in two years, unless some emergent occasion shall make it necessary, the judging whereof Wee leave to your discretion."[9] Berkeley decided that clearing the dust of the rebellion constituted a sufficiently "emergent occasion," so he called the assembly into session at Green Spring House the following February. Berry, Jeffreys, and Moryson seized the opportunity to insist

> That an Act of Assembly may passe for the future calling of a new Assembly to be Elected every two yeares ... , whereby to make those of the present Assembly more ready to comply with his Majestys Royall Commands for Retrenching their former Salary. Whereas by reason of their constant sitting, they Receive onely and Pay not; which this alteration will well Remedy, and make the Charges & Expence equall by alternate Receipts and Payments, and consequently alleviate the Present Pressure, which the People seeme soe much concerned in.[10]

Their urgings went unheeded, and the commissioners duly noted the assembly's recalcitrance.[11]

A Little Parliament

News of the insult to the king's wishes provoked a harsh reaction in London. The Privy Council sought advice from one of its committees, the Lords of Trade, on ways to impose on the assembly "a due sence & acknowledgement of their Duty & submission towards his Majestie."[12] Domestic uncertainties in England brought about by the Popish Plot, and the Exclusion Crisis delayed further action until late in 1679, when Governor Thomas Culpeper, second baron Culpeper of Thoresway, received new orders. The king forbade his calling an assembly without an express royal warrant except in instances of extreme emergencies. That rule put an end to regular annual meetings for the duration of the colonial era.[13]

Charles's instructions to Culpeper also required passage of a statute creating a permanent revenue to support the provincial government, which the king hoped would reduce the need for frequent legislative sessions. As the king's advisers envisioned, the desired income could be raised through customs duties assessed at two shillings on every hogshead of tobacco exported to England, at six pence per capita on all persons transported to the colony, and at one shilling and six pence, or three pounds of shot, on every vessel docking in Virginia. Culpeper announced the proposal in his opening speech to the General Assembly of 1680–1682. The burgesses rejected it out of hand. Not to be denied, Culpeper read them the riot act. Their refusal wasted time, he said, which was "totally unparliamentary and [would] make the Exercise of Assemblies, (which as most necessary ought to be most easy) wholly impracticable, if not impossible." He even accused the House of pretending "to the Sole Legislative power," which "noe house of Commons in England ever did" before the Civil War. Chastened, the burgesses voted to reconsider the measure, and they sent it to a joint committee for further deliberation but without assurances of final approval. It passed only after the governor accepted two concessions. One was an amendment repealing earlier revenue laws that exempted Virginia shipowners from the ship duties, and the other a petition to Charles II that justified the Culpeper bill. The statute, the first of its kind in Virginia, marked a pivotal reduction of the assembly's control over public finance.[14]

Having won that battle, the Crown reached for more. It next pushed for legislation empowering the governor and Council to raise taxes in emergencies without approval of the assembly. The underlying concept for such a law had originated with Berkeley, who had first received authorization from the General Assembly of March 1660/61 to levy as much as twenty pounds of tobacco per tithable "to defray the country debts and salaries." Revised in 1662, the law expired three years later, according to a sunset clause that was written into it.[15] Popular demands for resurrecting it were presented to the General Assembly of 1680–1682, whereupon Culpeper and the Council ordered that an "account thereof" be presented at the next legislative meeting. The report was never returned, perhaps because the second session of the assembly was abruptly prorogued on the king's order.[16] Later on, Culpeper took the further step of recommending the idea to London, as did Nicholas Spencer, who had succeeded Thomas Ludwell as secretary of the colony. Spencer argued that such authority would allow the governor and Council to "maintain & keep up the Dignity of the Government, and free the Inhabitants of the charge of too frequent Assemblies."[17] Acting on this advice, the king finally instructed Culpeper's replacement, Francis Howard, fifth baron Howard of Effingham, to "use your best endeavors" to pass such a law, but Effingham's success at carrying out the order was limited.[18]

Effingham had much better luck in ending the General Assembly's claim to sit as a court of last resort. Litigation initiated by Sarah Bland led in a roundabout way to his delivery of the fatal stroke. Her connections at court and her tenacity in pursuit of her objects alerted royal officials to yet another line of attack on the assembly's long-held prerogatives. Sarah Bland was the widow of the London merchant John Bland (d. 1680), who had devoted much of his life to developing huge landholdings and handsome business deals in Virginia, but had entrusted the management of both to a brother, Theodorick Bland, who served as Speaker of the House of Burgesses and was a member of the Council when he died in 1672, leaving a jumble of unresolved debts and claims against the family. His widow and executrix, Anna Bennett Bland, wrote to her brother-in-law, John Bland, and begged him to come to Virginia and settle her late husband's affairs. He sent his son Giles Bland instead. A sportive, quick-tongued fellow, Giles Bland quickly got at cross-purposes with his aunt and antagonized Berkeley. His rancor toward the governor led him to Bacon in 1676, a traitor's death, and the confiscation of the Bland estate. His mother, hearing of the execution of her son, resolved to succeed where he had not. She went out to Virginia to litigate the recovery of the family properties plus the arrearages that had been uncollected since before Theoderick Bland's death. Her attempts caused her to sue Anna Bland and the latter's new husband, St. Leger Codd, for their indebtedness to the Bland estate. The suit failed in the General Court, as did an appeal to the General Assembly. Back in London, Sarah Bland turned to the royal courts, only to be frustrated, and at length she petitioned the king-in-council for remedy. Charles II's advisers noticed the petition because of its potential for diminishing the power of the General Assembly, and they ordered Culpeper not to allow appeals from the General Court to the assembly.[19]

Culpeper carried out the order obliquely. When the burgesses in the General Assembly of 1680–1682 addressed him to learn "his Excellencies pleasure about a Committee for private causes" to determine which appeals the assembly should consider, Culpeper refrained from the usual naming of councillors, and no committee was appointed. No committee meant no hearings, which forced the burgesses to post a note "at the Assembly house doore" giving notice that "all private causes depending in the Assembly by appeall are refer'd to the Next Assembly."[20] During the abbreviated session of April 1682 the issue arose anew as the burgesses pushed Deputy Governor Sir Henry Chicheley to nominate councillors so as to avoid "great inconveniencyes" if not a "totall fayleur of Justice." Nothing came of their pleas because the meeting was prorogued, which spared Chicheley from offending the House.[21] The burgesses harangued him again when they reconvened the following November, but he put them off once more. So did Culpeper, who returned to his place in the middle of the session.[22]

There matters lay until Effingham became governor. His instructions, like Culpeper's, expressly forbade any appeals to the assembly. In addition, he had royal orders and a request from a Crown official, William Blathwayt, to settle the Bland litigation. Blathwayt and Sarah Bland were lovers, but Blathwayt was also one of Effingham's patrons. Shortly after Effingham arrived in Virginia in February 1684, he ordered the Bland case docketed for a rehearing at the General Court.[23]

Effingham and the House of Burgesses squared off on the larger appellate issue when he met the General Assembly of 1684. On 19 April 1684, Speaker Thomas Ballard appointed ten burgesses to the Committee for Private Causes and asked that the governor name several councillors to assist. Hearing that, Effingham immediately called the whole House into the Council chamber and treated them to a sharp chiding. He was "sorry," he scolded, "to see or heare of such obstructions in the beginning of this Assembly," especially because the burgesses paid no heed to "his Excellency the Lord Culpepers Command Received from his Majestie, that noe appeals should be from the Generall Courte to the Assembly, which he openly declared in the Generall Courte." Consequently, there were now "noe private Causes to be tried," and he saw no reason to assign councillors to other House committees either. He dismissed the burgesses with the rebuke that they "proceed to the businesse of the Assembly which now Gentlemen lies before you."[24]

New Realities

This was literally adding insult to injury. When their predecessors addressed Culpeper on 21 December 1682 asking for specific clarification of his position on the appeals issue, he had replied, "As to the last, all Private Causes debated & undetermined this sessions of Assembly, I agree that they stand referred to the next Assembly." His answer brought forth a further request. Because "noe private Cause hath been in debate this session of Assembly," the House asked if Culpeper's message "doth extend to private Causes, and other matters undetermined by this Assembly." To which the governor retorted, "noe Cause can be supposed to be Dismissed any Court, till the same be determined by some Judgment of that Court and therefore I conceive all Causes of Course remaine referred, and so noe need of any particular reference at all, besides I find it in the Journall of the Councill this particular provided for, however (for dispatch sake) I have agreed to the Generall termes expressed in the other paper."[25] Culpeper declined to show the burgesses his instructions; had he done so they would have seen the prohibition on appeals, and they would have caught him in the lie that he had spun for them. Of course, Effingham, who was under similar instructions, believed himself under no obligation to abide by assembly precedents, though he obviously tried to read Culpeper's statements in a fashion that gave him protective cover.

Abashed at such treatment, the burgesses retired to their quarters and promptly considered a response that took the form of a written rejoinder. In it they made two salient points. Virginia statutes, "Customes," and "Constitutions" invested the General Assembly with an "Inherent Right and Priviledge" to act as a "Courte of Judicature," and it had long been the practice for a "select Committee" to decide which causes to hear. As to Culpeper's pronouncement, the burgesses averred,

> This House is not sensible of any such Publiq declaration or expression of the Lord Culpepers but on the Contrary This House doe finde that by the Lord Culpepers answer to the then House, dated the 21st december 1682. He Concurred with the Honorable Councill and the House in Referring all private Causes to the next Assembly which seems to this House a Confirmation of what the House had before Received from the Honorable Lt. Governor the 28th November 1682. That if betwixt that time and the next Session of Assembly his Majestie should not please to give particular directions in the matter of proceedings in Appeales in private Causes to the Assembly then they should be heard and determined by Councill Assisting in Committees after the forme and manner of private Causes in Assemblies held before the yeare 1680.

The burgesses also asked to see relevant clauses of Culpeper's original instructions in order to "Yield their Ready obedience thereunto." Effingham did not reply, nor did he reveal Culpeper's orders.[26]

There things stood while the assembly worked on other business. On 26 April the burgesses adopted a resolution from the Committee on Propositions and Grievances, asking for Effingham's support for a petition to the king for his reconfirmation of the "antient Practice of this Country permitted and allowed by his moste Sacred Majestie and his Royall father of ever blessed Memory."[27] Piqued by the invitation, the governor chastised the House for its insult and then offered a compromise. If the burgesses reworded their memorial to say that appeals of more than £200 would go to the king-in-council, then he would support it. The House was not in a dealing mood. It adopted its petition unchanged and dispatched it to London in defiance of the governor's admonition against such a course. Effingham got the last word on 19 June when he announced a proclamation that annulled the statutory basis for the assembly's presumed "right."[28]

That the burgesses were so absorbed with the question of the assembly's authority in the appeals business was directly related to Sarah Bland's legal pursuit of Anna and St. Leger Codd. Bulldog-like, she pressed the Codds so unremittingly that they fled for sanctuary to Maryland to escape her bite. They returned just in time for the freeholders of Northumberland County to elect St. Leger Codd to the House. He sat as a daily reminder to many of his colleagues in the General Assembly of 1684, chiefly the irreconcilables among them, of the pernicious results of yielding to Effingham. Codd's predicament exemplified the "evill Consequence" that followed when "Ill disposed persons" harassed those of "honest & Quiet disposition" but also libeled and aspersed "the Government an instance whereof is most pregnant & visible, in Mrs. Sarah Bland."[29]

Reproving Effingham and petitioning Charles II availed burgesses little because their defenses of the assembly's claim to review General Court rulings lacked contemporary parliamentary precedent or royal sanction. Conceivably, the assembly might have salvaged a portion of its privilege had the irreconcilables accepted Effingham's offer of a deal, but their refusal to trade horses sealed the fate of another "antient right of Assemblies." More ominous, Effingham's resort to his proclaiming power to kill the prerogative opened a new avenue of assault on their presumed privileges.

Proclamations had been a feature of governance going back to the days of Samuel Argall, who seems to have been the first chief executive to use them with some regularity.[30] Argall and his successors depended on such instruments to address matters that lay beyond the reach of the General Assembly or affected military considerations. With the enlargement of the legislative purview of the assembly, however, gubernatorial proclamations became more a means of announcing public events and elaborating on the written law. Those employments were engrafted in colonial statutes as early as 1632, whereas the governor's proclaiming power was recognized statutorily two decades later, but with the pointed proviso that no proclamation could ever contravene an act of assembly. Significantly, however, no one in London paid heed to the implications of Virginia law.[31]

Indeed, the king's proclamations were always part of the governing mechanisms. James I introduced rule by proclamation, and his son expanded on it when he declared Virginia a royal province. The Crown seldom exercised its power after 1625, which allowed Virginians to disregard the likelihood that a sovereign might see in his proclaiming power a means of overturning colonial law or setting aside Virginia political customs. Bacon's Rebellion made likelihood reality after Charles II voided the acts of the June 1676 assembly. His proclamation was as radical a use of his residual authority as any since the 1620s, and it set the stage for more.[32]

In their capacity as the king's vice-regents, all of the postrebellion governors exercised their proclaiming power in the sovereign's name, but no one used it with the devastating ingenuity of Lord Howard of Effingham. He first recognized it for the forceful, flexible tool it was when he took on the burgesses in the appeals business. Time and again thereafter, whenever he wished to skirt the intent of Virginia law or thwart the assembly, he did so by proclamation. The tactic infuriated the Virginians but they were powerless to combat it.[33]

Effingham also exacted from the burgesses their traditional right of choosing their clerk. Longtime House clerk Robert Beverley provided the opening. He and the governor loathed one another. At the beginning of the Effingham administration, Beverley lay under arrest and indictment for his presumed part in the plant-cutters riots. Effingham presided at his trial and suspended his conviction for "high misdemeanours," thereby hoping to gain the Virginian's gratitude and loyalty. That was not to be. Second to Philip Ludwell, Beverley was the leading irreconcilable, and he continually found ways to aggravate Effingham.[34]

Things came to a head after Beverley embarrassed the governor by fiddling with the wording of a bill for the encouragement of towns, which was proposed during the first session of the General Assembly of 1685–1686. The quarrel over the text reached such heights that Effingham angrily prorogued the assembly.[35] Worse still, the governor wrote detailed accounts to London, singling out Beverley as the source of the trouble. In the letter he directed to the Privy Council, he observed that "your Lordships will now see how requisite, and advantageous it will be for his Majestys service, that the Clerk of the Assembly be hereafter appointed by his Majestys Governor." He requested and soon received the appropriate authorization, together with orders to dissolve the assembly, to declare Beverley "uncapable of any Office or Public Imployment," and to arraign the clerk for "altering the Records of the Assembly." A gleeful governor sent the assembly packing in October 1686, and he relished dismissing Beverley.[36]

Effingham made his move on the clerkship when he summoned the assembly in the spring of 1688. The burgesses proceeded to elect a Speaker in the usual fashion and picked another of the governor's foes, Arthur Allen. They were about to consider candidates for clerk when one of their number, the trimmer Francis Page, revealed his commission from Effingham naming him "Clerke to the House of Burgesses till I shall signifye my Will and pleasure to the contrary." Stunned, the burgesses inquired into the source of Effingham's action and only then learned of the king's order empowering the governor to name the clerk. In the face of a direct royal commandment they had no alternative but to acquiesce, and so the House, with little more than a murmur, lost the power to elect one of its primary officers.[37]

Effingham's zeal for further contests relented noticeably after he dissolved the General Assembly of 1688. Effingham suffered recurring illness that sapped his appetite for further confrontations, and with the king's permission he returned to England in February 1689, where he stayed until he resigned his office.[38]

Neither he nor Jeffreys nor Culpeper ever fully achieved their masters' goal of empire, though they strengthened the Crown's administration of its oldest American that empowered dominion. That reinforcement came at the expense of the General Assembly. Plainly, the Virginians had little chance of winning the scuffles that reduced their legislative independence of London. Imperial officials had picked their spots with some care, and in Jeffreys, Culpeper, and Effingham they found willing executives. Effingham, in particular, persisted by pressing the assembly at its most vulnerable points. Again and again, he struck down prerogatives and procedures that diverged incontrovertibly from political practice in Stuart England.

New Realities

Charles II and James II checked obstinate Parliaments by not calling any. Statutes of the realm were not yet absolute expressions of parliamentary will. They could on occasion be abrogated by royal proclamation, as James proved by his several declarations of indulgence that set aside religious conformity laws. Judgments in the law courts could not be appealed to Parliament. Appointments to the clerkships in the House of Commons were gifts of the sovereign, not the choice of the members. Royal favorites in the House managed its business and orchestrated the elections of its members. Therefore, Effingham could justify his so-called "great innovations"[39] as no more than mere attempts to bring the assembly into nearer conformity with the prevailing ways of Parliament. Demanding such modifications, he could easily argue, did no more than keep faith with his master's commands. And all loyal subjects had an affirmative duty to obey their king, even Virginians. His logic was as irrefutable as it was effective.[40]

Thus, when Effingham surrendered his commission in 1692, the General Assembly was not the same body it had been fifteen years earlier.[41] Not only was its authority diminished, but gone too was any pretense to a verisimilar equality with Parliament. Local concerns had defined politics in 1677, but localism yielded to issues of a more-pronounced provincial and imperial character. Cultivating royal bureaucrats became as vital as currying favor with Virginia freeholders. The office of governor-general was significantly reformed from what it had been in Berkeley's day. Whereas Berkeley had viewed himself as primus inter pares, his successors, acting under royal orders, distanced themselves from the burgesses and the councillors. As for the Council of State, it assumed a greater importance because it was the one element that continued to meet routinely once annual sessions of the assembly ceased to be the norm.[42] That alteration ushered in "the era of the Council," which lasted until well into the eighteenth century.[43]

Likewise, Effingham's successor, Sir Edmund Andros, encountered more pliant Virginians as death, retirement, or accommodation reduced the number of irreconcilables. Even the staunchest of them, Philip Ludwell, eventually made his peace with Stuart imperialism. The moderates, too, conceded that Virginia now belonged to an Atlantic community, the economic and political hub of which was London. With that concession came another realization.[44] Before 1677, few Virginians had thought much about how the General Assembly differed from Parliament. There was no need. Everyone on both sides of the Atlantic had accepted the departures as conditions of existence in the colony or had ignored them, so the attacks on the assembly caught colonial politicians off guard. They could not counter with justifications any more compelling than the uniqueness of their circumstances and the sanction of time. In the face of English precedents and determined governors, such defenses proved fragile shields, and that realization accounted for the origins of a distinctly Virginia line of political thinking.[45]

Jeffreys, Culpeper, and Effingham failed to achieve Stuart visions of empire. They hedged the General Assembly, and just as it stood at the breaking point, the downfall of James II and the accession of William and Mary directed the empire builders' attentions elsewhere. From the 1690s onward, the assembly's quest for power was as much a striving to recover lost ground as to claim new terrain.[46]

PART II

Membership

It being inconvenient and chargeable, in the Infancy of Government, to keep up many Officers, the usual Way is to trust all to one good Governor, who, like a tender Nurse, is sufficient to take the Management of the Infant Government, till it grow older, and wants other Tutors and Governors to Look after it.

All the great Offices in Virginia (being then an Infant Government) were at first heaped upon one Man, and, which is stranger, continues so to this Day.

—Henry Hartwell, James Blair, and Edward Chilton, 1697

The number of the Councellors when compleat is Twelve; and if at any time by Death or Removal, there happen to be fewer than nine residing in the Country, then the Governor has Power to appoint and swear into the Council, such of the Gentlemen of the Country, as he shall think fit, to make up that number, without expecting any direction from England.

—Robert Beverley II, 1705

According to an order of Court from the Governor and counsell for the Elexion of Burgesses out of this county, the commander with the consent of the commissioners appoynted the inhabytants of this county to meete togeather at the Sheriffs house wher the 15th day of February were come togeather and made choyce of mr. John How and mr. William Roper for Burgesses.

—Northampton County Court order, 1637

. . . there was by the unanimous vote of all then being present (being thirty in number) chosen Coll. Edward Hill Speaker, and being by them presented to the Governour from him received approbation.

—House journal, 1659

A Little Parliament

[The burgesses] have of long time been well knowing of the Loyalty faithfulness & good abillities of Robert Beverley *their Clerk and humbly pray your Lordship will please that he be continued and accordingly sworne.*

—House journal, 1680

Meetings of the General Assembly routinely gathered governors, councillors, burgesses, Speakers, and clerks. Those were occasions not only to discharge public business but also times for courting power, for forging friendships, for making enemies, for settling scores; sessions were opportunities to enliven the General Assembly as an institution and to enlarge its collective memory.

In countless ways—some recorded, many not—each legislator had a hand in the assembly's work, though not all equally. What then is to be made of those individuals? In a few words, a little and a lot. Some are now barely known figures, recognizable only by name and smatterings of personal detail. Conversely, others surface from the extant record and show themselves in considerable proportion. Profiling members highlights the interplay between personalities and the working of the assembly as it points to explanations of how individuals passed from neophytes to skilled politicians.

Chapter 4

Governors-General

❧❦❧

The historian Robert Beverley, writing in *The History and Present State of Virginia* in 1705, characterized the office of governor and its occupants for his readers. Governors were royal appointees who served at the monarch's pleasure and represented the Crown "in all things." Assemblies came and went at their bidding. Not only did they propose legislation, but also no bill became law without their assent and signatures. Governors presided "in all Councils of State," they established courts, they appointed civil officers, and they had charge of military affairs.

Among the chief executives who served before 1705, only Sir William Berkeley won praise from Beverley. His pen dripped vitriol on Culpeper and Effingham who made dangerous alterations of "an old Constitution so abruptly." Beverley mercilessly derided Francis Nicholson as a small-minded man who strove mightily to "gain himself a Character" but spared the others when he took scant notice of them singly or collectively.[1]

Beverley's commentary disclosed three salient features of the office of governor. It was the pivot point of the colony's government, it mingled political rule with military authority, and men of standing were supposed to fill it. All three attributes fit squarely within the meanings that Britons had ascribed to the word *governor* ever since its entry into their language. Those very properties had meshed precisely in the minds of the managers of the Virginia Company who erected the office in 1609. Sir Edwin Sandys's subsequent redesign of the colony's administration abated the absolute authority of the governor, making him first among equals with his councillors, and elevated his political responsibilities, but his martial duties remained untouched. Consequently, when the first General Assembly convened, the office already existed in the shape it retained until independence.[2]

Contemporary mores dictated who should be governors. Britons accepted social inequity as the natural order of things, and few doubted the timeless verity that some men were ordained to rule and others were meant to be governed. It was also an article of faith that exalted station bestowed on genteel English men the gifts required of good rulers. Those merits were palpable to anyone with eyes to see: riches, piety, forbearance, industry, and prudence.[3] Sir Thomas Elyot[4] set to words social concepts that his readers already understood when he explained the value of recruiting governors from the top ranks. "Where vertue is in a gentyll man," he wrote in the sixteenth century, "it is commenly mixte with more sufferance, more affibilitie, and myldnesse, then for the more parte it is in a persone rural or of a very base lineage, and when it hapneth otherwise, it is to be accompted loathesome and monstruous." Furthermore, he cautioned, when a leader was "worshypfull, his governance, though it be sharpe, is to the people more tolerable, & they therwith be the less grutch [i.e., complaining] or be less disobedient."[5]

Even men of merit required timely guidance in the execution of their duties. In the instance of Virginia's governors, that direction took its form in written orders known as commissions and instructions. The more general of the two, a commission constitutionally warranted an incumbent to execute his office by specifying the authority granted to him. Beverley mentioned some of the governor's powers, as well as others that invested any chief executive with broad control over the lives of Virginians. Instructions, by contrast, provided explicit dictates for how the powers conferred in the commission should be rendered effective.[6]

The basic contents of the two credentials dated from the company era. Wording of the instructions became stereotyped when the Crown appointed Sir George Yeardley in 1626. The substance of the commission was standardized at the renaming of Sir Francis Wyatt in 1639, if not earlier.[7] Crown bureaucrats modified the composition of both after Bacon's Rebellion, when they redrew each with a greater particularity that reflected imperial designs on the colony and the office itself. The Board of Trade recodified the two documents in 1696, after which they remained unchanged down to the Revolution.[8]

Commissions were public papers. Indeed, reading them aloud before the Council of State formed part of the ritual of any governor's inauguration.[9] Record copies were also filed with the secretary of the colony and were available to anyone who might wish to read them. Instructions were another matter. They came to be construed as privileged communications between monarch and vice-regent. Berkeley habitually shared his with members of the General Assembly, but postrebellion governors were not so forthcoming. Culpeper, an adept prevaricator who seldom honored orders to the letter, if at all, had good cause to hide what Charles II commanded of him. On the other hand, Effingham quickly found political advantage in keeping his instructions secret. The issue surfaced in 1685 when he and the House of Burgesses contested the extent of his veto power, and the burgesses "prayed most humbly" that he would furnish them with a copy. Effingham shot off a tart reply, saying that "not foreseeing any occasion, that I should have of it, I left it at home," which effectively left the burgesses to sputter in frustration. Such a tactic meant that no one could ever accuse him of acting contrary to his charge, and it was one his successors continued. Its poisonous side, however, was a festering irritant that annoyed burgesses and governors in the generations to come.[10]

Original commissions or instructions were fancy documents, elaborately done up on either parchment or fine paper. Each bore the signature of the appointing monarch. A wax impression of the Great Seal of England was laced to the commission. The instructions carried the lesser imprint of the king's privy seal. Signing and sealing authenticated the two records, and both were delivered to their recipient when he officially assumed his duties. On taking office, every governor swore an oath of office plus the customary vows of allegiance and supremacy. Following the passage of the Test Act in 1675, he also had to profess his belief that no "transubstantiation of the sacrament of the lord's supper, or in the elements of bread and wine, [occurred] at or after the consecration thereof."[11] These rituals of inauguration usually took place in the Privy Council chamber, often in the royal presence. Repeated soon after a new governor reached Jamestown, their reenactment represented the ceremonial start of a new administration.

Commissions, instructions, and ceremonies reinforced the centrality of the governor to public life in Virginia and drew notice to his enormous power. How a governor actually governed, though, depended on something more than the warrants and symbols of the office. That something embraced the properties that Sir Thomas Elyot specified as uniquely inherent in "gentyll men." The historian Robert Beverley, however, who would not have quarrelled a word with Elyot, discerned but one man who brushed close to Elyot's ideal of the good ruler. Some would debate Beverley's choice; nevertheless, it invites a closer look at the men who presided over the General Assembly throughout the seventeenth century.

Twenty-two men sat in the governor's chair between 1619 and 1700. Ten were councillors of state, who warmed the cushion as acting or deputy governors for intervals ranging from a few months to a few years. The Crown appointed two—

A Little Parliament

Herbert Jeffreys and Francis Nicholson—as lieutenant governors. Richard Bennett, Edward Digges, Samuel Mathews, and Berkeley were all elected governors. Sir George Yeardley, Sir Francis Wyatt, Sir John Harvey, Berkeley, Culpeper, Effingham, Sir Edmund Andros, and Nicholson each held a commission from the Crown as "Governor Generall of our Colony and Dominion of Virginia."[12]

What Sir George Yeardley (bap. 1588–1627) lacked in family pedigree he more than offset through experience. Reared plain George Yeardley, son of a London merchant-tailor, he chose to find his way in the world by adventuring rather than by tailoring. He learned lessons of command after he enlisted in a company of English troops that saw duty in the Netherlands. While in Holland he rose to a captaincy and associated with Sir Thomas Gates before the two of them went to Virginia in 1609— Gates to become lieutenant governor under Thomas West, baron De La Warr, and Yeardley to become captain of Gates's bodyguard. Although Yeardley "brought onely his sword with him," he gathered a favorable reputation as a dependable officer and a dedicated settler, which led to a stint as deputy governor once Samuel Argall left Virginia. Yeardley returned to England in 1617, where he busied himself in tightening his ties to company officials. He caught the eye of Sir Edwin Sandys, who engineered Yeardley's knighthood and appointment as governor.[13]

Knighting Yeardley added weight to his new office but did rather less to allay the apprehensions of colonists who had long clamored for men of "birth and quallyty" to govern them. For such settlers, as for others, it mattered little that Yeardley was now Sir George. Taps on his shoulders from James I's rapier may have graced him personally but could not automatically erase the stigma of his origins. He remained in the eyes of many a "meane fellow by way of provision."[14]

Yeardley smoothly executed the launch of the General Assembly, but on the whole his was not an easy administration. Some of his difficulties probably arose from his background and his personality, though how much is a debatable point. He was not Elyot's ideal governor. More likely, Yeardley's troubles stemmed from flaws in Sandys's scheme to avert impending disaster for company and colony, which the governor was obliged to implement. Among other things, a hasty buildup of population taxed the governor's abilities to cope with the new arrivals. Yeardley had little time to prepare for them and too few supplies from London to sustain them through their difficult first days in Virginia. As he saw the situation, the company never sent him adequate warning when it dispatched more shiploads of settlers. Worse still, some get-rich-quick ideas seemed all the more pointless in the face of sickly or inept colonists. Yeardley grew cross, which chafed his relationship with Sandys and company investors, who eventually wearied of continual complaints about their inadequacies, causing some to wish him gone. Frustrated, Yeardley finally asked to be relieved. No one raised a voice to dissuade him, and in the summer of 1621 the general court of the company voted to replace him with Sir Francis Wyatt.[15]

Five years later, Wyatt gave place to his predecessor. Yeardley's prospects were a bit more promising the second time around. The company was gone, and the settlers were struggling to save the General Assembly. Yeardley shared their concerns, even to the point of accepting an assignment of lobbying at Whitehall for royal confirmation of the assembly. His agency came to naught, though he fashioned his own connections with the court. When the Crown sought Wyatt's replacement, Charles I and his advisers turned easily to Yeardley. They knew him, he knew Virginia, and the colonists who counted now trusted him. Yeardley's political ties and abilities finally signified far more than his parentage. A mere eighteen months into his second administration death deprived Yeardley of an opportunity to impress additional marks either on the office or on Virginia.

Sir Francis Wyatt (ca. 1588–1644) was much that Yeardley never could be, or ever was. Born at Boxley Abbey, Wyatt descended from a cultivated, patrician Kentish family with long roots deep in the county's political and social life. Sir Thomas Wyatt, his great-grandfather, was a renowned Tudor poet, and his grandfather, also a Sir Thomas, perished as a traitor for raising up Wyatt's Rebellion against Queen Mary Tudor. That misadventure cost the Wyatt family its reputation and estates, though Francis's father recovered both. Elizabeth I even made George Wyatt a justice of the peace, but he devoted much of his time to studying and writing. Young Francis grew to manhood early in the seventeenth century in the comfortable embrace of the country squirearchy that was the source of England's governing classes. Tapped in 1618 for a knight, he married one of Sandys's nieces. An interest in colonial enterprises led him into the Virginia Company, and as a stockholder he took his turn filling various of its committee assignments. His ties to Sandys and his rising visibility within company circles explain the logic of his election as Yeardley's replacement.[16]

It was Wyatt's lot always to govern Virginia in times of great emergency. Scarcely had he settled in at Jamestown than he had to lead the settlers against the Indians. Mustering frightened colonists in the wake of the 1622 uprising and at the same time attempting to realize the policies of an equally crestfallen Virginia Company was a trial for anyone, let alone Wyatt, who had neither practical military experience nor political seasoning. The governor proved a quick study and won respect from everyone for his skill at steadying the Virginians and taking the fight to Opechancanough. That gift increased his standing with the planters who esteemed him as a "most just and sincere gentleman" who lacked "all manner of Corruption or pryvate ends."[17] Naturally enough, he emerged as the obvious choice as the Crown's first governor-general.[18]

Wyatt smoothed the transition from company to royal control, just as he played the lead in the effort to legitimate the General Assembly. That work ended abruptly because of his father's death in 1625, which required him to return to England. He surrendered his commission rather than muddle Virginia's political situation by naming a deputy governor.

Retirement from office did not translate into an abandonment of Virginia affairs. During the ensuing decade and a half Wyatt retained his contacts in the colony. At court he was clearly regarded as one of the king's more knowledgeable advisers about Virginia. That reputation resulted in the proffer of membership on the Dorset Commission, which he readily accepted. Many of its other members were former colleagues from the Virginia Company, so it was scarcely a surprise when the commission forwarded its recommendation that a similar entity should take over the management of Virginia. Wyatt's personal views of the report are now unrecorded, though he would not have opposed it, given his place on the commission and his background in the defunct company.

The ouster of Sir John Harvey turned the Dorset remedy into a nullity as the Crown moved to quiet rebellious Virginians. Although the king stood behind his governor, it was quickly evident that Harvey could not govern in the face of staunch hostility from his councillors. Lacking both the will and capacity to force Harvey on the colonists, the king let him go. Once again Wyatt loomed as the best possible successor. The available Wyatt became the indispensable Wyatt, and as Wyatt had done in the past, he calmed a troubled situation before selling his commission to Berkeley.

Wyatt kept his place on the Council of State as part of the deal that made Sir William Berkeley governor, though for how long is uncertain. Indications are that he returned to Boxley Abbey toward the end of 1642. His movements are difficult to trace once he got back to an England that was in the first throes of the Civil War. With whom he sided is not certain, but that did not matter very much because he died in 1644. Curiously, though, about the time of Wyatt's death, the Cavalier propagandist Peter Heylyn accused him of stirring up Virginia dissenters against Berkeley. By implication Heylyn seemed to suggest that the former governor leaned in the direction of puritanism and the parliamentary cause. The allegation is without independent corroboration, and Heylyn's charge is plainly inconsistent with other evidence of Wyatt's character.[19]

Sir John Harvey (d. 1646) was the antithesis of Wyatt. A seafaring man from the Dorset port town of Lyme Regis, Harvey was lured to the mariner's calling as a youth. He went from the forecastle to the quarterdeck, eventually joining the diverse cadre of merchant skippers who flew the English ensign round the globe as they plied blue water from England to the Baltic, to the Levant, to Africa, to the East Indies, to the Americas and back, ever in search of profitable cargoes. Such men were more than mere ship captains. Rough spun, ill-lettered, and badly graced though they sometimes were, they possessed a talent at once mysterious and highly desirable: the ability to navigate from port to distant port across seemingly trackless expanses of ocean. That gift elevated them to positions of importance. Great trading companies in London or Bristol were helpless without them. Backers of colonies needed them. Even kings looked to them, especially in times of international strife, when they armed their ships to prey on enemy commerce or harbor towns. In a word, mastery of celestial navigation and the other maritime arts gave them entrée that the best parlayed to great advantage. So it was with Captain Harvey.[20]

The sea furnished Harvey well, to judge from the scattered details of his early career. Once he became a skipper, he developed a sound reputation for his seamanship from the experience of regular runs to the East Indies, and he had the ear of the government on occasion. By the 1620s he held a stake in the Virginia Company and served on at least one of its committees. He owned at least one ship, the *Southampton*, which provided him an income once he leased her to the company to transport new settlers to Jamestown. When he first voyaged to the colony itself is unclear, though he eventually acquired land in the New Town quarter of "James Cittie," where he built a house.[21]

In 1623 the Privy Council named Harvey chairman of a fact-finding committee to report to James I on how he might govern the colony once the Crown took control. Harvey and his fellow commissioners could hardly have expected a warm reception at Jamestown, given the nature of their assignment, and they received none. Even so,

Harvey's conduct during the inquiry left something to be desired. A decidedly undiplomatic personality, the captain was known to intimates as a "proper man, though perhaps somewhat choleric and impatient." His disposition quickly set him at odds with members of the General Assembly. To make matters worse, Harvey tangled with several colonists in unseemly squabbles that credited no one. He complained bitterly to correspondents back home about his troubles, but the commission's work proceeded to its conclusion, and Harvey returned to England.[22]

The Crown eventually rewarded him for his service by slating him to succeed Yeardley as governor. Involvement in the English assaults on Cadiz and fending off attacks on British ports kept Harvey from returning to Virginia until 1630, by which time a knighthood adorned him, but he remained as prickly as ever. Only now his hand plotted Virginia's course, and to him charting it was no different than sailing his ship. At sea, he brooked no objections to his orders. He countenanced no debate with subordinates; neither did he solicit their votes at the officers' mess. Back talk equated with mutiny. His word was law. Anything less than unequivocal obedience courted disaster for the crew, the cargo, and the ship. His style suited a quarterdeck better than a council chamber, and it soon set him at odds with his councillors of state, who disagreed with his policies and who were just as determined to share in ruling as he was resolved that they should not. And so they ran him off. He died in disgrace, unnoticed and missed by none save, presumably, his relations.[23]

The disasters of Harvey's administration have always masked his successes as governor. Harvey ended the war with the Indians, which stopped the periodic campaigns of killing and pillaging that had dragged on for a decade. Uneasy peace freed colonists and natives for more productive purposes, just as it added a leavening of tranquility that Virginia had not enjoyed since 1622. The first Maryland settlers also had cause to be grateful to Harvey because he followed his instructions to assist them, despite stout opposition from his councillors. Harvey likewise deserves credit for altering the shape of local government. He got the General Assembly to adopt the recommendation of a commission headed by Archbishop William Laud that Virginia be subdivided into shires. The change was profound in that it set the foundations of the county courts and of the colony's ruling elite. Then, too, Harvey presided over the first full revisal of the colony's laws and prodded the assembly into adopting legislation that bettered Jamestown. The improvements he effected to the capital village went a considerable way toward turning a collection of nondescript buildings into the semblance of a town. At the distance of three and a half centuries, therefore, the irascible Harvey seems deserving of a kinder assessment than he ever received from his foes or from most historians.[24]

The appointment of Sir William Berkeley (1605–1677) broke a pattern. Every governor before him had invested in the Virginia Company, sat on its committees, had firsthand experience of the colony, or often advised the Crown on colonial matters. Berkeley brought none of that. Nor was he a made-up gentleman in the fashion of Yeardley or Harvey. He came from an influential gentry family, one that stood many rungs further up the social ladder than the Wyatts.

His branch of the Berkeleys located in the west of England near the town of Bruton in Somerset. His father, Sir Maurice Berkeley, sat in Parliament, was a justice of the peace, and held shares in the Virginia Company. Elizabeth Killigrew Berkeley, his mother, belonged to a well-bred Cornish family that also participated actively in company business. Born in Middlesex, at the estate of his maternal grandparents, Berkeley passed his early years there and at the Abbey, the family seat in Bruton. He earned degrees at Merton College, Oxford, and read law for a time at the Middle Temple. He traveled to the Netherlands and possibly to Italy before his relatives secured his appointment as a gentleman of the king's privy chamber. While that post may appear insignificant to modern eyes, it certainly was not seen so in the 1630s. Such places afforded opportunities for aspiring younger sons like Berkeley, and there was no forecasting how high he might go, given his lineage and abilities.

Things started out promisingly enough for the new privy chamberman. He wrote and published plays, one of which, *The Lost Lady, A Tragi-Comedy*, was performed before Charles I and Henrietta Maria. A circle of courtiers known as "the Wits" welcomed him into their society, while another group who gathered around Lucius Cary, second viscount Falkland, opened him to diverse intellects and political ideas. He also met men who had been to Virginia, and proximity to the mighty informed him about the policy debates over the colony's future direction.[25]

Years at court made Berkeley neither rich nor famous nor powerful, though they did gain him a knighthood. Lack of distinction vexed him as time went on. He grew especially uneasy once Charles I's vacillations and deceits caused the moderate royalist in him to suspect his master's rule. Doubt festered into alarm after he twice joined the forces that went north with the king to engage the Scots in the disastrous Bishops' Wars of 1639 and 1640. A crowd of subsequent events inched the nation nearer to the edge of civil strife and increased his uncertainties. The defining moment culminated for Berkeley about the time that Thomas Wentworth, first earl of Strafford, met his doom on 12 May 1641. The king's craven sacrifice of a hated but faithful minister convinced Berkeley to leave England. The question was where to find not just a refuge but also a place to start afresh.[26]

Constantinople beckoned first. Acting at the suggestion of a distant relation, Berkeley prepared to go to Turkey. All was actually in readiness when, for reasons no longer certain, Berkeley suddenly reversed himself and bought his way into the Virginia governor's chair. Exactly how he managed that feat remains a mystery, although the outlines are plain enough. Having seized on Virginia as the better prospect, he used friends and relations to level the way there. Wyatt seemed an easy mark, given the advantages Berkeley could bring to bear. The would-be governor pulled many more court strings than any Wyatt might tug in return. And bigger ones, too. His brother Sir Charles Berkeley was personally close to the king. Family and friends worked promptly. Indeed, they rushed Berkeley along with startling speed. Barely two and a half months after Berkeley decided to quit the court, Charles I ordered the warrants for his commission and instructions. The documents differed not a whit from the wording in Wyatt's credentials, apart from whom they named. Both papers passed the seals in a mere ten days, and they were in Berkeley's hand by 10 August 1641.[27]

For what reason, or reasons, did Charles I so readily toss aside the experienced Wyatt in favor of the novice Berkeley? The king's thinking is unrecorded. Berkeley never said, or if he did, his account is lost. Nor does a ready explanation lie elsewhere. The existing ancillary records are decidedly quiet on the subject of the appointment. In the absence of specific written documentation, circumstantial evidence provides a clue to a likely answer. The king had bigger things on his mind than who governed far-off Virginia, and he was in a hurry. His situation relative to the Long Parliament had gotten so bad by August that he quit London for Scotland. So his decision to cast Wyatt adrift came down to this. A distracted, shallow-minded king acted hastily to content an importunate subject. Significantly, Charles I handed Berkeley his credentials and left town the very same day.[28]

Previous royal governors received little help from the Crown beyond their orders, and neither did Berkeley, but he landed at Jamestown even more naked than they. Trouble in England bred trouble in Virginia because it forced the colonists to pick sides and threatened a rupture of ties that bound colony to mother country. Being governor under those conditions was trial enough, but the unusual and abrupt manner of Berkeley's appointment also put him at a disadvantage. He had neither friends nor allies among Virginians. The big men eyed him warily. Sir Francis Wyatt was a known quantity. Berkeley was not. A majority of his new councillors were the very men who had unhorsed Governor Harvey, and they were fully prepared to upset him, too, should that prove needful. The demands of office pulled Berkeley several ways at once and challenged his political wit. Serving colonist and monarch simultaneously meant following his instructions, holding Virginia loyal to the Crown, maneuvering between rival blocs of colonists, and contenting Charles's opponents in Parliament. The test, of course, lay in finding scales that balanced these conflicting demands.

Although inexpert at such things, Berkeley was by no means ill-invested for the job that lay ahead. Ten years' service at court had tutored him in the ways of politics, its theories and its pitfalls. His inherent powers as chief executive were an asset. Personal attributes benefited him, too. Distant yet approachable, he was an urbane, witty man with a playwright's talent for a clever phrase and a courtier's exquisite manners. He enjoyed the gift of a flexibly creative, quicksilver intellect that rendered him at once visionary and easily adaptable. Last, and by no means least, Berkeley shared an important similarity with the settlers themselves. Like them he sought an existence in Virginia that he had failed to attain in England. He parlayed connections, an office, a few thousand pounds sterling, and a several dozen servants into great fortune and power. His beloved Green Spring House near Jamestown testified to his success and personal wealth as it symbolized his abiding devotion to Virginia. Lavishly appointed, the sprawling mansion enveloped its owner in such grandeur and luxury that could be seen nowhere else in the English North America of his day. (Nor would great houses of comparable scale or embellishment rise in the Old Dominion until the eighteenth century.) The plantation fields provided the testing grounds for various diversification experiments that he ultimately projected as replacements for tobacco culture.[29]

Berkeley understood from the beginning of his tenure that his best chance of political success lay in joining hands with members of the General Assembly. Evidence of his ensuing relationship with the members is distressingly thin, although some of its outlining features are quite apparent. He judiciously curried potential friends as he isolated rivals. From his first assembly to his last, he acknowledged limits to his powers and stayed within those boundaries. In the Council of State, for example, he acted as primus inter pares, which allowed his colleagues a voice that comported with their sense of themselves. He handled the burgesses similarly. His greatest boon to them was encouraging them to sit as a separate house. He treated the entire General Assembly with a deference and deftness of touch that fostered the enlargement of its parliamentary privileges. A shrewd politician, Berkeley had an instinct for timing and an alertness to the character of others. Sometimes giving a little gained him more; sometimes a flash of wit or temper worked; sometimes the threat of retirement turned the trick; sometimes the proffer of a reward won an ally. By such means, Berkeley constructed a devoted corps of legislators who followed him willingly throughout most of his tenure.

His last years as governor were his worst, and they brought disaster. Undermined by failing health and discredited policies, an aging Berkeley overstayed his welcome. He misread the signs of his decline and the mood shifts among the planters. That blunder caught him up in the episode that destroyed him; Bacon's Rebellion defined him as no other event in his long, varied career. Seen entire, however, the whole Berkeley did more for the Old Dominion than cruelly suppress the revolt he helped cause.[30]

Profiles of the other governors elected during the Interregnum are considerably sketchier than Berkeley's. Richard Bennett (bap. 1609–1675) shared West Country origins with Berkeley as his family hailed from Wivelscombe, Somerset. An uncle, Edward Bennett, held the place of auditor for the Virginia Company. He started the Bennett presence in the colony when he founded a large plantation on land, in modern-day Isle of Wight County, that he received from the company.[31] Richard Bennett went to Virginia in the mid-1620s and subsequently established himself as a planter in the area that became Nansemond County. He sat as a burgess in at least one General Assembly before Charles I raised him to the Council of State in 1639. Wedding Ann Utie, widow of an important politician, further cemented his ties to the area's emerging leadership, as did the later marriages of their daughter, Anna Bennett Bland Codd.[32]

Puritan leanings and his overthrow of Berkeley in 1650 put the two men at political odds; nevertheless they remained personally cordial throughout a relationship that lasted nearly thirty years. As governor, Bennett not only reconfirmed Berkeley's title to Green Spring, but he also schemed to allow Berkeley to remain in Virginia after the parliamentary takeover. A few years later, when Bennett needed a

Jamestown residence, Sir William sold him one in his town-house complex. Bennett kept his Council seat after the Interregnum. Berkeley even named him a major general in the militia and then sent him to Maryland as an envoy in some of the negotiations aimed at limiting tobacco production in the two provinces.[33]

Governor Bennett faced a more difficult chore than Governor Berkeley. Answerable to the House of Burgesses in a way that Berkeley never was, Bennett operated from a position of weakness. His identification with Parliament's commercial policy haunted him, especially after the First Navigation Act provoked war with the Netherlands. Lack of finesse hurt, too. So did his squabbling with the burgesses over the choice of the Speaker. Remarkably, in the face of what should have been crushing obstacles to success, Bennett accomplished the task for which he had been elected. He led Virginia from royal to parliamentary government in a fashion that produced neither bloodshed nor lingering institutional upheavals.

Edward Digges (1621–1676) left a lighter mark. Yet another colonist of Kentish stock, he came from a family whose interests in Virginia also dated to the company period. He gained some legal education at Gray's Inn as a youth, but being a fourth son, his prospects in England were none too good, so in his thirtieth year he immigrated to Virginia, bought a plantation in York County, and rapidly acquired a reputation as an able planter who raised high-quality tobacco. The weed enriched Digges, but he achieved much wider notice for his experiments with silk production. Marriage to Elizabeth Page, whose brother John was a rising star in York County, opened political doors. Family ties, political connections, and wealth netted Digges a place on the Council of State in 1654, and a year later, the House of Burgesses elected him governor in Bennett's stead. He quit after eighteen months to become Virginia's agent in London, from which position Charles II promoted him to the Council for Foreign Plantations in 1660. Subsequently, Digges worked as one of Berkeley's operatives in the English phase of bargaining with Maryland authorities about limitations on tobacco production. The negotiations failed, and Digges returned to agriculture, becoming the man on whom Berkeley most relied to demonstrate the worth of silk as an alternative to tobacco. In 1670, Berkeley rewarded his "worthy frend" by appointing him a councillor of state and the colony's second auditor general, which posts Digges occupied for the remainder of his days.[34]

There are few traces of the first Virginia-born governor, Samuel Mathews (ca. 1630–1660), from which to reconstruct his life. He grew up at Mathews Manor, that "fine house, and all things answerable to it," that his father, for whom he was named, had built near Denbigh. In all likelihood, the elder Mathews engineered his son a spot on the Warwick County bench, which led to his election as a burgess in the General Assembly of April 1652. A few years afterward, the younger Samuel went on the Council before he was elected governor. His fights with his former colleagues in the House of Burgesses were his only memorable accomplishments, and his sudden death early in 1660 led to Berkeley's second administration.[35]

A new breed of chief executives came in the wake of Bacon's Rebellion. Except for Effingham, all were seasoned by decades of service commanding English troops in the home islands, on the Continent, or in North Africa. Career army officers and royalists at heart, they thought imperially. Postings to garrison towns taught them techniques of administration in the face of oftentimes unruly and hostile civilians. Loyalty, outlook, and experience fitted them neatly into the role the Crown assigned to them in Virginia after 1677.[36]

The first of them, Herbert Jeffreys (d. 1678), initially took up the sword for a living in 1642, when Charles I commissioned him a lieutenant in a regiment of foot. His taste for his calling and his skill soon earned Jeffreys a captaincy, but siding with a losing cause delayed his prospects for higher rank. Exiling himself with other defeated royalists, Jeffreys joined the staff of the young James Stuart, duke of York, in France. Following the Restoration in 1660, he saw duty in Dunkirk, Portsmouth, York, and France before the duke posted Colonel Jeffreys to Virginia to dispose of Bacon and his rebels.[37]

Lieutenant Governor Jeffreys was not an easy man. In outlook he came closer to Sir John Harvey than to the old man he dismissed in April 1677. After all, in the seventeenth century, English sea captains and army officers often rolled off the same bolt of cloth; background mattered, but the ability to follow orders mattered more. For such men, careers and livelihoods depended on the prompt, efficient execution of assignments. So for Jeffreys duty came down to this. The king and the duke wanted to tame the General Assembly and to return the office of governor to its central place in colonial administration. King's orders were king's orders; carrying them out was Jeffreys's sworn obligation, and enforce them he would.

That attitude set up a tension in Virginia unlike any since Harvey's day. Jeffreys possessed something not seen before in the colony as well, a resolute Crown buttressed by the presence of one thousand redcoats. Just how far would Jeffreys go? Not far, as it turned out, because he died after a mere eighteen months in office. That was time enough, though, for him to force three leading irreconcilables—James Bray, Thomas Ballard, and Philip Ludwell—from the Council of State and to displace lesser members of the faction from their offices as well.[38] A bout of illness then felled him. It came on him in the summer of 1677 and kept Jeffreys from presiding at the General Assembly that October. Winter's cold restored him, but he again worsened with the onset of warmer weather, and by summer's return, he was a sickly, miserable man once more. His weakness emboldened the irreconcilables to vex him at every turn. Those "troublers," noted William Sherwood, of Jamestown, contrived with all the artifice they could muster "to bring a Contempt ... [upon] our present good Governor." Death released Jeffreys in December 1678, and after he died the spite-filled irreconcilables succeeded in imprisoning his widow for her late husband's debts.[39]

The irreconcilables had cause to hope for better things once they learned that Thomas Culpeper, second baron Culpeper of Thoresway (1635–1689), held the commission as governor and captain general. Culpeper was Dame Frances Berkeley's cousin, and her brother, Alexander Culpeper, was longtime agent for the new governor's Virginia business. Surely, thought the irreconcilables, such blood ties would incline Culpeper to their views. On the other hand, Charles II expected him to carry out orders. Both the king and the irreconcilables soon learned that their optimism was misplaced. Culpeper never intended to fulfill either's expectations.

Culpeper had passed his early years at the family seat in Hollingbourne, Kent. He went abroad when he was sixteen to join his exiled father, and grew to manhood with the penurious outcasts who formed the Stuart court-in-waiting. Sir John Culpeper lived to see Charles II returned to his throne and his son married to a Dutch heiress but not so long as to enjoy his own deserved high place in the restored government. When he died in 1660, he left Thomas the king's indebtedness to anyone named Culpeper, a bankrupt barony of Thoresway, and a claim to a share of a proprietary land grant in Virginia. The young nobleman, armed with those assets, plus his wife's dowry and a generous dash of personal charm, set about recouping his fortune. Culpeper could not regain his father's old post as master of the rolls, though he secured rights to several clerical places in the rolls office, each of which had a reputed market worth of £1,500. Charles II quickly found another more visible and lucrative employment, giving him charge of the Isle of Wight and Carisbrook Castle. That appointment augmented Culpeper's wealth greatly, though it did little to enhance his talents for governance or his willingness to hone them. Even so, Culpeper continued a royal favorite. The king subsequently commissioned him an officer of an infantry regiment and named him to the Council for Foreign Plantations. The latter assignment ultimately enabled Culpeper to secure the Virginia governorship.[40]

Contemporaries regarded Culpeper as "one of the most cunning and covetous Men in England," and he cared little for governing Virginia.[41] His real interest lay in exploiting his claim to a huge tract of Virginia real estate that he had gained as part of his inheritance. His father, along with Berkeley's brother John and others, once formed a group that in 1649 Charles II designated proprietors of the Northern Neck. Exile prevented any of them from taking advantage of the would-be monarch's largess, though Sir John Berkeley went so far as to designate Sir William Berkeley his land agent.[42] No one made much of an attempt to develop the grant after the Restoration, and one by one the patentees died or disposed of their interests, leaving only Lord Culpeper and Henry Bennet, first earl of Arlington, as the 1660s closed. Seeking to rid Virginia of proprietors forever, Governor Berkeley instituted a series of complicated court actions and a round of hugely expensive, time-consuming negotiations. Dickering turned more complicated in 1673, after the king assigned all unpatented land in the colony and all of its quitrents to Arlington and Culpeper. Berkeley's raising of taxes to fend them off contributed to the rebellion of 1676, and that upheaval delayed further dealings, though Culpeper appointed land agents who issued patents in his name and collected rents for him.[43]

Culpeper took his oaths as governor only a few weeks after Berkeley's burial on 13 July 1677, but he tarried in London for months thereafter. Not even news of Jeffreys's death bestirred him, but blunt royal orders finally sent him packing in 1679, nearly three years after formally assuming office. Once in Virginia, Culpeper settled down at Green Spring House and into a brief fling with Dame Frances Berkeley. (The liaison had significant political repercussions because Philip Ludwell also courted, and eventually married, the Widow Berkeley.) Culpeper met the General Assembly, and once he had coaxed it into granting the Crown its desired permanent revenue, he cavalierly ignored the remainder of his instructions, prorogued the assembly, and took a ship for England without giving fair warning of his intentions or asking anyone's permission to abandon his post.

Culpeper savored the pleasures of London while desperate planters in Middlesex and Gloucester Counties cut up tobacco seedlings in a hopeless attempt to drive up the price. Members of the Council of State quickly and easily restored order well before the governor-general returned to the colony in December 1682 to launch his personal investigation into the episode. The so-called Plant-Cutter Rebellion had ominous overtones that boded ill for Culpeper's stewardship of his royal trust. Clearly, many Virginians remained in a mutinous frame of mind, and some of the irreconcilables, most notably Robert Beverley, were the likely ringleaders of the troubles. All of that suggested his lordship's failure to do a job, but that was not all. Culpeper also raided the provincial treasury to the tune of some £9,500. Once he had packed up the treasury, he suddenly announced to the Council of State that he was returning to England. An exasperated Charles II deprived him of office, and the Virginians got Lord Howard of Effingham in his stead.[44]

Francis Howard, fifth baron Howard of Effingham (1643–1695), fell from an Anglican sprig of the great family tree of Catholic Howards.[45] The eldest son of Sir Charles Howard of Great Bookham in Surrey, young Francis had a thoroughly conventional upbringing before his parents shipped him up to Oxford, though he left without a diploma. Actually Howard's purpose was not earning degrees but forming associations that he could translate to his advantage later in life. Nothing passed his way after he went home to Great Bookham, though in 1673 he contracted a proper marriage to Philadelphia Pelham. After his father died, he became both deputy lord lieutenant and a justice of the peace for Surrey. He might have stayed a country squire for the rest of his days but for the death of his cousin, Charles Howard, fourth baron Howard of Effingham. That put Francis in line for the barony. Succeeding to the title provided little by way of additional income or estates, though it raised the visibility of the new Lord Howard at court. His kinsmen, Henry Howard, sixth duke of Norfolk, and Henry Mordaunt, earl of Peterborough, introduced him to the duke of York and William Blathwayt, and by their contrivance he emerged as the leading contender to replace Culpeper.

Effingham considered the position an appealing prospect. Not only was it an opportunity to serve his sovereign, but it also carried a salary of £2,000 plus numerous other perquisites and potential rewards. The financial considerations especially caught his eye, given his need to support a large household. Moreover, as he wrote to his beloved wife, the income would provide "Advantages and Ease" that might sustain them into "our elder years."[46] Leaving his family behind, to join him once Philadelphia recovered from the birth of her eighth child, Effingham set sail for

Jamestown late in November 1683, big with expectations of how he would faithfully and rigorously execute all of the king's instructions.

His ship dropped anchor in the York River ten weeks later. The Council of State put on great shows of gladness at his coming, and "neare 300 horse" and dignitaries attended a welcoming reception.[47] Such displays masked the cautiousness with which the colonial leaders now approached any new governor. There was concern lest Effingham prove another Culpeper or Jeffreys, but there was hope, also, that he and they might, in the phrase of William Byrd, "proceed more for the countrys interest then formerly."[48]

Byrd and the others got neither a Culpeper nor a Jeffreys. Instead they got a minor peer of the realm of average intellect, who was rarely, if ever, reflective. Devoted to an Anglican God, a Stuart king, and the Howard family, Effingham took the world and his high place in it as both came to him. His unchallenging approval of the orthodoxies of his age rendered him easily amenable to the demands Stuart colonial policy required of him. In fact, he saw the opportunity to govern in Virginia as the chance of his life, and he resolved not to fail.

Determination to triumph where others had not was the very quality that distinguished Effingham. Until he chose to go home, not the tragic death of a wife whom he deeply loved, not his contests with the burgesses, not his own sickliness— in a word—nothing stayed his determination to give his masters what they wanted. Perseverance kept him in place, and that characteristic drew strong backing from Charles II, then James II, and finally William III and Mary II. His opponents among Virginia politicians found few effective ways to respond to such resolution, and they forfeited privileges that significantly diminished the General Assembly.

Poor health finally forced Effingham to return to England in February 1689. He arrived knowing that King James no longer sat on the throne and that the House of Burgesses was lobbying for his dismissal, so one of his first concerns was keeping his place. He fended off the burgesses' attempt to dislodge him, no doubt taking some delight at the ease with which he frustrated his arch enemy Philip Ludwell. And William and Mary greatly pleased him when they ordered a new commission for him as governor in February 1690. By then, it was fairly clear that his physical condition militated against ocean travel, so he acceded to the appointment of a lieutenant governor, who filled in for two years before Effingham resigned.[49]

Francis Nicholson (1655–1728) was another of those army officers who occupied various administrative posts throughout the empire over a lifetime. He had been lieutenant governor under Sir Edmund Andros in the Dominion of New England and resident in New York City. In the turmoil that overturned the Dominion in 1689, Nicholson gave up Fort James to rebellious militiamen and sailed away to England, a refugee under a cloud for supposedly abandoning his command in the face of danger. Neither his desertion of Fort James nor a change in reigns damaged his prospects for long, because William and Mary maintained James II's colonial policies and used the same officers to enforce it. Thus, Nicholson's patrons had little difficulty inserting him as Effingham's lieutenant governor.[50]

His first turn in Virginia went easily for Nicholson. Happy to have Effingham gone from their midst, the councillors and burgesses readily cooperated with the lieutenant governor, and a mood of magnanimity prevailed in the General Assembly as it had not since Berkeley's day. Nicholson's legislative proposals, especially one that resulted in the founding of the College of William and Mary, were partly responsible. He also chose not to challenge the assembly. His was a precarious position. There were no longer redcoats garrisoned about Virginia to back him up as they did for Jeffreys. Effingham might choose to return, which would displace him. Nor could Nicholson rely on the Crown in quite the same way as had Effingham. Good army officer that he was, he weighed the risks and ignored the potentially troublesome portions of his instructions.[51] Nicholson angled for the line to succeed Effingham, but that was not to be. The prize went instead to Sir Edmund Andros (1637–1714), and Nicholson got translated to Maryland.

Andros had the distinction of governing all of the royal colonies. Native of the Isle of Guernsey, he answered a call to arms as a youth and became one of the Crown's ablest soldier-administrators. More particularly, he attached himself to the household of James, duke of York, whose faithful servant he was. James dispatched him to govern the ducal province of New York in 1674, and as King James II he sent Sir Edmund to rule the Dominion of New England. Came the Glorious Revolution and the Massachusetts colonists overthrew the hated governor-general and clapped him in a dungeon on Castle Island in Boston harbor. Nine months of incarceration passed before Bay Colony authorities shipped him off to stand trial in London on charges stemming from his execution of James II's orders. The prosecution failed for want of evidence and because Andros's judges were also his allies.[52]

William Blathwayt, who had done much to advance Effingham, saw in Andros the successor to Lord Howard, and, as much as any single person, that wily bureaucrat maneuvered Sir Edmund into place. Andros reached Virginia by the autumn of 1692, and within a few months of his arrival he circulated a call for the legislature and writs for the elections of burgesses. The harmony of Nicholson's day quickly dissipated once Andros greeted the General Assembly of March 1693, and the relationship worsened in subsequent meetings. King William's War (1689–1697) soured it because Andros, on orders from London, pressed the assembly to contribute to the defense of New York. Burgesses and councillors held to the view that given Virginia's need of security they could furnish neither money nor men for the New Yorkers' protection. The assembly's attempts at revising the body of statute law aggravated Andros, too, although he conceded the desirability of the project. He grew quite out of sorts once it appeared to him that the assembly committed more of its time and energies to law revision than to matters he deemed of greater moment. But if there was a single issue that soured the well, it was the widening of differences between Andros and the Reverend James Blair.[53]

The cleric was a man on a mission. Ever since Bishop Henry Compton had designated him a replacement for John Clayton as his personal agent, or commissary,[54] Blair labored mightily for the establishment of a college for Virginia. Blair at first welcomed Andros, but when it became apparent that the governor did not share his enthusiasm for the college, they began to drift apart. The rift stretched once Blair, with help from his relatives on the Council of State, as well as Nicholson and influential patrons in England, forced a charter for the College of William and Mary past the seals. After Blair took the fledgling institution in hand as its first president, the breech with Andros became unbridgeable. Andros finally resigned, amid reports that Blair had greased the skids for his removal and for Nicholson's return.[55]

Governor and Captain General Nicholson began his second term well enough, but "he went not then with that Smoothness on his Brow, he had carry'd with him, when he was appointed Lieutenant-Governour." His second administration was as tempestuous as any in the Old Dominion's history. Even so, Nicholson compiled a record of considerable accomplishment. By the time his enemies drove him off in 1705, he had overseen the move of the capital to Williamsburg, reforms to the land system, a complete overhaul of the colony's statute law, and a reduction of conciliar privileges.[56]

Outwardly, the office that Nicholson assumed in 1698 differed little from what it had been eighty years earlier, though it had changed as it related to the workings of the General Assembly. Whether by necessity or design, the tendency from 1619 to 1677 was for governors to share their lawmaking authority with the assembly, which contributed to its growth as a parliamentary entity. That trend reversed after Bacon's Rebellion, when the Stuart imperialists set about reasserting the Crown's control over the colony. Success depended greatly on the character of the men charged with carrying out imperial designs. Although none of the governors after 1677 succeeded precisely according to plan, Jeffreys, Culpeper, Effingham, Andros, and Nicholson achieved one cumulative consequence. In humbling the General Assembly, they made every future governor-general a potential enemy, and that alteration of Anglo-Virginia politics had significant consequences throughout rest of the colonial era.

Chapter 5

Councillors and Burgesses

A parliament man, wrote Sir Edward Coke, "should have three properties of the elephant; first, that he hath no gall; secondly, that he is inflexible, and cannot bow; thirdly, that he is of a most ripe and perfect memory."[1] To Coke's way of thinking, England's governors shared such qualities natively. The representatives who took turns in the General Assembly exhibited similar elephantine assets, though they were political novices, who, apart from John Pory, never sat in Parliament or held local office in England. Another common earmark distinguished them from the traditional ruling classes. They more nearly resembled those thousands of Britons who swarmed into the Old Dominion than the men of whom Coke spoke.

The demands of a tobacco economy kept Virginia a society of immigrants throughout the seventeenth century, and a diverse multitude alighted before the migration peaked in the 1660s. Although some settlers were misfits, the colony never was a rubbish heap for England's social weeds. Dispossessed royalists hung up their hammocks in Virginia-bound vessels, too, but well-off cavaliers usually kept their loyalties to themselves, prayed or plotted for the Stuarts' return, and stayed home. The immigrants, in fact, mainly belonged to a middle rank of Stuart Britons who stood socially above poverty but below greatness.

They hailed from all over the kingdom, though most colonists originated in southeastern England and the counties that ran from the Thames Valley to the West Country. Moving from place to place seemed natural enough because they had flocked from rural communities into London and other port cities before turning westward for the Chesapeake. How they got to Virginia dictated their fate.

Colonists with nothing to venture save their labor sold themselves into indentured bondage for the price of a voyage. Young, single, and mostly male, they accounted for more than three-quarters of Virginia's white settlers.[2] Capital and personal connections graced a second, smaller contingent. Young men too, they not only paid their own way but also that of families and bondservants as well. Links with the Virginia Company or to established residents gave the group a leg up on their fellow settlers and enabled some to fasten their collective grip on colonial politics. There were gentlemen, army officers, lawyers, doctors, surgeons, apothecaries, coopers, innkeepers, bakers, salters, mariners, bookbinders, husbandmen, and yeomen in that number, but the majority were the offspring of mercantile families. Some were well-educated, some had little more than a grammar school education or an apprenticeship, and some could barely read or write.[3]

With a thirst for money and an eye for power, the second group of immigrants quickly fell to tobacco farming and other commercial pursuits. Using their mercantile contacts, they enlarged the range of their business ventures and extended the reach of their economic influence. Officeholding especially attracted them because a place in the colony's emerging political order opened conduits to land, laborers, social networks, and strategic marriages that consolidated power as it elevated status. Public service also enhanced the chances of shaping the direction of the colony in their favor. Above all else, office was a badge of success that symbolized arrival at the head of Virginia society. An itch for eminence and fortune was the ultimate prick for settling in the Old Dominion. Salving it seemed more than a remote possibility. A high death rate, a predominately male population, and a ready supply of offices appeared to assure steady opportunities after 1619. Founding the General Assembly opened a range of new positions from burgess to clerk. In turn, when the assembly created the county courts, it brought batches of justices of the peace, sheriffs, clerks, surveyors, escheators, and other lesser local officials into the mix.[4] Provincial openings also multiplied with the addition of a signet office,[5] the places of attorney, auditor, escheator, and receiver general, and numerous collectorships.[6]

Appearances were not entirely as they first seemed. Unfavorable demographic conditions produced a steady turnover of places, to be sure, though not at a rate that was wholesale. Besides, significant numbers of officeholders passed on gains to their progeny. After 1619, and without interruption, those men, their sisters, their daughters, their sons, and their widows intertwined with one another's families, thus plaiting a mazy patchwork of kin that eventually enveloped Virginia's political establishment.

At first, the chief claim to authority was mere ability to survive and thrive in Virginia. Leaders without experience, the men who filled available openings were predatory creatures who traded the intricate legalities of England for the freedom to stalk personal gain in Virginia. Their aggressiveness abated as they learned the politician's craft and gained the acceptance of those they presumed to govern. They thereby not only consolidated their hold on political power, but they also eventually acquired attributes of rulers similar to the men Sir Edward Coke had in mind.

This then was the great planter elite, which never numbered more than a few thousand, that supplied the General Assembly between 1619 and 1700. Making a full roster of the assembly is an impossibility because of incomplete records. At a minimum, however, 148 men sat as councillors and another 623 as burgesses.[7]

Councillors were Crown appointees, except during the Interregnum, when the House of Burgesses elected them. Unlike the governors, they received no formal sign of office; being named in the gubernatorial commission warranted their authority. There were no set requirements for membership either. Tenure was for good behavior, and governors avoided nominating "necessitous people, or people much in debt."[8] Force of habit kept the number of Council chairs between ten and eighteen, one of which belonged to the secretary and one to the treasurer. Wealth, proximity to Jamestown, experience in Virginia politics, and personal and kinship ties counted in the calculation for nominees, too.

If land ownership is taken for a measure, then all 148 councillors were men of great wealth in comparison to their fellow colonists. A typical holding was in excess of seven thousand acres.[9] Ostensibly, personal fortunes mattered for another reason. Custom dictated that councillors discharge their duties without compensation, so they received neither salaries nor expenses for their services. Nonetheless, there were opportunities for recompense. By statute, councillors and up to ten members of their households were exempted from all taxes except parish levies.[10] Moreover, the secretary, the treasurer, and any councillor who collected standing revenues, fort duties, special assessments, or customs also took fees for their troubles. Indeed, as the seventeenth century progressed, councillors monopolized all the lucrative provincial places that were at the governor's disposal. Multiple officeholding provided them with considerable income, though the practice also occasioned "great Confusion, especially in such things wherein the Places [were] incompatible."[11]

From an early date, councillors tended to live in the immediate vicinity of "James Cittie," and for a plain reason. Travel was slow; distance added to the difficulties of attending meetings, especially those called on short notice or in emergencies. Therefore, as settlement radiated outward from Jamestown, place of residence figured increasingly in determining membership. By the 1660s, if not sooner, men from Charles City, James City, and York Counties occupied half the Council seats. Others who lived in counties that either fronted the James River or lay immediately adjacent to Charles City, James City, or York took the most of the remaining places, which left the Eastern Shore and the frontier fringes consistently underrepresented.

At first, members also tended to be a mix of newcomers and hardened colonists, who were graced more by their skill at planting settlements and fending off the natives than by their political acumen. That trend continued until after the founding of the county courts, but after 1650, virtually all appointees were longtime residents who had spent years in local government or in the House of Burgesses.

Half the councillors held their seats less than five years, but roughly 8 percent lasted two decades or more. Length of service is not a good measuring stick of influence or continuity. No penalties attached for absences, as was the case in the House of Burgesses, nor was a full Council necessary because the governor and any three members could conduct business.[12] Almost the only time everyone tried to assemble was after a change of reigns or at the start of a new gubernatorial administration, but even those occasions could not always guarantee full attendance. At Effingham's inauguration, for instance, only five of twelve councillors swore their oaths with the new governor.[13]

Despite occasional problems of absenteeism, a core group routinely showed up at nearly every meeting. Among those who attended regularly up through the Restoration in 1660, nine—Richard Bennett, William Claiborne, Samuel Mathews, George Menefie, William Peirce, Richard Kemp, Argoll Yeardley, Thomas Willoughby, and John West—were among the most influential. They all landed in Virginia about the same time. Similar in outlook, they saw in the Council an engine of their distinction and Virginia's welfare, the two being inseparable in their minds, but the nine diverged over ends. Claiborne, Mathews, Bennett, Menefie, and Peirce shared commercial and political interests, and they formed an alliance linked to London merchants of a Puritan bent and to Parliament. Kemp, Yeardley, and Willoughby inclined to opposing views, which left West as something of a swing man. The nine thus represented issues that often divided the Council from 1619 to 1660. They also illustrate how certain great planter families maintained their grip once their places were assured.

Bennett, who joined the Council in 1639, reached a pinnacle when the burgesses chose him governor. His election in 1652 may have owed as much to his religious convictions as to other considerations, for he was the most-overtly Puritan of his faction. Whatever the explanation, he slipped into the background after a difficult administration, though he was the only one of the nine who kept his place after the Restoration. His child, Anna, was twice married, first to Theodorick Bland, a councillor and Speaker of the House of Burgesses, and then to St. Leger Codd, a justice and sometime burgess for Northumberland County. It was the latter union that led to the Sarah Bland litigation that cost the General Assembly its appellate jurisdiction.[14]

Sir Edwin Sandys recruited Claiborne (1587–1677) fresh out of Pembroke College, Cambridge, for the colony's surveyor. Shipping over in Governor Wyatt's retinue, Claiborne landed in 1621. His first job was laying out the New Town section of Jamestown, and he did other surveying while scouting opportunities for himself. He soon parlayed his surveyor's skills into substantial real estate holdings while relying on his business connections to forge broad and lucrative trade networks that reached from the Chesapeake to London. His commerce put him crosswise with the Lords Baltimore and the Maryland settlers, resulting in the extinction of his trading operations at Kent Island and his lifelong, intense animosity toward Maryland and the Calvert family. Growing wealth and influence placed him squarely in Virginia's emerging political elite, and in 1624 he was named to a seat on the Council of State. A year later he followed Christopher Davison as secretary of the colony, a place he held for a decade before it passed to his rival Richard Kemp. Standing with those of his fellow councillors who sought a wider hand in governing, Claiborne helped drive Governor Harvey from office after that abrasive fellow refused to accede to their demands. Subsequently, Councillor Claiborne acted as intermediary for Wyatt in the negotiations that culminated in the summer of 1641 with Berkeley's appointment as governor.[15]

Berkeley named Claiborne treasurer of Virginia, but there was always an edge to their relationship.[16] The treasurer rivaled the governor for leadership of the planter elite. They disagreed over the prosecution of the Anglo-Powhatan War of 1644–1646, just as they held opposite views on the issues that led to civil war back home and the overthrow of royal government in the colony; then, too, Claiborne was one of the commissioners to whom Parliament entrusted the task of bringing Virginia under its dominion, and in that capacity he negotiated the terms by which Berkeley surrendered in March 1652.

The House of Burgesses reelected Claiborne secretary throughout the Interregnum. He and Berkeley remained on civil terms, despite their differences, and he eased Sir William's resumption of power in March 1660. Berkeley retained him for a few months, but Claiborne was too deeply implicated in the parliamentary cause to continue. Delivering up "all the records belonging to the secretaries-office" to Thomas Ludwell, Claiborne retired from public life in March 1661 and returned to his plantation on the Pamunkey River in New Kent County.[17] Berkeley subsequently put two of Claiborne's sons on the bench of New Kent, and one of them also sat in the House of Burgesses. Claiborne surfaced momentarily after Bacon's Rebellion, when he mounted one last attack on the Marylanders in a vain attempt to recoup financial losses they had inflicted on him nearly half a century before.[18]

Samuel Mathews (d. 1657), a well-connected Londoner, arrived in the colony the year after Claiborne. Ironically enough, he sailed as a passenger aboard Sir John Harvey's ship *Southampton* as a member of the Harvey Commission that investigated the condition of Virginia for the Privy Council in 1622. Even though the colonists viewed the commissioners with considerable suspicion and some reacted harshly to Harvey's highhandedness, they accepted Mathews as one of their own, especially after the Powhatans attacked the colonists. His military training, an adeptness for besting the natives, plus his successes as a trader made him an obvious selection when Charles I named his first Council of State in 1625.[19]

An intermittent conflict, the Anglo-Powhatan War allowed Mathews ample time to make of himself a great planter. The foundations of his success were two large tracts of real estate he had received from the Virginia Company as compensation for his work on the Harvey Commission. One sat across and a bit downriver from Jamestown; the other lay at Blunt Point on the north side of the river in the present city of Newport News. On the latter he raised a house, variously known as Denbigh and Mathews Manor, which may well have been the largest residence in Virginia before Berkeley's Green Spring House. Marriages with a pair of rich widows related him to several prominent planter families, and the bond reinforced the scope of his commerce, which centered on Mathews Manor. He built a thriving trade that moved tobacco, corn, furs, and other goods throughout the James River watershed, around the Chesapeake Bay, and thence to London, where he exchanged his Virginia goods for finished products to distribute to his colonial customers. Partnerships with the likes of his friend Claiborne and London merchants such as Maurice Thompson and William Cloberry fastened this far-flung latticework together and brought handsome returns.

The chair at the Council table produced monopolies on trade with the natives. Various lucrative contracts routinely came Mathews's way, too. Among others were ones to raise a palisade across the Peninsula, a fort at Old Point Comfort, and new settlements amid unfriendly Indians in areas north and west of the York River. Ventures such as these involved risks, but their rewards far outweighed their dangers. Take the engagement for the palisade as an example; Mathews and his partner Claiborne invested none of their own capital. Instead, they received from the assembly £1,200 "in readie money to be laid out by our selves in servantes and such other necessaries as wee shall thinke requisite." They also got land, plus an annual payment of £100 out of the public treasury for "soe long as wee shalbe required to maintayne" the palisade. The agreement imposed few restrictions on the contractors and left the provincial government with no clear recourse in case they defaulted or shortchanged the taxpayers.[20]

Politically, Mathews tolerated the feisty Harvey until the governor interfered in his trade in the upper Chesapeake; then he teamed up with Claiborne, Menefie, and Peirce to drive off the hapless governor. Mathews's view of Virginia's trading relationships set him at odds with Governor Berkeley, who held him and his faction at arms length. The two men never came to blows because the basis of their opposing one another was less personal than philosophical. Though Berkeley often bested him throughout the 1640s, Mathews finally triumphed when Parliament reduced Virginia. Like Claiborne, Mathews devolved much of what he gained politically on his children. His namesake sat for a time in the governor's chair, where he never did. Another son became a justice in York County, and a grandson was a member of the Warwick County Court late in the 1680s.[21]

George Menefie (d. 1647) was one of the few trained lawyers[22] who immigrated to Virginia, though the practice of law supplied him little in the colony. He settled in 1623 and almost immediately started trafficking in land, tobacco, and laborers. Within a few years he ranked among the wealthiest planters in the colony and owned a plantation renowned for its flower gardens and orchards. Politics summoned him, too. His route to the Council was a bit unusual in that a single term as a burgess for Jamestown in the General Assembly of 1629 preceded his Council appointment six years later.[23] Menefie first met Claiborne when the latter surveyed a house site for him in New Town. He seems to have remained independent of the Mathews-Claiborne connection for several years before a second marriage eventually connected him to it through Maurice Thompson. The political and economic bonds grew tighter once Menefie got on the Council. He had barely grown comfortable in his seat before he fell afoul of Harvey and joined in thrusting him out. Arrested by royal warrant, Menefie returned to England to answer for his actions but was cleared of all charges. Resuming his Council seat, he became one of the stalwart regulars on whom Mathews and Claiborne usually depended. The effects of age or poor health steadily overtook him, and he stopped attending sessions about two years before his death. He had no sons, but his only daughter married Henry Perry, who was elected to the Council in 1655.[24]

William Peirce (d. 1645) and his family quit England in the company of a large contingent of colonists who shipped to Virginia in 1609. A soldier, Captain Peirce billeted aboard the convoy's flagship, *Sea Venture*, with Sir Thomas Gates and other officers; his wife and daughter were passengers on another vessel. A hurricane scattered the fleet, sinking some ships and foundering *Sea Venture* on the rocks off the Bermuda coast. The Peirces all survived and eventually made their separate ways to Jamestown. A variety of assignments followed before the captain took command of James Fort in 1623, and he later led several expeditions during the Anglo-Powhatan War. Like his colleagues, Peirce, who turned to tobacco, trade, and land speculation whenever time permitted in the early years, laid the ground for his wealth as well. He, too, lived at New Town, but he also had an estate on Mulberry Island in what became Warwick County. Claiborne surveyed both properties, and that association explains the beginning of their political relationship. Peirce served twice as burgess, and by the 1630s he was a councillor and close to the Mathews-Claiborne group. His last-known appearance in the Council occurred in October 1643, about a year before his death.[25]

Richard Kemp (ca. 1600–1649) was much at odds with Peirce and the rest of the Mathews-Claiborne faction. One source of friction stemmed from his support of Governor Harvey. Another was his displacing Claiborne as secretary. How Kemp got to be secretary is far from obvious. The only certainty is that he landed at Jamestown with his commission in hand, which clearly did not endear him to his new colleagues. A man of means, perhaps he flaunted his money, for he built the first brick house at Jamestown, which he sold to Governor Wyatt when he moved to an even more elegant dwelling on the mainland at Rich Neck, near Middle Plantation. He surely harbored a great dislike of George Menefie, who had brought the Reverend Anthony Panton to Virginia and found him a place in York County. The clergyman and the secretary thoroughly detested each other and feuded continually. Kemp finally persuaded a majority of the Council to banish Panton for an alleged affront, which sparked protracted litigation that bounced back and forth across the Atlantic for years. Wyatt and Kemp had their differences, too.[26]

Kemp was in England defending himself against Panton when Berkeley became governor. Whether the two knew each other beforehand is uncertain, but both men were sworn into office before the Privy Council on the same day. Once in Virginia, they developed a tolerable working relationship that quieted Kemp. Moreover, Berkeley designated Kemp deputy governor when the Anglo-Powhatan War of 1644–1646 forced his return to England. Kemp, a royalist at heart, died before the overthrow of the monarchy had had much effect in Virginia. His widow married Robert Smith, who served with Berkeley in the Council after the Restoration.

Argoll Yeardley (1617–1655) differed in temper from Secretary Kemp. The eldest son of Sir George Yeardley, he grew up on the Eastern Shore and gained a seat on the Council in 1639 while still in his twenties. An active merchant-planter, he enjoyed the advantages of inherited wealth and position. He also derived much of his livelihood from commerce with the Dutch and he was a leader in a combination of colonists who joined Virginia to Rotterdam.[27]

Dutch mariners first started scouring Virginia waters for opportunities not long after the initial settlement at Jamestown. Some were even acquainted with colonial leaders who had soldiered in the Netherlands before going to Virginia. As the visits increased, a number of the Dutch stayed behind, settling on the Eastern Shore and along the lower James, where they formed connections with men such as Yeardley. The other members of Yeardley's loosely woven network included his brother Francis, Councillors Nathaniel Littleton, Richard Lee, Thomas Willoughby, Ralph Wormeley, Secretary Kemp, and Adam Thoroughgood, a justice of the peace in Lower Norfolk County. Blood as well as money counted for Yeardley. His second wife, Ann Custis, belonged to one of the Anglo-Dutch families who were an important element in the Rotterdam mercantile community. Beyond that, Yeardley was instrumental in setting up Ann's brother John Custis as a planter in Northampton County, thereby launching him on a career that eventually led to the Council of State.

The Netherlands-Virginia trade grew to such a magnitude by the 1640s that it threatened to eclipse England's commerce in the Chesapeake, which was one reason the Mathews-Claiborne faction opposed the Dutch traffic as stoutly as it did. By the same token, personal ties and an expansive view of economic relationships were among the considerations that drew Yeardley and his group to Governor Berkeley. Of a similar outlook, Berkeley got major pieces of legislation through the General Assembly that widened Virginia markets to Yeardley's friends and relatives in Holland.[28]

A Little Parliament

The group's position deteriorated after the execution of Charles I and the passage of the early navigation laws, which provoked the First Anglo-Dutch War (1652–1654). Even so, Yeardley held onto his Council seat after Berkeley surrendered. He soon gave it up in order to stand as a burgess for Lower Norfolk, and he and his brother were elected to the General Assembly of 1653. Two years later, he was dead.

Thomas Willoughby (1593–1658) had a more prototypical career than Yeardley. In 1610, as a youth of seventeen, he bid farewell to home and kin in the Kentish town of Rochester to scratch out a niche in Virginia. He may have acquired a soldier's veneer before he emigrated or shortly thereafter, because the early references to him in the extant records consistently mention "Ensigne Willoby." He was styling himself "gentleman" in the 1620s, by which time he was also accumulating land and offices. During the Anglo-Powhatan War of 1622–1632, as Lieutenant Willoughby, he commanded a force that burned the fields and village of the Chesapeake Indians that lay near his own plantation. Thereafter, he was appointed judge of one of the monthly benches that antedated the county courts, and he sat in the General Assemblies of 1630 and 1632. One of the first justices for Lower Norfolk County, he joined the bench soon after its creation in 1637. He rose to the Council of State in 1641 but was turned out a decade later and died while on business in London.

His son and grandson followed in his footsteps to the Lower Norfolk Court, though that was as high as either ascended the political ladder. Daughter Elizabeth made more of an impression than her brother or nephew. She first married Simon Overzee, a Dutch merchant, who dealt up and down Chesapeake Bay and along the James River. Within a year of his death in 1660, Elizabeth took a second husband, George Coleclough, the younger sibling of a prospering London grocer. Coleclough had immigrated to the newly developing Northumberland County about 1651, and by 1656 he was both a magistrate and burgess for the county. Following his death, Elizabeth wed yet again, this time to Isaac Allerton, the son of a New Haven, Connecticut, merchant. About the time of that marriage, Allerton was commissioned a justice for Northumberland. He went on to the House of Burgesses before Effingham found him a chair at the Council table in 1687.[29]

The last of the nine, John West (1590–1659), descended from a titled Hampshire family, and he was one of four brothers who figured in Virginia's early years. The eldest, Governor and Captain General Thomas West, third baron De La Warr, saved Jamestown from abandonment after the Starving Time. Nathaniel West soldiered in the colony but died within a short time of his arrival. Francis West sailed with Christopher Newport in 1608 and joined the Council the next year. His colleagues picked him to succeed Yeardley in 1627, thus making him the first councillor ever elected acting governor. As for John West, he was affiliated with the colony's military forces from the time of his landing in 1618. He led a troop of men after the outbreak of the Anglo-Powhatan War of 1622–1632, and toward the end of that conflict was commander of one of the outlying settlements across the river from Jamestown. After turns in the General Assemblies of 1629 and 1631, he wound up on the Council.[30]

West seems not to have associated commercially with either the Mathews-Claiborne or the Yeardley groups but went his own way. In his mature years, his business was confined mostly to the upper end of York County, especially in the region that was carved off as New Kent, and at West's Point, where the Pamunkey met with the Mattaponi and became the York River. Politically, West appears also to have remained aloof from many of the disagreements that polarized the Council during his tenure. His election as acting governor after Harvey's overthrow was natural enough, but not because he was Mathews's ally. Rather, he was the senior member of Council, and seniority entitled him to the top spot, much as it had his late brother Francis when he had succeeded Yeardley. Then, too, from the standpoint of the moment, West was a figure of impeccable political and military credentials. His reputation as a longtime leader stood him well with planters of all stripes, and it added the cover of legitimacy to the conspirators who deposed Harvey. Moreover, his arrest and trial in England allowed him the chance to enlist his family in removing Harvey and lobbying for Wyatt's reappointment.[31]

West continued as something of the grand old man of conciliar politics throughout Berkeley's first administration and the Interregnum. After West's death, Sir William and the General Assembly of March 1659/60 acknowledged as much when they commended West for the "many important favours and services" he had done for "the countrey of Virginia." Furthermore, Berkeley signed an order that the levies of West's son "and his family be remitted, and that he be exempted from payment thereof during life."[32]

In profile, the Restoration councillors looked much like West and the others of his era. The younger ones dated their arrivals to the 1640s and 1650s, or earlier, although only three immigrated to Virginia after 1660. Except for those three—the rebel Nathaniel Bacon and the Ludwell brothers—the rest were men who climbed up through the ranks of the county courts and the House of Burgesses. Some followed fathers or brothers, and others passed their places on to their sons. Despite these similarities, there was an appreciable difference: councillors after 1660 lacked the combativeness and inclination to rival the governor that characterized their predecessors. That distinction resulted more from the way Berkeley related to them and to the nature of conciliar politics than from a want of vigorous personalities.

Council politics had none of the bite of earlier decades. Adjusting to the English trade laws, diversifying the economy, renewing Jamestown, defending against the Dutch, and voiding the Northern Neck Proprietary drove the political agenda. Although there were disagreements over how to address those issues, the governor and Council were mainly of one accord on the prescriptions for treating them all. Such harmony resulted in considerable measure from Berkeley's handling of the Council.

For starters, there was no wholesale emptying of seats when Berkeley returned to power in 1660. Instead, he permitted holdovers from the parliamentary regime to stay in their chairs and merely added others who were more to his liking. The arrangement made for an unusually large Council at first, but death soon whittled it down to a more traditional size by the mid-1660s.[33] Roundhead or royalist, follower or foe, newcomer or oldtimer, no one was a stranger to Berkeley. Four councillors were actually his kinsmen, and others ranked among his neighbors or confidants and dearest friends. He won them all by the sheer force of his charm and his deference to the Council as an institution. Generous in his employment of the perquisites at his disposal, he distributed his gifts so that everyone got something and in a way that usually strengthened loyalty to him. His treatment of Thomas Stegge, the son of a former adversary, stands as a good example. Berkeley nominated the younger Stegge to fill a Council vacancy and then gave him the newly created and highly remunerative office of auditor general, both of which kept Stegge a steady supporter until he died in 1670.

Different times, different issues, and different people led to a relatively harmonious Council that for a time subordinated itself to the governor. Nevertheless, it was a collection of strong-minded men who sometimes went their own ways or exerted considerable influence on Berkeley.

One of these was Abraham Wood (ca. 1614–ca. 1683). Emigrating when he was ten, Wood grew from a boy into one of the colony's greatest Indian traders. He spent his young years with the first Samuel Mathews, who trained him on the ins and outs of commerce with the natives, and he became an adept dealer, scout, fighter, and explorer.

Using Fort Henry, at the falls of the Appomattox River, where sits modern Petersburg, Wood oriented his activities toward Virginia's southwestern frontier and tapped a highly rewarding custom in furs. The fort/trading post also doubled as the jumping-off point for probing the interior as he and others, with Berkeley's eager encouragement, sought to find the Pacific Ocean by tracking westward deep into terra incognita. Wood led one such expedition in 1650. He scouted the land along the Chowan and Nottoway Rivers, which piqued interest in colonizing the entire region south of Virginia. Likewise, the trek was partially responsible for Berkeley's becoming one of the proprietors of Carolina, although the Interregnum deterred such schemes for years. Wood in the meantime developed additional market outlets closer to Fort Henry and encouraged greater settlement at the edges of Henrico and Charles City Counties.[34]

The expansion of his operations throughout the 1660s and 1670s raised the pressures on the area natives and made Wood more protective of his interests. By then he had passed up the ranks to the Council of State, where he was regarded as the premier expert in Indian affairs. He had Berkeley's ear because he and the governor frequently partnered in the fur trade and because for decades Berkeley trusted his advice on how to defend against possible attacks from enemy tribes. Indeed, Wood, as much as anyone else, helped Berkeley formulate the strategy that dictated overall Indian policy from the end of the Anglo-Powhatan War of 1644–1646 to the outbreak of Bacon's Rebellion. In addition, Wood won Berkeley's respect as a military officer, especially for his hand in revamping the Charles City and Henrico militia that became the model for reforms colonywide, and he held one of the major general's commissions. "Lamenesse and other infirmities" of advancing years reduced his usefulness in the critical months preceding Bacon's Rebellion, and the consequences were disastrous for trade, for the Indians, for Wood, and for the equally aged Berkeley.[35]

Francis Moryson (ca. 1628–ca. 1680) and Berkeley shared an altogether different relationship. Moryson's family was related by marriage to Berkeley's patron Lucius Cary, second viscount Falkland, and Moryson's brother was Berkeley's first commandant of the fort at Old Point Comfort. In 1649, Moryson, Richard Fox, and Berkeley's cousin Henry Norwood, royalist army officers all, booked berths aboard *The Virginia Merchant* for the Chesapeake. They were treated to a harrowing passage. Off Cape Hatteras, a fierce storm overtook *The Virginia Merchant*, blowing her far off course as towering, wind-whipped seas dismasted her and nearly drove her under. Jury-rigged, the crippled ship pressed on in search of her destination. Months of short rations and near starvation greeted crew and passenger alike before they raised a landfall on the Eastern Shore and a weakened Moryson finally reached Green Spring House.[36]

Once he recovered from the effects of his near-fatal voyage, Moryson lived with his widowed sister-in-law before he acquired property of his own, some of which lay near Green Spring House. He may also have become a James City County magistrate, and in 1656 he was elected to the General Assembly, where he became Speaker. He entered the Council four years later.[37]

Thereafter, Moryson secured the command of the Old Point Comfort fort and the place of deputy treasurer. Berkeley named him deputy governor before Sir William returned to England in 1661. In that capacity Moryson oversaw both the final stages of the return to royal authority and the fifth revision of Virginia's laws. Berkeley next made him the colony's agent, which was unquestionably Moryson's most important assignment to date. As such, he resided in England for thirteen years and handled the colonial government's negotiations with the Crown in its attempt to limit tobacco production and to overthrow the Northern Neck grant.[38]

Somewhere along the way Moryson turned on his benefactor. Perhaps he came to resent Berkeley's habit of sending others to assist him; perhaps he changed his mind about the governor's view of the relationship of colony to Crown. It was a different Moryson who returned to Virginia in 1677 as a member of the royal commission of inquiry into the causes of Bacon's Rebellion. He was now Charles II's man, not Sir William Berkeley's, and he showed little friendliness to his old champion. Nor was he anything more than correctly cordial to his former planter and Council colleagues. His intimate knowledge of them, and of Virginia politics, made him especially dangerous to their concerns in the post-Berkeley era. Death prevented him from harming their interests as much as he might have had he lived longer.[39]

Thomas Ludwell (1629–1678) was someone who likely got under Moryson's skin, especially after Berkeley dispatched him to London in 1674 in the company of another councillor, Robert Smith, to lobby against the Northern Neck grant. Moreover, Ludwell and his brother Philip (ca. 1638–1717) enjoyed an unmatched intimacy with Berkeley. Some at the time actually supposed the Ludwells' proximity amounted to an undue influence on their old governor.[40]

It had not always been so. Berkeley did not know the brothers until they showed up in Virginia in 1660. Natives of Bruton, Somerset, they were children when he left England. Their initial contact with him was through his brothers, Sir Charles Berkeley, who inherited the Abbey in Bruton, and John Berkeley, second baron

Berkeley of Stratton. Both were close to Charles II, and one or the other was the instrument by which Thomas Ludwell gained a royal warrant for the office of secretary of the colony shortly after the Restoration. He made his brother his deputy, and the two struck up a relationship with Berkeley that deepened down the years. The governor graced the secretary with the profitable place of escheator general after its creation in 1669. He also persuaded the absentee surveyor general, Alexander Culpeper, who was his brother-in-law, to create the post of deputy surveyor general for Philip Ludwell, and then put him on the Council, too. Secretary Ludwell, had he lived longer, would have been a force for the Crown to contend with. As it was, he was mobilizing the irreconcilables when he died. Philip Ludwell stepped forward to fill his shoes and became their principal leader. For fifteen years he used his considerable gifts to struggle against Berkeley's successors before finally making his peace with Stuart imperialism.[41]

Of course, Nathaniel Bacon the Rebel affected the Ludwells, Berkeley, the Council, and all of Virginia like no other member. Son of a Suffolk squire, he came up in the comfortable world of the English country gentry. Time spent at Cambridge and touring the Continent educated him in the ways of his privileged station, though it did little to settle him into a fixed place among his like. Returning home, he tried by means both fair and foul to enrich himself, and, against his parents' will, he also married Elizabeth Duke, the daughter of a neighboring family. A shiftless young man before the marriage, after it Bacon was shiftless still, without prospects and a family man to boot. His exasperated father intervened and did what others with means and in similar situations sometimes did in those days. He gave his son and daughter-in-law money and furnishings and shipped them off to Virginia where they might amount to something. Not only would they start with a grubstake, but they also had relatives in the colony who would surely look after them. And what kin! One was Auditor General Nathaniel Bacon, who was influential and childless and a member of the Council. Another was the governor's wife, Dame Frances Berkeley.[42]

Nathaniel and Elizabeth Bacon arrived in the summer of 1674. The Berkeleys entertained them while Bacon scouted for a permanent residence. He soon contracted with Councillor Thomas Ballard to buy a large plantation in Henrico County at Curles Neck. (The James River made a series of big bends at the site, hence the name.) Among Bacon's neighbors were Abraham Wood and William Byrd, who was already rivaling Wood as a fur trader and expert on Indian affairs. Early in the new year,

Berkeley gave Bacon a vacant Council chair. Seldom had a newcomer flown so high so fast, but his wings got singed after he presumed to advise the governor on the proper way to deal with Indians and to importune him for his own share of the fur trade. Never one to take direction from his juniors, relatives or not, Berkeley was not amused, all the more so because in the fall of 1675 he faced the greatest military threat from the natives in thirty years. And so he acidly told his young in-law to mind his own business. Things between the two of them soured further after their wives quarrelled.[43]

The situation with the Indians along the frontier went from bad to worse to horrible, and as the winter of 1675 became the spring of 1676, the prospect of war with the natives threatened rebellion of the colonists. Bacon, not knowing the measure of the governor, nor caring, infuriated Berkeley even more by taking command of a troop of unauthorized volunteers and sallying forth to kill "Indians." That was the first in a series of missteps that turned a disagreement over Indian policy into a duel that plunged Virginia into civil war. When it was over, Berkeley was discredited, Bacon, not yet thirty, was dead of dysentery, and the Crown was bent on reforming the General Assembly.[44]

Factiousness reigned for the remainder of the century as the councillors adapted to the new realities of the postrebellion era. Gone was a neglectful Crown. Irreconcilables, moderates, and trimmers sparred over a response to royal designs on the General Assembly. That contest dominated conciliar politics to the end of Effingham's tenure, when it gave way to other disputes that characterized succeeding administrations. Gone, too, was a governor whose outlook was Virginian. Berkeley's successors took a decidedly different view of the Anglo-Virginia connection, putting royal wishes ahead of those of the colony, and that fostered frequent confrontations after 1677. Although the parallels are not exact, the relationship between governors and councillors was more reminiscent of the 1630s, 1640s, and 1650s than of the 1660s and 1670s.

Retirement, dismissal, and death gradually brought new faces to the Council table. They belonged to men who, in the words of Francis Nicholson, earned their "estates and places of honour ... More by accident than any extraordinary honesty or ability." Nicholson may be excused for his dismissal of them, given their hostilities toward him; nevertheless, the governor's councillors walked the same paths to their chairs as had their antecedents. They were forbidding personalities for any governor to contend with, and none was more formidable than James Blair.[45]

Blair is now remembered as the principal founder of the College of William and Mary and not as the exceptional politician he surely was. Unlike the others, he was neither native-born nor a longtime resident of Virginia, and he was the only man of the cloth to sit in the Council of State during the seventeenth century. Disagreeable he was, but he was arguably the single most commanding political presence of the postrebellion era.

A native of Edinburgh, Scotland, Blair (ca. 1655–1743) was the son of a clergyman of episcopal leanings. When he was twelve, his parents sent him to Marischal College, Aberdeen. He remained for two years before moving on to the University of Edinburgh, where he took his master of arts. An inner call to holy orders led to an additional six years of theological studies before his ordination. Like his father, Blair was a staunch champion of a Scottish episcopacy, so he sought preferment from the bishop of Edinburgh, who assigned him a small parish. Steadfast protestantism caused trouble when Blair gagged at swearing an oath recognizing the Catholic duke of York as head of the Church of Scotland on his succession to the throne as James II. That refusal cost the young priest his livings and closed Scottish doors to others. Bereft of prospects in his homeland, he journeyed south to London, where he became acquainted with Henry Compton, bishop of London, and other prominent Anglican divines. Compton, who held territorial jurisdiction over the colonies, offered his protégé the rectorship of Varina Parish in Virginia and with it the chance of advancing the church's cause. In 1685, Blair booked passage for America and never looked back.

His dedication to the needs of his fellow Virginia clerics and to revitalizing the institutional church gained the clergy's confidence, which soon made him a recognized leader in ecclesiastical matters. Blair quickly cast his eye beyond his priestly responsibilities for ways to improve his standing and the weight of his purse. Marriage to Sarah Harrison not only joined him to one of Virginia's most influential ruling families, but it was also an opening to wealth and politics as well. The overthrow of James II also favored Blair, for it returned his patrons to their former positions of power in England. In 1689, Compton thrust him into greater prominence by naming him his commissary, or personal representative. Being commissary, in effect, made Blair Virginia's chief priest, and it endowed him with broad authority in ecclesiastical matters great and small. That assignment, together with his lobbying for the chartering of the College of William and Mary, resulted in appointment to the Council in 1694. From then until he died, Commissary Blair made and unmade governors almost at will, or so it surely seemed to colleagues whose ties to London were weak in comparison to his.[46]

A Little Parliament

The symmetry of Blair's long, turbulent career was an absolute zeal for the two enterprises he took up as his own particular causes: the College of William and Mary and the colonial church. He expected the same dedication from everyone else. When he found such devotion lacking in Sir Edmund Andros and Francis Nicholson, he attacked them and used every means at his disposal to brush them aside. Nothing deterred him, not even his suspension from the Council. Indeed, after Andros put him out, he merely looked to patrons in England for aid in restoring him. They did, and Andros lost his job.

Blair's example as a councillor lay in his constant cultivation of English officials to protect him and to support his goals. In Berkeley's day, looking east was a sometime thing; after 1677 it became a necessity for colonial politicians who sought to mitigate Whitehall's intrusions into their affairs. Blair demonstrated the potential benefits of influencing Crown policy by winning friends and influencing people in London. That lesson was not lost on his colleagues on the Council, or in the House of Burgesses.

As for the burgesses, one significant trait distinguished them individually and severally. A burgess held the only elective office in Virginia, and those who sought it had to win the affections of the voters at the polls. Election thus became the measure of political ability.

In principle, the colonists linked voting and officeholding to the ownership of real property. In fact, however, Governor Yeardley effectively enfranchised all adult male colonists when he required every free man and company tenant to vote in 1619. Yeardley's standards remained in effect for years. The first limitation came in 1670, when the General Assembly restricted the vote to landowners and taxpayers on the grounds that

> the usuall way of chuseing burgesses by the votes of all persons who haveing served their tyme are ffreemen of this country who haveing little interest in the country doe oftner make tumults at the election to the disturbance of his majesties peace, then by their discretions in their votes provide for the conserva[t]ion thereof.

Berkeley suspended the statute in the elections of May 1676 in an attempt to undercut Bacon's popularity. It was revived by the direct order of Charles II after the rebellion, and the link between the right to vote and property ownership remained unchanged for the duration of the colonial era.[47]

Councillors and Burgesses

No law prevented any freeholder from standing for the House of Burgesses. As a practical matter, though, the candidate pool was always a small pond, especially after the counties became the basis of house membership. By midcentury they were the exclusive units of representation in most sections of Virginia. Once the General Assembly eliminated church parishes as electoral districts in 1662, few men who were not justices of the peace sat in the House of Burgesses. The sole mandates thereafter were laws requiring the appearance of two representatives from each county under pain of stiff fines. There were few known violations of those statutes after 1620 when the assembly sanctioned the benches of Henrico and Middlesex Counties for noncompliance.[48]

The noteworthy thing in all of this was the linkage between representation and groups of freeholders who lived in particular parts of the Old Dominion. Here was a custom created by local magistrates aiming to control local affairs that fostered a later American idea of the representative as a person whose principal obligation lay with the voters of the district. Such an accidental development diverged from the seventeenth-century English understanding. In that view, the constituency of a member of the House of Commons was the whole of the body politic, not just the voters who elected him.

What determined which justice got to sit in the House of Burgesses is not always readily apparent, though for much of the century certain justices avoided election. Every commission of the peace named the four most senior judges justices-in-quorum. Their designation required the presence of at least one of them for any session of court to be legal; on the other hand, the four could act in place of the full bench. Because courts sat monthly, duty ordinarily kept quorum justices out of the assembly. Law as well as duty eliminated sheriffs, at least until the 1680s. Chief among the sheriff's responsibilities, apart from conducting elections, was his role as county police officer. He served warrants, impaneled juries, seized property for judgment of debts, arrested and detained criminal suspects, held those bound over for trial, inflicted corporal punishment, and collected both county and provincial taxes. Often he acted as bailiff and crier for his court as well. Clerks of court also stayed out of the assembly in most instances. Their presence at county sessions was essential because they prepared the agenda, kept the dockets in order, attended to all the other purposes that attached to their jobs, and collected the fees for each of the transactions, which made their places attractive and lucrative.

A Little Parliament

Some drawbacks reduced the lure of being a burgess. The financial perquisites were modest because, unlike councillors, burgesses had far fewer opportunities for holding multiple provincial offices. For his troubles, each burgess received a per diem of 150 pounds of tobacco, plus expenses for lodging and travel to Jamestown. The allowances paled in comparison to the rewards that went with being a sheriff or a clerk of court. House service also required periodic absences from one's normal routines that ranged from days to weeks. Making the trip to Jamestown itself could be difficult, especially for anyone who lived in the remoter parts of the colony. Those circumstances compelled choices that some justices obviously found unacceptable, and so they never offered themselves.[49]

Until Effingham's day, the ability of the governor to manipulate the choice of candidates was limited. True, he might hold a particular group of burgesses together by proroguing the assembly—as Berkeley did with the Long Assembly—or he might dissolve it in the hope that a new poll would result in a more pliant house. As Jeffreys and Culpeper and then Effingham discovered, however, dissolution proved a blunt weapon as long as the sheriffs retained unchallenged control of the elections.

Sheriffs had complete charge of polling. They published election writs, fixed election dates, set the hours for polling, selected the venue, and conducted the oral voting. Freeholders themselves, they could also cast deciding votes whenever ties occurred. Such authority allowed local justices enormous influence over who went to Jamestown, and it circumscribed the executive's ability to pack the House with placemen.

Postrebellion governors learned to their frustration that unless they found ways to outbid the courts they had few means to tip the course of elections in their favor. That is why Effingham continued Culpeper's practice of commissioning the sheriffs annually, thereby transforming the shrievalty into a tool of gubernatorial patronage. However much those who would be sheriff may have despised Effingham, he made them dependent on his favor, and that gave him and later executives some sway in electoral politics. Contemporaries described the impact of Effingham's innovation this way. A governor, they said, had great stroke in an election because the

> Sheriff's Place being granted anew every Year, either by the Continuance of the old Sheriff or the Nomination of a new one, is a constant fresh Temptation to a great many Pretenders to exert their utmost Skill and Interest in managing the Elections of the Burgesses of their several Counties for the Governor. Then after these two Burgesses are actually chosen, one of them is very apt to be gained by the Hopes of this same Sheriff's Place next

Year; or if either of them is a bold Man in the House of Burgesses, the appointing him Sheriff takes him out of the House, and by this Art the Governor can either oblige and gain one of the two Burgesses of a County, or at least lay him aside, that he can do him no Hurt.[50]

In an age when constitutionally fixed terms of office were as yet an-unheard-of thing, burgesses came and burgesses went frequently. The incidence of turnovers ran about six in ten from the mid-1650s onward, which suggests little continuity from one assembly to the next. Incumbency may have had small value in the seventeenth century. Colonial legislators were not representatives in the modern meaning, which is to say no burgess regarded electoral politics as his profession or his chief means of livelihood. Besides, the concerns of government were generally private or parochial in nature, which made local magistrates the most visible agents of authority, so counties remained centers of power and activity until localism receded to the political shadows. Consequently, a justice might stand for election, sit in an assembly or two, and then drop out for a while before gaining reelection.

To be sure, there were justices who made election to the House something of a habit and continued to serve for years on end. Most notable among these was Lemuel Mason (1628–1702). Virginian by birth, he sprang from a well-connected Lower Norfolk family and married into another. As a young man, he took his father's seat on the county bench and kept it for fifty-two years. His freeholder neighbors first sent him to the House of Burgesses in 1654, when he was twenty-six. They reelected him time after time during the better part of four decades thereafter, and he dealt with every governor from Richard Bennett to Sir Edmund Andros. Something other than mere popularity may also account for his longevity. Like other durable incumbents, Mason represented a county that lay within easy reach of the capital. Proximity, it seems, made it easier for some to serve longer than others.[51]

Itself a tiny place, the House before 1700, even at its largest, contained fewer than fifty members. Seats passed among justices who all knew or were related to one another, and each acquired familiarity with House business and procedures. On the other hand, such old hands as Lemuel Mason gained generous measures of experience and institutional memory that they could share or employ to influence less seasoned colleagues.[52]

The House of Burgesses that lasted from March 1661 to March 1676 makes a good case in point. All told, seventy-seven men sat in this so-called Long Assembly, of whom thirty-four were elected in March 1661. Various burgesses in the preceding House did not return, either out of loyalty to the parliamentary regime or because they lost to challengers. Two went to the Council of State, and there was no election in one county. Even so, an unusually high number, twenty-seven, carried over from the old House. Their ranks soon thinned. Berkeley named six to the Council. Three were dismissed on order of the House, one for his "illegall proceedings" against the natives, another for being "loving to the Quakers and ... well affected towards them," and the third for killing someone in a fit of rage. Others quit to take turns as sheriffs and never returned. Death or retirement caused the greatest number of turnovers, accounting for about a quarter of the total. As a result of all the changes, the average tenure was only about five years, and a mere six burgesses (8 percent) stayed for the entire life of the Long Assembly.[53]

An even more dramatic turnover happened because of the election that produced the General Assembly of June 1676. In that poll, thirty-nine out of a possible total of forty-one burgesses were elected. Of them, twenty-two can now be identified by name and constituency.[54] Bacon, despite his being an outlaw, was one, and so were his close allies Richard Lawrence and James Crewes. As for the remaining nineteen, four had no identifiable prior political experience; five, maybe six, carried over from the late assembly; the rest were incumbent justices of the peace.[55] And, although Augustine Warner, the immediate past Speaker, returned as a member for Gloucester County, he evidently lacked the votes to regain the Speakership. The chair went instead to Thomas Godwin, a man who had been out of the House since 1659.[56]

The complexion of the House changed again as the dust from Bacon's Rebellion settled and the assembly scrambled to protect itself from the Crown's attacks. Virtually a fresh cohort of burgesses entered after 1677, and though new to the House, the members all belonged to the political establishment. About half were immigrants, the rest Virginia-born; among the latter, eight of ten followed fathers or grandfathers. Partisan divisions among irreconcilables, moderates, and trimmers continued into the 1690s, with trimmers in the decided minority. Those factions declined after the Effingham administration as the House came increasingly to terms with its diminished role, and as the century closed, other issues drove politics.

No matter how the burgesses grouped politically, the greater part who filled the House after 1619 are barely recognizable figures, save those who became Speakers or rose to the Council of State and a handful of others who left records of some note.

Among the latter were the Armistead clan, William Carver, Francis Grey, William Fitzhugh, and Lemuel Mason.

The story of the Armisteads' rise to political fortune[57] began when William Armistead, his wife Anne, and their children left Kirk Deighton, Yorkshire, for Virginia in the mid-1630s. Alighting in Elizabeth City County, they put down roots and set about the tasks of prospering. Destruction of the Elizabeth City records bars any detailed account of their activities, though William's amassed landholdings of 2,500 acres and the pivotal placement of his children indicate success at raising the family into the ranks of the great planters. A daughter, the thrice-wed Frances, related the Armisteads by turns to one clergyman and two councillors of state, and sons John and Anthony each made his way to a seat in the House of Burgesses.

John Armistead (fl. 1650s–1690s) was born probably in Virginia soon after his parents settled in the colony. When he came of age, he moved to Gloucester County to manage properties the family had acquired after the area north of the York River was opened to English settlement. Those lands came to him at his father's death, and they made him one of Gloucester's most substantial planters. In the 1660s, he and Robert Beverley engaged in various joint business ventures. Their relationship grew closer still when he married Beverley's sister-in-law, Judith Hone. The match resulted in four children. One of the daughters married Robert "King" Carter and another became the second wife of the second Ralph Wormeley, a member of the Council.

Armistead held a place on the Kingston Parish vestry before Governor Berkeley named him to the Gloucester bench and as an officer in the county militia. He became sheriff in 1676 and again in 1680. Elected to the House of Burgesses in 1680, he and Beverley parted company politically as Armistead inclined toward Stuart colonial policy. Armistead also helped suppress the plant-cutter riots, which apparently kept him out of the second session of the General Assembly of 1680–1682 and widened his distance from Beverley.

By the time he returned to the House in 1685, Armistead was on friendly terms with Governor Effingham, who often quartered at Gloucester Hall, the plantation of Armistead's neighbor and fellow justice, Thomas Pate. That association benefited Armistead in 1688, when Effingham named him to a vacancy on the Council. His tenure was brief because he refused for conscience' sake to swear allegiance to King William and Queen Mary. The Crown restored him to his place in 1698, but Armistead died before the order reached Virginia.

A Little Parliament

Anthony Armistead (d. by 1705) grew up in Elizabeth City County and married Hannah Ellyson, daughter of a James City County justice of the peace, sheriff, and burgess who enjoyed a closeness with Governor Berkeley. Proximity to Ellyson, and thus to the governor, accounted for Armistead's advancement to a place on the Elizabeth City County Court and a captaincy in the militia by the mid-1670s. During Bacon's Rebellion he sided with Berkeley, who put him on a court-martial that condemned one of the rebels to death. Elected a burgess in the third session of the General Assembly of 1680–1682, Armistead had a seat on the Committee on Public Claims. He did not seek reelection in 1684 and remained out of provincial politics throughout the Effingham administration, though he retained his offices in Elizabeth City.

Armistead returned to the House in October 1693. At that time he helped to draft a bill regulating tanners, but the bill never passed into law. Subsequently, he won reelection to every General Assembly but one that sat for the next decade. Successive Speakers appointed him to another standing committee, Propositions and Grievances. That committee recommended changes in existing law and received petitions from the voters for which it proposed remedies. His assignment thus gave Armistead a voice in crafting most of the legislation that the House enacted. He frequently participated in conference committees that negotiated with the governor and Council on the passage of bills and other legislative matters. In addition, he sat on a joint committee of burgesses and councillors who laid the groundwork for the revised legal code of 1705, although he did not live to see the fruition of their work.

Despite his position, Armistead sometimes ran afoul of House procedure, and he was not immune to opposition at home. His irregular attendance at the sessions resulted in a number of reprimands. Those censures nearly cost his seat in 1699, when some Elizabeth City voters petitioned for his removal, charging that his reelection was "undue." The House sustained him, and Armistead was never absent again. He died while a member of the General Assembly of 1705.

William Armistead (d. 1715), the third of that name, was the son of Anthony and Hannah and the most prominent member of the family's third generation in Virginia. He held an officer's commission in the Elizabeth City militia as well as a place on the county court. Elected to the General Assembly of March 1693, he was subsequently reelected in 1702. From that date he sat in the House of Burgesses until 1710, when he lost to Francis Ballard. He regained the seat, which he held until his death. Like his father, Armistead sat on the Committee on Public Claims and several conference committees, and he had one other distinction of note. He was among the very few burgesses ever to serve in the House with his father and two of his brothers. Father and son were members from 1703 to 1705. One brother was with him in the General Assembly of 1705–1706, and the other one joined him in 1714.

None of the Armisteads stood in the first tier of House leaders, but neither did they rank among insignificant members. What separated them from many of their more powerful colleagues was the fortune to have sons who kept the family at the head of Virginia society for the rest of the colonial era and beyond.

William Carver (1623–1676) left a different mark. Born in Bristol, England, he took to blue water in his youth and grew up to be a successful merchant and sea captain. His pursuit of trade led him to settle in Lower Norfolk County about midcentury, and by 1663 he was a member of the county court. His appointment turned out to be one of Berkeley's unwise choices because Carver proved a troublesome justice who nevertheless sat in the House through several sessions of the Long Assembly. Contentious, erratic, even dangerous, he frequently accused his neighbors of slandering him. Sometimes he settled his disputes with blows instead of words. In 1672 he allegedly stabbed to death a seaman, Thomas Gilbert. At his examination before the county court, Carver admitted to the killing. He vowed, however, that he was in a "distracted Condition," which rendered him incapable of recollecting the deed and so not responsible for its outcome. His fellow justices found otherwise. They ruled his conduct felonious and bound him over for trial at Jamestown. An acquittal followed, but his reputation as a violent man shadowed him for the rest of his days.[58]

In a curious way, that fame brought him to rebel against Berkeley in 1676, though what drew Carver to Nathaniel Bacon remains a puzzle. There is nothing in the known record that connects him to Bacon before the revolt. They lived miles apart and on opposite sides of the James River, Carver on its south shore, near its mouth, and Bacon on its north bank, closer to its falls. On the other hand, Carver perhaps had some prior acquaintance of Giles Bland, the Crown customs collector who became one of Bacon's chief lieutenants, though again the two cannot be positively linked before they sided with Bacon. The attraction may have been only what Thomas Mathew recollected thirty years after the fact: that Carver "was resolved to adventure his old Bones against the Indian Rogues."[59] Whatever it was, rebel he did, and in September 1676 Bacon dispatched Carver, Bland, and a squadron of vessels across the Chesapeake Bay to dislodge Berkeley from his stronghold at Councillor John Custis's Arlington House on the Eastern Shore. While the governor dickered with the sea captain, Berkeley's henchmen overpowered the entire rebel flotilla without much of a struggle, and Carver soon died at the end of a rope.[60]

A Charles City County resident, Francis Grey (d. 1679) arrived in Virginia about the same time as Carver. He too was of mercantile origins, though his rise to the bench was swifter than Carver's. Elected a burgess in 1663, he sat for one session of the Long Assembly before he vanished from the provincial stage. He was soon out of local politics too. The source of his fall is uncertain, though it seems to have stemmed from his personality. Like Carver, Grey was given to violence. His wife, Grace Grey, was a particular object of his abuse. He tormented her "by private unspeakable Devices, by the worst of words, by desperate & unmercifull blowes, & by Cutting her eares." She finally grew so desperate that in 1665 she took the extraordinary step of seeking help from Governor Berkeley. In a direct appeal she implored him to compel her husband to treat her "in the quality of his wife" or to provide her with separate maintenance. Berkeley responded by ordering the Charles City court "to enquire into the barbarous usage" and to give her "all redresse ... and all security & maintenance for the future." Thereafter, Francis Grey dropped from view.[61]

William Fitzhugh (1651–1701) first went to the House in that crop of burgesses who served after Bacon's Rebellion. A native of Bedfordshire and a woolen-draper's son, Fitzhugh showed up in Virginia about 1670 and settled in Stafford County. Marriage to Sarah Tucker tied him to a kinship network with links to important families along the upper Potomac watershed. His commercial experience opened doors to economic advancement. He translated his practical exposures to the law into a profitable sideline as an attorney. Among his most prominent clients were the second Ralph Wormeley, of the Council, and Robert Beverley, whom he represented when that arch irreconcilable was suspected of fomenting the plant-cutter riots.[62]

Elected to the General Assembly of February 1676/77, Fitzhugh was among the first postrebellion burgesses who came to the House with no prior political experience as a justice of the peace. Indeed, he sat in the House for ten years before his appointment to the Stafford bench. He served in four consecutive assemblies, during which successive Speakers gave him various assignments, including a place on the influential Committee for Propositions and Grievances. At one point he ranked third in committee seniority and seemed destined for higher things, but then his political fortunes crashed. A moderate, he took an unsuccessful run at the Speakership in 1684, which put an edge on his relationship with the irreconcilables. His moderation cost Fitzhugh more because longtime rival Martin Scarlet unseated him in the 1685 elections. Scarlet then induced the House to investigate allegations that Fitzhugh had misappropriated Stafford County funds. The inquiry came to naught after Governor Effingham backed Fitzhugh, which tainted him all the more. He did not return to the House for nearly a decade, and even then there were rumbles against him because of his lukewarm enthusiasm for the overthrow of James II. Nevertheless, he won his old place on Propositions and Grievances and chaired the committee. Beyond that, he labored to revise the statutes in force, though nothing came of his work once the Council of State shrank from seeing the revisal through. His career as a burgess ended after Governor Andros dissolved the General Assembly of October 1693.[63]

Like everyone else who held places in the General Assembly after 1619, Fitzhugh assumed the mantle of gentility and helped fashion Virginia's great planter elite. Their linkage of social position with political authority was another of the unintended consequences of the founding of the General Assembly.

Chapter 6

Clerks and Speakers

Clerks and Speakers ensured the expeditious, orderly dispatch of the General Assembly's judicial and legislative deliberations. As leaders of the House, Speakers ranked in stature just below the governors and councillors, and their power to influence the work of the assembly was considerable. They bore a political trust, too, which shaded their office with overtones that always colored the choice of Speakers. Clerks, being primarily record keepers, carried no such responsibilities, but the incumbents and the manner of their election also became controversial subjects after 1676.

The place of clerk originated in the customs of Parliament, but the office differed from its Westminster equivalent in certain notable respects. There were, according to William Hakewill, "two principal Clerks of the Parliament ... who ... enroll[ed] all the Pleas and business of the Parliament," one for the Lords and another for the Commons. Commissioned by royal letters patent, both kept their offices for life and received "ancient salaries," plus fees, and each employed batteries of deputies to assist with the clerical chores. To begin with in Virginia, John Pory clerked for the Council of State and the General Assembly, and he doubled as secretary of the colony as well.[1] That arrangement remained in effect until the mid-1620s, when the two offices were separated by executive fiat. The apparent reason for the separation was the Council's displeasure with Edward Sharples, who as acting-secretary-clerk betrayed Council confidences to the Harvey Commission. He reported things said in private and gave the committee "Copyes of our wryteings & Letters to the Kings majesties & the L[ord] of the privye Counsell ... out of promise of reward." His offenses had sharp political repercussions, and they manifestly violated his sworn pledge not to reveal "matters Committed unto [him] and all things that shall be treated secretly at the Counsell table." For his indiscretions, Sharples lost his position and his ears.[2] Wyatt and the Council then stripped the office of secretary of its direct clerical duties, and instead assigned them to a clerk. As a sop, future secretaries retained supervision of the clerk and the gift of nomination, but their nominees were subject to confirmation by the full Council.[3]

A Little Parliament

Successive Council clerks maintained the journals of the assembly and its other legislative papers until 1643. Their role grew more refined once the House of Burgesses came into being; thereafter it bespoke the greater specialization of the Council of State as a high court of judicature and as the second branch of the General Assembly. As clerk of the General Court, incumbents issued process, they docketed cases for hearing, they enrolled judgments, and they maintained case files; as clerk of the Council of State, they drafted orders-in-council and kept minutes; as clerk of the assembly, they prepared amendments to bills, they took minutes, and they acted as messengers to the House of Burgesses.

In lieu of fixed salaries in cash, clerks received statutory fees rated in tobacco for certain of their transactions. Suitors, for example, paid them two pounds of tobacco for "everie petition, answer and reply, or any other writing that shall pass under the hand of either plt. or deft." Likewise, clerks collected charges for filing suits, issuing subpoenas, or entering judgments on the record. As an added tangible compensation, there were allowances for work done during legislative sessions and the title "clerk of the Assembly." Proximity to the great officers of state carried considerable reward, too.[4]

Its benefits certainly made the post among the colony's more remunerative positions, and it drew its share of grasping colonists. Covetousness alone was insufficient for appointment. Patronage of the secretary or the governor was obviously important, but literacy and familiarity with clerical routines were the crucial considerations. Incumbents learned those skills in various ways. Some who could read and could write in a fair hand acquired the necessary technical competence through mastery of a clerk's manual such as William West's *Symboleographie*. Others relied on experience gained in business. Untrustworthy though Sharples may have been, it was his mercantile experience that helped him to his appointment in the first place. Similarly, Thomas Brereton, Francis Kirkman, and Richard Awborne, who clerked for the Council throughout the 1660s and 1670s, had commercial origins. On the other hand, John Meade, Samuel Abbot, and perhaps Henry Hartwell were among those who, "by their Function, or Course of Life, practice their Pen in any Courts, or otherwise," actually trained for the calling of clerk before they left the British Isles.[5] A few, William Edwards being one, learned by apprenticing in the county courts. Formal legal education boosted another, Edward Chilton.

Chilton (d. 1707) studied law before he showed up in Virginia sometime after 1676. He acquired property at Jamestown, married a daughter of the second Speaker

Clerks and Speakers

Edward Hill, and caught the eye of Secretary Nicholas Spencer, who named him Henry Hartwell's successor in 1682. His tenure was controversial, especially during the General Assembly of 1684 when he fell in behind Effingham, whose views of the imperial connection accorded with his own at the time. The governor thought he saw a way to undermine the burgesses by elevating Chilton's importance as a legislative officer. Appointing Chilton "clerk of the General Assembly," Effingham demanded that the House raise Chilton's allowances to equal those of its own clerk. The burgesses balked. They argued that Chilton had little to do besides keep the "Journall of your Excellency and the Councell proceedings." They claimed that "Imployment Labour, and Care, by the Method now used in Assembly proceedings" greatly added to the work of their clerk, which was why he deserved twice what they voted to pay Chilton. Neither side budged until a frustrated Effingham finally caved in, conceding, he said, so that "noe further time be wasted in this nature." He never broached the issue again, and the role of the clerk of the assembly remained ambiguous.[6]

Chilton gave way to William Edwards in 1687 and was attorney general for several years in the 1690s before returning to England. There he collaborated with Henry Hartwell and James Blair during the summer of 1697 to indite an account of Virginia for the Board of Trade. As the Privy Council had once queried Sir William Berkeley about conditions in the Old Dominion, so the new board sought similar information from the three authors. Overall, Chilton and the others pitched their answers in tones that spoke for the benefits of a properly fitted and managed empire, though they clearly disdained the concentration of power in the hands of the governor and Council. Specifically, they were highly critical of the many ways in which Virginia's legal and political order deviated from English standards.[7] They noted, for instance, that clerks of Council "neither take an Oath to discharge their Duty, nor give any Security," and they commented on how the House of Burgesses lost control of its clerk.[8]

A clerk of its own became a necessity once the House of Burgesses sat apart from the Council, and from the start, the office closely resembled its like in the House of Commons. Early clerks, it seems, deliberately copied the English model as far as their understanding and colonial circumstances permitted. For example, when Clerk John Meade adopted the Latin title "clericus domus communis" for his own in 1643, he merely arrogated the style of his counterpart at Westminster.[9] Meade's successors followed his lead, though the habit of referring to themselves as "clerk of the house," "clerk of the burgesses," or "clerk of the assembly" soon crept into routine usage, too. (Used interchangeably, these terms implied nothing beyond the likelihood that later clerks, or the burgesses, had little command of Latin.) Then, too, by the 1640s Virginia clerks also could rely on procedural manuals, which laid down their duties with some specificity. Their inclination to emulate what they read was natural enough because the cover of the printed word from authoritative texts sanctioned them.[10] The work was comparable, too. It involved maintaining journals, preparing draft bills, enrolling acts, and authenticating copies of records, among other things.[11] In addition, the clerks swore similar oaths that bound them to secrecy and the bidding of their respective Houses.[12]

Despite these likenesses, Virginia clerks differed from their English cousins in three respects. First, they employed fewer subordinates, such as the bevy of copyists, tellers, enrollers, and reading clerks who assisted in the Commons. Second, because the colony lacked a secure record office, clerks retained physical custody of all assembly archives, which they stowed in their own private houses between sessions. Finally, they were elected by the burgesses, not appointed by the governor. The latter distinction dated to when the House came into being. At the time, Berkeley, seeing an advantage to himself, allowed the burgesses to pick John Meade as clerk. Thereby, the House laid down a precedent that went unchallenged until Effingham set it aside in 1688.

Meade, Henry Randolph, Robert Beverley, Thomas Milner, and Francis Page stand out as the more notable clerks. Secretary Richard Kemp recruited Meade (b. after 1612–1645) out of England, quite possibly bringing him over on a return trip from London in 1641. Meade accomplished a lot in his short tenure, which ended at his death in 1645. He set important and lasting precedents. None was more important than the formal written journals that documented the votes, proceedings, and orders of the House. The journals, in brief, recorded the actions that defined the House as an institution. Indeed, as Hartwell, Blair, and Chilton later made the point, "to know the Pressures, Humours, common Talk, and Designs of the People of that Country, perhaps there [was] no better Way than to peruse" those volumes.[13]

Randolph (1623–1673), a merchant of Northamptonshire stock, wound up in the colony while still in his teens. Alighting on Turkey Island in Henrico County, he set himself up as a planter and eventually translated his writing talents into an appointment as clerk of the county court. Association with Francis Moryson explains why the burgesses first elected him. In 1656, Moryson was Speaker, so when Charles Norwood's departure caused a vacancy, he put Randolph's name forward. Randolph remained clerk longer than anyone else in the century. Of greater significance than sheer longevity was his contribution to two thoroughgoing revisions of the statutes in force.[14]

No seventeenth-century clerk was more controversial than Robert Beverley (bap. 1635–1687) or more powerful. Born in Hull, Beverley had a varied background in commerce before he moved to Virginia about 1663. He became the surveyor for Gloucester and Middlesex Counties and had a talent for advocacy, too, which he whetted as a regular suitor and one of the best attorneys in the colony's courts. The income from both pursuits combined with commerce and tobacco-raising to enrich him, and he ranked among the wealthiest planters in Virginia.[15]

Politics beckoned too. Once the General Assembly lopped off part of Lancaster County to form Middlesex in 1668, Governor Berkeley put Beverley on the first commission of the peace for the new county and named him one of its militia officers. Beverley then took a turn as sheriff before he was appointed attorney general pro tempore. He also acted as clerk for the House Committee on Propositions and Grievances, which signaled his developing interest in taking on assignments for the General Assembly.[16]

Such quiet, unexceptional openings were but preludes to an otherwise tempestuous career in public life that broke stormy in 1676 and blew troubled until Beverley's death ten years later. He "approved himselfe" during Bacon's Rebellion "to be most loyall, circumspect, and couragious in his Majesties service for the good of his countrey."[17] Efficient and ruthless, he displayed a singular adeptness for capturing rebel ringleaders and taming their followers. His harshness of method left a sour, lingering aftertaste that made him a target of complaint; nevertheless, his prominence as a Berkeley loyalist led to his election as clerk of the House in the General Assembly of February 1676/77.

Several weeks after that assembly rose, the royal commissioners inquiring into the rebellion insisted that Beverley give them the House journals and other papers. He refused. His duty to his masters in the House prevented him from complying, and he could not gain their permission because they were no longer in session. Unimpressed, the commissioners forcibly seized the documents. Angry burgesses who attended the General Assembly of October 1677 protested the blatant, "great violation of our priviledges" both to Lieutenant Governor Jeffreys and to the Privy Council. The upshot of their complaints were orders from the Crown dismissing Beverley from all civil offices and a mandate to send duplicates of House and Council journals to London regularly.[18]

For Beverley, the entire episode came as a turning point. It angered him against Jeffreys, and it thrust him into the emerging irreconcilable faction. Dismissal cost him nothing. It and his resistance suddenly raised his stature with the burgesses and councillors who shared his opinions or were of a more moderate persuasion. A majority in the House merely ignored the royal commandment and reelected him in 1679. Such was his popularity that Governor Culpeper dared not oppose his becoming clerk again in 1680. (Culpeper later claimed that his approval of Beverley actually gained him the power to appoint the clerk, but it did no such thing.) Beverley overreached when he encouraged his fellow planters in Gloucester, Middlesex, and New Kent Counties in events that preceded the tobacco-cutting riots. Moderates and even some among the most hardened of his irreconcilable allies publicly drew back at that, and on 12 May 1682 a warrant went forth for his arrest and deprivation of all places of public trust.[19]

Incarcerated aboard various vessels, Beverley remained in custody while the authorities pondered what should become of him. His enemies among the trimmers on the Council blamed him wholly for the plant cutting but were fearful of proceeding against him. Culpeper might have preferred to hang him, but he held back too because the evidence of Beverley's culpability was hardly compelling. The governor therefore avoided a decision and went back to England, leaving the matter to his deputy, Sir Henry Chicheley, who sympathized with the rioters but disapproved of his neighbor's alleged misdeeds and died before he could decide what to do. That left Beverley to languish at the king's pleasure. So Beverley continued a prisoner until the spring of 1684, when on the order of Charles II he was tried before the General Court. Found guilty of ambiguous charges, he confessed his error and received pardon. His exoneration came well after the assembly had gone into session, so the burgesses chose Thomas Milner as their clerk.[20]

Like Beverley, Thomas Milner (d. 1694) applied an aptitude for surveying to a successful hunt for riches and position. In 1650 he settled in Nansemond County, where his movements are difficult to track because the county's seventeenth-century records have been lost. Available information reveals a steady improvement in his fortunes. By 1676 Milner had gained a seat on the county court, a militia officer's commission, and landholdings of at least thirty-three hundred acres. He also held the district surveyorship for Nansemond, Warwick, and Elizabeth City Counties, a job that linked him to Beverley and to Philip Ludwell, who gave Milner the appointment. All that fitted him to join with the irreconcilables, and it made him a good candidate in April 1684 to succeed Beverley.[21]

From the irreconcilables' point of view, the choice of Milner seemed little short of inspired. His command of the records or procedures may not have equaled Beverley's, but he showed every bit as much relish for confounding governors. He drafted a memorial to Charles II wherein the House sought royal confirmation of the assembly's right to hear appeals from the General Court. After Effingham chastised the burgesses for their presumption and they rejected a compromise proposal, Milner drew up the version that went to Whitehall "in the Name of the House of Burgesses only." Following the session, Milner and the burgess William Sherwood left for London, intent on presenting the address to the king and lobbying against the governor.[22]

Effingham got word of what Milner and Sherwood were up to via William Blathwayt and confessed in angered amazement that "I did not think any person would have had the Impudence to have owned that Addresse, for besides what you find on the Joynall by my messages, I sent for the house of Burgesses, and gave them a severe aprehention for Entertaining any such thoughts." Effingham promised Blathwayt that he would "turn out Sherwood from practicing as an Atturney" and oust Milner from all his offices. "It would be very much to the advantage of the Government," he concluded, "if the Clerk of the Assembly were for the future nominated by the Governor, as by the King in England." And so he planted in his patron's mind the seed of an idea that cost the House its right after another of Effingham's tussles with Robert Beverley.[23]

The pesky Beverley had emerged from his ordeal seemingly triumphant. No doubt he delighted when the voters in Middlesex elected him to the House of Burgesses in 1685, and his vindication appeared complete after his House colleagues quickly reelected him as clerk that November. Their choice annoyed Effingham, though he held his irritation to himself out of hope that the recent brush with the law would calm Beverley. It did not, and the two men soon ran athwart one another over the wording of a bill, among other disagreements. Effingham's patience wore to the breaking point, whereupon the governor drove Beverley from office one last time.

Effingham, with James II's blessing, named Francis Page to replace him. The gleeful governor plainly intended to prosecute his enemy too, but Beverley's sudden death in March 1687 denied Effingham that pleasure.[24]

While Beverley's removal cleared the way for Francis Page, his death gave the governor an unexpected bit of leverage for forcing the burgesses to accept the loss of their right of election. Within weeks of Beverley's demise, Effingham and the Council issued an order that claimed the records of the assembly "usually Committed to the Care, Custody, and keeping of the Clerk of the Assembly." The documents were immediately entrusted to Council clerk William Edwards who would hold them "Safely and Securely preserved ... untill his Excellency shall think fitt, to Dispose them into the Care and Custody of a person fitt for soe Weighty a Concerne."[25] They remained in Edwards's hands for nearly a year because Effingham did not "think fitt" to call an assembly until the following April.[26]

When the House gathered on 24 April 1688, Effingham sprang his appointment of Page on the burgesses. Left with only one choice, they accepted the fait accompli, though not without a rearguard action that extracted a concession from the governor. The opening presented itself when two councillors came to the House and brought "a Form of an Oath for the Clark" that Effingham had written. "Comparing the same with the usuall Oath," the burgesses observed two changes that departed "materially" from the one "which hath been administred heretofore." One was a clause acknowledging the clerk's appointment "by his Excellency the Governor," and the second removed the vow to "Keep Secret all proceedings of the said House of Burgesses so far as shall by the said House be found necessary."[27]

The second alteration was immediately seen as the more serious of the two emendations; it would irreparably damage the House because it would enable the governor to know what was being said in committee or to hamper floor debate. Such an assault on their privilege of free speech was more than the burgesses could tolerate, and they fired off an immediate rebuttal. While they "Yeilded" to Page's appointment, they remarked plainly that "the person so nominated is still our Clark, & therefore as much our Servant as any former Clarke of Assembly." Therefore, they "humbly Supplicated" Effingham to allow Page to take the "usuall Oath," a copy of which they appended to their resolution.[28]

Effingham, wishing to avoid a distraction, backed down a bit. He said in his reply that the House had misunderstood him. He had no "desire, that the Clark should be a spy upon your actions." What he intended was to be informed "what were the Votes & Resolves of your House" and so avoid having business "come upon me, as it were by way of Surprize." Being thus "not willing to intrench upon any privilege of your House," he proposed inserting the words "you shall keep secret all private Debates."[29] The burgesses accepted after some reflection, and Page was duly sworn clerk. It was a small victory, one that hardly offset the diminution of the House's freedom, but it was all the burgesses could get.[30]

Page (1657–1692) himself seems to have been personally acceptable to the House. He shared a common background and experience with many who sat there. Son of Councillor John Page, he was a member of the York County bench, a former sheriff, and a vestryman for Bruton Parish, and the York freeholders thrice elected him as one of their burgesses. Like his father, he aligned himself with the trimmer faction, which would account for why Effingham nominated him. Retiring at the end of the session, his one accomplishment was copying "Severall Antient & usefull Records" into a "fair book," which unfortunately has long since disappeared.[31]

With Effingham out of the way, the burgesses tried to reclaim their right. They "elected" Page's successor at the General Assembly of 1691, which Lieutenant Governor Nicholson allowed to slide by without challenge. A similar attempt met a swift, harsh rebuke from Governor Andros when the House convened the following year. To all intents and purposes, it was he who finally closed the argument "by giving a Commission to one they had formerly chosen, *viz.* Mr. Peter Beverley," the son of Effingham's steadfast enemy, who later became the first Speaker of the House in the new century.[32]

The roots of the Speaker's office trailed back to England and struck deeply into the history of the House of Commons. "That the Commons have ever had a Speaker, I think none will doubt," declared the author of a widely used parliamentary manual. Henry Elsynge could not say for certain just when the office originated, though he believed that it dated to the fourteenth century, but when he came to explain the reason for it, he wrote with greater assurance. Someone had to preside, he observed, and someone had to act as spokesman for the house. Hence the office and title of Speaker.[33]

For hundreds of years the Commons chose "whom they would of their own House"; invariably, however, their choices were the reigning monarch's creatures. Nominated by their sovereigns, Speakers simultaneously held Crown offices, and in Henry VIII's time they began to receive royal stipends as well. (For example, that great champion of Commons, Sir Edward Coke, was simultaneously Queen Elizabeth's solicitor general and Speaker in the Parliament of 1593.) A nominee, once chosen, always declined his election in a short speech and begged to be excused for his insufficiencies. His colleagues customarily denied the request, whereupon the new Speaker approached the throne to pray for the ancient privileges of the House: freedom from arrest during the session, liberty of speech, and access to the throne. The Speaker then returned to the House, and it got down to business, with him in the chair.[34]

Although the Speaker's role as presiding officer was important, it long stood second to his purpose as his colleagues' intermediary between Crown and Lords. Those parts swapped places during the seventeenth century. The exchange happened gradually as kings and Commons disputed the question of who held the ultimate constitutional authority of rule. Along the way, the conflict inspired in Stuart Englishmen a keen interest in parliamentary procedures, and curiosity joined opportunity to beget the Virginia Speakership.[35]

A "mouth of this house"[36] grew necessary once the burgesses sat apart from the governor and Council; however, many important details about the maturing of the institutional Speaker are lost to us. Two things are nonetheless abundantly clear. Certain members of the General Assembly possessed a deep knowledge of the English Speaker, his duties, and how he was chosen. Presumably, they got the information out of works such as Elsynge's and others that touched on contemporary English politics or by word of mouth and correspondence between family and friends. Whatever the sources of inspiration, the creators closely patterned the Virginia Speakership after the English model down the decades after 1643. The Speaker also passed from go-between to leader of the House. Beginning with the founding of the office itself, that transition accelerated during the postrebellion decades.

Just as in England, when the burgesses assembled for a new legislature, their first order of business was organizing their House. Certifying the returns followed the reading of the election writ; then the burgesses sent a delegation to the governor to inform him that they were gathered as a House and to ask leave to elect their Speaker. An election followed. The newly chosen Speaker gave his disabling speech and was installed in the chair. Finally, a committee from the House presented him to the governor for approval, which was never denied.

Biographical information about all the Speakers consists mainly of small details, so weighing their merits becomes something of a guessing game. Nevertheless, the overall impression that emerges is of men who commanded loyalty and respect sufficient unto their elections as the principal officer of the House. That judgment merely reinforces the obvious, but it in no way forms the basis for conclusions about any Speaker's legislative skills or political acumen, as the case of Robert Wynne (1622–1675) plainly illustrates.

Wynne draws notice by virtue of his having been the longest-serving colonial Speaker but one. His twelve-year tenure (1662–1674) embraced a period when the General Assembly rose to its zenith as a little parliament and compiled an impressive legislative record. With Wynne in the chair, the burgesses contributed to the restoration of royal authority, to the fifth general revision of the statutes, and to the enactment of diversification laws, defense bills, and legislation to defeat the Northern Neck Proprietary. Beyond that, Wynne joined a delegation of burgesses and councillors that negotiated with the Maryland government to limit tobacco production. He was also the first Speaker to whom any governor accorded the privilege of signing official messages to Whitehall. That Berkeley so graced him signified his personal regard for Wynne and recognition of the Speaker as an adroit leader of the House.

For all of that, Speaker Wynne remains a shadowy fellow. The known facts of his existence require but few words to recount. Born and reared in Canterbury, he grew up in a family conspicuous for its wealth and position. His paternal grandfather, for whom he was named, was once lord mayor of the cathedral city, and other close kin represented Canterbury in Parliament. What Wynne did before he set himself up in Virginia is mostly mysterious. Very possibly he read law, a supposition that is borne out by the survival of one of his books—a first edition of Sir Edmund Plowden's *Commentaries*—which he inherited. (His ownership of that set, printed in law French, argues Wynne's familiarity with that arcane tongue, and that clearly set the Speaker off from most of his colleagues.) Presumably a younger son seeking enlarged prospects or an open royalist seeking a fresh start, Wynne landed in Virginia before midcentury and had become a member of the Charles City County bench by 1656. Two years later he showed up in the House for the first time. He sat out a session but returned in March 1660 to participate in Berkeley's recall. He ran again when Berkeley called the election that brought the Long Assembly into being. Death's sudden claim on Speaker Henry Soane thrust Wynne into the office. Wynne himself died the owner of considerable property in Virginia and in Canterbury.[37]

A Little Parliament

The likelihood is that the choice of Wynne and other Speakers was contested from the origin of the House of Burgesses, though the first instance of an election dates no earlier than 1653. To the extent that there was competition between candidates, those rivalries probably turned at first on the same issues that divided the Council of State. That many in the House opposed the politics of the Mathews-Claiborne-Bennett faction throughout the 1640s and 1650s would explain why, with the exception of the first Thomas Stegge, early Speakers identified with planters who inclined to Charles I and Virginia-Dutch commerce. The second Edmund Scarburgh, the Speaker in the General Assembly of 1645–1646, traded extensively with the Netherlands, and in 1653 he was debarred from office for his loyalty to the Stuarts. Likewise, the first Edward Hill, who preceded Scarburgh, was a Berkeley ally, whereas Scarburgh's successors, Ambrose Harmer and Thomas Harwood, had no identifiable political or personal links to the Mathews group.[38]

Not unexpectedly, Edward Major and Thomas Dew, the first of the Interregnum Speakers, espoused strong Puritan views. Each of their replacements, however, was a royalist. An explanation for that phenomenon lies in the composition of the House throughout the Interregnum. Burgesses tended to cleave between those who favored the new regime and those who remained mildly loyal to the Stuarts. On the whole, the balance usually favored the royalists. The latter bowed to what they could not immediately change, pinched their noses, and voted in chief executives acceptable to the parliamentary regime in London. But when it came to picking their leaders in the House, the royalists always mustered votes enough to elect one of their own for Speaker. On at least one occasion, they even succeeded in engineering the unanimous reelection of Speaker Hill, who presided at the General Assembly of 1654–1655. Even if candidates opposed one another, they came out of the royalist camp. Hill ran again in 1659 and won, but the royalist Moore Fauntleroy, a member for Lancaster County, "moved against him as if clandestinely elected and taxed the House of unwarrantable proceedings therein." The election stood, though the burgesses suspended Fauntleroy until "uppon his submission he may be readmitted."[39]

Besides Henry Soane and Robert Wynne, Augustine Warner and Thomas Godwin also sat in the Speaker's chair during the second Berkeley administration. The extant House journals, far from complete, are silent about whether Soane or Wynne had opposition. If so, their opposition may have been merely pro forma. On the other hand, there is a case to be made that Warner and Godwin faced each other at the June

1676 legislative session. Warner presided at the final session of the General Assembly of 1661–1676, which committed the colonists to a passive, expensive, hugely unpopular war with the Indians, and he identified with Governor Berkeley, who later named him to the Council of State. Standing for reelection as burgess for Gloucester County, Warner easily won his seat in the May polling. Godwin, who was absent from the House for fifteen years, came out of retirement and was also elected. Other than holding a place on the Nansemond County Court, he bore no overt political or personal obligation to Berkeley; neither was he directly connected to any of the Baconians. His evident lack of partiality toward either side explains why "ill-Humoured" burgesses preferred Godwin over Warner. That inference gains additional weight from Warner's reelection as Speaker in February 1677 by a House that was unquestionably pro-Berkeley.[40]

Challenges for the Speaker's chair again grew commonplace during the 1680s and 1690s. They sometimes reflected partisan divisions among the burgesses. In other instances, they appear on the record as contests more personal than factional. All, however, are indicative of the burgesses' keen desire to put someone in the chair who reflected the will of the House and who was capable of standing up to the Council or the governor. Thomas Ballard's election in 1680 and its consequences illustrate both situations.[41]

Ballard ran against the trimmer Matthew Kemp, late Speaker in the General Assembly of 1679, whom he narrowly defeated; then someone nominated another trimmer, Isaac Allerton, and Ballard handily prevailed over him. Ballard's victories represented more than the triumphant return to power of a top irreconcilable, whom Lieutenant Governor Jeffreys had earlier driven from the Council. They were smart defeats for the trimmers. Kemp, at least, found unguent in his elevation to the Council shortly after the session. His supporters, though, never nominated another of their following.

Speaker Ballard hoed hard as leader of the General Assembly of 1680–1682. He convened a House in which expectations were high that the new governor would be attuned to the irreconcilables and the moderates, and there were aspirations of relieving economic pressures raised by the glut in tobacco. Those hopes were not realized because Culpeper showed himself no more sympathetic to Virginia sensibilities than had Jeffreys. Worse still, from the burgesses' vantage point, the governor checked the Speaker at nearly every turn. Deputy Governor Chicheley was no easier match either. As a result, the House emerged at its dissolution considerably weaker than it had been at its call, and much of the blame came back to haunt Ballard.

A Little Parliament

Two years passed before another legislative session. Effingham's election writ for the General Assembly of 1684 resulted in a House more strongly irreconcilable than the last. Ballard returned as the burgess for Jamestown and offered himself as a candidate for Speaker. William Kendall and the younger Edward Hill (1637–1700) opposed him, and Ballard fell in the initial round of balloting, as did Kendall. Hill then faced a challenge from William Fitzhugh but beat it back, only to have Charles Scarburgh advance himself before Hill finally won. That the House denied Ballard his bid for reelection because Culpeper and Chicheley had bested him seems self-evident in light of the burgesses who ran against him. Both Kendall and Hill were irreconcilables; Fitzhugh was a moderate.[42]

No doubt it pleased Hill to sit where his father had once sat, but he fared little better than Ballard as Speaker. Hill had the misfortune of chairing the House when the General Assembly lost its right to take appeals from the General Court. He staunchly defended the prerogatives of the House throughout the dispute, but that was a fight neither he nor the burgesses could win in the face of the Council's acquiescence and the determined Effingham, who had strong backing from Whitehall and the full weight of English constitutional precedents in his favor. And so the House grudgingly yielded another of its privileges. Hill lost, too. At the next general election, either he decided not to stand, or the Charles City County freeholders rejected him; whatever the cause, Hill dropped out of provincial politics. He surfaced again in 1691 to take a place at the Council table. That appointment symbolized an end to the irreconcilable phase of his public career.[43]

The man who succeeded Hill, William Kendall, was another of the irreconcilables. He led the burgesses during the contentious first sitting of the 1685–1686 legislature and worked closely with Robert Beverley to frustrate Effingham. Kendall died in the interval between sessions, however, so the governor never had a chance to try to even the score.[44]

Bereft of their leader, the burgesses replaced him with Arthur Allen (ca. 1652–1710), yet one more of the irreconcilables. Allen gave place by turns to two others, Thomas Milner and Philip Ludwell. Milner won without apparent opposition, but Ludwell had to beat back five challengers to climb into the Speaker's chair. Although the journal does not name Ludwell's adversaries, they were most probably younger members; more than half the House consisted of newcomers, and none of them had any evident irreconcilable connection. Being an irreconcilable no longer mattered in 1695, not even to Ludwell, who had by that time made his peace with the new order. He had walked his road to Damascus a few years earlier after the burgesses sent him to London to lobby against Effingham. The attempt to unhorse the baron was a miserable failure. Deeply disappointed, Ludwell came to a critical choice: convert or continue to fight and risk losing everything. He converted. Nevertheless, his past explains why some opposed his election as Speaker. Governor Andros, for one, was so concerned that he sought his Council's opinions about Ludwell's fitness and whether he "should speak to the Members ... before they chose their Speaker or after"; the Council advised forebearance.[45]

The Speakers after Ludwell all beat back challengers. Their opposition was far from token because each victor usually stood against a field of four or five other candidates. When William Randolph ran in 1698, it took several days for him to round up the winning margin. Robert Carter confronted a similar situation at the next assembly. Despite Lieutenant Governor Nicholson's impatience at "haveing waited these two daies Expecting a Speaker would have been presented," a third day passed before the deed was done.[46]

These and all the preceding contests delineate one salient difference between the Virginia Speaker and his English cousin. No governor dictated to the House of Burgesses in the same manner as the Crown manipulated the House of Commons. Truth to tell, however, no governor was exactly diligent in taking on the House either, least of all those who ruled after 1677. Andros's inquiry about Ludwell and Nicholson's rebuke are the sole recorded hints of anything that might be read as interference. To the extent that both represent dictation, they stand as rather puny examples of gubernatorial boldness.

The want of sterner stuff is a curiosity. In view of the effort to minimize the General Assembly, the Crown ought to have assailed the Speakership in a fashion that parallelled its attack on other House prerogatives, but it did not. Why?

No governor commanded resources comparable to the king's. Back when the Speakership was new, Berkeley showed more concern for placating the Council than for controlling the Speaker because his councillors posed a far greater political threat to him than anyone in the House. He therefore allocated the provincial places at his disposal to them instead of to the burgesses, and he continued to do so for the remainder of his first administration. Gubernatorial influence attenuated to an even greater degree once the parliamentary settlement made the House of Burgesses master of its own fate. The burgesses fortified their mastery still more in 1653 after they backed down Governor Bennett for meddling with their election of Walter Chiles. Bennett's retreat acted as a caution for Berkeley throughout all of his second administration. Consequently, the record, such as it is, shows little sign of any willingness on his part to tamper with the Speaker's election.[47]

These precedents left postrebellion governors few tools with which to fashion a Speaker who was beholden to them or who would put the Crown ahead of the House. Precedent worked against them in another way as well. Since 1643, once the burgesses announced their wishes, no governor denied the House. That privilege relied on more than mere Virginia practice, it carried the imprimatur of parliamentary custom. "The King," wrote Henry Elsynge, "never rejected any whom they [the Commons] made choice of."[48] What the sovereign accepted, therefore, no governor could reject on constitutional grounds.

The office of Speaker itself stood as a bulwark, too. From the beginning the burgesses cut it as close to its English pattern as they knew how. They perfected the fit as their understanding increased, and by the last decades of the century the resemblance between the two offices approached exactness. That likeness surely checked the postrebellion governors. Not even Effingham dared claim that the institutional Speaker departed from contemporary procedures in Parliament and so must yield to his refinements. Cunning, not stupid, he would not battle for what he could not win, so he picked on the more vulnerable clerkship.[49] Thus, while the House of Burgesses lost the privilege of picking its clerks, its unhindered right to elect its presiding officer remained secure.

Chapter 7
Lessons for Legislators

Councillors, burgesses, Speakers, and clerks all perceived Virginia as a place where they might reinvent themselves in an environment unshackled by England's labyrinthine legalities. They quickly learned that living in Virginia demanded more than a mere quest for opportunity. Survival was their foremost need, and aspiration alone ensured neither endurance nor success. Staying alive in a strange country was hazardous, but as dexterity at coping in a new land grew, the cadences of colonial life required greater regulation. Without rules there was no order. Taxes would not be raised and malefactors would not be punished; laborers would not be bound and property would not be acquired; estates would not descend and debts would not be collected. Because these and dozens of similar political issues remained imperatives, the assemblymen never entirely slipped the trammels of their background. Freedom invited chaos and the loss of cultural identity. The latter possibility was an especially terrifying prospect, made the more dreadful by separation from England and discontinuities that punctuated life in Virginia throughout the seventeenth century. Confronted thus, members of the General Assembly harked back to their roots to pluck from them a legal means of giving their society definition.[1]

The idea of law signified something to every seventeenth-century Briton. One of them expressed that universal meaning this way. "Good is the Law," wrote James Wooley,

> and to Doe good Designed
> But if the Executors for gaine Doth grind
> The face of Justice And Oppress the Poore
> There is Another Law for them in Store
> Which neither Judge nor Jury can withstand
> Noe Lawes nor writs can Frostrat heavens high hand.[2]

Wooley and his countrymen recognized law as the bond that held everyone in civilized communion with one another. Like other legal systems, England's law comprehended society's priceless possessions: beliefs and family, property and reputation, life and liberty. Its form gave it distinctiveness, which led the English to call it by an expressive phrase—"the common law." Common law likewise represented an ageless wisdom regarding the right construction of English polity. It afforded the kingdom protection, and it fixed standards of taste, manners, and morals. Its shapes and its rituals acted as reminders to all and sundry that it was the arbiter of their conduct. It was all of these things, and it was more than these things. Construed in the broadest of senses, common law was the utmost expression of English culture because it delimited an identity that set the English off from other Europeans, from Africans, from Asians, and from the peoples of the Americas.[3]

Englishwomen or -men required no formal instruction to understand how law formed them even as it regulated them in their daily lives; they needed only to look about them. From childhood they absorbed precepts that governed the household when they observed the relations between themselves and their parents. As they matured, they imbibed rules that controlled political authority, social gradations, the church, and the distribution of wealth in the larger society. When they took up a calling, married, produced children, changed residences, left the country, came into property, or committed crimes they again discovered themselves constrained by time-honored norms of conduct. At every turn, they saw law as an inevitable condition of life itself. Step by step, they grew to comprehend that a well-regulated realm was an ordered community that held its subjects in place, at peace with one another, and out of harm's way. Naturally enough, by the time they reached adulthood, they instinctively accepted a fundamental maxim of common law, "the safety of the people is the chief law."[4]

Then, too, the men who filled the General Assembly after 1619 brought practical exposures to law to their tasks. Those with groundings in commerce or the skilled trades gained a working familiarity with instruments and legal proceedings that touched on the routine courses of their occupations. They learned how to prepare bonds, indentures, bills of exchange, charter parties, and wills. Collecting or discharging debts imparted lessons in filing litigation, testifying, and acting as attorneys. In a similar vein, those of more genteel origin knew something of land law and the intricacies of conveyances, trusts, or tenures. By these means, councillors and burgesses acquired a lay knowledge of how England's legal institutions worked, just as they were led to view law from a special vantage point.

For men without academic legal education, the phrase "common law" meant something quite different from that conveyed to lawyers. The latter attached several shades of meaning to the expression. They used it to differentiate between English and Continental law, as well as between law and equity, or the judicial opinions that regulated proceedings in the courts of King's Bench and common pleas, and it distinguished the customary law of immemorial usage from parliamentary statutes. In Virginia the words meant something much narrower: they betokened the branches of law that were most familiar to the burgesses and councillors: equity, the law merchant, and unwritten local law.[5]

Members of the assembly also found much inspiration from books. After the introduction of movable type into the British Isles late in the fifteenth century, books about English law burgeoned in number and subject matter. That single technological innovation revolutionized the spread of legal information because it not only speeded and cheapened production costs, but it also increased the availability of given titles. English printers were quick to see a ready market for law books. Soon after William Caxton set up his first press, legal publishing became staple fare as printers and booksellers struggled to keep pace with rising demand. By the time the first settlers alighted at Jamestown, dozens of titles were already in circulation, but the quantity and assortment grew greater still as the political contests between king and commoner intensified the zeal of literate Britons for things legal. Thus, the variety of accessible texts to which colonial legislators might turn at any point after 1619 fell into several broad classifications: case reports, statutory compilations, treatises, judicial biographies, how-to manuals, and guides to parliamentary procedure.[6]

Written opinions of high-court judges were an English lawyer's stock-in-trade; they formed the basis of legal arguments and judicial decisions. Before printing, selected decisions were gathered in manuscript volumes known as yearbooks. Case reports started to appear about 1535. The earliest reports bore marked resemblance to the yearbooks in that they consisted of little more than rough notes or sketchy summaries of fact and opinion. Coverage broadened with time, which enhanced the reports' usefulness and marketability.[7]

Among the many volumes of reports that circulated throughout the seventeenth century, those by Sir James Dyer,[8] Edmund Plowden,[9] and Sir Edward Coke[10] were especially prized for their expansiveness and erudition. Copies of all three showed up in Virginia, though their initial utility to colonial lawmakers is difficult to gauge. The first editions were rendered in law French, a bastard variant of Norman French, middle English, and Latin that was the speech of reportage, but one that many in the General Assembly could not read. That impediment lessened at midcentury, when

English translations generally came on the market and law French slowly receded from fashion.[11] The second Richard Lee, the second Ralph Wormeley, Arthur Spicer, and William Fitzhugh, each of whom sat in the assembly after 1660, owned reports in translation. Fitzhugh's correspondence also reveals how he customarily consulted an English version of Coke's reports.[12] Likewise, George Talbot, a Maryland councillor of state, invoked Coke's authority in 1685, when he sought to quash his murder indictment before Governor Effingham and the General Court.[13]

Statutory compilations represented successive attempts to surmount what one bookwright styled a "multiplicity" of parliamentary acts that made "knowledge of the law … less clear and certain."[14] Compilers devised two solutions to that inconvenience. The more unwieldy of them consisted of statutes printed in full text and arranged chronologically. Such collections amounted to bulky tomes whose content was difficult to navigate even with the indices and tables that performed as finding aids.[15] The remedy for these "evils" involved reducing the acts to their essentials and ordering the abstracts in some logical manner. Hence the origin of books known as abridgments. They organized statutes alphabetically by topic, abstracted the content, and indexed the summaries. The result was a compact reference work that usually fit within the covers of a single, handy volume.[16]

Full-text compilations afforded colonials with models of statutory form and language, just as they likely served as patterns for Francis Moryson's *Lawes of Virginia Now in Force* (London, 1662), and John Purvis's unauthorized, corrupt *Complete Collection of All the Laws of Virginia Now in Force* (London, 1684).[17] Of the available abridgments, Virginians most commonly turned to those of Sir Anthony Fitzherbert,[18] Ferdinando Pulton,[19] William Rastell,[20] and Edmund Wingate.[21] The extent of their influence is conjectural because no direct link between one of these abridgments and an act of assembly has ever surfaced.

Treatises embraced everything from legal philosophy to the technicalities of specific branches of law. Copies of Coke's *Institutes of the Laws of England* (London, 1628–1644) found their way to Virginia. Coke ranks high among the peerless legal minds of the ages. His contemporaries revered him in his own day for his staunch advocacy of parliamentary prerogatives and the primacy of common law. Although later generations of would-be lawyers on both sides of the Atlantic struggled for mastery of the *Institutes* as an obligatory part of their education, the great work showed up less frequently in seventeenth-century colonial libraries and so left fewer discernible marks on Virginia lawmakers than the treatises of Sir John Fortescue, Sir Thomas Littleton, Christopher St. German, Sir Thomas Smith, Sir Francis Bacon, or Sir Henry Finch.

In *A Learned Commendation of the Politique Lawes of England* (London, 1567), Fortescue drew attention to the limited character of the monarchy and the rule of law. He fashioned his commentaries on those twin themes in the form of a Socratic exchange between himself and a young Prince Edward (1470–ca. 1483) in order to instruct the future king in the ways of English law. St. German directed *Dialogues in English, Between a Doctor of Divinity, and a Student of the Laws of England* (London, 1554) to prospective lawyers, and it resembles a modern introductory textbook in reach and substance. One of the earliest books ever printed in England, Littleton's *Tenures* (London, 1481) was a technical treatment of fifteenth-century property law. Done in parallel law French and English settings, the various editions all dealt with the doctrines of real estate in a thoughtful style that reduced the intricacies of property law to an orderly statement. Smith's *De Republica Anglorum: The Maner of Governement or Policie of the Realm of England* (London, 1580) explained the nature of English polity in the late Elizabethan age. Published posthumously, Bacon's *Elements of the Common Lawes of England* (London, 1630) provided a more contemporaneous summary statement of the underlying general principles of English law. Finch aimed *Law, Or, a Discourse Thereof* (London, 1627) primarily at neophytes. It was not filled with much imagination or art, but the singular thing about the volume was its appearance in Virginia libraries, not its lackluster content. That presence suggests an eclectic tendency on the part of councillors and burgesses to take enlightenment wherever they could find it.

Biography of the period concentrated on exemplary lives for didactic purposes. Consequently, biographers drew their renderings in hues that highlighted faith, virtue, honor, integrity, and adherence to duty as the central characteristics that made judges worthy of imitation. Like all mighty men, judges merited attention not merely because of their greatness but also because of their office. Their central place in the legal order made their careers valuable object lessons for all who followed the law or governed. Such themes found ready voice in such books as Thomas Fuller's *History of the Worthies of England* (London, 1662) or Gilbert Burnet's *Life & Death of Sir Matthew Hale* (London, 1682).

Though not properly a law book, John Brown's *Merchants Avizo Verie Necessarie for Their Sonnes and Servants, When They First Send Them beyond the Seas* ... (London, 1589) contained generous helpings of legal wisdom aimed at young men preparing to become merchant-venturers. It drew particular notice to commercial papers such as bills of exchange, letters of attorney, bonds, and contracts, all of which were essential to the exchange of goods or services. Once mastered, *The Merchants Avizo* pointed to more-sophisticated legal manuals.

How-to manuals enjoyed an especially wide readership in Virginia. This type of law book ran a gamut that spanned dictionaries; directories for clerks, sheriffs, constables, justices, or attorneys; and handbooks for drafting testaments, conveyancing, pleading cases, or other legal instruments. Often composed in a piquant style, each work offered its content in a forthright presentation that was practical and easily comprehensible, even to a reader with no more than a passing acquaintance of the law. John Cowell's dictionary *The Interpreter* (Cambridge, 1607), William West's *Symboleographie: Which May Be Termed The Art, or Description, of Instruments and Presidents ...* (London, 1590), Henry Swinburne's *Treatise of Testaments and Last Wills* (London, 1590), and Michael Dalton's *Countrey Justice* (London, 1677), ranked with the finest examples of their species, and each left visible marks in Virginia law and practice.

Cowell, a Cambridge don with a fondness for lexicography, first published the *Interpreter* in 1607. Deep research and lucid explanations set it off from previous legal dictionaries, such as John Rastell's *Terms de la Ley* (London, 1519), from which Cowell borrowed quite freely. Cowell's definitions provided etymologies and traced the precedents that invested words and phrases with their particular legal meanings. Nevertheless, Cowell's learning brought trouble because Sir Edward Coke regarded the *Interpreter* as derogatory to Parliament, and it was suppressed. Reissued in 1637, three years after Coke went to his grave, it remained in print for another nine decades.

The *Symboleographie* was a clerical manual. In it West discussed the derivation of legal records and their purposes. What made the book especially valuable to Virginians was its large collection of sample documents. West provided texts in Latin, which still enjoyed standing as the language of written instruments, but he helpfully included English translations. A reader who needed a proper deed form or the appropriate wording for an indenture or a will had merely to scan the examples to find one that suited his particular situation and copy it. West also gave pertinent advice on record keeping in general, which proved beneficial to clerks of court and in the General Assembly.

A biblical admonition— "Put thine house in order, for thou shalt die, and not live"—printed on the title page of the *Treatise of Testaments and Last Wills*—prepared users for Swinbune's ensuing advice on disposing of one's earthly goods in an appropriate legal fashion. Swinburne, a sixteenth-century probate judge, opened the book with an extensive discussion of the origins and purposes of wills. From there he proceeded to such important considerations as the types of wills, qualifications of testators, possessions that could be conferred by will, the appropriate wording of the will, and the role of executors. He buttressed his observations with generous references to inheritance law, and he included various useful tips about avoiding mistakes or complications that might delay probate or void a will.

Dalton focused on justices of the peace in a like manner, adorning his commentary with profuse citations to appropriate statutes and case law. *The Countrey Justice* began by tracing the development of the office down to 1618, the year the first edition appeared. Dalton described the justices' powers and duties, explained their administrative responsibilities, and told readers what constituted criminal conduct and how to make arrests, gather evidence, conduct trials, and execute sentences. He rounded off *The Countrey Justice* with several tables of authorities and indices.

Of more direct interest to councillors and burgesses when they met in the General Assembly were books that dealt with parliamentary procedure. Smith's *De Republica Anglorum* and the concluding volume of Coke's *Institutes* both contained treatments of how Parliament operated, but they tended to be more general than practical. Although Coke referred to an "ancient treatise, called modus tenendi parliamentum &c.,"[22] procedural manuals of a sort recognizable to modern eyes dated only from the era of the Civil War and the Interregnum. Those volumes found their way to Virginia, and very likely copies of one or the other of them eventually wound up in the General Assembly's legislative reference library.[23]

Someone started that library while the assembly was still new. In 1621, for example, Councillor George Thorpe wrote Sir Edwin Sandys, entreating him "to send us the newe booke of thabrigement of Statutes and Stamfords please of the Crowne and mr west presidents and what other Lawe books you shall thinke fitt."[24] The collection apparently had grown large enough by 1661 for Secretary Thomas Ludwell to catalog it.[25] (His list burned in 1865, unfortunately.) The library was augmented a few years later after the assembly voted to buy copies of "all the former statutes at large and those made since the beginning of the raigne of his sacred majestie that now is and a few other approved bookes of law." Among the latter were Swinburne's *Treatise of Testaments and Last Wills*, and both Dalton's *Countrey Justice* and his *Officium Vicecomitum. The Office and Authority of Sheriffs* (London, 1623).[26]

A Little Parliament

In the end, books helped lay foundations for Virginia law, but they did more. They chinked holes in the education of men who lacked formal legal training. In that sense, they guided and solaced, for they provided an authoritative assurance that only the printed word can convey. Together with culture and experience, they constituted the lessons that transformed neophytes into skilled lawmakers.

PART III

Assemblymen at Work

It is the request of the house that the right Hon Sir William Berkeley would take into his care the building of a state-house and what agreements he shall make, or shall be by his order expended for the same, it is ordered to bee paid out of the publique levie, and to bee raised by act of Assembly.

—Order of the General Assembly, 1660

Which Jury being impaneled and sworne to inquire of the said Indictment delyvered vpp there verdict, that the said [William] Reade was guilty of Manslaughter who being asked what hee had to say for himselfe that he ought not to dy demanded his Clergy wherevppon he was delyvered to the ordinary, &c.

—Verdict in the Quarter Court, 1629

The 3 differences between Mr. Richard Lawrence plt And Mr. William Dudley deft about accts concerning a vessell is dismist, Lawrence haveing past his bill for the ballance and pay costs als exec.

—General Court judgment, 1671

The Difference Between Mr. Thomas Pate and Christopher Charltone vppon An Appeale from Glouster Court to the Generall Court about the Said Charltones Freedome and referred to this Court where it is ordered that the Said Charlton Serve Six yeare from his first Comeing into this Country According to Agreement And the Said Pate be Satisfied by Service from the Said Charltone for his Absence from his Said Master From which Judgment the Said Charltone Appeales to the Assembly.

—Notice of appeal to the General Assembly, 1673

THAT there shall be in every plantation, where the people use to meete for the worship of God, a house or roome sequestred for that purpose, and not to be for any temporal use whatsoever, and a place empaled in, sequestered only to the buryal of the dead.

—Act of Assembly, 1624

A Little Parliament

Need for a place to hold the General Assembly turned Jamestown into the capital of Virginia. From the beginning, the assembly resorted to the expedient of convening in the church, private residences, even alehouses. Twice a purpose-built capitol was raised, and twice it burned. Fire and politics made locating a proper house for the General Assembly a perennial problem that went unresolved until the founding of Williamsburg.

Councillors advised governors on appointments and every other concern that fell under the rubric of what is now called "policy." They also legislated, and after the assembly became bicameral, they constituted its upper house. Where once they were Virginia's only court, they gradually assumed the guise of an appellate bench, though they retained original jurisdiction in felony cases and certain other litigation. Theirs was not always the final word in civil causes because the General Assembly acted as the court of last resort during much of the century.

The business of councillors, burgesses, and governors, met in the General Assembly, was making laws, and in time few areas of colonial existence were immune from their legislative reach. Thus, the body of the statutes testifies to the passage of assemblymen from novices to capable legislators with a sound grasp of the implications of power and its uses.

Chapter 8

A House for the General Assembly

Virginia Company officials left the decision of where to convene its proposed general assembly to the colonists. Governor Sir George Yeardley picked Jamestown. His was an obvious choice. Jamestown was the principal settlement and within its precincts lay the only building—the church—spacious enough to accommodate large gatherings. By those accidents Yeardley turned Jamestown into Virginia's first capital, and for eight decades the General Assembly met there.

If wishing alone resulted in capital towns, then "James Cittie" should have succeeded as a seat of government, given its hold on the colonists. Every royal governor from 1625 forward was under king's orders to build it up, and the settlers were generally hostile to locating their capital anywhere else. Harvey, Wyatt, and Berkeley wrought major improvements during their administrations, though Nathaniel Bacon's firing of the town in 1676 undid their work. Postrebellion politics impeded rebuilding efforts, and nearly two decades passed before the town returned to a semblance of its former self; then it burned again, and the seat of government moved to a new place that the colonists named in honor of King William III.

Even in the best of times Jamestown amounted to little more than a village. Its several dozen buildings sheltered a small resident population, some of whom kept taverns, ran breweries, or mixed commerce with agriculture. As a whole, "James Cittie" exhibited few discernable signs that one now associates with capital cities. It lacked distinct public spaces, and neither a grand capitol complex nor an imposing governor's palace symbolized the little metropolis as the vital center of colonial political life. Instead, successive governors, burgesses, and councillors made do with the church, residences, and taverns. These were the buildings that they and other colonists referred to as "state houses" for much of the seventeenth century.[1]

Fighting the Anglo-Powhatan War of 1622–1632 claimed a higher priority than building up Jamestown. A bankrupt Virginia Company and the Crown takeover raised questions about the very legitimacy of the assembly and its continued viability. Small in size and unicameral in form, the fledgling legislature itself required only a meeting room that could be pressed into service as the occasion required. The "Quire" of the church served that purpose well enough. As for the governor and Council, when they sat in their executive or judicial capacities, they met for a time in a structure known as the country house.[2] The company furnished that building as the governor's quarters, but it was abandoned about the time William Claiborne laid out New Town; afterward governors began living in homes of their own. Hence, their residences, also loosely styled "country houses," periodically doubled as Council chambers and courthouses. In like fashion, the secretary of the colony employed space in his house as a record office.

Arrangements such as these proved satisfactory enough for as long as the pattern for the General Assembly remained that of a corporate appendage rather than a miniature Parliament. The model changed as the colonists pushed Charles I to recognize the assembly and as it acquired more of the attributes of a legislature. Then, too, the number of burgesses increased and annual sessions grew commonplace, so the little frame church seemed a less serviceable venue. Peace with the natives at last allowed colonial politicians breathing space in which to address ways of finding the assembly permanent lodgings, and the push to enhance Jamestown lasted from the Harvey administration to Berkeley's surrender in 1652. In response to a direct royal order, for example, Governor Harvey secured the assembly's authorization for a levy to cover the costs of "the building of a State howse at James Cittie." Soon after Wyatt started his second term in 1639, he renewed the statehouse tax and navigated into law a bill that denominated Jamestown the colony's "chief town" and compelled governors to maintain a dwelling there.[3]

For his part, Wyatt complied with the statute by purchasing Secretary Richard Kemp's brick house, which he later sold to Berkeley, who kept the place until about 1650, by which time he had completed his three-unit row-house complex. One unit of the latter then became his official residence, and it was sometimes denoted as the state, or country, house, too.[4]

Harvey retired before he could engage an undertaker to raise the statehouse for the assembly. What to do next fell to Wyatt. Instead of contracting for a new building, he opted to convert a private dwelling. That seemed the expedient thing, especially after ready-made quarters suddenly became available. Opportunity appeared in the person of a financially strapped Harvey. Bankrupt, the former governor needed ready capital to satisfy his creditors, so he hurriedly liquidated all of his Virginia assets. Consequently, in April 1641 he conveyed to Wyatt and the General Assembly his "tenement now used for a court house ... situate and being within James city island," plus an adjoining "old house and granary, garden, and orchard." Because Harvey was desperate for funds, the negotiators for the assembly haggled hard, and the selling price of 15,700 pounds of tobacco benefited the colony financially. The bargain was profitable in another way, too. It provided Wyatt the chance to consolidate the provincial government within a single complex of buildings, and that was something no other governor had accomplished.[5]

Harvey's tenement remained as a courthouse that met the immediate requirements of both the Council of State and the James City County Court. Part of the larger "old house" was meant for a town hall and a record office for the secretary of the colony, which was another step toward investing Jamestown with the attributes of a "chief town." Almost certainly some portion of the old house also provided space for the assembly, which needed a new facility in 1641 because it had grown too large to fit comfortably in the choir. The choir itself had become unavailable during the construction of a new church on the foundations of the old. And some of the more devout colonists surely objected to the continued mixing of the sacred with the mundane, all of which made quartering the assembly in Harvey's "old house" a timely move.[6]

These political uses of the Harvey properties were consistent with the multiple meanings that seventeenth-century Virginians attached to "state house." Traditionally, the word conjured images of a building, or buildings, appropriated for a town hall, an official residence, ceremonies of state, or other similar public purpose, and it was used synonymously with "country house." But the colonists gradually gave "state house" another definition, one that came closer to the modern American use of "capitol"—a structure dedicated to the use of the legislature and other officers of state. That meaning acquired additional significance once the General Assembly became bicameral.[7]

Creation of the House of Burgesses prompted a reconfiguration of the assembly's meeting facilities because one chamber that seated burgesses and councillors together no longer sufficed. The burgesses required a hall of their own, where they could conduct their separate business without interruption or in secret. Their clerk needed work space too, as did house committees. Extant records do not reveal how Harvey's old house was modified to adjust to the burgesses's needs. Conceivably, Berkeley and the Council withdrew to the courtroom in the tenement and used it for their legislative chamber. Perhaps, too, Berkeley projected a new capitol complex. Charles I had instructed him to raise "a convenient house" in which to transact public business. If Berkeley contemplated such a building, he was slow in carrying out his plan. He concentrated instead on erecting his mansion at Green Spring and his town house block until construction on both was interrupted by the Anglo-Powhatan War of 1644–1646 and his sudden trip to England in search of weaponry. After the war, he worked toward boosting Jamestown's urban amenities and its commercial possibilities, but all of that came to full stop as well once he surrendered to the parliamentary regime.[8]

Fire swept the Harvey buildings away in 1655. Homeless, the Council contracted with Thomas Woodhouse, who furnished chambers in his ordinary, a public house whose bill of fare was fixed by law. The House of Burgesses made similar provisions, though the identity of its landlord is recorded no longer. These arrangements continued until the provincial government acquired another ready-made statehouse in 1657. That one lasted a short while because a blaze destroyed it about the time Berkeley returned as governor pro tempore. Once again, Woodhouse accommodated the Council, and another tavern keeper, Thomas Hunt, rented to the burgesses.[9]

At its meeting in October 1660 the General Assembly asked Berkeley to take "into his care the building of a state-house," it authorized the necessary funds, and it permitted the governor to impress up to "tenne men of the ordinarie sort" as common laborers. Tidying up the reversion to royal authority and increased concern over Stuart colonial policy seemed the greater priorities, so Berkeley delayed action on the assembly's request. He went instead to England, intent on guarding Virginia's interests and promoting his vision of a diversified economy. When he returned, he brought instructions from Charles II to build towns on each of the colony's major rivers and the express command "that you begin at James River, which being first seated wee desire to give all Countenance, and to settle the government there."[10]

The king's orders set off a bustle of rebuilding at Jamestown, and in 1663 the General Assembly again asked Berkeley to undertake the design and construction of a new statehouse. The assembly argued for fiscal responsibility, noting that rents the government paid for holding sessions in private houses "would in two or three yeares defray the Charge of a State house." Another benefit was aesthetic and in keeping with the renewal of the town. A purpose-built capitol would remove "the dishonour of our Lawes being made and Judgments given in Ale-houses." As if to stiffen Berkeley's resolve, the assembly also earmarked 30,000 pounds of tobacco from the current budget and promised an additional appropriation of "what ever more it shall amount to next yeare." The House also appointed a committee to treat with the governor about planning the new facility.[11]

Berkeley's design is not among his surviving papers, and his records that documented the progress of its execution are gone, too. Nevertheless, the project went forward at such a pace that partial occupancy occurred within a year. Thomas Ludwell reported as much in the spring of 1665, when he informed one of the English secretaries of state that the new capitol accommodated "the publique affaires of the country." The onset of the Second Anglo-Dutch War and a diversion of resources to defend against a feared invasion slowed or stopped work on the statehouse. Construction picked up again at war's end, and it apparently finished about the time the assembly assigned Secretary Ludwell "the Eastern garret over the Statehouse to make an office of."[12] The finished structure lasted only a few years before the 1676 fire gutted it.[13]

As the embers of revolt flickered out and the ashes of the metropolis cooled, the problem was what to do with Jamestown. Conducting the business of government promised to be a trying, sometimes messy affair unless the town recovered. Recognizing the difficulties, certain freeholders who lived in Lancaster and Rappahannock Counties petitioned to move the capital across the York River to Tindall's Point (present-day Gloucester Point). That location, they argued, was more central and thus more readily accessible to all colonists. The General Assembly of February 1676/77 greeted the petitions favorably and even went so far as to resolve

> that whereas the state house being now Burnt downe by that Arch Rebbell and traiter Nathaniel Bacon the younger, and allso the houses in James City And for as much as Tyndalls poynte is supposed and accompted, to bee the most Convenient place for the Accomodation of the Country, in gennerall to meet att, that therefore the state house for the time to Come, Bee Built att Tindalls poynte.

Opposition from the Jamestonians was immediate and evidently of such strength that it squelched action on the resolution, at least for the moment. Nevertheless, the idea lingered until 1680, when by a vote of eighteen to twenty-one the house finally killed it.[14]

Repairs to Jamestown limped along for nearly twenty years. Torpor, lack of craft, or the want of building materials do not entirely explain why the "unhappy Town did never after arrive at the Perfection it ... had."[15] Politics, however, will explain the repeated delays in restoring the statehouse.

Postrebellion assemblies hesitated to raise the necessary taxes, and for good reason. Their predecessors gambled a massive investment in a renewal of Jamestown that greatly increased the load on already burdened ratepayers who saw few rewards from the expenditure. Steep provincial levies and no immediate prospect of relief from more taxes were among the reasons many planters rebelled with Nathaniel Bacon. Their revolt was something that did not soon fall from the memory of anyone who served in the assembly after the uprising, especially in the face of a bad economy that stagnated into the 1680s.

Rebuilding a gubernatorial residence and the statehouse fell hostage to the struggles between the assembly and the governors, too. Out of his own pocket, Berkeley had erected and maintained an official residence at Jamestown, but no other governor could or would follow his example. After the fire his successors had little success in cajoling the assembly into paying for a publicly financed house for them. Jeffreys did not even try. Instead, he billeted a while with his troops before moving to more congenial quarters at Middle Plantation. Culpeper "infinitly desire[d] the Houses in James City should be built out of hand," but the assembly declined to budget funds. He backed off and stayed with his cousin Dame Frances Berkeley at Green Spring House.[16] On the other hand, Effingham saw a gubernatorial residence as a perquisite and a manifest symbol of the royal authority he represented. More important, he also had Charles II's order that the assembly build a house for him in the "usual place of Your Residence."[17] He tried to get the necessary appropriations out of the General Assembly of 1684; failing that, he accepted an interim housing allowance. Venomous relations with the assembly killed any prospect that he would get his house, and there would be no official residence until the Governor's Palace was built at Williamsburg in the new century.[18]

Movement on a new facility for the assembly fared rather better, though progress to that end inched along. Immediately after the fire, the assembly met at Green Spring House before moving on to the houses of Otho Thorpe and William Sherwood at Middle Plantation.[19] It returned to Jamestown in 1679, by which time publicans William Armiger, Susannah Fisher, and Ann Macon were able to accommodate the burgesses. When the Council sat legislatively or in General Court, it used Macon's facilities. It rented from Henry Gauler as well, at least until it engaged Sherwood, whose refurbished house on the old Kemp-Wyatt site offered a more capacious great hall. (Executive sessions sometimes convened at various councillors' plantations, too.) The councillors also depended on Armiger for supplies of candles, a painting of the "Kings Armes for the Generall Courte," and other appointments that dignified their meeting room with a hint of majesty.[20]

There things stood until the Effingham administration. In his opening address to the General Assembly of 1684, the governor indirectly signaled his interest in reconstructing the statehouse by remarking on the need to build towns throughout the colony. The burgesses took the hint, and within a matter of days a committee drew up a building contract and identified a prospective contractor. Effingham concurred, and on 22 May 1684 William Sherwood was empowered to draft "Articles between his Excellency and the Speaker in behalfe of the Generall Assembly And the Honorable Collo. Phillip Ludwell for the Rebuilding the state house."[21]

Eighteen months later, a partly completed statehouse welcomed the assembly. There was a hall for the House of Burgesses on the ground floor and a chamber above. Too small for the Council, the upper room seemed a suitable place to lodge the house clerk, which is what the burgesses proposed. Effingham and the Council balked, noting that the garret, or "Porch room," had been the secretary's office before the fire. The burgesses conceded the point, though they retorted how in the past "there [was] nothing Spoken or proposed in the house, that was not equaly to be heard there, as wel as in the Assembly room itselfe, besides the same gave continual opportunity to all sorts of persons to crowd before the Assembly room, under pretence of coming to the office." They suggested the alternative of putting the secretary's office in the basement "under the Assembly room." A bit of haggling followed, but once the burgesses sweetened the deal by agreeing to continue lodging the Council in William Sherwood's "Hall, small back room, and Cellar," Effingham and Secretary Nicholas Spencer accepted the proposal. The bargain struck, a House committee drew up a new contract with Ludwell for the additional construction, though he never performed the work.[22]

Ludwell's part in the town bill fiasco widened his breach with Effingham beyond bridging. Consequently, an enraged governor retaliated in a fashion that prevented his adversary from proceeding with the statehouse renovations. On 13 December 1685, Effingham abruptly prorogued the assembly while it was in midmeeting and before any bills were signed into law. In effect, there was no session, which cast Ludwell's contract into legal limbo. Then Effingham sought royal permission for Ludwell's removal. James II willingly granted it, and in the fall of 1686 the governor happily dismissed the secretary from all public employment.[23]

The renovation dragged on. In 1686 the House authorized Henry Hartwell to buy "a Convenient Table & Turky worke Carpet," chairs, lanterns, brass candlesticks, sconces, and other fixtures, all of which he was to have in place by the next session. That order suggests that Hartwell had replaced Ludwell. The specified items of furniture indicate that work on the burgesses' side of the statehouse was nearing completion.[24] By contrast, the Council's quarters remained unfinished as late as 1695, when Sherwood ended his leasing arrangement with the councillors. Thereafter, he rented the space to the burgesses for use of the Committee on Propositions and Grievances.[25]

By the mid-1690s, the statehouse had returned to an approximation of its condition before Nathaniel Bacon set the town alight. Its days numbered fewer than anyone associated with the reconstruction could have imagined. On 20 October 1698 another fire swept the statehouse to ashes, after which the capital moved to a site at Middle Plantation that flourished into Williamsburg.[26]

Chapter 9

A Court of Judicature

Until 1700, the Council of State served as Virginia's highest regular court, while the General Assembly sometimes acted as its court of last resort. To believers in separation of powers between coordinate branches of government as a mighty fortress against tyranny, mixing judicial with executive and legislative authority may seem a quaint, even dangerous, design. Councillors and burgesses saw nothing sinister in such an architecture of polity. They could not envision arranging power in the same way the framers of the American Republic thought possible after independence because that construction represented an as-yet-unimagined break with the wisdom of ages past.[1] The very lack of distinctions appeared natural enough, for that was the way it was in England, and that was how it would be in Virginia until the Revolution.[2] Consequently, after 1619 no one regarded the Council and the assembly in their respective judicial capacities as aberrant or threatening to liberty. And so the seventeenth-century configuration of both as courts should be viewed from the vantage point of archaic theories of governance rather than from the prospect of post-1776 constitutionalism.

Virginia Company officers intended the Council as the colony's sole court of law. As such, it combined the powers of English civil, admiralty, ecclesiastical, and criminal courts into a single jurisdiction, and it would sit quarterly. (Hence the name "Quarter Court," an appellation it carried until 1662.) One of its four sessions coincided with meetings of the assembly, during which time burgesses might join councillors in a judicial capacity.[3]

Nothing worked precisely according to plan. Among other reasons, the volume of legal business proved larger than anyone in London anticipated. Coping with cases consumed so much time that judging them soon intruded on the Council's equally important advisory, legislative, and executive duties. Councillors resorted to more meetings in hopes of relieving the situation, and by the time of the company's bankruptcy, monthly sessions were common.[4] Additional sittings helped, but they only palliated rather than cured, and councillors, with the assembly's assistance, searched for a more appropriate arrangement. First, proprietors of particular plantations received limited power to dispatch petty civil and criminal actions that arose within the precincts of their settlements; then, in 1624, the assembly shifted parallel judicial responsibilities for the remainder of Virginia to a new series of monthly courts.[5]

Little is known about either of those benches, though the proprietary ones were presumably patterned after English courts baron and leet. Particular plantations were themselves modeled on the manors and hundreds that had dotted rural England for countless generations. By contrast, the plan of the monthly courts approximated certain features of an English court of quarter sessions. A local military commander presided over a panel of commissioners, and together they took into their care "the conservation of the peace, the quiet government and safety" of colonists who lived within the territorial limits of their court. They also had "power and authority to heere and determine all such suits and controversies ... as exceede not the value of one hundred pounds of tobacco." Civil litigants could "appeall" their judgments "to the cort at James Citty."[6]

These arrangements allowed the "cort at James Citty" to revert to quarterly sessions, but they sufficed only a little while. Virginia's expanding population soon widened "the ... distance of many parts of this collony from James Citty" and added more numbers to those already seeking legal audience in the Quarter Court.[7] Increased appeals and other filings once again threatened to engulf the councillors, but the burdens were not all one-sided. Petty actions made up the majority of trials, so the expenses associated with initiating a suit at Jamestown or appealing a local court decision often exceeded the value of the case. Moreover, resolving a case in the Quarter Court could be a frustratingly slow affair given the hardships of travel, the inconvenience of lengthy absences from home, and the effort of preparing for trial. Litigants frequently neglected to answer summonses on time or at all. On occasion, an attorney, a plaintiff, a defendant, or a witness failed to appear at the appointed day, with the result that the suit was postponed or it failed altogether. The combined effect of such impediments not only annoyed everyone, but it also threatened to defeat the very purpose of the Council as court. Justice delayed was in fact justice denied.

Repeated tinkering from the 1630s onward resulted in elegant remedies that gradually met some colonists' legal needs more efficiently. The hodgepodge of provincial and local courts that sprang up after 1619 was scrapped in favor of a series of county benches that answered judicially to the Quarter Court. Greater uniformity of structure led in turn to refinements of the Quarter Court, and those embellishments touched everything from when the Court met to its jurisdictional boundaries to the rules of criminal and civil procedure.[8]

By an act of 1632, the Quarter Court convened every March, June, September, and December. Subsequent amendments modified the cycle, but the sequence remained more or less intact for thirty years. In 1662, noting that the existing schedule was "not equally distributed into the quarters of the yeare," the General Assembly required the court to sit in March, September, and November. That change rendered the designation "quarter courts" altogether unsuitable, so the legislators chose "Generall courts" as a more agreeable name.[9] Experience ultimately compelled the assembly in 1684 to limit the terms of the General Court yet again. As the preamble to the enabling statute intimated, it was "very grievous and burthensome" to hold "two generall courts" in the autumn because suitors could "scarce returne home before they [were] exposed, to the danger and charge of returning againe, to their great hazard and detriment." The act therefore eliminated the September term and reset the two remaining for April and October.[10]

Regarding the boundaries of the General Court's jurisdiction in civil, maritime, ecclesiastical, and criminal matters, the assembly initially turned over to the justices of the peace all civil actions of less than £10 sterling, or an equivalent value in tobacco. (The threshold figure ultimately rose to £16.) On the other hand, the General Court continued to hear any cause that surpassed those amounts as well as all civil appeals.[11]

English law of the sea covered everything from disputes over shipping contracts and seamen's wages to piracies and wrecks, which were tried before the High Court of Admiralty. In Virginia, such litigation first came under the Council's charge, though in 1658 the county courts gained an explicit statutory right to hear them as well. The act merely sanctioned a custom of long-standing because justices and councillors had jointly administered "all things pertaining to seafairing" for many decades before the assembly finally got around to enacting its authorizing law. This joint jurisdiction continued until 1697, when Governor Sir Edmund Andros received word from London to "appoint Judges, Registers, Marshalls & Advocates" for a new Crown court of vice-admiralty that embraced both North Carolina and Virginia. As much as anything, Andros's instructions responded to Parliament's passage of the

Navigation Act of 1696, which incorporated the American colonies within the bailiwick of the High Court of the Admiralty for the purpose of enforcing the trade laws. But the orders also answered a longtime wish of the councillors to rid themselves of judging maritime causes.[12]

Generally speaking, English ecclesiastical law governed issues of worship or ecclesiastical discipline and, as it related to the laity, embraced matters of morals, family relations, and the descent of estates. It was administered by a set of church courts that had their own rules of procedure and evidence that were more derivative of civil law than common law. Church courts never made the crossing to Virginia, and so their jurisdiction became the province of secular courts. Church law concerned morals, estates, and family relations, in addition to issues of worship or ecclesiastical discipline. The General Assembly shifted routine responsibility for enforcement of the canons to the county courts. Devolution began in 1640, when the justices of the peace were first assigned the task of punishing bastard bearers, fornicators, or adulterers, and it culminated in the statutory revisal of March 1661/62, when county magistrates acquired most duties of English ecclesiastical judges.[13] Thereafter, the General Court intervened in canonical affairs only in instances of controversies between vestries and rectors or between parishes and secular authorities. It also retained appellate authority whenever parties disputed county court judgments that involved the validity of wills, the distribution of decedents' assets, or similar concerns.[14]

In criminal matters, the county courts took charge of petty offenses and exercised a limited role in capital prosecutions. Apart from a short time during the 1650s, however, the General Court tried all "causes that concerne life or member." The predicate for this limitation found its rationale in a belief that only "men of the greatest abilities both for judgment and integrity"—the councillors—should exercise the dreadful power to condemn their fellow Virginians to death or maiming as just retribution for their most heinous misdeeds.[15] Even so, there were two departures from the rule. Any governor-general, as the king's vice-regent, could issue a commission of oyer and terminer to any county court.[16] That warrant enabled the named justices to try a specific capital suspect, but once guilt or innocence had been established their authority immediately lapsed. The assembly applied the mechanism in a perversely novel way near the end of the century, when it crafted special courts of oyer and terminer to try slaves who stood accused of felonies. Made up of local justices, those benches relieved the Council of hearing such cases ever again.[17]

A Court of Judicature

Trials of whatever nature moved through the General Court from start to finish in successive stages. Rules governed each step along the way, and every stride was intended to lead to a proper conclusion in an orderly fashion. This regularity, or due process, as an expression of legal principles, conveyed something rather different in the seventeenth century than it does at present. Citizen, advocate, and jurist alike now revere the precept of due process of law as a sturdy shield against the state's capricious interference with persons and belongings, or as a central component of constitutional interpretation. Colonials viewed due process in much less soaring terms.

Parliament minted the phrase "due Process of the Law" in a fourteenth-century statute, but the expression attracted little attention until the 1630s. During a war between France and Spain, the Parliament of 1626 dissolved without passing subsidies, and dissolution left Charles I scrambling for money to keep his armies afield. Extraordinary requirements demanded extraordinary measures, so the king resorted to the imposition of a forced loan to underwrite the troops.[18] His opponents, in search of a legal argument to counter the levy, seized on the ancient words and hesitantly joined them with a hallowed assurance from Magna Carta. A connection seemed evident because the great charter warranted a free man harmless from loss of life, liberty, or property except by the "lawful judgment of his peers, or by the law of the land."[19] Keenly critical of the forced loan, Sir Edward Coke manufactured this tenuous linkage into an especially sharp foil with which to prick the constitutional claims of his sovereign. "Due process of the law" and "by law of the land" meant the same thing to Coke. With characteristic canniness, he examined the precedents and contrived an elaborate validation of his equation, which he set forth thoroughly in the second part of his *Institutes of the Laws of England.* His proofs came from scratch at times, but no matter their source, they led unswervingly to his grand conclusion: the king's adversaries, not Charles I, had right, custom, and law on their side.[20]

Coke's erudition was sure and sustaining to those who believed it, but it did not divert the king, nor did it comport with the views of other contemporary authorities whose reputation for scholarship rivaled Coke's. Indeed, one could, and can, rummage hard the works of John Cowell, Michael Dalton, and like compilers of legal texts without discovering any commentary that joined due process of law to Magna Carta as Coke had. But the word *process* caught their eyes, and those writers ascribed to it discrete meanings that had little to do with the great charter. When, for example,

Cowell discussed process, he wrote, "Sometimes that only is called the Process, by which a Man is called into the Court, because it is the Beginning or the principal Part thereof, by which the Rest of the Business is directed." Process likewise entailed "the Manner of proceeding in every Cause,"[21] Those definitions comported with what "due process of the law" meant in the fourteenth century, they had not changed much by the seventeenth, and they were ones the colonists freighted to Virginia. How the Council and the assembly actually applied those meanings can be recapitulated in a perusal of the steps they devised for the conduct of criminal and civil trials.

English criminal law first arose as a distinct species in the thirteenth century, and by the time Jamestown was settled, it had its own rules and customs.[22] Foremost among its organizing premises was its junction of felony with evil. Felons were sinners, whom Satan had enticed into treason, murder, rape, arson, burglary, and thirty other capital crimes.[23] Felonious acts justified the stern, fleet chastisement of lex talionis—the law of an eye for an eye. Even so, before an accused received punishment, she or he had to be arrested, examined, charged, tried, convicted, and sentenced. Those steps embraced what passed for criminal due process, but they differed profoundly from present-day usage. A prisoner was detained on "just cause, or some lawful and just susptition," though nothing obliged an arresting officer to inform the suspect of a guarantee of silence or of counsel. No lawyer attended the interrogation, and, apart from that "birthright of every Subject of England," a jury, the suspect was accorded few rights at the trial itself.[24]

Before coming to the bar, the defendant usually remained in close confinement, as bail was automatically denied to an alleged felon. He did not always face his accusers, and he usually lacked the privilege of presenting witnesses in his behalf. Even if permitted to call them, he had no way of requiring their presence or of ascertaining beforehand what they might say in open court. Testimony of co-defendants or confederates was taken at face value, as were confessions or other statements, even those gained under duress. Indeed, hearsay and almost any means of proof could be introduced under rules of evidence that were modest at best and nonexistent at worst. No matter the source, incriminating information was kept from the defendant, who had no right equivalent to the modern guarantee of discovery. He did not know the charges against him until he stood in the dock, and then he had to refute them without an attorney's advice.[25]

A Court of Judicature

The trial itself had less to do with fairness or justice in any modern sense; its primary intent was establishing culpability and apportioning exemplary punishment. In the words of felony indictments, a defendant had not "the feare of God before thine eyes but [was] moved and seduced by the instigation of the devil."[26] Trial therefore represented a ritual way of holding someone answerable for wicked deeds in a predictable fashion. Consequently, its processes weighed heavily against an accused.

Such were the ideas about criminal law that educated the English colonists. After 1619, the councillors fashioned their version of criminal procedure largely on the advice they took from such books as William Staunford's *Pleas of the Crown*, Michael Dalton's *Countrey Justice*, and William Lambarde's *Eirenarcha*. Dalton, in particular, gave the clearest direction for what to do. *The Countrey Justice* provided extensive commentary on the nature of capital crimes, the probative value of physical evidence, the weight that attached to witness testimony, and related subjects. It also went through trial proceedings in infinite detail. When, for example, Dalton explained the empaneling of juries, he began the discussion, "This is that happy way of Trial, that notwithstanding all kings of State and revolutions of Time, hath continued from time beyond all memory to this present day." In this, as in other instances, Dalton never failed to remind his readers of underlying precepts or techniques that led to the desired end of bringing a felony suspect to his rightful reward.[27]

Thus, Dalton's careful guidance allowed the councillors to apply the English law of crimes to the colonial setting just as they read it. For that reason, as much as any other, the General Assembly seldom bothered defining criminal procedures. On those rare occasions when it did, it put Virginia departures from English practice into written word.

Its prohibition against justices of the peace trying felons stands as one of those notable exceptions. So were its prescriptions for picking petit juries for the General Court. Britons believed that jurors must be the peers of one's neighborhood. Applying that principle to the General Court presented a stumbling block. The Court sat at Jamestown, and it did not ride circuit. So, unless a felony offense happened in or near James City County, an accused could not easily be tried by jurors drawn from the vicinity of his abode. To hurdle that obstacle, legislators adapted a means that English courts had long used to complete a deficient jury. On orders from a judge, that method, known as tales de circumstantibus, permitted a sheriff to require the participation of a requisite number of jurors from among the bystanders around the courthouse. In Virginia, a county sheriff picked six of the "neerest inhabitants of [the] county to that place where the fact was committed," who accompanied the witnesses and defendant to Jamestown. Then on trial day, the General Court directed its writ of venire facias ("you cause to come") to the sheriff, ordering him to produce a jury. The sheriff in turn served the six men he had brought with him and any six male onlookers who lounged about the Council chamber or in the yard. The assembly thus solved a procedural difficulty that English law had not anticipated in a way that both fulfilled a colonial need and kept faith with tradition.[28]

There was yet a third exception. This one provided a modicum of explicit, written protection against self-incrimination in criminal trials. Reacting to a petition from the burgesses for Accomack County, the assembly decreed in 1677 that "noe law [could] compell a man to sweare against himselfe in any matter wherein he is lyable to corporall punishment." Here was a grain that came to full flower in both the Virginia Declaration of Rights and the Fifth Amendment.[29]

The progress of an actual trial may be seen in the case against a Northampton County colonist named Katherine Pannell, who was arrested in February 1660 on suspicion of murdering her maidservant Eleanor Cowell. When the justices of the peace examined Pannell, they developed testimony and other information that she had beaten Cowell, striking her in the face with a wooden "scure." A jury of inquest found that the latter blow caused an infection that "corrupted the Opticke Nerve of the left Eye; & putrifaction thereby had Issued into the Braine," which led to Cowell's death. That finding provided enough cause to charge Pannell with murder. Accordingly, the justices bound her over to the General Court and remanded her to the custody of Sheriff Anthony Hoskins. Hoskins imprisoned Pannell until he could transport her across the Chesapeake Bay to Jamestown, where she sat in the town's jail to await trial.[30]

Pannell was initially slated for a hearing in March 1660, but for unknown reasons, she requested, and won, a continuance to the following October. According to a habit established during the 1620s, the fourth day of each General Court term was reserved for clearing the criminal docket, which meant 17 October in this instance. That day court bailiff Thomas Ballard, who was also sheriff of James City County, empaneled a grand jury before the Court got down to cases. Twenty-four men composed a grand jury, so Ballard rounded up that many of the nearby locals and swore them to their task, which was to determine whether the indictments against all those slated for trial were sufficient.[31]

A Court of Judicature

Court opened when the crier, who was usually the undersheriff of James City County, stood up and announced:

> O Yes O yes O Yes silence is commanded in the court while his Majesties Governor and councell are sitting, upon paine of imprisonment. All manner of persons that have any thing to doe at this court draw neer and give your attendance and if any one have any plaint to enter or suite to prosecute lett them come forth and they shall be heard.[32]

That done, Governor Berkeley accompanied by the rest of the Court filed in and were seated. (The governor and any three councillors made a quorum.) When Council clerk Thomas Brereton called Pannell's case from the docket, the grand jury considered her indictment and determined it was billa vera—a true bill. Pannell was brought into the courtroom and heard the charges against her read aloud; then Berkeley told her to plead.

At this point, Pannell faced several options, which she may or may not have known. She might confess and throw herself on the mercy of the Court. Or, she could claim a defect in the charges by alleging that she was not the person named in the indictment. Another tactic lay in challenging the jurisdiction of the court or the law under which she had been arraigned. As a final possibility, she might advance a special plea that alleged her previous acquittal or conviction for the same offense, or a pardon.[33]

Pannell pleaded her innocence, and once she did, Berkeley asked how she would be tried. "By God and my country" came the customary reply. Her answer caused Brereton to serve Sheriff Hoskins with the writ of venire facias, and Hoskins in turn produced the six residents he had gathered up from Northampton, plus six spectators. As soon as those prospects stood in the jury box, Pannell could challenge any of them peremptorily and remove them from the jury. By contrast, if the attorney general[34] wished to contest someone, he had to argue for an exclusion. As Dalton remarked, with "Life, Liberty and Estate all at stake," counsel for "The King must shew his cause."[35] Once twelve men were selected and a foreman chosen, all of them vowed to render a verdict "according to the best of [their] cunning," and the jury took its place.[36]

Pannell's trial then began. Brereton read her indictment for the jurors' benefit. The attorney general then called his witnesses, all of whom testified openly on oath to the facts as they knew them. Pannell was allowed to interrogate any who spoke against her, though she had no opportunity to introduce exculpatory or mitigating evidence. After the last witness had spoken, Berkeley probably allowed Pannell a few moments to reassert her innocence before the attorney general summed up his case.

Berkeley instructed the jurors, telling them to make one of three findings: guilty as charged, guilty of a lesser crime, or not guilty. The jury then retired to consider the case. Their conference lasted for only a short while because they were kept from food, drink, and relief until they reached a verdict.[37] (There was no possibility of their becoming a hung jury because they were not let out of the jury room until they arrived at a decision.) Having concluded their deliberations, the jurors reassembled in the Council chamber. Sheriff Ballard brought Pannell to the bar, and Berkeley commanded the jurors to gaze on her as the foreman delivered the verdict. Guilty as charged.

Once convicted, a defendant could fall back on several ploys to stay the sentence and its execution. One was to claim benefit of clergy. A custom rooted in medieval English criminal procedure, benefit of clergy was originally meant to protect clerks in religious orders and to shield ecclesiastical jurisdictions from secular interference. In time, it enabled some convicts to escape punishment by reading or reciting the so-called "neck verse" out of Holy Scripture (Psalms 51:1).[38] Benefit of clergy had found its way into General Court practice by 1628.[39] It was granted rather sparingly thereafter, though it was not available to Pannell because she was female.[40] For women in her situation, another possibility lay in declaring pregnancy. If "a jury of matrons" concluded a convict was quick with child, then judgment might be respited until she gave birth. Pannell made no such declaration. A final expedient was to seek an arrest of judgment and a new hearing on the grounds of procedural error, but that maneuver required more legal skill than Pannell could muster.

So Berkeley pronounced judgment. Using words that came directly out of Dalton, he delivered the sentence of the Court. "You shall be carried back to the Prison from whence you came," he intoned, "and from thence be had to the place of Execution, and there be hanged by the neck until you be dead, and the Lord have mercy upon your soul."[41] All was not lost. There was a final avenue of escape. Pannell could beg for mercy and Berkeley's pardon. She did precisely that, and "forasmuch as the Kings most gratious Pardon extendeth so farr as to acquit her from the said offence, It [was] therefore Ordered that she bee discharged from the same By Proclamation at the next Court held for Northampton County she paying the sheriffs & Clerks fee."[42]

A Court of Judicature

Pannell was indicted, tried, convicted, and pardoned, all within a matter of hours. There was nothing unique in that. Trials in the General Court always moved swiftly. Customarily, the interval between indictment and judgment seldom surpassed a day or two. Sentences were carried out almost immediately as well. Clemency was a rare gift, which is the only thing that marked Pannell's brush with the law as extraordinary.

If the outcome of her hearing was unusual, the charges that led to it were not. Capital trials were the norm in the General Court, but there were others besides cases of murder or manslaughter.[43] Some, such as the abortive Berkenhead Conspiracy and an equally vain slave "Plott" on the Northern Neck, involved colonists in bondage. Others arose from rebellions or piracies, and at least one resulted from an assault on a Crown customs official.

On 6 September 1663, a group of Oliver Cromwell's former soldiers, who had been sold as servants to various planters in Gloucester and York Counties, plotted a mutiny. They gathered at a small house in a wood in Gloucester, where they agreed to meet a week later at midnight, with whatever additional men and arms they might recruit; then all would file off to Councillor Francis Willis's plantation and steal a large cache of weapons and a drum. The conspirators planned to go from plantation to plantation amassing more supporters and guns and killing anyone who stood in their way. Their ultimate aim was a march on Jamestown to demand their freedom from Governor Berkeley. Failing that, they would troop off and settle as free men elsewhere.[44]

As often happened with such intrigues, a lukewarm follower, John Berkenhead, betrayed this one before it ripened.[45] Berkenhead exposed all to his master, former Speaker John Smith, who alerted his fellow magistrates. In short order, the ringleaders were caught, examined, and turned over to the General Court. On or about 13 September, a grand jury indicted them at Jamestown for violating a provision in the English law of treason, and they were put on trial and very likely condemned.[46] Playing Judas won Berkenhead freedom and a reward of five thousand pounds of tobacco instead of thirty pieces of silver. A shaken General Assembly, which was in session at the time, instituted a pass system for servants and declared the "thirteenth of September, the day this villanous plott should have been putt into execution," a perpetual holy day of commemoration.[47]

Increasing numbers of slaves raised the likelihood of their trying an escape en masse or worse. Just such a attempt was foiled in 1680, when Secretary of the Colony Nicholas Spencer informed his Council colleagues of "a Negro Plott, formed in the

Northern Neck for the Distroying and killing his Majesties Subjects the Inhabitants thereof, with a designe of Carrying it through the whole Collony of Virginia." The principal actors were soon caught and sent to Jamestown for a "Speedy Tryall." Subsequently, the assembly hastily passed its law that established the special courts of oyer and terminer for trying slaves charged with felonies.[48]

The rebel Nathaniel Bacon died from dysentery and so escaped punishment for leading the uprising that bears his name. His chief confederates were less fortunate. Berkeley, aided by the ever ruthless Robert Beverley, rounded them up, all except Richard Lawrence, who vanished into the interior and was never seen again. Revolting against the governor was treason against the Crown, and being taken in active rebellion was prima facie evidence of high crimes. No other proof of guilt was necessary for conviction in any court of law. Trial of the captive rebels was a mere prelude to an inevitable fate. Several faced courts-martial, but most were tried in the General Court before all danced for the hangman.[49]

Some among the plant-cutters met a similar fate, though provincial authorities initially inclined toward leniency. Deputy Governor Sir Henry Chicheley played down the disturbance, holding it to be little more than a disorganized riot. In law, such a finding allowed him to issue a general pardon "to all then present in the feild without naming who."[50] Chicheley, however, incarcerated Robert Beverley on suspicion of having been the instigator, and he required several other principals to post bonds for good behavior and restitution. When Governor Culpeper returned to Virginia in December 1682, he launched his own investigation. Though he was "little used to the practical part of Criminal matters," he nonetheless concluded that "the universal cutting and actual destroying of the Tobacco-plants by force of Arms, though none killed to bee Treason" under English law.[51] After he pressed the Council of State to concur with his opinion, he issued orders on 10 January 1682/83 for the arrest of Somerset Davies, Bartholomew Austin (alias Black Austin), John Cocklin, and Richard Baily for trial at the next General Court.[52]

The trials stirred considerable feeling in York, Gloucester, and even James City. Culpeper reported to his superiors in London that grand jurors were under pressure to refuse indictments. "High words and threats" fell on the petit jurors as well, but Culpeper's stern admonitions stiffened them so that Davies, Austin, Cocklin, and Baily were convicted and sentenced to die. Davies was hanged at Jamestown. Because Culpeper "thought fitt to mingle mercy with Justice," he reprieved Baily, who was "extremely young not past 19, meerly drawn in and very penitent." As for Black Austin, Culpeper ordered him executed "before the Court house in Glocester-County, where the Insurrection first broke out, and where the Justices had too much enclined that way."[53]

Suppressing pirates was difficult in a colony whose geography made it easily accessible to buccaneers and whose provincial government lacked naval resources to pursue them. Moreover, the line between privateering and piracy was a narrow one, especially because the same people frequently indulged in both, and being seafaring people, they did not always know if England was at war or at peace. Two piracy cases that came before the General Court during the 1680s illustrate the difficulties that confronted Virginia authorities.

The first implicated a band of corsairs who sacked plantations along the mouth of the York River and preyed on coasting vessels that plied the Chesapeake Bay. Efforts to catch the raiders proved futile until they were captured in Rhode Island. They were extradited and jailed in Middlesex County, but they soon broke prison. Two were caught and immediately transported to Jamestown. Tried, convicted, and sentenced to hang, they escaped, and for three days there was no sign of them anywhere. On the third day, they returned to prison and, "with Cheerfull Countenances," they announced to their startled jailers that they had repented and were quite prepared to go to the gallows. The "unlike heard of" behavior so moved Deputy Governor Chicheley, who had presided at the trial, that he reprieved the penitents and turned the case over to the Crown for its dispostion.[54]

In the second case, the legal issues were muddier. It began in July 1688, when Governor Effingham ordered the arrest of Edward Davis, Lionel Delawafer, and John Hinson on "Vehement susptiton of Pyracie."[55] Caught together with a "Considerable quantity of Plate and Mony," the three instantly became the object of extensive legal wrangling. They sought to save their necks and their fortune by intimating that they were innocent traders. That claim convinced no one, so they insisted that they had come to Virginia to avail themselves of a royal proclamation of pardon for any privateer or pirate who surrendered on or before 20 January 1688/89. Indeed, they went so far as to petition Effingham "to discharge us with our money etc."[56] Apparently unsure of himself, Effingham demurred and referred the matter to London, which left the three to languish in the Jamestown jail. Almost a year passed before Davis, Delawafer, and Hinson convinced the Council of State to bail them so that they might go to England and plead their case. Once there, they engaged the services of Micajah Perry, a well-connected merchant with ties to the Crown and leading Virginians. Perry negotiated their pardon and the return of their treasure in exchange for their gift of £300 to the fledgling College of William and Mary.[57]

The three philanthropic pirates were the last to be haled before the General Court. Piracy remained as vexing as ever, but the councillors surrendered their jurisdiction over future suspects to the court of vice-admiralty, which Governor Andros set up in 1697.

Institution of the navigation system brought Crown customs officials to the Chesapeake. Not unexpectedly, their attempts to enforce the penal provisions of the trade laws evoked hostility from Marylanders and Virginians alike, though the colonists mostly managed to keep their animosities in check. One of those officers, Christopher Rousby, however, displayed such singular gifts for inspiring belligerence that he wound up dead. Rousby settled in Maryland in the 1660s, entered into the colony's political life, and caught the approving eye of Charles Calvert, third baron Baltimore. On the proprietor's recommendation, Rousby won a royal commission in 1680 as a customs collector for the upper reaches of Chesapeake Bay; thereafter he quickly fell out with his patron. Baltimore lodged a complaint against "this Knave Rousby," charging that the collector's harsh ways discouraged shippers and damaged commerce.[58] That protest caused Rousby's return to England, where he was vindicated and restored to his post. Once back in Maryland, he became the antagonist of George Talbot, Baltimore's kinsman and president of the Maryland Council of State.

The root of the trouble between the two was tied to Rousby's office. Rousby could arrest those he accused of smuggling or breaking the trade laws, but it was the business of the Maryland courts to decide what infringements, if any, had taken place. Rousby's interest in prosecuting his allegations was not solely doing the king's service. He had a stake in seeing that the accused were found liable because he collected fees from the sales of condemned cargoes and vessels. Frequently, the judgment of the courts was a finding of no violation, and Rousby went away empty-handed and believing that the outcome resulted from Talbot's collusion. Besides, although Rousby had the king's commission, nothing in it made Talbot answerable to Rousby. Unhappily, as time passed the feud between the two men assumed mortal proportions.

On an October afternoon in 1684, Talbot sailed out to HMS *Quaker*, which lay anchored in the mouth of the Patuxent River with Rousby aboard. The skipper, Thomas Allen, invited Talbot to dine at captain's mess. Drink overcame both, and they squabbled. Rousby, who was smoking topside, heard the clamor and went below. He started arguing with Talbot. Quarrel turned to scuffle, whereupon Talbot drew his dagger and slashed his enemy to death.[59]

The fight sobered Allen, who immediately arrested Talbot for murder and sequestered his sloop. As soon as the Maryland councillors heard what had happened, they insisted that their president be handed over to them for trial. Allen declined, saying that because the killing had occurred on his majesty's ketch, Talbot must be tried under admiralty law. He would therefore turn his prisoner and his vessel over to Governor Effingham, who was vice-admiral for the whole Chesapeake watershed. The Marylanders lodged a protest, which Effingham ignored, and less than a month after the killing, Talbot was haled before a special meeting of the General Court.[60]

Talbot admitted guilt at his arraignment hearing, but he knew some law, too.[61] He immediately challenged the Court's jurisdiction, pointing out how the homicide had occurred in the Patuxent River, a fact that vitiated the application of admiralty law and entitled him to a trial at common law in Maryland. For proof of his argument, he cited a statute from the time of Richard II, which defined basic admiralty jurisdiction. That law, said he, limited the admiral's authority to murders committed at sea, not in territorial waters. He also invoked Coke's *Institutes* and Lord Baltimore's proprietary rights as a further justification of why the General Court lacked power to judge him. Actually, Talbot was playing a fast game. Contrary to his construction, the statute expressly provided that when homicide or mayhem was "done in great ships hovering in the mainstream of great rivers, beneath the ports near the sea, and in no other places of the same rivers, the admiral shall have cognizance." Furthermore, Coke's commentary on that very passage noted quite emphatically how the clause limited the authority of common law courts.[62] Neither Effingham nor the rest of the General Court knew their law well enough to confound Talbot. Instead, his apparent learning so bedazzled them that they remanded him to the custody of the sheriff of Gloucester County while Effingham sent letters to London for instructions as to what he should do next.[63]

The sheriff of Gloucester was an inept jailer.[64] Talbot easily got away from him and ran off to Maryland. Effingham pressed the Marylanders for his return until the spring of 1686, when Talbot finally stood trial at Jamestown. Considering Talbot's confession and the other testimony, the outcome was never in doubt, and Effingham sentenced the prisoner to hang. Lord Baltimore lobbied to save his relative, as did several Virginia councillors. Secretary Nicholas Spencer wrote to Whitehall, "I haveing heard all the tryall, from thence can not but be soe charitable to say I suppose that unfortunate strooke given by Col George Talbott was the effect of passion heightened by the rage of drinke." The pleas worked, and James II reduced Talbot's sentence to five years' banishment.[65]

Criminal trials of whatever variety were always far fewer in number than civil litigation. That reality coincided with another. The private side of English procedural law was of greater complexity than its penal twin, and much of it did not easily fit the types of cases that arose in Virginia. Finding ways of navigating disputes to resolution after 1619 aroused feelings of urgency that spawned elaborate, statutory specifications of civil procedure.

Something else was afoot as well. In England, a civil action was a costly and drawn-out venture. Employing lawyers ensured that one's suit proceeded in the appropriate court according to an intricate set of tactics, which ran the gamut from the writs that opened the case to the pleas, rejoinders, rebuttals, and surrebuttals that set forth facts and answered counterclaims of an opponent. Writs wrongly used or flaws in the filings fatally prejudiced the suit because defects, however trivial, could be advanced as a block to further proceedings. And, unless one commanded Latin and law French, what went on in the courtroom was a puzzlement, too. The technicalities of common-law pleadings seemed to lay litigants as so much trickery that served only to enrich lawyers and to defeat the ends of justice. William Shakespeare caught his contemporaries' frustrations with the legal system when he put these words into the mouths of his characters the butcher Dick and the rebel Jack Cade:

Dick. The first thing we do, let's kill all the lawyers.

Cade. Nay, that I mean to do. Is not this a lamentable thing, that of the skin of an innocent lamb should be made parchment? that parchment, being scribbled o'er, should undoe a man? Some say the bee stings, but I say, 'tis the bee's wax; for I did but seal once to a thing, and I was never mine own man since.[66]

The resentment Shakespeare captured in that colloquy animated sentiments for law reform in England throughout the first half of the seventeenth century, some of which cropped up in Virginia, too. Councillors and burgesses often emigrated to avoid stings akin to Cade's, and they lacked formal legal education, which relieved them of abiding attachments to law as a professional calling. Virginia, being a smaller and ruder society than England, also had little use for England's numerous courts with their highly complex procedures and technicalities. That difference was something Virginia Company officers recognized when they originally planned the Council as court.

Rule-making fell first to the councillors, who crafted procedures in response to the needs of the moment or in concert with the General Assembly. An early example of rule making at work was the adaptation of a technique called "bill pleading." Borrowed in the 1620s from the practices of the High Court of Chancery, the Court of Requests, and the Court of Wards, and based on models in William West's *Symboleographie*, bill pleading quickly became the accepted method of initiating trials and appeals in the General Court.[67]

The beauty of bill pleading was its flexibility. Plaintiffs and appellants were free to tailor their bills according to the complexities of their individual cases. Elasticity allowed councillors plentiful leeway in determining what evidence to admit or which appeals to accept. Bill pleading, as it developed in Virginia, also minimized the importance of writs, a command of Latin and law French, or the services of lawyers. The few writs that actually made their way into General Court practice were uncomplicated in form and always rendered in English.[68] Bills themselves seldom came to more than rehearsals of the facts that were cast without concern for technical style or legalisms. Substance mattered more than form, especially after the General Assembly of 1657/58 required "all courtes of judicature" to ignore any imperfections of figure and "give judgment according as the right of the cause and the matter in lawe shall appeare unto them."[69] That mandate, in effect, also kept suitors "within the first Limmits of The Merritts of their cause."[70]

Although statutory definition of court rules was routine after midcentury, the General Assembly was slow in asserting a rule-drafting prerogative of its own. It adopted only two procedural statutes before it became bicameral—the one that fixed term times, and another that required furnishing defendants with copies of plaintiffs' bills.[71] Dividing the assembly, coupled with its second major overhaul of the statutes in force, opened the door to a more activist approach after 1643. Indeed, those two events seem to have made the catalyst for the first code of civil procedure. The authors pruned a thicket of repetitive, ineffective, or outdated practices down to a set of logically arranged rules. Beyond that, the assembly guaranteed jury trials to anyone who "desire[d] the verdict of a jury for the determining of any suite," it set filing fees, and it regulated attorneys.[72] Later assemblies amended the code, polishing or annexing rules that defined or regulated juror compensation, oaths, bonds, subpoenas, witness testimony, and depositions, among other subjects. Those additions were themselves buffed even further in the general revisions of 1652, 1658, and 1662. The end consequence, as Secretary Thomas Ludwell once remarked, was a series of rules that made "Lawes and pleadings upon them easy & obvious to any mans understanding."[73]

Those rules were a boon to litigants, because "any man" could sue or be sued in the General Court. Plaintiffs and defendants ranged from slaves to great planters. Even governors answered, and none of them ever asserted "executive privilege" to prevent suits against them. On those occasions when they were parties, governors or councillors merely recused themselves so as to avoid the appearance of impropriety. Prestige of office seemingly shielded them from being sued continually. The known instances of such actions are few.

Whoever the litigant, a trial of the first instance worked this way: A plaintiff prepared and presented a bill, sometimes called a declaration, a petition, or a complaint, which alleged harm at the hands of someone else, and prayed for relief. The court accepted the bill and summoned the defendant to answer the allegation. A summons took the form of a written mandate that the councillors directed to an appropriate sheriff. The sheriff served, or "arrested," the defendant and took a bond for his response. Next the defendant answered in writing, whereupon both parties had additional opportunities to file rejoinders on the record. The defendant, personally or through an attorney, appeared in court to plead to the bill, and the case moved to trial. Each party called witnesses or presented depositions and other facts in open court. After those presentations the advocates, or the parties themselves, argued their evidence. If there was a jury, the governor charged the jurors before they retired to consider a verdict. If not, then the governor and councillors decided according to the facts, the applicable law, or the common sense of the matter. Once the ruling was established, the governor pronounced it and ordered execution of the judgment; then the clerk called the next case.

Trials did not always follow this precise routine. Some never made it to a full hearing or stopped in midstream. An admission of responsibility resolved the cause, and the court immediately ruled for the plaintiff. A defendant might persuade the court that it lacked jurisdiction, which ended the litigation. If a plaintiff failed to prosecute, his complaint was dismissed, and the defendant collected costs. Conversely, if a defendant did not show up, the plaintiff won by default. "The discovery of some Error or Defect when the [trial was] so far proceeded in" led to a nonsuit, or termination, of the case. Postponements were always another possibility, given the problems with travel or other contingencies. A motion for a "refference" continued a case and spared the petitioner from adverse consequences arising from delay.[74]

One party or the other might opt for a jury trial. The tradition of civil juries was an ambiguous legacy that colonial authorities did not adapt immediately.[75] Even after it was grafted onto Virginia law, litigants rarely resorted to juries either in the county court or the General Court. They preferred bench hearings instead. This marked penchant may appear strange now, but it had a certain logic for the colonials. The outcome of a case was no more certain if reached by jurors or judges, so there was no evident advantage in employing the one as opposed to the other. Time was an additional consideration. So was cost. Jury trials took longer because of the greater intervals needed to seat juries and for them to decide. Juries were also expensive. By law, the litigant who wanted one paid a fee for swearing it and another to compensate the panelists.[76] Those payments ran up the price of a lawsuit, and many colonists chose speedier and cheaper bench trials, which became the preferred mode of resolution.

No matter the method, the cases that the General Court tried in the first instance usually turned on economic matters, with issues of debt being the most common. At the simple end of the scale were suits akin to one filed in 1671 by a Gloucester County justice of peace, Humphrey Gwynn. He sued Richard Young to collect a gaming debt. (The size of the alleged bet is unknown, although it would have equaled at least £16, since otherwise the Court would not have accepted Gwynn's bill.) Young denied gambling, so the issue before Governor Berkeley and his colleagues was "whether it were a wager or not." After due deliberation, "It was the Judgment of this Court that [there] was a Legall wager and he that lost ought to pay."[77]

At the complex end of the yardstick were suits such as that of *Farvacks* v. *Scarburgh*. A London merchant, Daniel Farvacks (or Fairfax) dealt in the Virginia trade, and among his customers was Edmund Scarburgh, a prominent Northampton County merchant-planter and former Speaker.[78] Sometime about 1660, Scarburgh ran up a huge account in bills of exchange, cash, and commodities. Years passed, and when Farvacks tried to negotiate payment, Scarburgh refused "not onely to Satisfy [him], but defyeth him and the Agents he haith Imployed, threatning them with great Actions, if they Intermeddle there In."[79] Frustrated, the well-connected Farvacks looked to the Crown for assistance in collecting his debt. In November 1668, the Privy Council instructed Governor Berkeley to straighten out the mess, and several of its members wrote personally to the governor, urging him to intervene. Shortly after Farvacks engaged Secretary Ludwell as his attorney, Farvacks died, which put his son John into the picture.[80]

A year went by while Berkeley and Ludwell moved things to the place where young Farvacks agreed to settle for £2,000, payable in three annual installments. Ludwell wrote to his client in February 1670, informing him of the potential agreement. He cautioned patience and urged Farvacks to honor his father's promise "which was that he would keep very secret the receipt of his debt least all [Scarburgh's] other creditors fall like a rain on him." Ludwell also explained how Scarburgh had recently sustained great losses that drove him ever deeper into debt. Consequently, few in Virginia were eager to pursue him through the courts, and that, Ludwell continued, complicated the case all the more.[81]

Scarburgh backed out of the agreement. Pulling a trick from his pocket, he attempted a bit of pressure in London through his younger brother, Sir Charles Scarburgh, who was the king's personal physician. Doctor Scarburgh tried to maneuver the Privy Council into arranging a favorable settlement.[82] In the meantime, Ludwell engaged in a subterfuge of his own. He turned to Alderman John Jeffreys, a powerful London merchant, for help in securing an order-in-council to force Scarburgh into the General Court. As he wrote to Jeffreys, that maneuver was the only feasible way to end the suit. Jeffreys did as Ludwell bid, and on 6 July 1670, the Privy Council commanded Berkeley to

> use your best Endeavours that [Farvacks] may have speedy Justice done unto him, and in order thereunto, that you forthwith cause ... Edmond Scarborough to appeare before you, and not to suffer him to depart out of your Government untill he hath either paid the said Debt, or given sufficient Security to satisfy the same if upon a tryall at Law it shalbe found due. And of your Proceedings herein to give an Account to this Board.

As further signs of the Crown's firm intent, both James, duke of York, and Secretary of State Henry Bennet, first earl of Arlington, sent admonitory letters too.[83]

The ploy worked. Scarburgh appeared at the General Court the following October. He and Ludwell dueled for advantage. Knowing that he could not argue his way out of the debt entirely, Scarburgh aimed to minimize it as best he could. Here he had an advantage because Ludwell wanted a resolution and was willing to accept something as better than nothing. The jousting went on for a week, which was uncommonly long for a civil suit. Finally, Ludwell tendered an offer: £840, payable in two annual installments as "full Satisfaction of the whole debt as well principal as interest and charges," plus court costs and a performance bond. Scarburgh "desired until morning" to think it over. Next day, he accepted, though he extracted an amendment that adjusted the payment schedule from two to three years.[84]

The long-suffering John Farvacks had no cause for celebration. Scarburgh died of smallpox in March 1671. He died intestate. The absence of a will muddled an already chaotic estate even further. Ludwell filed a caveat to establish the priority of his client's claim above all others. In all likelihood, however, Farvacks came up empty because there is no record that Scarburgh's administrators ever paid him so much as a farthing.[85]

Cases appealed to the General Court often approximated the content of the Farvacks and Gwynn lawsuits. Many others concerned issues of no monetary value whatever. For example, because any litigant could contest any decision of any county court, there was even a cluster of appeals from African Virginians who sought their release from bondage.[86]

An appeal started with a motion in the county court to stay judgment until a hearing before the General Court.[87] As prescribed by law, the appellant posted the necessary bonds and drew up a bill setting forth the particulars of the appeal and asking for remedy.[88] Bills contained all sorts of reasons for the appeal—procedural irregularities, unspecified acts "contrary to law," the mere recitation of the facts of the original trial—however, none asserted constitutional violations. The very idea that the General Court might overrule the assembly or the county courts on that basis was an unimagined possibility during the seventeenth century. In reality, most appellants predicated their bills on the hope of obtaining a reconsideration that would result in better outcomes than the county court judgments.[89]

Which bills the governor and councillors actually favored was more a matter of their discretion than statutory definition. Generally, they took vastly more than they rejected. The intent of such latitude was to content great numbers of suitors, but its principal effect was to raise both the volume and variety of the court's entire case burden. Short of limiting the bases of appeals, which the General Assembly in 1662 ultimately declined to do, no one figured out a way to fix that problem, and a solution went begging for most of the century.

One of several things happened after the court docketed an appeal. Considering the particulars and the arguments, it dismissed a portion on the grounds "of noe cause appeareing," while it upheld some or reversed others. If the last, then the governor and councillors had two choices: order a new trial in the county court or try the case themselves. When they adjudicated an appeal, they did not normally hear it before a jury, though they might call one to assess damages if recompense was warranted. The court occasionally impaneled juries of inquiry to propose settlements, which formed the basis of its judgment. Or it might employ an arbiter. (Arbiters, or "umpires" as they were called at the time, were disinterested persons of learning, such as surveyors, mariners, merchants, or perhaps governors themselves.) By whatever method the high bench achieved its decisions, its ruling was deemed final. Unless, that is, some disgruntled suitor "appealed from this Court to the next grand Assembly."[90]

That route of relief first opened in 1619, following its introduction by the Virginia Company. The road ran more securely once the General Assembly grew in stature and acted the part of the high court of Parliament. Loss of pertinent documents obscures its use before midcentury. Even so, when the rules of civil procedure were codified in 1642, there was provision for "Appeales to lie from the quarter courts to the Assemblies with the former cautions." Succinct as the rule was, it nevertheless argues for the existence of a well-established practice by that date.[91]

To initiate an appeal a plaintiff moved to refer the case to the assembly. The General Court automatically granted the motion, whereupon the appellant posted the requisite securities for his appearance at the ensuing legislative session. (A drawback was the long interval between filing and hearing.) Meantime, the suitor drew up his bill and directed it to the Speaker, through the clerk of the House. The clerk in turn docketed all bills in the order in which they crossed his desk. At the next meeting of the assembly, he gave them to the Speaker, who turned all such petitions over to the standing Committee on Private Causes. That committee and its councillor assistants examined each appeal, dismissing those without merit and recommending remedies for the worthy ones. If the full House, the Council, and the governor concurred in those suggestions, they were enacted as official orders of the General Assembly, which gave them the force of law.[92]

The earliest-remaining examples of those orders dealt mostly with land disputes, which suggests that appealing to the General Assembly was first employed primarily as a device for settling real estate controversies; then it became something more. As of the 1660s and 1670s, the scope of what suitors brought to the Speaker, and what the assembly reviewed, had broadened considerably. The procedure, in its mature phase, was thus applied to virtually any situation, and for as long as it lasted it provided a useful remedy for a significant number of suitors.[93]

It survived until the Crown set about reclaiming its authority in Virginia. Intervention undermined the assembly's independence by striking at those practices that departed from contemporary parliamentary custom. The assembly's "right" to take appeals was easily among the most vulnerable, founded as it was on a misreading of Parliament's history. Except for impeachments and trials of peers, by the 1600s Parliament had all but ceased, if it ever had been that at all, to be a judicial entity in the same way that the General Assembly pretended to be. And so the idea of "the high court of Parliament" signified something different for the later Stuarts and their advisers than it did for Virginia legislators and jurists. The Crown, which had the whip hand after 1676, carried the day, though not without a resistance that proved futile in the end.

Chapter 10
The Art and Mystery of Legislation
✦✧❀✧✦

For as long as the General Assembly heard appeals, its work as a court of last resort always dimmed in the face of its making statutes out of bills. Old as the assembly itself, the power to legislate originated in the Great Charter of 1618, in which the Virginia Company first authorized the governor, councillors, and burgesses to enact general laws and orders.[1] Constitutional mandates, parliamentary precedents, colonial customs, and politics greatly enlarged that prerogative once the assembly took on attributes of a little parliament. As if by blade on whetstone, the General Assembly perfected its legislative skills, using the collective practice for a hone. Accumulated experiences likewise schooled members in the ramifications of their authority. They learned the often-noisy-but-always-subtle mysteries of the politician's art as they went about the business of making laws.

The assembly's habits of meetings were mainly in place before midcentury. A call to assemble brought councillors and burgesses to Jamestown. Burgesses organized their House and chose their Speaker. They joined their Council colleagues to hear the rector of James City Parish or some other cleric invoke God's watchful eye over their deliberations. The governor-general then gave an address that marked the formal beginning of the session. House and Council members retired to their respective halls where resolutions were introduced, debated, amended, rejected, or adopted. Favored measures went to the governor, who signed them into law, and they were enrolled with the colony's other permanent records. Its business complete, the General Assembly adjourned until it was summoned on another day.

All members partook in the deliberations, but all votes and voices were not equal. The governor-general spoke loudest of all. No assembly ever sat without his permission; he prorogued or dissolved assemblies at will, too. As the king's vice-regent and the colony's chief executive, he determined much of the legislative agenda, which he often charted in his opening address. He negotiated directly or informally with committees or individuals from the House of Burgesses, and he controlled debate in the Council of State. His assent determined which bills would pass into law. His dissent automatically killed any measure he opposed, for there was no such thing as the House and Council's overriding his veto.

The Speaker owned a loud voice, too, though it registered in a different range from the governor's. His place as principal officer of the House endowed him with enormous authority over legislation. He had the power to assign bills to committees. Measures came up for consideration at his discretion. If he ruled a bill out of order, it usually died because his fellow burgesses rarely overturned his decisions. The length and direction of floor debates yielded to his direction as well. His voice modulated to a dissonant sound after 1676, when as political leader of the House the Speaker turned into a frequent opponent of postrebellion governors and imperial policies.

Clerks were important to the process also, especially those who worked for the House of Burgesses. Their faithfully kept journals held the institutional memory that instructed the burgesses in the traditions and privileges of their House. In addition, clerks guided the course of lawmaking, for it was they who reduced petitions to drafts and cast bills into the words and adornments of statutory language. They did all of that and more besides. Some, such as Henry Randolph, were principal authors of full-scale overhauls of the statutes in force. Robert Beverley and Thomas Milner had leading parts in legislative intrigues that frustrated the Crown's designs on the General Assembly.

The actual convening of a General Assembly differed from the ways of bringing a Parliament to Westminster. Unlike Parliament, annual sessions of the assembly were largely routine, and its meetings were customarily timed to coincide with the convenience of the Council of State. Until 1676, the assembly sat in spring or in autumn. Afterward there was a marked preference for fall meeting dates. In England, the Crown sent the Lords writs of summons to gather in their House. The habit never caught on in Virginia because governors were not monarchs, councillors were not peers of the realm, and the Council of State was not the House of Lords. Consequently, the writ of summons lacked purpose in the colony. In its place, a note from the governor sufficed, though not all chief executives resorted to that small formality.[2] Getting the burgesses to Jamestown usually required elections. As in England, the warrant for voters to choose their representatives took form in a paper instrument known as an election writ.

Issued over the governor's signature, that document originated in 1619. Because Governor Sir George Yeardley received no specific guidance regarding the mechanics of electing the first burgesses, he was thrown on his own devices. The English example was of only marginal value to him; the writ was cast in Latin, and its content was too complex for Virginia's needs at that moment. Most important of all, though, Virginia Company officials, the governor, and the colonists did not think the prospective assembly as an equivalent of Parliament or of Yeardley as the king's surrogate.[3] Nevertheless, some formal mandate was needed to initiate the election, so Yeardley and the Council crafted a writ of their own.

That text has not come down to modern times. Very likely it was the same as the wording of a writ that Governor Sir Francis Wyatt circulated in 1624:

> Whereas the Governor and Councell of State are determined to call a generall Assembly for the better setling of the affaires of this Cuntrie. These are to will & require you [blank] to assemble all the freemen and Tenants inhabiting those Plantations and by pluralitie of voices to make ellection of two sufficient men. Willing & require the persons so chosen to give theire attendance at James Cittie the 14th day of February next comeing.[4]

Wyatt's form remained the standard after Virginia became a royal dominion, though it had fallen from fashion by 1676. In substance, later writs acquired a nearer correlation to English usage than to Wyatt's. Their tone expressed more overtly political purposes as well. Those differences hint at the evolution of the writ into a state paper that served governors much in the manner its English counterpart enabled sovereigns to steer Parliament and English voters.

When Sir William Berkeley broadcast his writ in the spring of 1676, he clearly meant to court the electorate and to plot specific goals for a new General Assembly. And for good cause. He stood next to disaster. His own apathy, a ruinous war with the Indians, and the suddenly popular Nathaniel Bacon had all undermined the aging governor. Shaken to action, he planned a snap election as a prop for righting himself. So he indited an unusually long writ in which he grandly pitched his case why the electors, which he expanded to include all freemen, should look to him instead of to Bacon.

Lamenting that the continuation of the General Assembly of March 1660/61–March 1675/76 was "looked upon as a Greivance by many of the Inhabitants of this Country," Berkeley dissolved that assembly and told voters to elect "the most sage best experienced and most understanding persons" as their representatives. The new assembly would convene in the statehouse on 5 June, there to "redress of all such

Greivances as the Country might justly complaine of and for the better security of the Country from our Barbarous Enemies the Indians and better settling and quieting our domestick disorders and discontents." He challenged the soon-to-be-chosen burgesses to "discharge that duty of their owne personall charge for the ease of the Country as the Councell shall." Falling back on a gambit that had always served him well, he dared voters a gamble of their own. "Supposeing," he wrote, "I who am the head of the Assembly may be [the] greatest Greviance I will most gladly joine ... in a Petition to his sacred Majesty to appoint a new Governor of Virginia and thereby to ease and discharge mee from the great care and trouble thereof in my old age."[5]

His ploy bore mixed results, not because it was misbegotten but because Berkeley tossed away the very leverage he hoped to gain by it. He easily wooed and won an obstreperous General Assembly, which passed a bevy of reform statutes and begged him to stay on as governor. Tyche, fortune's goddess, smiled on Berkeley, too. She made Bacon his prisoner, but he squandered that advantage. He not only pardoned his adversary and returned him to his place on the Council of State, but he also inexplicably let Bacon slip his clutches.[6] That stumble cost the governor dearly; it allowed the young hothead to regroup his supporters, and together they threw Virginia into civil war.

The election writ became a political contrivance of an altogether different sort in the post-Berkeley era. By then governors were under imperial instructions to call assemblies sparingly, and only in the king's "Royall Name."[7] More particularly, when they ordered elections, they styled their writs in a way that symbolically humbled the assembly. The preamble pointedly stated:

> Whereas by his most Sacred Majesties Commands, I have many matters of great moment to Communicate to a Generall Assembly, greatly tending to the well being and advancement of this his Majesties Collony, and subjects Inhabiting. I have therefore thought fitt ... that as soone as possible, a Generall Assembly, be held.[8]

That sentence conveyed a none-too-subtle reminder to elector and burgess alike. The General Assembly was absolutely dependent on the Crown and answerable to royal commands, which were funneled through the governor-general. Elections writs, in short, had become an institutional means of voicing realities that lay at the heart of Anglo-Virginia politics after 1677.

A governor's opening address approximated a modern State of the Commonwealth or State of the Union address in that it set forth certain political aims and legislative agendas. The tradition for such speeches, which found parallels in a parliamentary custom that harkened all the way back to the fourteenth century, began with the first General Assembly.[9] Secretary John Pory, not Governor Yeardley, gave the first one, when he "delivered in briefe to the whole assembly the occasions of their meeting."[10]

To suppose that Yeardley yielded to Pory as the better orator is to miss the more pertinent explanation why the governor deferred to the secretary. Pory knew from his days in the House of Commons how "the Chancellour of England or some other fit, honest and eloquent" person frequently "pronounced the causes of the Parliament" for the king, and he presumed to do likewise.[11] The duty eventually passed from Pory's successors to Yeardley's. Unfortunately, the remaining legislative journals do not record either the reasons or the precise moment for the changeover. The extant speeches offer no clues either. A mere fifteen exist in full text, but none dates earlier than 1651; another is from 1660; the rest all trace to the concluding decades of the century.[12] Few as they are, these specimens testify how time, circumstances, and individual governors fashioned the opening speech as a legislative tool.

Berkeley's clever messages, laced with artfully elegant images, were among his keenest political appliances. At first he governed with little help from the Crown and even less backing from the colonists. That realization rapidly translated into an axiom that guided him all the days of his administration. Persuasion counted for more than crude threats or naked application of force.

His two surviving opening addresses exemplify the principle in action. He delivered the first to an assembly that he convened in March 1651. Months earlier, the House of Commons had issued its declaration interdicting English trade with the colonists. It had also adopted a statute to foreclose commerce with the Dutch, and when Berkeley got wind of the two measures, he instantly realized their potential for harming Virginia and displacing him. Determined to forestall both possibilities, he summoned the burgesses and councillors to resist the threat. The address itself attacked "the men of Westminster" in typically Berkeleian style. "Surely Gentlemen," cried he at one point, "we are more slaves by nature, then their power can make us if we suffer our selves to be shaken by these paper bulletts." Should defiance meet with force, "do but follow me," he cajoled, and "I will either lead you to victory, or loose a life which I cannot more gloriously sacrifice then for my loyalty, and your security." His words were to good effect. They so impassioned his audience that both houses unanimously adopted a joint condemnation of Parliament's restraint on English trade and the "pretended Act" against the Hollanders.[13]

A Little Parliament

The second speech came nine years later, almost to the day, on the occasion of his election in March 1660. As in the earlier one, Berkeley capitalized on the moment. The death of young Governor Samuel Mathews had suddenly propelled Berkeley toward his old place, and in an extraordinary manner. Not everyone in the House of Burgesses entirely welcomed his recall, and neither did he. The terms of his restoration troubled him, too.[14] More generally, there was uncertainty about how events in England might affect him, the assembly, and the colony. To compose those disquiets, Berkeley talked without ever mentioning any specific legislative aims or voicing his own inner qualms. He reached for broader goals instead. "And now, Mr. Speaker," he concluded,

> since you have thought me worthy to be nominated for your Governour, it will be noe unpardonable boldness, if I presume to interpose my advice to you, which is, that you make choice of one, who hath more vigorous quallities to manage and support your affaires, and who hath more dexteritie to untie those knotts which I can neither unloose nor break amongst the Councill; there are many in your own body, which are more sufficient for it, which I dare not name because it were an injury to give any (soe equally worthie) precedence, though it were but in the Catalogue of their names. And now, Mr. Speaker, give me leave to return where I began, which is, to give the honorable House most Humble Thanks for their intended munificence to me, which I shall the more Cheerfully doe; because those are engredients to put an acceptable Tincture upon this Apologie; For considering my present Condition (if I had not irrefragable reasons on the Easiness it is proposed to dissuade me from it,) I should be worthily thought hospitall mad, if I would not change povertie for wealth—Contempt for honour. But many urgent reasons obstruct the way of those desired assents. But it is now time to beg pardon for troubling you this long.[15]

Berkeley deliberately gauged his remarks to echo a Speaker's disabling speech. The gesture adroitly deferred to the burgesses as it signalled a readiness to partner with them as in days of old. He thereby eased himself gingerly into his former chair and prepared the ground for a cooperative relationship that smoothed the restoration of royal government. He and the burgesses strengthened the alliance in subsequent assemblies and sustained it almost to the end of his second administration.[16]

By contrast, Culpeper's address to the General Assembly of 1680–1682 lacked the grace of Berkeley's rhetoric or the proffer of cooperation, but Culpeper was little concerned with pretty words and smart phrases. He intended to intimidate, not form coalitions, and he greeted the burgesses and councillors with less courtesy than he might allow one of his own servants. He announced three specific pieces of legislation that he expected the assembly to enact verbatim. The first promised amnesty and full pardons for "all persons whatever Except Bacon that died & Lawrence[17] that fled away & such as were Condemned by Legall Juries." The second allowed for naturalization of foreigners[18] so as "to Invite persons to Come to this place." The third required raising a permanent revenue to support the provincial government. To dispel any misconstruction of his demands, he announced imperiously that he had the king's "particular Commands to tender you the three Acts ... which upon mature Consideration with the Advice of the privy Councell, he hath sent you by me under the great seale of England with full power to give the Royall Assent to them." In effect, he was ordering the assembly merely to ratify what Charles II had already decreed. Culpeper continued by outlining other legislation that the Crown urged, and he concluded by admonishing, "If you have any grievances, you Can'ot have better time to offer them." And with that, he sent the members off to complete their tasks with "Speedy Resolution."[19] The assembly proved highly quarrelsome and anything but "speedy." Nonetheless, Culpeper extracted some of what the Crown demanded before he dissolved the assembly in December 1682 and Charles II cashiered him.

When Effingham approached his first General Assembly in 1684, he did it with greater cunning. Scorning Virginia politicians as much as Culpeper, he veiled his contempt, disguising it in the excessively cordial language of the courtier. "Gentlemen," he began,

> Since it hath pleased his most sacred Majestie to thinke mee worthy to serve him in this Circumstance I doe own my Selfe very happy that hee hath sent mee hither, not so much in Relation to the place as the worthiness of the persons Inhabiting in it For Gentlemen I observe in you such ... Readiness to Testifie your Loyalty to his Majestie That I Consequently promise my self an happy Issue of my Endeavours which next to the satisfaction that I have within mee that they shall bee always Zealous for his Majesties service, and you would Crown my wishes.

He then spelled out the proposals that the Crown had dictated as his legislative agenda, all of which he "Earnestly Recommended" for "Carefull and Speedy dispatch."[20] Sweet words soured quickly as the burgesses balked at complying with his wishes.

The lesson was not lost on him. His addresses to the General Assemblies of 1685–1686 and 1688 dropped any pretence of politeness. They also evidenced how Effingham's adroitness for making words sting reached a point of diminishing returns. When he greeted the assembly in 1688, for instance, he demanded a law to prohibit the exportation of bulk tobacco. The requirement for such a statute came directly from James II, who, said the governor, had acceded to colonial petitions for the ban out of his "speciall grace & favor." This pregnant sign of the king's graciousness must not go unheeded. After all, Effingham needled,

> his Majestie by his Royall prerogation [prerogative] might have only said Fiat, let it be done, & it should have been so, yet he hath referr'd it to you Gentlemen to be your own Carvers, & please your selves in the method of a law, for the prohibition of it; I need not use arguments to induce you to it, the shortest sighted person may easily foresee the benefitts that will insue.

Those words galled members who had grown to despise the governor, but then Effingham struck deeper. Without the king's "particular directions," he said, "I had not call'd an Assembly so soon." But since he had, he also required funding for the defense of New York against possible attacks from French Canada.[21]

Despite his repeated prodding, the assembly did little of what Effingham set forth in his speech. Instead, the House wrestled with him over his appointment of its clerk and lost. It also complained about his application of his proclaiming powers and higher fees for the use of the colony's great seal, all to no effect. For much of the time, though, the burgesses worked on a petition to Whitehall for his recall. Things went that way until an aggravated Effingham finally dissolved the assembly.[22]

Sir Edmund Andros and Francis Nicholson lacked gifts of tartness or apt phrasing, and neither was as intentionally provocative as Effingham or Culpeper. Andros's opening addresses read like marching orders to his troops.[23] Nicholson's were no livelier.[24] Oratorical abilities aside, the two men dealt in a different legislative milieu than that of their immediate predecessors. Death, enforced retirement, or political conversion reduced the number of irreconcilable members and rendered the bases of their opposition increasingly irrelevant. And, once Andros finally settled the matter of the governor's right to appoint the burgesses' clerk, there were fewer direct challenges to the assembly's prerogatives. The net effect of those changes made for a more tractable General Assembly throughout the 1690s, with the result that whenever Andros or Nicholson opened sessions, their speeches fell on receptive ears. Consequently, if those conduits of royal policy were not always greeted with enthusiasm, the addresses rarely provoked intense opposition. Instead, they were accepted for what such speeches always were, one of the two indispensable sources of legislative proposals.

The Art and Mystery of Legislation

The other lay with the General Assembly itself. As early as 1619, burgesses began seeking their constituents' grievances, and in time canvassing the electorate became a matter of settled law even to the extent of having county court clerks certify complaints to the assembly in writing.[25] Inquiring "into the necessities & greivances of the Country" implied something more than mere conversations about complaints; it embraced a far wider exchange of suggestions that passed from voters to representatives to laws.[26]

More often than not, the exact nature of that dialogue remains hidden, though there are occasional glimpses. Berkeley afforded just such a peek in a memorial he addressed to the Privy Council, wherein he described the Virginia legislative process.[27] Preambles to the acts themselves often provide another because they justified why the assembly adopted the statute—justifications that clearly suggested voter influence.[28] Propositions presented to the burgesses in 1663 and the session laws of June 1676, however, furnish the keenest insights into the process at work.

In September 1663, Northampton County burgess Edmund Scarburgh introduced a series of bills that ranged from revising debt recovery law to regulating the Indian trade. All were adopted, more or less, as Scarburgh presented them.[29] That he took the lead in moving the measures not only reflected his constituents' wishes, but also spoke to his personal stature. Having been once Speaker of the House, he still carried weight with his colleagues, and any legislation he sponsored had a reasonable chance at passage. His constituents clearly understood that when they petitioned him, and he delivered for them.

The acts of June 1676 illustrate a rather different side of the voter-burgess relationship. They passed through a General Assembly quite unlike any other in the century and under equally extraordinary political conditions. Five statutes—the defense act, the two Indian commerce laws, the general pardon act, and the bill that debarred two Charles City County justices from office—indicate the leverage that Bacon and his men exerted when they held the assembly hostage in the last days of the session.[30] Another act gave the color of statute to Berkeley's expansion of the franchise in his election writ.[31] Significantly, though, all the remaining laws addressed the complaints that welled up as a result of Berkeley's orders to the voters in his election writ.

Of these, one invoked "the lawes of England" against "unlawfull assemblies, routs, riotts, and tumults" as it "requested" the governor "to raise sufficient force at the publique charge to suppress the same, and inflict condigne punishment upon the offenders."[32] Another was clearly directed at newcomers like Bacon, for it denied public office to any immigrant who had not "bin constantly resident and abideing in the country for the space of three yeares."[33] That same act took aim at various abuses of local magisterial authority that had gone unchecked for years. A third law prevented councillors from voting in county court proceedings, which removed their direct involvement in local matters, and a fourth eliminated their poll tax exemptions, thereby lessening county taxes for everybody else. Similarly, a fifth statute extended the time allowed debtors to pay their debts, an extension that eased some of the economic hardships that had plagued planters as a result of the Third Anglo-Dutch War and the restrictions of the navigation system. A sixth law enabled justices-in-quorum to certify probates or letters of administration on the estates of intestates. That measure rid Berkeley of a routine chore and saved the affected colonists the additional expense of traveling to Jamestown. The remaining acts opened up vestry elections, placed additional restrictions on sheriffs, and suppressed most tippling houses or other establishments that sold liquor by the drink, among other things.[34]

However these and other laws originated, all moved through the General Assembly in a similar fashion.[35] Bills were classified as either private or "Publique." Public ones—those that touched government, church, or revenue—commenced in the House of Burgesses. For instance, appropriations measures started in the House Committee on the Public Levy. Committee members calculated ordinary revenues, estimated expenses, and arrived at a levy that balanced income against outgo. As the latter was always greater than the former, the committee then recommended an amount to be collected from all colonists who were liable to a head tax. That committee calculated that figure by dividing the total of the levy by the total number of tithables, that is, taxable persons.[36]

In making its determinations, the committee depended on information that came from several sources. Sheriffs supplied lists of taxable persons, and the colony's fiscal officers figured the provincial government's take from customs collections and other standing impositions. Anyone who performed any service for the colony could petition the committee for compensation. Those claims varied in number from assembly to assembly, so much of the committee's job lay in sorting through them and deciding which ones to honor.[37]

The practice of encouraging such petitions antedated the existence of the House and the committee by more than a decade. Although the number of those pleas increased over time, the burgesses were slow to regulate them much before late in the

1670s. By then annual sessions were no longer the practice, which sometimes left claimants dangling for long periods. The House adopted a standing rule of order in 1677 requiring county courts to certify all claims to the committee. The rule was eventually perfected into a statute.[38]

As soon as the committee finished its work, the draft appropriations bill went to the House floor for further consideration before it passed on to the governor and Council for their concurrence. Their approval was largely routine throughout the Berkeley era; at least that is the impression that emerges from the governor's correspondence and the extant House journals. It was a different story after 1677, when foot-dragging on appropriations and other bills became a favored tactic in the burgesses' struggles with postrebellion chief executives.

Every bill received three readings in the House. The first was a formality in the sense that it merely introduced the bill for consideration. After the clerk finished reciting the proposal, the Speaker repeated its title, summarized its content for his colleagues, and, as necessary, referred the bill to an appropriate committee for additional refinement. At least a day passed before the second reading, after which the bill was debated, amended, and voted on. If the vote was favorable, the Speaker instructed the clerk to prepare a fair copy. That work took time, so several days customarily lapsed before the bill received its third reading. A third reading was tantamount to adoption by the House, though further debate remained an option that the Speaker might allow.[39]

Once the House approved, the measure went on to the councillors, who had three choices. They could accept the bill as received, they could amend it, or they might reject it out of hand. Their procedure for reaching a decision was similar to that employed in the House, which is to say they also gave each item three successive readings. If the Council made amendments, the House considered the amendments and either approved them or reconciled the texts in what would now be called a conference committee, which consisted of few burgesses and councillors. They sat down and thrashed out compromise language that was subject to debate in both bodies.[40]

Much of the legislation initiated in the House passed through the Council without change, though disputes were not unknown. Berkeley and the burgesses scrapped on several occasions in the 1660s. In one instance, they disagreed on the contents of several bills relating to limits on tobacco cultivation. The House opposed limitations on the number of plants each colonist could raise per season and on a warehouse system. Even though scaling back production was the keystone in his diversification plans, Berkeley eventually yielded and agreed to drop both proposals from the statutes he finally signed.[41] During the Second Anglo-Dutch War, the burgesses demanded that Berkeley protest "to his most Sacred Majesty" the costs of raising a new fort at Old Point Comfort. He agreed "most willingly" but then went on to remark that if the "Assembly does not pay the Agent he shall not expect more from the Country neither shall he do anything." The House, after much grumbling, caved in and authorized the payment of Francis Moryson's expenses. In a third instance, Berkeley urged that councillors "Joyn with the House in Granting and Confirming the Sum of the Levy." The burgesses would have none of that because they conceived "it their priviledge to lay the Levy." Berkeley accepted the rebuke, admitting, "This is willingly assented to and desired to remain on Record for a Rule to walk by for the future which will be Satisfactory to all."[42]

For spectacle, for rancor, or for long-term effects on the assembly, these and later disagreements paled in comparison with a quarrel between Effingham and the House of Burgesses over an urban development bill. Fostering towns had been a goal of the Crown, the provincial government, and the colonists themselves since Virginia's earliest days.[43] The firing of Jamestown during Bacon's Rebellion renewed schemes to promote towns, and they climaxed in 1680 with the adoption of "An act for cohabitation and encouragement of trade and manufacture."[44] Charles II disallowed the law on the recommendation of his advisers, who objected to several features in the statute. Consequently, when Effingham became governor, he received instructions to "endeavour all you can to dispose the Planters to build Towns."[45] He first tried to coax an acceptable law from the General Assembly of 1684 only to give up once he and the House of Burgesses could not find common ground.

Neither the burgesses nor the governor denied the need for urban growth. Their disagreement centered on the location, number, and purposes of the towns. In the calculus of the burgesses, towns spurred economic growth and reduced reliance on tobacco, which was why the House favored restricting tobacco exports and building numerous towns. As the voice of imperial authority, Effingham saw a few well-founded port cities as a necessary means of enforcing the trade laws and supervising the colonists, which was why Charles II had ordered him to build one town "on every great River."[46]

At the first session of the General Assembly of 1685–1686, Effingham let the burgesses take a stab at crafting a tolerable statute. The burgesses in turn directed

Robert Beverley, their clerk, who had written the 1680 law, to draw up a proposal for their consideration. His draft contained two principal sections. One part allowed for the building of up to forty-five towns, one each sited along the James, the York, the Rappahannock, and the Potomac, respectively, with the rest to be distributed on the lesser rivers and certain smaller waterways that accommodated deep-sea shipping. The second portion enlarged the number of customs collectors to include one for every new town. Beverley's bill provided that the collectors' fees would be financed with a long-established fund that existed to pay incumbent collectors.[47]

Beverley finished his work about mid-November. The House gave it a speedy hearing before it came up for a third reading on 25 November, when it passed "as it is without amendment." It then went to Effingham and the councillors for their approbation. Two days later, Beverley recorded in the House journal that the Council returned the bill with several exceptions and amendments, all of which were considered on 28 November. The ensuing floor debate reconciled every difference but one, so the amended version was again delivered to the Council and appeared destined for adoption. Beverley noted on 1 December how the bill came back "from his Excellency and the Councell, Assented to bee fairly Engrost ... to the end the same may pass into law." A week later, he recorded the further notation that "a Rough draught of the whole body of the engrossed bills for lawes [was] read in the House. And resolv'd the same be sent to his Excellency and Councell for their perusall."[48]

Effingham refused to sign the town bill. The burgesses shot off a tart message that the "Rough draught" was "perfectly agreeable with the bills fully voted in this house and which have the test of your Excellencys and the Councells assent which gives the same the full force of Lawes and cannot (without the authority of another Assembly) admitt of or receive any alteration or addition."[49] Effingham responded that the text of the act no longer contained the Council's two most material amendments, which limited the number of towns to eight and raised new duties to pay the extra collectors. Without those modifications, he asserted, the law would be impractical, and he would not consent to it as it stood.[50]

In their sharply phrased rebuttal, the burgesses accused Effingham of trying to thwart them by exercising his veto ex post facto, which was unprecedented in the annals of the General Assembly. Beyond that, they contended, the act was law even without his signature. That reply provoked from Effingham an equally biting comeback. No bill in Parliament ever passed into law without the king's consent, and surely the General Assembly was not higher than Parliament. "Should I allow It otherwise to be Authentick," he continued, "I should destroy his Majesties Prerogative in his negative voice, which Jewel he hath entrusted to me, which God willing, I will preserve, therefore shall not passe that Law for Ports &c" unless the Council amendments "be allowed of." Snared untenably in the novelty of their reasoning, the burgesses recalibrated their argument, asserting that Effingham and the Council had actually approved the bill without the amendments. The proof, they claimed, was this. The bill, minus its questionable changes, had come back from the Council marked "assented to."[51] To the burgesses, those words anciently signified the Council's approval because no bill that bore them could ever be "questioned, disputed or altered."[52]

Battle lines drawn, Effingham declined to stir. The burgesses refused to budge. Legislative business stood still until someone yielded ground.

The tug of war sprang from the Council's amending procedure. As in the House of Lords, whenever the councillors changed a bill from the burgesses, they instructed their clerk to write their amendments in the margins of the copy that came from the House.[53] As Effingham himself remarked in one of his messages to the burgesses, however, "there was no room in the margin to write the alteration therefore it was wrote in a piece of paper and affixed to the Act which hath alwaies been the way without signeing."[54] In effect, he asserted that the bill to which he had agreed and the bill that the burgesses insisted was law were absolutely not the same.

Finally, the burgesses acknowledged the truth of the governor's claim when a delegation met with him on 8 December. Beverley's minutes of the conference included the statement that when the bill was returned to the House a week earlier, it bore "a certain paper no waies authenticated." Because the attachment lacked Effingham's signature, the house adopted the bill without it, thereby permitting the burgesses to contend that they had enacted only what the governor had "assented to."[55]

Whether a genuine error or a purposeful plot to foil Effingham lay at the root of the problem is difficult to say. At a distance of three centuries after the fact, plausible cases can be made for either explanation.[56]

The mistake, if there was one, belonged to Effingham, who was not wholly in possession of his faculties throughout much of the session. His wife had died just weeks before he journeyed to Jamestown to convene the assembly. She had lingered in agony many months before scurvy finally killed her. The length and horror of her exit pained her adoring husband deeply. As he helplessly watched her waste away, he was stricken too, felled by a recurrent urinary ailment that nearly carried him off. Profoundly grieving and desperately sick, he was forced to delay the start of the assembly for almost a month while he arranged the shipment of his wife's body back to England, and he tried to recuperate. Still weak, he met the councillors and burgesses on 2 November. His opening address resounded sourly to burgesses, who put the irreconcilable William Kendall in the Speaker's chair and named Robert Beverley clerk. Arguably, therefore, loss and illness confused Effingham into forgetting to sign off on that "certain paper." If so, then his distractions boxed him into an embarrassing place, and he turned excessively combative as he tried to extricate himself.[57]

On the other hand, it is possible that Beverley, Kendall, and other irreconcilables saw opportunity in Effingham's distress. Although the paper scrap that contained the Council's amendments is gone, there is significance in Effingham's reason for not validating it with his signature. He said that he had merely followed established custom. No one—certainly not Speaker Kendall or Clerk Beverley, who surely knew the traditions of the House as well as anyone else—challenged the governor. Silence therefore suggests that Effingham's understanding of assembly procedure was close to the mark. That being so, then it is improbable to suppose that the burgesses inadvertently overlooked the Council's amendment or lost the paper on which it was written. The weight of evidence, on balance, leads to the conclusion that the irreconcilables deliberately tried to embarrass the sickly, mourning Effingham by sneaking into law a bill that failed to meet his specifications. That was precisely the conclusion Effingham drew, and from the moment he reached it he set his face against Beverley.

Once it became evident that Effingham would not yield, the House delayed the appropriations bill in the belief that the withholding of revenues would bring him around. He countered with an offer to sign all the laws but the town act in exchange for the money measure, but the House stood firm. Its obduracy finally forced his hand. On 12 December, Effingham suddenly called the burgesses into the Council hall. Severely chastising them, he ended their dressing down by saying,

> I must confesse, considering your proceedings and obstinacys I doe not now treat you in a Parliamentary way, for that would have been much shorter and sharper, but doe as it were Parly with you, that you may be Convinced of your Errors, which I hope you will, when you have consulted your Pillowes, which is the motive that I doe not at present dissolve you, but only Prorogue, and you are hereby in his Majesties Name Prorogued till the 20th of October next unless I shall thinke fitt in the interim to Dissolve you, or Convene you by my Proclamation.[58]

Nothing like that had ever happened before. Worse was to come.

A Little Parliament

In February 1686, Effingham sent separate accounts of the aborted session to his patron William Blathwayt, to the Privy Council, and to James II. His letters told of his difficulties in a straightforward fashion that explained the nature of the trouble in detail. He took special care when he accused Beverley of fiddling with the town bill and encouraging the burgesses to resist him. Such behavior, he advised, required harsh censure, and he outlined what he argued were the appropriate punishments. First, he asked the king to affirm the governor's prorogation, a vivid sign of the king's support for the governor. Second, he begged for a direct command to dissolve the assembly. That order would, in his words, "be so great a rebuke to them ... that I hope it will deterr them for the future to be so obstinate and peevish." Third, he asked for authorization to appoint the clerk of the House. Finally, he requested permission to proceed against Robert Beverley.[59]

When Effingham faced the burgesses in October 1686, the House was even more refractory than the one that he met a year earlier. Speaker Kendall was dead. Several other members were gone too. Irreconcilables filled their places. Things got off to a bad start when Effingham made his opening address. Desiring a short, "happy" session, he proposed little new legislation, but his sarcasm insulted his listeners, who had come to Jamestown stewing for a fight. And fight they did while Effingham waited on the Crown's reactions to his letters.

He had timed his missives with the hope that he might have answers before the assembly reconvened on 20 October. Dispatched on 1 August, the king's approving response did not reach Jamestown until 10 November, but Effingham withheld publishing it until the appropriations bill passed and he had signed it into law. He then summoned the burgesses, read them the royal letter, and pointedly remarked that this was the first time a monarch had ever had cause to order a dissolution. Expressing the hope that the burgesses would learn from this sharp lesson, he sent them packing. He also gave orders that copies of the king's letter be dispatched to all the county courts with commands to have it read on court days and in parish churches to the end that the voters would learn how displeased the king was with the General Assembly.[60]

Effingham removed Beverley as clerk and intended to do more, but Beverley's death spared the pesky Virginian further punishment. Others were not so fortunate. Effingham deprived Philip Ludwell of his Council seat, removed Speaker Arthur Allen and Thomas Milner from their places as surveyors, denied William Sherwood his attorney's license, jailed William Anderson, a burgess for Accomack, and disciplined several others among the irreconcilables.[61]

The Art and Mystery of Legislation

From the assembly's point of view, turning these men out served as a caution against vigorous resistance to Crown policies. Fear of losing place softened members and made them more amenable to direction from Whitehall. The example schooled them in the limitations of their authority. A determined Crown represented a power that they could neither match nor master, and so they accommodated.

Chapter II

Acts of Assembly

B urgesses and councillors came to their legislative tasks imbued with three abiding certainties. Law ordered the goings and comings of civilized society, Virginia was a wilderness place, and the General Assembly had an affirmative obligation to lodge the colony within a fitting cabin of laws. Until they had gained actual practice of crafting statutes, however, none of them could say which parts of their intellectual baggage could be trimmed to the peculiar conditions of their new world. So they scoured their individual experiences and knowledge of law for guidance. Occasionally their search proved deficient, sustained as it was by an imperfect awareness of English legal traditions. Sometimes they encountered contingencies for which the past afforded uncertain remedy, or nothing at all, so they struck off in new directions. Often their purposeful departures from English customs brought them to statutory destinations that graced the fortunate few rather than the mass of colonials. But whatever they deemed suitable they cut to shape as acts of assembly.

Early acts little resembled later ones, much less statutes of the realm.[1] The difference proceeded as much from the original conception of the General Assembly as from ignorance, though want of knowledge surely played a part. As a managerial adjunct to the Virginia Company, the assembly obtained limited powers of legislation, which stretched no further than the bounds of the Great Charter of 1618 and the company's amplifying instructions.[2] Accordingly, acts from the company period appear more in the quality of corporate bylaws or town ordinances than prescripts of Parliament, and they carried the same approximate value as social rules.

A bankrupt company and an inattentive Crown abruptly altered the statutory landscape. Whether fledgling legislators liked it or not, they were thrown precipitously onto their own resources. The primary lawgivers for Virginia after 1624, they faced the predicament of wrestling with problems and powers that necessarily surpassed their initial mandate. Turning to available collections of legal texts, they patterned their legislation after parliamentary norms, borrowing a design that originated in Tudor times.

A Little Parliament

Their model took shape as the Tudor monarchs used their Parliaments to change church and state from the reign of Henry VIII to the death of Elizabeth I. Its development not only coincided with a heightening presence of Parliament in English politics, but it also advanced the use of legislation in a way that exalted the prominence of statutes in the English system of government.[3] Sir Thomas Smith captured the drift of both tendencies. He asserted at one point in *De Republica Anglorum* that the "most high and absolute power of the realme of England, consisteth in the Parliament." Continuing in the robust, meaty cadences of Elizabethan vernacular, he noted how acts of parliament

> abrogateth olde lawes, maketh newe, giveth orders for thinges past, and for thinges heereafter to be followed, changeth rightes, and possessions of private men, legttimateth bastards, establisheth formes of religion, altereth weightes and measures, giveth formes of succession to the crowne, defineth of doubtfull rightes, whereof is no lawe alreadie made, appointeth subsidies, tailes, taxes, and impositions, giveth most free pardons and absolutions, restoreth in bloud and name ..., condemneth or absolveth them whom the Prince will put to that tryall.[4]

His enumeration drew notice to something else. It iterated the timeless relationship of lex scripta to lex non scripta: statutes set down in writing took precedence over unwritten common law. But when Smith observed how "the consent of the Parliament is taken to be everie mans consent," he advanced the more novel idea of legislative supremacy; that is, the sovereignty of Parliament gave statutes their sanction as law because "everie man," through king, lords, and commons had willed them. Smith also understood statute-making as no mere abstract exercise. For any legislation to have effect it must be applied in the workaday world, and application depended on meaning and interpretation. Though he did not say so directly, Smith, like others among his contemporaries, understood the key to any statute's purpose and intent resided in its preamble.[5]

Statutory preambles were another Tudor innovation. Henry VIII and his minions in the Parliament of 1529–1534 first employed preambles as exuberant polemical justifications to state the case for the English Reformation and other policy changes they had set afoot.[6] Structurally, a preamble was thereafter one of three elements that composed any sixteenth- or seventeenth-century statute of the realm—the other two being an enacting clause that rehearsed Parliament's power, and a body that set forth things regulated by the act.[7]

Acts of Assembly

After the 1630s Virginia statutes approached nearer to this parliamentary model. Initial results, hasty responses to the pressures of a colony radiating outward from Jamestown and warring on its native neighbors, caused difficulties, but the clumsiness of the councillors and burgesses vexed everyone even more. Laws lacked preambles, others had no enacting clauses, and some were little more than rudimentary statements of regulatory purpose. Remedies were often as inept as the defects they were meant to cure. For example, when an assembly modified a standing law, rather than enacting its change as a new piece of legislation, it merely tacked its alteration on to the offending statute. If an amendment did not mesh smoothly with the rest of the law, then the entire act became difficult to understand, let alone enforce. Such ineptness, in a curious way, led to beneficial results. Ever mindful of their deficiencies, successive General Assemblies overhauled the entire body of laws on five occasions. And there was agitation for a sixth revision during the waning decades of the century, though that one did not come to pass until 1705.[8]

The first remake started with the General Assembly of February 1631/32.[9] Members designated someone—precisely who remains a mystery—to survey existing statutes with a hard eye toward purging the useless laws and clarifying the useful ones. With carefully directed pen strokes, he or they stripped away ill-conceived legislation, redundancies, and other blemishes that bred bewilderment and proposed a mere forty-eight acts. In and of itself, that single change represented a momentous advance, but the redactors went further and drafted laws according to subject matter and cast them in parliamentary language and shape. The draft opened with ecclesiastical regulations. A series of economic laws came next, followed in turn by acts that governed local courts, elaborated privileges of the assembly, set secretarial fees, and related to defense. Concluding the revision was an order for broadcasting the proposed laws "throughout this colony" and a stipulation that "the commissioners, for the mounthlie corts doe at the beginninge of theire corts always read or cause to be read, all these acts."[10] By such method the assembly codified Virginia laws. Reducing them to an orderly, plain restatement was a significant first for colonial legislators.[11]

Despite the achievement, the code lasted but a short while. The next General Assembly set it aside in favor of another. That substitution did not signal rejection of the earlier effort or of law reform itself. On the contrary, the work of the previous session was an intermediate step in a several-stage process that was completed in September 1632. First came a search for ways of rectifying jumbled masses of existing legislation, a process the General Assembly of February 1631/32 commenced. Members then debated the proposal, enacted it, and declared it the law of the land. Even though the compilation might not have entirely matched every expectation, there was merit to it nonetheless. It provided order where none was before, it reduced confusion, and it was conditional. Litigants and magistrates alike could test its strengths and isolate its flaws, knowing that something better would follow in due season. Enter the General Assembly of September 1632.[12] Its role was to complete the task by producing a more finished revision.

The pertinent legislative journals are gone, but in lieu of them, the next best evidence—the compilations themselves—clearly documents this procedure. A comparison of the second to the first reveals the close, evolutionary relationship between them. Their classification systems, their subjects, their language, their forms, and their purposes were alike. On the other hand, the acts in the second version were often longer and frequently more precise. There were other substantive refinements. Most prominent was the explanatory general preamble that in good parliamentary fashion explained the motives for the revision. New statutes also bridged gaps not closed earlier. Other adornments were incorporated as well. A new and explicit provision voided "all other acts and orders of any assembly heretofore holden" and settled the question of what was then the law in Virginia.[13]

The Revisal of 1632 lasted only for a decade. Even so it left its enduring mark. It was the prototype of later revisions.

A bustle of legislative activity produced a torrent of additions to the revisal.[14] The freshet of "many and sundry acts and laws" had predictable consequences. "Mistakes & pretenses" swept in through "misinterpretation or ignorance," which left colonists in a "very prejudiciall" legal environment. And so the General Assembly of March 1642/43 again distilled the laws in force "into a more exact method and order."[15] The restated acts more nearly resembled statutes of the realm than their forerunners. Of even greater note, the Revisal of 1643 ranked as the first significant legislative deed of a bicameral General Assembly. That feat in effect deepened the assembly's sense of itself as a sovereign legislature. In that regard, the process of revision represented one large step in the assembly's becoming a little parliament.

Surrender to the commonwealth of Oliver Cromwell brought about the third overhaul. Passed by the General Assembly of April 1652, and rudely cobbled, it met the immediate concern of establishing Parliament's writ in Virginia. Very likely, the burgesses regarded it as temporary and looked to the day when a later assembly might craft an elegant, more comprehensive codification.[16]

Governor Richard Bennett displayed little taste for taking on that chore after he angered the House of Burgesses for interfering in the election of Speaker Walter Chiles. Bennett's successor, Edward Digges, showed no such inclination either. The job finally landed on the General Assembly of March 1657/58, which met for the specific purpose of discharging it.[17] Samuel Mathews and the burgesses stoutly resisted one another over the content of the revision, so much so that the young governor almost lost his place. In the end, despite all of the tumult, the burgesses, Mathews, and the councillors produced the longest, most encyclopedic codification to date.[18] That exploit is yet another indication of legislative maturity, but it points equally to the role of House clerk Henry Randolph, who did much of the preliminary work.

Randolph performed similarly when he joined Francis Moryson to prepare the draft for the fifth revision. Adopted in March 1662, the new compilation completed the return of royal government, which was the ostensible reason for its undertaking. Apart from that, the revisal was noteworthy in two other respects. It codified the paramount authority of the assembly over the colony's institutions, it solidified the rule of the burgesses over their internal affairs, and it brought the General Assembly the fullness of its powers as a little parliament.

The Revisal of 1662 stood for forty years, far longer than Randolph, Moryson, Berkeley, or anyone else probably expected it to last. As the assembly augmented the revisal, addition after addition hugely distended the "whole body of the laws of … Virginia." Eventually the acts came to "lye in great disorder and confusion by reason that many of them are repealed, others obsolet and out of use some expired and many made in the infancy of this country inconsistent and hardly intelligible."[19] Clamor for reform started in the Culpeper administration and grew louder during the Effingham and Andros years. That din rattled in the ears of the authors of *The Present State of Virginia, and the College,* who caught the tenor of the complaints nicely when they remarked that the "Laws want Revisal, not only to bring them into a good Order and Method, but in order to the paring away several of them that seem inconsistent with Law and Equity, and are apt to bring Disparagement on the Legislative Power of their Country."[20]

The longevity of the Revisal of 1662 had less to do with its inherent excellence than with a persistent annoyance of the post-Berkeley era. After 1677, the Crown, the governors-general, and the assembly wanted statutory revision, but they rubbed each other sore disputing how to proceed. Officials in London viewed law reform as one means of bringing Virginia nearer to their visions of empire. Governor Effingham saw it as a way to undercut the assembly, which was reason enough for the assemblymen to drag their feet. Sir Edmund Andros had little patience with it because it distracted attention from matters he deemed higher priorities. Then, too, the councillors and burgesses were not entirely of one mind about how law reform should go forward, and so it languished into the 1690s. Governor Nicholson and the General Assembly of April 1699 broke the impasse by striking a bargain over means and ends. They embodied their deal in "An act appointing a committee for the revisall of the whole body of the laws of this his majesties colony and dominion" of Virginia. The statute spelled out in fine detail the who, the what, and the how of the revising process. Its foremost stipulation created a nine-man commission. Three came from the Council (Edward Hill, Matthew Page, and Benjamin Harrison) and six from the House (Miles Cary, John Taylor, Robert Beverley the historian, Anthony Armistead, Henry Duke, and William Buckner). Peter Beverley performed clerical duties, and Benjamin Harrison and Bartholomew Fowler were designated committee assistants. The act clothed the commission with

> full power and authority to revise, alter, add to, diminish, repeal, amend or revive all or any ... Laws and reduce the same into bills in such manner and forme as they shall think fitt and necessary, which said bills ... Shall by the said comitee be reported to the next meeting of the assembly and so from time to time till all the said laws be fully and absolutely revised.

Its remaining provisions set forth the committee's work schedule and various other procedural matters.[21]

The committee's membership mixed experience and interest. Councillor Hill brought to the table a wealth of institutional memory and legislative savvy, having been Speaker of the House and a leader among the irreconcilables. Harrison, in addition to his political stature in Charles City County, was the Reverend Councillor James Blair's father-in-law. Matthew Page was of a conciliar family and brother to the lately dead Francis Page, whom Effingham had forced the burgesses to accept as clerk back in 1688. He also sat on the Board of Visitors of the College of William and Mary, which linked him to Blair's interests as well.[22] Miles Cary followed his father and grandfather as burgess for Warwick County, starting with the General Assembly of 1684. Anthony Armistead belonged to another durable family of colonial politicians, and Robert Beverley was a son of Effingham's old nemesis. Henry Duke was a relative newcomer who had represented James City County off and on since 1691; so was William Buckner, who was just in his second term as a member for York County.[23]

As for the committee staff, they were seasoned to their responsibilities, too. Benjamin Harrison served as clerk of the Council until he resigned, apparently so that he could more readily assist his father. Bartholomew Fowler was a deputy clerk of the Council before he became the colony's attorney general. Peter Beverley, eldest son of Robert Beverley, held his father's old post as clerk of the House of Burgesses.[24]

The committee sat down for the first time on 5 July 1699, though it did no more that afternoon than listen to a reading of its enabling legislation. During the next several days, it went about the business of organizing for work. It swore in Peter Beverley. He then indited an address to Nicholson, requesting the same "Liberty and freedome of Speech and debate as is accustomed to be allowed to the Members of the Generall Assembly in their proceedings." While the committee awaited Nicholson's reply, it perused "Certain Instructions of the Lords Justices of England." Councillor Harrison then promised to furnish law books, "Two gallons of best Recording Ink, Two Thousand of best dutch Quills, A pound of pounce," and other writing supplies, which tidied up the last of the organizational details. A year of regular meetings and steadily progressive labors seemed to augur success, but then work suddenly stopped.[25] Thereafter, the work moved haltingly until it was finally finished in 1705.[26]

Many reasons account for the delays. Changes in committee membership, moving the capital to and founding the city of Williamsburg, and the protracted feuds that produced Nicholson's recall all figure into any blend of explanations. Death called Hill, Page, and Armistead, all of whom were gone by 1704. Duke moved up to the Council of State. Peter Beverley quit the committee to become Speaker of the House in the General Assembly of 1700–1702. His half-brother Robert (the historian) sailed away to England bent on lobbying against Nicholson. He had grown to despise the governor, whom he excoriated for removing the capital from Jamestown, "where there were good Accommodations," to Williamsburg, "where there was none."[27] Nicholson's contretemps with Blair and squabbles with other councillors distracted the governor and finally cost him his job.

Kinks that knotted the course of law reform before 1699 were mostly unavoidable in the long run, given the stakes and the players. Hitches aside, even a hurried glance at the revisals in conjunction with the session laws discloses just how far the General Assembly traveled after 1619. Early acts, little resembling statutes of the realm, lacked specificity and controlled a narrow range of activity. Later ones, closer in kin to the parliamentary model, were more explicit, arbitrated wider areas of daily existence, and more precisely defined institutions that distinguished Virginia from England or set Virginians apart from one another. Glimpsed more closely, the acts illumine the evolution of those distinctions. Laws that controlled local government, the church, land, labor, and Anglo-Indian policy are among the prime examples.

Once the colonists spread from Jamestown, the scramble for an effective local administration was on. The Virginia Company addressed the issue in the Great Charter of 1618 by consolidating existing settlements into the boroughs of Charles City, Henrico, James City, and Kicoughtan.[28] Certain judicial duties quickly devolved onto the commanders of private plantations, too. Monthly courts surfaced in the 1620s, when the General Assembly raised them in Charles City and Elizabeth City (formerly Kicoughtan); it subsequently increased the number of benches to five.[29] By these means the members aimed to supply local governments that matched the needs of extra settlements, but in their zeal to be helpful, they merely layered jurisdictions atop one another, which confused rather than alleviated the problems the assembly wished to correct.

Prodded by Governor Sir John Harvey, and armed with the recommendations of the Laud Commission, the assembly abandoned its dilapidated arrangement in the 1630s, opting instead for county courts. The change promised the colonists an efficient, uniform administration that was readily expandable to new locales. Eight counties became ten before the close of the 1630s, and ten multiplied to twenty by 1668. The pace of immigration slowed, and twenty did not become twenty-two until the assembly divided Lower Norfolk and Rappahannock Counties in the 1690s.[30]

Of equal importance, the county court system signaled a statutory demarcation between locality and province. Overall policy making, legislation, and higher judicial decisions stayed with the governor, the General Assembly, and the General Court, leaving routine governance and legal administration to the county courts. This bounding of responsibility occurred gradually but purposefully as the assembly assigned greater powers to the courts, and it culminated with the local government provisions of the Revisal of 1662.[31]

Each court consisted of justices of the peace, a sheriff, and a clerk, who were all gubernatorial appointees, and various lesser officials. Justices were first called "commissioners of the peace," a denomination that carried over from the old monthly courts. The label did not stick because everyone from the governor on down loosely called them "justices of the peace" until the assembly legalized the usage in the Revisal of 1662. Individual justices quieted petty broils, took bonds, gathered depositions, issued warrants; together at monthly sessions, they heard cases as they tended to the administrative needs of their bailiwicks. Aided by his deputies, the sheriff executed court orders and policed his county. The clerk kept the records.[32]

All of this had the comfortable look and feel of an English court of quarter sessions, which afforded the General Assembly its model. Despite outward resemblances, the two courts never were a perfect match. The General Assembly did not allow the justices the power over life and limb, and it modified their competence in ways that united administrative, admiralty, criminal, civil, and ecclesiastical powers that in England lay within the ambits of different courts. In the end, while a colonial magistrate could "act, and doe all such things as by the laws of England are to be done by Justices of the peace there," his powers of office differed noticeably from those of his English counterpart.[33]

The county court as a public repository for wills, land titles, business and commercial transactions, contracts, and even private writings varied from English custom, too. So did the office of clerk itself. In the kingdom, a custos rotulorum—the senior justice of the peace—held his court's trial rolls. The clerk of the peace, the senior justice's deputy and a scrivener, actually took down the record of court business, but he had no judicial purpose. In Virginia, the county clerk was an officer who merged the record-keeping responsibilities of a custos with the scribal duties of his deputy. A colonial clerk, moreover, exercised no judicial power either, because as long as he continued in place he was lawfully forbidden a seat on the bench.[34]

Harvey named the first sheriffs in 1634. His selections initiated the gradual makeover of that office in its Virginia setting. A letter from the governor sufficed as a sheriff's warrant of office until the Culpeper administration, when a formal commission replaced it. Appointees were not restricted to members of the bench until midcentury, though they always were thereafter. An act from the Revisal of 1662 embedded that practice in statute as it reiterated an earlier rule that incumbents hold office "an whole yeare and noe longer."[35] Then, too, the assembly molded the shrievalty more as an instrument of local power than as a direct extension of provincial authority. Consequently, Virginia sheriffs possessed few of the ministerial duties that attached to their opposite numbers in England. And the want of judicial license to hold sheriffs' courts constituted an even more pronounced difference between them.[36]

As for the Church of England, its precepts and its organization solaced the soul and buttressed secular mores. Members of the General Assembly always understood the value of a religious establishment, so they strove from an early date to provide a congenial place where the church might increase and multiply and have dominion over all Virginia souls.[37] On the other hand, church fathers in England tended their colonial stripling halfheartedly or not at all. Virginia was neither a diocese itself nor canonically affiliated with an existing one. It nominally belonged instead to the Diocese of London, except for a time in the 1680s when it briefly attached to the See of Durham.[38] A scheme to consecrate Alexander Moray, rector of Ware Parish in Gloucester County, went nowhere in the 1670s, so no bishop donned mitre, cope, and crosier in the Old Dominion until after the Revolution.[39] Parish priests were always in short supply, too. Colonists frequently viewed those who held cures as ignorant, trifling, or debauched. (When Sir William Berkeley answered a query about the colony's clergy in 1671, he acidly commented, "but as of all other Comodityes so of this the worst are sent us.")[40] Compounding these deficiencies was the absence of ecclesiastical courts to correct moral lapses, to handle family relations, and to oversee the descent of estates.

The failings of the church to take root institutionally sent the General Assembly off in search of alternatives. It assigned many ecclesiastical responsibilities to the laity and secular authorities, it drew parish boundaries, it empowered justices of the peace with the administrative and prosecutorial authority of church courts, and it manufactured vestries into vehicles of lay control in local parishes. Without a diocesan bishop to qualify parish priests, the process of selection fell to the vestries and to the governor. Vestries acquired an almost exclusive right of nominating rectors.[41] By virtue of an act from 1642, governors exercised a bishop's right of inducting (that is, admitting) ordained clerics into their temporal rights as parish priests. Whether they could collate, or present, unsolicited candidates of their choice for parish vacancies remained open to question, though there is no evidence of any such attempts until the eighteenth century.[42]

Not having a bishop raised an added difficulty in regard to weddings. Matrimony, as the Book of Common Prayer put it, "was an honourable estate instituted of God," not "to be enterprised, nor taken in hand unadvisedly, lightly, or wantonly." Under canon law a couple needed a license from a diocesan that attested to the absence of any impediment to their union.[43] Governors assumed the right of licensing for themselves until the assembly provided otherwise. Recognizing in 1662 that no governor's "knowledge of persons [could] possibly extend over the whole country," the assembly authorized the senior justice in each county to issue licenses in the governor's name. That arrangement continued until Effingham used a proviso in the legislation to appoint Thomas Pate as the colony's registrar of marriages.[44]

The General Assembly of March 1660/61 addressed the shortage of priests. One of its acts encouraged the building of a "colledge"; another instructed the London-bound Governor Berkeley to solicit royal letters patent and charitable funds for the school.[45] Nothing came of the legislation, so the prospect for a college went begging until James Blair's efforts in behalf of the College of William and Mary. Once that redoubtable cleric-councillor secured the college charter, the assembly responded with the necessary enabling legislation and financial support in the form of a duty on the hides of deer and certain other fur-bearing creatures.[46]

Seventeenth-century Britons cherished land above all material possessions. Moths could corrupt personal belongings, and thieves could break in and steal money, but land remained steadfast. Owning it conferred might and stature, for it was the very ground of England's ruling classes. It filled a like place in Virginia.

Colonial acts that regulated land use after 1619 never reached the intricacies of the English law of real property that had developed down the centuries into a tangle of rules about ownership and other uses. Labyrinthine though it might be, there was purpose to the maze: the intent was to keep the limited land of a tiny island kingdom within the clutches of a few powerful hands. By contrast, Virginia land seemed abundant beyond English imagination, waiting to be possessed and to yield its splendid bounty. That someone else—the natives—already had claims on the land mattered not at all because the colonists presumed Virginia was theirs by right of settlement. Indeed, the General Assembly never considered the Indians' property interests when it set about devising land laws.[47]

Once colonists claimed Virginia, all of it theoretically belonged to the king; they were his tenants and obliged to pay him quitrents. Of medieval origin, the concept of monarch as landlord-in-chief was the fundamental premise of English land law. It made its way to Virginia as the assembly put various quitrent statutes on the books.

Colonists ignored those acts until the Crown took a more aggressive approach to collecting its due, which happened during the late Berkeley years and after Bacon's Rebellion.[48] Other ancient tenures never gained a similar hold because they were without institutional supports or the confines of little England. As a result, settlers mainly appropriated a few traditional tenures such as freehold and leasehold.

Introduced by the Virginia Company to lure immigrants, the headright system soon became the preferred means of obtaining initial title to land.[49] Anyone who paid his own passage, or someone else's, could collect a fifty-acre headright per person. To receive this bounty, a claimant had to present an affidavit vouching that he had brought family members or servants or others. By law, a prospective patentee included a survey along with the other paperwork. When all documents were in order, the governor issued a patent, which conferred both proof and right of ownership to the requisite acreage. A record copy remained on file in the office of the secretary of the colony as a tally of the property's disbursement.

The need for surveys produced a corresponding need for surveyors. Land surveying required special mathematical skills that graced few settlers. William Claiborne was one, and the Virginia Company employed him as the colony's first surveyor general. In time he developed a network of local and regional subordinate surveyors that reached into every county and part of the colony. The assembly abetted him in 1624 when it enacted a law that fixed the course of all future regulation of surveys and surveyors. In the end, the posts of surveyor general and local surveyorships became among the more lucrative of Virginia offices, which made them highly coveted.[50]

After 1634, the General Assembly placed responsibility for validating land claims with the county courts, and they likewise performed as places of record for most real estate transactions. Indeed, one motive that initially persuaded the assembly to establish the courts was its wish to unburden the Council of State of such mundane matters. Designating the courts as registries worked to another purpose: it assisted settlers in establishing an undoubted record of all activities that related to titles or anything else to do with land tenures.

Other than the foregoing provisions, the General Assembly mostly refrained from regulating transfers of land. There was no need. For one thing, conveyances, whether by sale, lease, or will, were private business and not necessarily matters of legislative concern. For another, colonists knew about conveyancing from experience and could find appropriate deed forms in such books as William West's *Symboleographie*. That said, the assembly tried to reduce the likelihood of deceitful dealings when it outlawed unrecorded conveyances.[51] Also, it adapted a technique known as escheat. Escheat came into play when an accidental circumstance, most commonly the death of an heirless landholder, disrupted tenure and descent, in which instance possession returned to the grantor. Accordingly, whenever a colonist died without heirs, his lands reverted to the king, who for a fee could give them to someone else—or so went the theory. Theory did not accord with practice in the Old Dominion. Settled statutory requirements evolved tentatively. The first of them did not appear on the books until 1662. Up to that date, it seems, properties of heirless landowners passed back to the control of the county courts, which disbursed them as best they might. The arrangement sufficed, but only to a point, because it could not warrant clear title should the king wish to assert his rights. Hence the 1662 act. It allowed anyone who held escheated land for more than two years to confirm rights by payment of a fee into the Virginia treasury. The act hinted further that if Charles II demanded it, an escheator would be named to "find all such lands for the king," and in due course Sir William Berkeley appointed Secretary Thomas Ludwell escheator general. (Whether Ludwell actually received quitrents is an uncertainty because of the disappearance of the account books from his time in office.) There things rested until the post-Berkeley era, when the Crown vigorously pressed for quitrent collection. In the end, the Revisal of 1705 codified the Virginia law of escheats in a way that matched royal wishes with an effective procedure for regranting escheated real estate.[52]

The General Assembly addressed another contingency that arose from death's intervention, an inordinate rate of parental demise. This demographic quirk meant that most Virginia children came to adulthood having lost a mother, a father, or both.[53] What brought the assembly into the picture was its concern for the security of minors' estates. A first rule appeared in the Revisal of 1643 mandating that guardians "of all orphants shall carefully keep and preserve such estates as shall be comitted to their trust," that they educate their wards in the "rudiments of learning," and that they "provide for them necessaries according to the competence of their estates." Furthermore, the act compelled custodians to render annual accounts to the county courts of "the said estates and of the increase and improvement." That law stood more or less intact until the General Assembly of December 1656 changed its educational clauses. The principal alteration dealt with wards whose inheritances "be

so meane and inconsiderable" that they would not support a "free education."
Children in such circumstances were to "be bound to some manuall trade till one and
twenty yeares of age." Evidently, the amendment failed the test of time because it
disappeared from the act "Concerning Orphans" in the Revisal of 1662. That most
comprehensive of orphan legislation remained in force until 1705, though it was
twice modified. One of those changes, which related to slaves, pointed to the worth
of a singular species of personal property that colonials who owned it valued only
slightly less than their land—bond laborers.[54]

Land conferred rank, but land without workers yielded small profit. John Rolfe's
successful cultivation of West Indian tobacco turned the weed into something, as
Ralph Hamor said, "which every man may plant, and with the least part of his
labour, tend and care will returne him both cloathes and other necessaries."[55] Rolfe
thereby stoked the great tobacco boom that cursed Virginia with a single-crop
economy that remained perennially dependent on the sweat of indentured servants
and chattel slaves.

On its face, colonists in bondage toiling for the aggrandizement of planters was
anything but novel. Stuart Britons knew about service. The Bible, which some could
read and all heard preached, abounded in tales of good servants and bad. Many a
well-to-do English family could trace its fortune to the rewards of serving the
monarchy. Uncounted Englishmen and -women served the households of their betters.
Young men learned skilled crafts or industrial occupations through another type of
service, apprenticeship. Britons knew of slavery, too. The Bible told them so. Legal
writers remarked on slavery. Some contemporaries—Captain John Smith among
them—were themselves slaves for a time; English wanderers like Smith, however, fell
into slavery by accident of war or capture on the high seas, not by accident of birth
or color of skin.[56]

The novelty of bondage in Virginia rested elsewhere. It lay in how the General
Assembly whittled old-fashioned ideas about service into indentured servitude and
chattel slavery. Those institutions met peculiar labor conditions in Virginia in a
peculiar way. Neither took much substance from precedents drawn out of English
history or from common law.

To be sure, indentured servitude looked like apprenticeship. A contract known
in law as "a covenant merely personal," but which everyone called an "indenture,"
bound servant and apprentice alike.[57] By it an apprentice bargained with a master

artisan to work for a period of years in exchange for maintenance and training. At the end of his term, he got a written release that stood as proof of his having lawfully completed his indenture, and he was free to ply his craft. If, in the course of the term, either party breached the specific stipulations in the indenture, the other had remedy in the courts for there was ample statutory and case law to bolster contracts. Masters secured recompense from runaway, thieving, or scoundrel apprentices. For their part, apprentices gained protection from excessively harsh usage and release from masters who failed in their bounden duty. Indenturing meant loss of liberty that subjected apprentices to their masters' beck and call. It also reduced them to chattels for the duration of their contracts because their mentors could sell or will indentures much as any other personal property.

These similarities spoke to appearances rather than to substance. Apprenticeship answered two social goals: it allowed craft guilds sway over certain occupations and, after Parliament adopted the Statute of Artificers in 1563, it enjoined a kingdomwide method of training on those who would embark on industrial trades.[58] Apprentices signed their contracts knowing that if they performed willingly and faithfully they might attain useful employment.

Indentured servitude responded to something altogether different. It existed not to inculcate skills but to recruit footloose young Englishmen and then to break them into compliant agricultural laborers. Of course, its promise was that of a fresh start for would-be colonists who could venture no more than their labor. That lure hooked such settlers in their willing thousands. Once snared, they found themselves caught up in a system that wore them out and gave them little in return. Those that survived the rigors of their temporary condition seldom passed above a rootless underclass who made up the next-to-bottom rung of Virginia's social ladder.

The meanness of servitude raised endless annoyances for planters. Servants pilfered household belongings. Others sought release in illicit sexual liaisons or in drink. Some broke tools, malingered, set on their masters violently, or, as in the case of the Berkenhead Conspiracy, ganged up to rebel. More commonly, many ran away at the first opportunity. Planters saw in these reactions clear harm to their own economic interests and constant threat to a well-kept community. They therefore sought cures from the General Assembly, which needed few spurs because the members themselves contracted for servants in large numbers.

Servant laws were among the first acts to pass the General Assembly of 1619. They became an integral part of settled Virginia law as virtually every subsequent assembly worked out statutory ways to define relationships between masters and servants. Harshly punitive, the acts were weighted heavily in the master's behalf, even though they permitted servants access to the courts. Servants contracted with planters to work specified periods of time, usually four to seven years depending on the type of indenture. Planters in turn defrayed the expenses of passage and paid the costs of maintenance. Servants were liable for extra time if they ran off or bore bastards, and those who stole or were violent answered to the criminal laws and faced added service, too.[59]

The General Assembly fabricated slavery more gradually, though no less purposefully. Applied only to Virginians of African descent, the law of slaves cast its captives into perpetual bondage as it pared away their humanity and reduced them to the same status as an ox or a stick of furniture. Africans probably alighted in Virginia even before an unknown Hollander famously landed his human cargo in 1619. That arrival signaled neither a ponderable African migration nor the start of slavery itself. African Virginians were still a tiny population until the 1660s, but not every one fell automatically into slavery.[60]

For a long time, previous condition and religious beliefs dictated which black colonists were fated for lives of endless bondage. English opinions figured prominently, too. Britons suspected all who were not of their kindred; more especially, they mistrusted Africans who were of a different color and of decidedly un-European ways. Still, the General Assembly proceeded cautiously when it came to articulating legal relationships between whites and blacks. Slavery therefore abided in fact years before it existed in the statutes, and it seemed a convenient alternative to servitude once the English began to regard it as a way to alleviate their vexations with a trying class of their own people. Now and again a few slaves escaped to freedom through the courts and passed into the ranks of the colony's free people. Like servants, slaves stole and broke things, they ran away, and they fornicated, sometimes with whites. Such behavior was common enough for it to foster choruses of constituent complaints at midcentury. In reply, the assembly initiated an intermittent series of statutory definitions, beginning with the legislative session of December 1662, that culminated in the Revisal of 1705. It reinforced masters' rights of ownership, reduced access to the courts, and restricted the freedom of slaves to move about. Intermarriage was banned too, and the natural children of slave women were declared slaves also. Furthermore, the assembly erected special courts to try slaves accused of capital crimes.

Acts of Assembly

By 1705, in short, colonial law regarded slavery as the permanent condition of most African Virginians, and it deemed them things rather than persons.[61]

Statutory regulation of Anglo-Indian policy developed slowly, much in the fashion of labor law. Considerations of security, commerce, and control always drove the relevant legislation. From the day settlers first beached their longboats on the Jamestown shore until the historian Robert Beverley declared a hundred years later that "the Indians of Virginia are almost wasted," Algonquian, Iroquoian, and Siouan-speaking tribes posed a formidable obstruction to the English.[62] The Powhatan chiefdom dominated much of the region east of the fall line. Siouan speakers ranged west of the falls. Those who spoke Iroquoian lived to the southeast of the Powhatans, who were the greatest threat to the colonists. The English fought the Powhatans in three wars between 1622 and 1675 before they broke the natives' strength.[63] Desultory insults and injuries always occurred in the uneasy quiet of peacetime and came as frightening reminders of the constant hazard of living close by hostile neighbors; small wonder then that the General Assembly reacted to dangers—real or imagined—with various types of defensive legislation. The pertinent laws dealt with everything from armaments, militias, and fortifications to waging war and making peace.[64]

Passing such laws was not without unintended consequences. For example, the requirement that colonists own muskets, powder, and shot broke with custom in England, where statutes expressly forbade firearms to anyone worth less than £100 in lands, leases, or offices. The prohibition effectively put guns out of reach of honest subjects, except for when they drilled in county trainbands or signed up to wear the king's red coat.[65] In Virginia, however, arming free white males at their own expense was an important component in colonial defense. The assembly's mandate spared provincial and county governments the trouble of stockpiling weaponry, though it put "peeces" and ammunition in virtually every planter's household.[66] In no time at all, widespread ownership made firearms seem no different from any other tool employed to roll back the wilderness. Such ready access put guns within easy reach of servants, slaves, and Indians, despite the assembly's acts to the contrary.[67] Handiness also posed dangers for provincial authorities at times like the overthrow of Sir John Harvey or Bacon's Rebellion, when it was all too easy for the disgruntled to take up their weapons and violently vent their frustrations.

Even though the English perceived the Indians as threatening, they also saw commercial possibilities in their foe. Indeed, the prospect of trade with the "naturals" motivated the investors in the Virginia Company to found the colony in the first place. Their colonists arrived well-stocked with trade goods, including ample supplies of sheet copper. Indians prized copper because of its rarity, and geometrically shaped copper ornaments conferred high status on their owners.[68] Exchanges of copper and other barter items for grain prevented the Jamestown venture from collapsing altogether, but trucking with the natives signaled something more. Great rewards could fall into the pockets of Englishmen who mastered the business of the trade itself.[69]

The General Assembly established ground rules. Its regulations usually favored the likes of William Claiborne, Abraham Wood, William Byrd, and other bigwigs who held the lion's shares of the trade for themselves and their partners. Encouragement of westward explorers opened up new areas for enterprise. Forts built with taxpayer money worked as trading posts just as well as bastions. Provision for public interpreters served the general welfare, though it also spared traffickers an expense and gave incumbent translators a leg up on potential rivals. Trading licenses brought governors additional income and gave them considerable say about who could participate in the commerce.[70]

As the English saw the situation, trade and security ultimately depended on their ability to control the natives. They took hostages, whom they tried to "civilize"; just as they played on tribal enmities as a tactic to divide and conquer. Their victory in the Anglo-Powhatan War of 1644–1646 presented a singular advantage. Defeat weakened the Powhatan chiefdom as never before, which allowed Sir William Berkeley to deal hard for peace. Necotowance, paramount chief after Opechancanough, surrendered most of the homelands to the colonists while he acknowledged English title to an area his people retained north of the York River. He also agreed to pay "unto the King's Govern'r the number of twenty bever skins att the goeing away of Geese yearely" as tribute. More important, the peace treaty was the century's first Anglo-Indian agreement accorded the imprimatur of legislative fiat. Beyond that, it set forth Berkeley's comprehensive scheme for controlling Indian affairs. He envisioned a chain of forts strung along the frontier as a defensive perimeter. He also aimed to reduce tensions by keeping the two peoples as separate from one another as conditions permitted. Hence the English were denied access to the Indians' reserve land without gubernatorial warrant, and the Indians were required to wear identifying coats and badges whenever they entered English settlements. Berkeley grounded the entire plan on subjugating all Indians who lived within or near English precincts.[71]

For the next thirty years, the assembly added to this core design. The treaty was recodified in 1658, and again four years later. Otherwise, various assemblies held the tributaries accountable for their misdeeds in the colony's courts just as it required the natives to use the English judicial system to redress their complaints against the colonists. At the same time, legislators continued down the path of separation with further restrictions on contacts, outlawing what the assembly defined as the "casual" killing of natives and holding them above slavery, among others.[72]

Nevertheless, the provincial government faltered, and it turned a blind eye to lax enforcement of the statutes. An increase of colonists after 1646 soon flooded the reserve lands north of the York River, where three new counties were established by 1653. This and other violations kept relations always simmering just below flash point. Occasional flare-ups got tamped down until the summer of 1675, when the frontiers burst into open warfare that inflamed Bacon's Rebellion. In the end, the hapless tributary tribes suffered most, for it was they who bore the brunt of destruction.[73]

The General Assembly had no hand in the peace agreement the English signed with the remaining Powhatans in 1677. Lieutenant Governor Herbert Jeffreys and his colleagues on the royal commission of investigation negotiated the so-called Treaty of Middle Plantation. Instead of seeking the assembly's ratification, as had Berkeley in 1646, Jeffreys dispatched the pact to Whitehall for the Privy Council's approval.[74] Jeffreys's course reached beyond Indian affairs. His snub equated with the Crown's intent to diminish the assembly, and that had implications for colonial legislation.

Acts of assembly, whatever else they were, attempted to relate Virginia law to English law. Crown assaults on the assembly's legislative prerogatives went to the very heart of that relationship. Already by 1677 English officials had inclined to a position that Sir William Blackstone later stated as conventional wisdom. When he remarked on the nexus in 1765, he observed how in the colonies

> the common law of England, as such, has no allowance or authority there; they being no part of the mother county, but distant (though dependent) dominions. They are subject however to the control of parliament; (though like Ireland, Man and the rest) not bound by any acts of parliament, unless particularly named.[75]

What was common conviction among Englishmen in Blackstone's day was hardly so a hundred years earlier. The nearest thing to settled opinion in England came from a Court of King's Bench decision handed down in 1608. In *Calvin's Case*, the court ruled that any Scot born after James I took the English Crown was no alien and was therefore fully capable of inheriting land like any natural-born English subject. The section of the judgment that appeared pertinent to Virginia explained the circumstances under which a monarch might procure lands outside his realm and the effect different ways of acquisition had on the laws of those territories. In the instance of King James, England passed to him in right of succession, and only Parliament could change the law of the kingdom. Conquest from another Christian king was a second possibility, in which case prevailing law continued until the new prince set it aside. The king might also forcibly grab the territories of infidels. His seizure immediately annulled local law, and the lands automatically passed under royal dominion.[76]

Virginia had not come under royal authority by any of the means reckoned in the King's Bench analysis. From the start, colonists regarded Virginia as having "no Original Laws" among natives "so barbarous & rude that they had no other direction & Government amongst them but the Law of Nature, & what civility they since have, arrives to them from their Commerce with us."[77] Indeed, members of the General Assembly seemed quite unaware of Calvin's Case. Nothing in the extant legislative records directly connects any of them to the ruling or to an act of assembly. Actually, the sole Virginia reference to Calvin, more implied than explicit, dates to the 1680s, but it derived from some private litigation that William Fitzhugh undertook for Councillor Ralph Wormeley rather than from legislation.[78]

The thing that seemed more pertinent than Calvin was this. Once the colony passed into royal hands, members of the assembly could believe that it was entitled to enjoy a status more like that of the Isle of Man or the Channel Isles than of a heathen terrain. Virginia belonged to the Crown, it was not generally subject to Parliament, and it had "peculiar laws or customs" of its own.[79] Furthermore, when Charles I proclaimed Virginia his province, he declared it "a part of Our Royall Empire, Descended upon Us and undoubtedly belonging and appertaining unto Us, … As any other part of Our Dominions."[80] Members could also read the reference to "Our Territory and Dominion" in Charles II's commission to Sir William Berkeley as governor in 1650. Similar allusions cropped up in the great seal of the colony and in other public records as well.[81] And there was the long-standing, often-repeated injunction that the colonists rule themselves as near to the English law as their circumstances would allow.[82]

Circumstances allowed, indeed demanded, that the assembly take large portions of English law for the colony's own. Those takings were not always by legislative action, as in the example of criminal law. On the other hand, when the General Assembly deemed particular English statutes appropriate, it specifically enacted them as Virginia law.[83] Where there was nothing, members made something from whole cloth.

Left alone, the assembly acted freely in ways that awakened feelings of equality between itself and Parliament and its acts and statutes of the realm. A novel illustration of that sensibility appeared in a declaratory paper that passed the General Assembly of April 1647. The document responded to parliamentary legislation curtailing Anglo-Dutch commerce in the Chesapeake and the Caribbean. Rather pointedly, it noted,

> For wee may not presume on such a thought that the most honorable houses of Parliament would conclude [i.e., bind] us in a Case of right & priviledge granted unto us by ancient Charter (vidzt) that it should bee lawfull for the Planters to entertaine trade with any nation or people in amitye with his Majestie, especially without hearing of the parties principally interested, which infringeth noe lesse the libertye of the Collony & a right of deare esteeme to free borne persons (vidzt) that noe lawe should bee established within the kingdome of England concerninge us, without the consent of a grand Assembly here.

Perhaps, the legislators continued, "the most honorable houses [had] bin abused & by the wylie & spetious pretences of Merchants, or Seamen trading to the Collony" persuaded to pass the law. No matter the reason, Parliament had overstepped and intruded on "the rights, immunities & priviledges of our Charter by as due a Clayme belongeinge to us, as is the wages of an hirelinge that hath laboured for it, ... [that] were the Conditionall reward & guerdon [i.e., recompense] expounded for our Undertakings in those rugged paths of Plantation."[84]

The contention that Parliament's authority had its limits in Virginia was unusual. It is the earliest-known example of such a pronouncement by the General Assembly, but it arose from what members in 1647 took as good precedent. They found sanction for their posture in a provision in the Virginia Company charter of 1606, which had promised to the original colonists and their descendants "all liberties Franchises and Immunities within anie of our other domynions to all intentes and purposes as yf they had been abyding and borne within this our Realme of Englande or anie other of our saide Domynions."[85]

Their claim roiled muddied constitutional waters—the as-yet-ill-defined relationship of the General Assembly to Parliament. The challenge passed unmet, though the failure to confront it heightened the assembly's sense of itself. Silence seemed tantamount to consent. For as long as members continued to approximate English law, and no one inquired into the width of variation from that benchmark, the assembly possessed spacious leeway to do as it pleased. Of course, Stuart imperialists eagerly promoted just such inquiries after 1677, and by their actions they implied what Blackstone wrote explicitly. But even they drew back from insisting that Virginia law follow English practice down to its last jot and tittle. The assembly yielded, but when it came to legislating on provincial and local matters, its power continued intact.

Refined, polished, and refined again, the acts of assembly changed in design and purpose many times over. Seen whole, they make an almost yearly chronicle of how the burgesses and councillors slowly imposed their ideas of order and civility on Virginia. As such, the laws in force offer precise, measurable evidence of the General Assembly at work from 1619 to the close of the century. This record offers conspicuous signposts along the route untrained men walked to become handy legislators. It speaks to widening legislative mastery and of the assembly's transit to a little parliament. It indicates how answers to momentary exigencies were fashioned from wholesale appropriations of English law. It discloses unmistakable and extraordinary prescriptions that had little precedent in common law, or none whatsoever. And it testifies to the subordination of the General Assembly and the reconfiguration of Anglo-Virginia politics after 1677.

Afterword

❧❧❧

Just shy of its eightieth birthday, the General Assembly gathered in April 1699. Its impending anniversary drew no one's notice because burgesses, councillors, and a new governor-general all fixed their minds on more-immediate concerns. Fire had destroyed the statehouse the previous October, so there was need for meeting space, and as had often happened in past years, Jamestonians accommodated the House and Council as best they could. An abundance of aspirants turned the choice of the new Speaker into a horse race. Sorting through the crowded pack made for extended balloting that left an anxious lieutenant governor Francis Nicholson to fidget in frustration. Finally, Robert Carter ran to the head of the field, won the prize, and relieved the governor of his impatience. Business could begin. Nicholson opened the session with an address that charged the assembly to plan for law reform and a new capital city at Middle Plantation. Done with their work by the first week of June, the members adjourned to await the governor's summons on a future day. The call never came. Instead, in October 1700 Nicholson circulated election writs that ordered another assembly to meet with him at "his Majesties Royall College of William and Mary adjoyning to the City of Williamsburgh."[1]

A new assembly, sitting in a new place on the eve of a new century, marks the conclusion of this portion of the history of the General Assembly of Virginia. Before 1700 lay decades of development, during which the assembly lost its resemblance to the scheme of its originators and acquired the guise of a bicameral legislature. Where once the assembly's authority had been narrowly bounded, its powers in 1700 reached into every colonial household and for a time even exceeded those of Parliament. Through the assembly, fortunate planters also united high social rank with the right to govern in an ancient, English way. And while assemblymen experimented with the skills and mechanics of governance, they passed from novice politicians to artfully capable lawmakers.

For all of that, something unpleasant jostled the thoughts of the older burgesses and councillors who crossed from the seventeenth to the eighteenth century—a gnawing, deep distress about prospects for the General Assembly. Former irreconcilables and moderates, to whom accommodation came hard, saw more loss than improvement in the Crown's aggressive reconfiguration of Anglo-Virginia politics after 1677. They no longer met annually as a matter of right. Gone too was the burgesses' free choice of their clerk. The full assembly had lost its privilege to sit as a court of last resort, and its laws were easily set aside by gubernatorial proclamations or royal commandments. Sir William Berkeley had been friendly, even deferential, to the assembly, but his successors were more often enemies than allies. Indeed, the combination of assertive chief executives and a forceful Crown led to a seemingly dangerous gathering of power in the governor's hand. The accumulation not only upset legislative privileges, but it also abruptly altered Virginia's old constitution. Weakening the assembly shifted political weight from the burgesses to the Council of State and lessened their sense of themselves as the colony's rightful rulers.

Such disquiets fed an equally palpable concern for the future of Virginia. By any measure, little about the colony had come up to expectations. Dreams of diversified agriculture remained what they had been when the assembly voted in the 1660s for Governor Berkeley's schemes—dreams. And costly ones, too. Tobacco-raising remained the principal means of livelihood, but prosperous cultivation of that ubiquitous plant meant an ever-more stratified plantation economy and increased dependence on slave labor. Socially, Virginia continued as a collection of rude, dispersed settlements that still lacked even a single town worthy of the name. And however much leading planters aped England's landed gentry, their pursuit of refinement seemed as nothing in the eyes of the very Britons whose benediction they desperately sought, but who refused it and instead mocked them for their pretensions.

Such concerns played in the minds of native-born members who lived into the eighteenth century, too, albeit in a different key. Like the trimmers of Jeffreys's and Effingham's days, these creoles thought of Virginia as part of an Atlantic imperial community that centered on London. They accepted a diminished General Assembly as a reality that separated their political landscape from their fathers, and they learned the lesson of Parson Blair's assiduous currying of favor with imperial authorities. Moreover, they understood life in the colony as somehow different from life in the metropolis, though they fancied re-creating the Old Dominion as a little England as nearly as their circumstances permitted. Natives and sons of natives filled nearly every seat in the county courts, the House of Burgesses, and the Council of State. When the General Assembly met in the hall at the College of William and Mary, the drift toward critical mass was one among the currents that carried the Little Parliament toward its next stages of development.

Note on Sources

When retreating Confederate government officials set fire to the military warehouses in the business district of Richmond in April 1865, the blaze consumed the bulk of Virginia's seventeenth-century provincial archives. A measure of the loss can be gauged by an inventory of the office of the General Court that Conway Robinson prepared in 1829 and various memorandums that Thomas Jefferson had compiled earlier. The inventory and the memorandums appeared as appendices to the second edition of H. R. McIlwaine, ed., *Minutes of the Council and General Court of Colonial Virginia, 1622–1632, 1670–1676, with Notes and Excerpts from Original Council and General Court Records, Into 1683, Now Lost* (Richmond, 1924; 2d ed., Richmond, 1979). Despite the destruction, a considerable horde of information, albeit widely dispersed, has survived. What follows is a short discussion of those manuscripts, many of which are readily accessible to researchers in microform or in print.

The Virginia Colonial Records Project brought together 963 reels of microfilmed manuscripts that relate to Virginia in the period 1607 to 1783. Those films reproduce duplicate texts of lost originals that are housed mainly in British repositories. Record groups range from public documents to private papers. Individual reels are available via interlibrary loan from the Alderman Library at the University of Virginia or the Library of Virginia. They may also be consulted at the Virginia Historical Society and at Colonial Williamsburg Foundation's John D. Rockefeller Jr. Library. An online guide to the collection is searchable on the Library of Virginia's World Wide Web site at http://www.lva.lib.va.us.

Housed at the Library of Virginia is a collection denominated the "Virginia Colonial Papers, 1630–1778," which includes remnants salvaged from the 1865 fire. Individual items are mainly petitions, judgments, or other showings that attached to suit files from the General Court. Many of them were printed in abstract or garbled renditions in W. P. Palmer et al., comps., *Calendar of Virginia State Papers and Other Manuscripts* ... (Richmond, 1875–1893). The documents have been microfilmed by the Library of Virginia, and reel 1 contains a modern calendar that serves as a guide to the collection.

Series 8 of the microfilm edition of the Thomas Jefferson Papers at the Library of Congress includes various seventeenth-century and later transcripts of papers relative to the General Assembly that Jefferson acquired during a lifetime of research. William Waller Hening and H. R. McIlwaine printed most of these records. Deserving of special note, however, are two bound volumes, identified as "Virginia Miscellaneous Papers, 1606–1692" and "Virginia Foreign Business and Inquisitions, 1665–1676," which contain seventeenth-century file copies of provincial records. They originally belonged in the record group that Conway Robinson styled "Inquisitions etc." in his inventory. Jefferson appropriated the volumes for his own uses before he sold them to the federal government with the rest of his library, and that happenstance saved them from the fire of 1865. Portions of the contents appeared in early issues of the *Virginia Magazine of History and Biography*. Film copies are accessible via interlibrary loan from the Library of Congress, and the original records can be viewed at the Library of Congress Web site at http://memory.loc.gov/ammem/mtjhtml/mtjhome.html.

County court records are another fertile ground for miscellaneous legislative papers, correspondence, fugitive copies of statutes, orders-in-council, General Court judgments, and similar items. There were twenty-three counties in Virginia by 1700. Of these, most of the records for ten, including James City County, no longer exist. Only the records of Accomack, Lancaster, Lower Norfolk, Northampton, Northumberland, Surry, and York Counties span the seventeenth century in more-or-less unbroken series, beginning with the year when each county came into existence. The range for the remaining counties goes from a few fragmentary files to runs that cover years or even decades. For further details, consult Morgan P. Robinson, "Virginia Counties: Those Resulting from Virginia Legislation," *Bulletin of the Virginia State Library* 9 (1916). Copies of all bound volumes are on microfilm, and they are available on interlibrary loan from the Library of Virginia. Discussions of the Virginia County and City loose papers at the Library of Virginia and other records on microfilm are found at the Library's Web site at http://www.lva.lib.va.us/whatwehave/local/county_formation/index.htm. Lists of available Burned Record County records are found at http://www.lva.lib.va.us/whatwehave/local/va22_burnedco.htm. Lists of the available county and city records for loan on microfilm are at http://www.lva.lib.va.us/whatwehave/local/local_rec/county_city/index.htm.

Original suit files and other loose papers are not to be overlooked. When they exist, they are kept at the county courthouses or at the Library of Virginia. Those for Northampton County, now at the Library of Virginia, are especially noteworthy, and the clerks of court in the City of Chesapeake and Surry County retain seventeenth-century recordings of the acts of assembly passed in 1647 and the revised statutes of April 1652. The Library of Virginia holds a photostatic copy of the acts of assembly,

1642–1647, from the City of Chesapeake that is available for consultation in the Library's Manuscripts Reading Room.

That portion of the William Blathwayt papers at Colonial Williamsburg Foundation's John D. Rockefeller Jr. Library is an important source for exchanges between William Blathwayt, a well-connected English bureaucrat, and Virginia officials from the Restoration to the end of the seventeenth century. These records are also on microfilm, along with a guidebook, and can be borrowed on interlibrary loan.

Henry and William Coventry held high places at the court of Charles II after the Restoration, and they accumulated a mammoth quantity of manuscripts. Their collection now belongs to their descendant, the incumbent marquess of Bath, and it resides in the library of his great seat, Longleat House, near Warminster in Wiltshire. Volumes 76–78 of the Coventry Papers include many items that relate to Virginia, especially in the time of Bacon's Rebellion, but volumes 2, 3, and 12 are useful as well. The entire collection is available on microfilm that may be borrowed on interlibrary loan. Consult Lester K. Born, comp., *British Manuscripts Project: A Checklist of the Microfilms Prepared in England and Wales for the American Council of Learned Societies, 1941–1945* (Washington, D.C., 1955), for a complete list of reels and a short description of their contents.

The Ferrar family papers, which are in the library at Magdalene College, Cambridge, bear mainly on the period when the Virginia Company of London controlled the colony. Portions of the collection were microfilmed for the Virginia Colonial Records Project, but the collection was reproduced in its entirety on film in *The Ferrar Papers, 1590–1790, in Magdalene College, Cambridge,* ed. David Ransome (East Ardsley, Wakefield, West Yorkshire, Eng., 1992). Ransome prepared a helpful introduction and finding aid, both of which appear on reel I.

Samuel Hartlib's papers are as yet a relatively unknown collection to most Virginia scholars. A polymath, Hartlib maintained a broad circle of international correspondents, and his surviving papers (about twenty-five thousand manuscripts) are housed at the University of Sheffield. Hartlib had close ties to Parliament during the Interregnum through Benjamin Worsley. Consequently, the Worsley correspondence file is especially pertinent to the parliamentary takeover of Virginia in 1652. The Samuel Hartlib Papers Project produced the first electronic full-text edition of the entire collection in 1996. A second electronic edition, including additional Hartlib material from other repositories in the United States and Europe, became available in the summer of 2002.

When Conway Robinson inventoried the provincial archives, he took copious notes, and in more than a few instances he also made verbatim transcripts of individual documents. Significant portions of his compilations appeared in early issues of the *Virginia Magazine of History and Biography*, and some are in H. R. McIlwaine, ed., *Minutes of the Council and General Court of Colonial Virginia*, 2d ed. (Richmond, 1979), but a search of the actual notes themselves, which are among the Conway Robinson Papers at the Virginia Historical Society, yields nuggets of high quality that are found nowhere else.

Lyon Gardiner Tyler, longtime president of the College of William and Mary, had access to private family papers and other documents that have gone missing since his day. His gleanings, like those of Robinson, sometimes provide useful tidbits, providing one is willing to plow through quite large, oftentimes tedious, files of correspondence, notebooks, and other materials. The Tyler collection is in the Earl Gregg Swem Library at the College of William and Mary.

Supplementing these manuscript collections is a variety of printed documents. William Waller Hening compiled the majority of the legislative acts into *The Statutes at Large; Being a Collection of All the Laws of Virginia, From the First Session of the Legislature, in the Year 1619 ...* (Richmond, New York, and Philadelphia, 1809–1823; reprint, Charlottesville, 1969). A thoughtful scholar-editor, Hening approached his task with a care and thoroughness that is remarkable for someone in a day when travel and the means of scholarship were decidedly primitive. Fugitive statutes that escaped his notice have been printed in early issues of the *Virginia Magazine of History and Biography* and the *William and Mary Quarterly*. The most comprehensive collections are Warren M. Billings, ed., "Some Acts Not in Hening's *Statutes*: The Acts of Assembly, April 1652, November 1652, and July 1653," and Jon Kukla, ed., "Some Acts Not in Hening's *Statutes*: The Acts of Assembly, October 1660," *VMHB* 83 (1975): 22–76, and 77–97.

Susan Myra Kingsbury, ed., *The Records of the Virginia Company of London*, 4 vols. (Washington, D.C., 1906–1935), documents the company years. William J. Van Schreeven and George H. Reese, eds., *Proceedings of the General Assembly of Virginia, July 30–August 4, 1619, Written & Sent from Virginia to England by Mr. John Pory Speaker of the First Representative Assembly in the New World* (Jamestown, Va., 1969), provides the definitive edition of Pory's journal.

Henry Read McIlwaine was chiefly responsible for gathering and publishing the majority of the extant legislative and higher judicial records. Those renditions appear in his *Journals of the House of Burgesses of Virginia, 1619–1776* (Richmond, 1905–1915); *Legislative Journals of the Council of Colonial Virginia* (Richmond, 1918–1919); *Executive Journals of the Council of Colonial Virginia, 1680–1775* (Richmond, 1925–1966); and

Note on Sources

Minutes of the Council and General Court of Colonial Virginia (Richmond, 1924). Despite an occasional misapprehension of the nature or purpose of what he printed, McIlwaine was a scrupulous scholar. His editions retain the usefulness he intended for them. Equally important, his work testifies to the persistence of a dedicated historian who labored under conditions and financial constraints unknown today.

As for papers of the governors-general, only those of Sir William Berkeley; Thomas Culpeper, second baron Culpeper of Thoresway; Francis Howard, fifth baron Howard of Effingham; and Francis Nicholson exist in sufficient quantity to merit scholarly editions. The Library of Virginia issued my edition of Effingham's under the title *The Papers of Francis Howard, Baron Howard of Effingham, 1643–1695* (Richmond, 1989), and I have prepared the Berkeley papers for future publication. The Culpeper and the Nicholson papers await their editors.

Richard Beale Davis, ed., *William Fitzhugh and His Chesapeake World, 1676–1701: The Fitzhugh Letters and Other Documents* (Chapel Hill, 1963), and Marion Tinling, ed., *The Correspondence of the Three William Byrds of Westover, Virginia, 1684–1776* (Charlottesville, 1977), provide glimpses into the political activities of two men who loomed prominently in the activities of the General Assembly. These editions are unique in the sense that Fitzhugh and the first William Byrd were two of only three Virginia politicians of the period whose extant personal papers exist in quantities bulky enough to justify letterpress editions. The remaining manuscripts of the third, Secretary Thomas Ludwell, have yet to be reconstituted.

Not to be slighted are legal dictionaries, clerks' manuals, statutory compilations, formularies, case reports, treatises, and parliamentary practice manuals that circulated in Virginia before 1700. In addition to the titles discussed above in Chapter 7, two bibliographic studies are helpful in identifying the range of available texts: William Hamilton Bryson, comp., *Census of Law Books in Colonial Virginia* (Charlottesville, 1978), and Warren M. Billings, "English Legal Literature as a Source of Law and Legal Practice in Seventeenth-Century Virginia," *Virginia Magazine of History and Biography* 87 (1979): 403–416. The actual volumes themselves can be difficult to use because they are now scarce and highly desired, meaning that they are housed in rare book collections at research libraries or they are in private hands. The Early English Books in Microforms series, produced by University Microfilms of Ann Arbor, Michigan, provides an alternative means of access. That resource is keyed to A. W. Pollard and G. R. Redgrave, comps., *A Short-Title Catalogue of Books Printed in England, Scotland and Ireland, and of English Books Printed Abroad, 1475–1640* (London, 1926), and Donald G. Wing, comp., *Short-Title Catalogue of Books Printed in England, Scotland, Ireland, Wales, and British America, and of English Books Printed in Other Countries, 1641–1700* (New York, 1945–1951).

Abbreviations and Short Titles

Locations

BL	British Library, London.
DLC	Library of Congress, Washington, D.C.
HLRO	House of Lords Record Office, Westminster.
PRO	National Archives (Public Record Office), Kew, Richmond, Surrey.
LVA	Library of Virginia, Richmond.
ViHi	Virginia Historical Society, Richmond.
ViU	Alderman Library, University of Virginia, Charlottesville.

Manuscript abbreviations

ADWI	Accomack County Deed, Will, and Inventory Books. (All county court record group abbreviations refer to microfilm copies of original manuscript records, LVA.)
AOB	Accomack County Order Books.
Add.MSS	Additional Manuscripts, BL.
C	Chancery Papers, PRO.
CCOB	Charles City County Order Books.
CO	Colonial Office Papers, PRO.
HCA	High Court of Admiralty Papers, PRO.
LNDWI	Lower Norfolk County Deed, Will, and Inventory Books.
LNOB	Lower Norfolk County Order Books.
MOB	Middlesex County Order Books.
NoOB	Northampton County Order Books.
ORDWI	Old Rappahannock County Deed, Will, and Inventory Books.
PC	Privy Council Minutes, PRO.
RDWI	Richmond County Deed, Will, and Inventory Books.
SDWI	Surry County Deed, Will, and Inventory Books.
SP	State Papers, PRO.
WDWI	Westmoreland County Deed, Will, and Inventory Books.

Short titles

AHR	*American Historical Review.*
Adventurers of Purse and Person	Virginia M. Meyer and John Frederick Dorman, eds., *Adventurers of Purse and Person: Virginia, 1607–1624/5*, 3d ed., rev. (Richmond, 1987).
Beverley, *History*	Robert Beverley, *The History and Present State of Virginia*, ed. Louis B. Wright (Chapel Hill, 1947).
Billings, Selby, and Tate, *Colonial Virginia*	Warren M. Billings, John E. Selby, and Thad W. Tate, *Colonial Virginia: A History* (White Plains, N.Y., 1986).
Billings, *Old Dominion*	Warren M. Billings, ed., *The Old Dominion in the Seventeenth Century: A Documentary History of Virginia, 1606–1689* (Chapel Hill, 1975).
Bruce, *Institutional History*	Philip Alexander Bruce, *Institutional History of Virginia in the Seventeenth Century: An Inquiry into the Religious, Moral, Educational, Legal, Military, and Political Condition of the People Based on Original and Contemporaneous Records*, 2 vols. (New York, 1910).
Cay, *Abridgment*	John Cay, comp., *An Abridgment of The Publick Statutes in Force and Use From Magna Carta, in the ninth year of King Henry III. To the eleventh year of his present Majesty King George II. Inclusive* (London, 1739).
Clarendon Papers	Edward Hyde, first earl of Clarendon, Papers, Bodleian Library, University of Oxford.
Colonial Papers, LVA	Virginia, Colonial Papers, 1630–1778, State Government Records Collection, LVA.
Coventry Papers	Henry Coventry Papers, Longleat House, Wiltshire.
Cowell, *The Interpreter*	John Cowell, comp., *A Law Dictionary: Or, the Interpreter of Words and Terms Used either in the Common or Statute Laws of Great Britain, and in Tenures and Jocular Customs* (London, 1727).
Craven, *Dissolution*	Wesley Frank Craven, *The Dissolution of the Virginia Company: The Failure of a Colonial Experiment* (New York, 1932).
Craven, *Southern Colonies*	Wesley Frank Craven, *The Southern Colonies in the Seventeenth Century, 1607–1689*, vol. I in *A History of the South*, ed. Wendell Holmes Stephenson and E. Merton Coulter (Baton Rouge, La., 1949).
Effingham Papers	Warren M. Billings, ed., *The Papers of Francis Howard, Baron Howard of Effingham, 1643–1695* (Richmond, 1989).

Executive Journals of Council	H. R. McIlwaine, Wilmer L. Hall, and Benjamin J. Hillman, eds., *Executive Journals of the Council of Colonial Virginia*, 6 vols. (Richmond, 1925–1966).
Hakewill, *Modus tenendi Parliamentum*	William Hakewill, comp., *Modus tenendi Parliamentum: Or, The Old Manner of Holding Parliaments in England* (London, 1660).
Hartwell, Blair, and Chilton, *Present State of Virginia*	Henry Hartwell, James Blair, and Edward Chilton, *The Present State of Virginia, and the College*, ed. Hunter Dickinson Farish (Williamsburg, 1940).
Hening, *Statutes*	William Waller Hening, ed., *The Statutes at Large; Being a Collection of All the Laws of Virginia from the First Session of the Legislature, in the Year 1619*, facsimile edition (Charlottesville, 1969, originally published at Richmond, New York, and Philadelphia, 1809–1823).
Journals of the House of Burgesses	H. R. McIlwaine and John Pendleton Kennedy, eds., *Journals of the House of Burgesses of Virginia, 1619–1658/59; 1659/60–1693; 1695–1702* (Richmond, 1914–1915).
Kingsbury, *Records of the Virginia Company*	Susan Myra Kingsbury, ed., *The Records of the Virginia Company of London*, 4 vols. (Washington, D.C., 1906–1935).
Kukla, *Speakers and Clerks*	Jon Kukla, *Speakers and Clerks of the Virginia House of Burgesses, 1643–1776* (Richmond, 1981).
Kukla, *Political Institutions*	Jon Kukla, *Political Institutions in Virginia, 1619–1660* (New York, 1989).
Legislative Journals of Council	H. R. McIlwaine, ed., *Legislative Journals of the Council of Colonial Virginia*, 2d ed. (Richmond, 1979).
Leonard, *General Assembly Register*	Cynthia Miller Leonard, comp., *The General Assembly of Virginia, July 30, 1619–January 11, 1978: A Bicentennial Register of Members* (Richmond, 1978).
Minutes of Council and General Court	H. R. McIlwaine, ed., *Minutes of the Council and General Court of Colonial Virginia*, 2d ed. (Richmond, 1979).
Proceedings of the General Assembly	William J. Van Schreeven and George H. Reese, eds., *Proceedings of the General Assembly of Virginia, July 30–August 4, 1619. Written & Sent from Virginia to England by Mr. John Pory, Speaker of the First Representative Assembly in the New World* (Jamestown, Va., 1969).
Randolph MSS	Virginia Company of London, Records, 23 April 1619–7 June 1624, vol. 3, the Randolph Manuscript (bearing bookplate of John Randolph of Roanoke), Mss3 V8192 a, ViHi.

Robinson, "Notes"   Conway Robinson, comp., "Notes and Excerpts from the Records of Colonial Virginia," 1624–1689, Conway Robinson Papers, Mss5:9 R5613:3, V:Hi.

VMHB   *Virginia Magazine of History and Biography.*

WMQ   *William and Mary Quarterly.*

Notes

FOREWORD

I. For example, see Beverley, *History*, 47–48; Hartwell, Blair, and Chilton, *Present State of Virginia*, 40–44; William Stith, *The History of the First Discovery and Settlement of Virginia: Being an Essay towards a General History of this Colony* (Williamsburg, 1747); Thomas Jefferson, *Notes on the State of Virginia*, ed. William Peden (Chapel Hill, 1955), 110–117; Hening, *Statutes*, I:iii–xxiv; Alexander Brown, *The First Republic in America* (New York, 1898); Bruce, *Institutional History*, 2:229–521; Thomas J. Wertenbaker, *Virginia under the Stuarts, 1607–1688* (Princeton, N.J., 1914), esp. 29–59; Charles M. Andrews, *The Colonial Period of American History* (New Haven, Conn., 1934–1938), 1:180–205; Craven, *Southern Colonies*; Bernard Bailyn, "Politics and Social Structure in Virginia," in *Seventeenth-Century America: Essays in Colonial History*, ed. James Morton Smith (Chapel Hill, 1959), 90–115; Richard L. Morton, *Colonial Virginia*, 2 vols. (Chapel Hill, 1960), esp. 1:45–61; Jack P. Greene, *The Quest for Power: The Lower Houses of Assembly in the Southern Royal Colonies, 1689–1776* (Chapel Hill, 1963), 22–28; Greene, "Changing Interpretations of Early American Politics," in *The Reinterpretation of Early American History: Essays in Honor of John Edwin Pomfret*, ed. Ray Allen Billington (San Marino, Calif., 1966), 151–184; exchange between Bailyn and Greene in *AHR* 75 (1969): 337–367; Wesley Frank Craven, "... And So the Form of Government Became Perfect," *VMHB* 77 (1969): 131–145; Martin Herbert Quitt, "Virginia House of Burgesses, 1660–1706: The Social, Educational & Economic Bases of Political Power" (Ph.D. diss., Washington University, 1970); Wesley Frank Craven, *The Colonies in Transition, 1660–1713* (New York, 1968); John C. Rainbolt, "A New Look at Stuart 'Tyranny': The Crown's Attack on the Virginia Assembly, 1676–1689," *VMHB* 75 (1967): 387–406; J. Mills Thornton III, "The Thrusting Out of Governor Harvey: A Seventeenth-Century Rebellion," *VMHB* 76 (1968): II–26; J. R. Pole, *The Seventeenth Century: The Sources of Legislative Power* (Charlottesville, 1969); John C. Rainbolt, *From Prescription to Persuasion: Manipulation of Eighteenth* [i.e. Seventeenth] *Century Virginia Economy* (Port Washington, N.Y., 1974); Stephen Saunders Webb, *The Governors-General: The English Army and the Definition of Empire, 1569–1681* (Chapel Hill, 1979), 329–425; Warren M. Billings, John E. Selby, and Thad W. Tate, *Colonial Virginia: A History* (White Plains, N.Y., 1986), 47–172.

2. Inquiries from the Council for Trade and Foreign Plantations, 29 Sept. 1670, CO 1/26, fol. 196, PRO.

3. Ibid., fol. 197. Berkeley sent his reply on 21 June 1671.

4. Transcripts of the assembly journals were not routinely sent to London until the 1680s, so those that found their way into Crown hands before that time did so more by chance than by design.

5. Elyot, *The boke named the Governour, devised by Sr. Thomas Elyot, knight* (London, 1531), The Proheme.

6. Dalton, *The Countrey Justice* ... (London, 1677), I, 9.

7. Treasurer and Company. An Ordinance and Constitution for Council and Assembly in Virginia, 24 July 1621, in *The Three Charters of the Virginia Company of London, With Seven Related Documents, 1606–1621*, ed. Samuel M. Bemiss (Williamsburg, 1957), 127–128.

8. Warren M. Billings, "'Virginias Deploured Condition,' 1660–1676: The Coming of Bacon's Rebellion" (Ph.D. diss., Northern Illinois University, 1968), 85–119; Billings, "The Growth of Political Institutions in Virginia, 1634 to 1676," *WMQ*, 3d ser., 31 (1974): 225–242; Billings, *Old Dominion*, 39–50; Billings, "The Transfer of English Law to Virginia, 1606–50," in *The Westward Enterprise: English Activities in Ireland, the Atlantic, and America, 1480–1650*, ed. K. R. Andrews, N. P. Canny, and P. E. H. Hair (Liverpool, 1978), 215–244.

9. Jon Kukla, introduction to Leonard, *General Assembly Register*, ix–xii; Kukla, "Robert Beverley Assailed: Appellate Jurisdiction and the Problem of Bicameralism in Seventeenth-Century Virginia," *VMHB* 88 (1980): 415–429; Kukla, *Speakers and Clerks*, 3–20; Kukla, "Order and Chaos in Early America: Political and Social Stability in Pre-Restoration Virginia," *AHR* 90 (1985): 275–298; Kukla, *Political Institutions*, the printed version of his 1979 University of Toronto dissertation.

10. For example, Wesley Frank Craven, *White, Red, and Black: The Seventeenth-Century Virginian* (Charlottesville, 1971); Edmund S. Morgan, *American Slavery, American Freedom: The Ordeal of Colonial Virginia* (New York, 1975); Thad W. Tate and David L. Ammerman, eds., *The Chesapeake in the Seventeenth Century: Essays on Anglo-American Society* (Chapel Hill, 1979); Darrett B. Rutman and Anita H. Rutman, *A Place in Time: Middlesex County, Virginia, 1650–1750* (New York, 1984); Lois Green Carr, Philip D. Morgan, and Jean B. Russo, eds., *Colonial Chesapeake Society* (Chapel Hill, 1988); James R. Perry, *The Formation of a Society on Virginia's Eastern Shore, 1615–1655* (Chapel Hill, 1990); and James Horn, *Adapting to a New World: English Society in the Seventeenth-Century*

Chesapeake (Chapel Hill, 1994), provide a generous sampling of the scope, direction, and findings of writers who have dominated Chesapeake studies since the early 1970s.

11. David W. Jordan, *Foundations of Representative Government in Maryland, 1632–1715* (Cambridge, 1987).

CHAPTER 1: BEGINNINGS

1. Craven, *Dissolution*, 1–80; Sigmund Diamond, "From Organization to Society: Virginia in the Seventeenth Century," *American Journal of Sociology* 63 (1958): 457–475; Theodore K. Rabb, *Jacobean Gentleman: Sir Edwin Sandys, 1561–1629* (Princeton, N.J., 1998), 319–353; Samuel M. Bemiss, ed., *The Three Charters of the Virginia Company of London, With Seven Related Documents, 1606–1621* (Williamsburg, 1957), 95–108, 127 (quotation). The original versions of the Great Charter and the two commissions are lost. Copies that Yeardley made in 1621 for Sir Francis Wyatt were Bemiss's source texts.

2. Craven, *Dissolution*, 36–39.

3. John Chamberlain to Sir Dudley Carleton, 28 Nov. 1618, in *The Letters of John Chamberlain*, ed. Norman Egbert McClure (Philadelphia, 1939), 2:188.

4. Pory to Sir Dudley Carleton, 28 Nov. 1618, in William S. Powell, *John Pory, 1572–1636: The Life and Letters of a Man of Many Parts, Letters and Other Minor Writings* (Chapel Hill, 1977), 74–75.

5. The date when Yeardley issued his writs is based on an approximation in John Smith, *The Generall History of Virginia, New-England, and the Summer Iles . . .* (1624), Fourth Book, in *The Complete Works of Captain John Smith (1580–1631) in Three Volumes*, ed. Philip L. Barbour (Chapel Hill, 1986), 2:267. No copy of Yeardley's writ survives, but a text of its probable wording, quoted here, survives in Kingsbury, *Records of the Virginia Company*, 4:448–449.

6. No official transcript, that is one signed and sealed by the officers of the General Assembly, remains. Pory, in all likelihood, produced such a document in his capacity as secretary of the colony, but it went missing centuries ago. That record formed the basis of his "reporte," copies of which he sent abroad. One of the latter eventually came to rest in the Public Record Office in London, but it was forgotten until the 1850s, when Conway Robinson—a founder of the Virginia Historical Society and dedicated antiquarian—noted its existence. Thereafter, the historian George Bancroft secured a transcript, which he annotated and published in 1857 (Bancroft, ed., "Introductory Note to Proceedings of the First Assembly in Virginia, 1619,"

Collections of the New-York Historical Society, 2d ser., 3 [1857]: 331–334). Subsequent printings occurred in 1874 and 1907 (Powell, *John Pory*, 96). The most recent and best rendering from the manuscript is *Proceedings of the General Assembly*, which reproduces Pory's text in both facsimile and print. It is the source of the quotations employed throughout this chapter.

7. Powell, *John Pory*, 25–30.

8. *Proceedings of the General Assembly*, 15–17.

9. Cay, comp., *Abridgment*, s.v. "oaths"; Hakewill, *Modus tenendi Parliamentum*, 12, 15–20; Henry Elsynge, comp., *The Ancient Method and Manner of Holding Parliaments in England*, 4th ed. (London, 1679), 147–156, 166–181. Pory was present in the Commons in 1610 when the members debated at length the role of the Speaker. Mary Patterson Clarke, *Parliamentary Privilege in the American Colonies* (New Haven, Conn., 1943), 61–92; Wallace Notestein, *The House of Commons, 1604–1610* (New Haven, Conn., 1971), passim.

10. Kukla, *Political Institutions*, 51–52.

11. See, for example, Bruce, *Institutional History*, 2:403–407; Thomas J. Wertenbaker, *Virginia under the Stuarts, 1607–1688* (Princeton, N.J., 1914), 36–39; Wesley Frank Craven, "... And So the Form of Government Became Perfect," *VMHB* 77 (1969): 131–145.

12. *Proceedings of the General Assembly*, 17–19.

13. Ibid., 19 (1st quotation)–25, 37 (2d quotation).

14. John Hatsell, comp., *Precedents of Proceedings in the House of Commons: With Observations* (London, 1785), 1:120–129; Clarke, *Parliamentary Privilege*, 132.

15. *Proceedings of the General Assembly*, 25 (quotation); Notestein, *House of Commons*, passim.

16. The foregoing account derives mainly from Craven, *Dissolution*, 148–336, Billings, Selby, and Tate, *Colonial Virginia*, 41–45, and Rabb, *Jacobean Gentleman*, 353–389. A modern facsimile of the proclamation is *A Proclamation for setling the Plantation of Virginia, 1625*, ed. Thomas Cary Johnson Jr. (Charlottesville, 1946). Ironically, the king sealed the proclamation on 13 May, which was the eighteenth anniversary of the day the first settlers landed on Jamestown Island. The London printers Bonham Norton and John Bill issued it in broadside in a single edition of an unknown quantity soon thereafter. John Cook Wyllie, "The Printing of the Proclamation," in Johnson, *Proclamation*, 31–38.

17. Johnson, *Proclamation*, [27], [29].

18. Kevin Sharpe, *The Personal Rule of Charles I* (New Haven, Conn., 1992), 3–62; Alison Plowden, *Henrietta Maria: Charles I's Indomitable Queen* (Thrupp, Stroud, Gloucestershire, Eng., 2001), 1–53.

19. Although Yeardley prorogued the first General Assembly to 1 Mar. 1620, he subsequently dissolved it (*Proceedings of the General Assembly*, 71). There are no records of a session in 1620, but the historian Robert Beverley writing in 1705 observed that "Burgesses met the Governour and Council at James-Town in May 1620." Given that his father, his brother, and he were all clerks of the House of Burgesses, his statement assumes some credibility on its face because he had access to documents now lost. However, the remark is a bit suspect, because he styled this meeting "The First General Assembly that ever was held there" (Beverley, *History*, 48). The latter mistake, plus the absence of any acts, caused William Waller Hening to aver it was "extremely doubtful whether such an assembly was, in fact, ever held" (Hening, *Statutes*, 1:119). Circumstantial evidence suggests it was improbable that a May 1620 assembly actually convened. The next session for which a record remains was the General Assembly of 1621 (Hening, *Statutes*, 1:119). So far as known, there was no meeting in 1622, perhaps because of the onset of war with the natives, so the assembly seems not to have convened again until Mar. 1623/24. Hening, *Statutes*, 1:121.

20. Hening, *Statutes*, 1:128 (1st quotation); Robert Johnson, "The Humble Petition of the Sundry Adventurers and Planters of the Virginia and Summer Ilands Plantations," and Nathaniel Butler, "The Unmasked Face of Our Colony in Virginia as it was in the Winter of the Yeare 1622," Kingsbury, *Records of the Virginia Company*, 2:372–376; *Journals of the House of Burgesses, 1619–1658/59*, 21–25, 25–26 (2d–7th quotations), 27 (8th quotation).

21. Commission to Sir Francis Wyatt, 26 Aug. 1624, *WMQ*, 2d ser., 8 (1928): 161 (1st quotation)–163 (3d–5th quotations); *Minutes of Council and General Court*, 56 (2d quotation); Charles M. Andrews, *The Colonial Period of American History* (New Haven, Conn., 1934), 1:193–195; Petition to James I, May 1625, *Journals of the House of Burgesses, 1619–1658/59*, 43–44; "Divers heads wherin the Lords are to be moved," May 1625, *WMQ*, 2d ser., 8 (1928): 161–163, esp. 162. Andrews, *Colonial Period*, 1:194, and H. R. McIlwaine in an editorial note in *Journals of the House of Burgesses, 1619–1658/59*, xxx, contend that the session was a "convention," not an assembly. The basis of that claim seemed to rest on the assumption that because James I had not warranted the assembly, Wyatt was powerless to call one. That reading, as Jon Kukla has noted, ignored the general provision in Wyatt's commission that enabled him to act as he had under the company's authority. Kukla, *Political Institutions*, 72–75.

22. *Minutes of Council and General Court*, 104–107, 120 (quotation on 105). Wyatt was out of office on or about 28 July 1626, which was the first day Yeardley presided at the Council as governor. Ibid., 104.

23. Ibid., 107–157; commission to Sir George Yeardley, 14 Mar. 1625/26, Conway Robinson Papers, ViHi.

24. Yeardley died on an unrecorded date and was buried on 13 Nov. 1627. *Minutes of Council and General Court*, 157.

25. The Council elected West acting governor on 14 Nov. 1627 (ibid.); Sir Robert Heath to governor, Council, and burgesses, 1627, and Francis West and the Council of State to the Privy Council, 20 Dec. 1627, CO 1/4, fols. 86, 88–89, PRO; Kukla, *Political Institutions*, 76–79; *Minutes of Council and General Court*, 168; *Journals of the House of Burgesses, 1619–1658/59*, 44–51, 121–124.

26. Michael Strachan, *Sir Thomas Roe, 1581–1644: A Life* (Salisbury, Wiltshire, Eng., 1989), 221; Petition to the Privy Council, 6 Mar. 1631/32, Virginia Papers, Sackville Mss 712/2, Cambridge; Kukla, *Political Institutions*, 81–95; Instructions to Sir Francis Wyatt, 11 Jan. 1638/39. Wyatt's instructions are lost, but they were exactly the same as those to Sir William Berkeley in Aug. 1641, and it is the latter from which the quotation derives. Instructions to Sir William Berkeley, 10 Aug. 1641, CO 5/1354, fols. 224–241, PRO.

27. Hening, *Statutes*, 1:179–180. The other revisions occurred in 1643, 1652, 1658, and 1662.

28. Hening, *Statutes*, 1:122–124 (2d quotation), 125 (1st quotation), 126, 128, 139–146, 155–163, 171, 172, 196, 224; Warren M. Billings, "The Growth of Political Institutions in Virginia, 1634 to 1676," *WMQ*, 3d ser., 31 (1974): 225–242.

29. 6 Will. & Mar., cap. 2; Cay, comp., *Abridgment*, 2: s.v. "Parliament."

30. *Minutes of Council and General Court*, 55–56, 168.

31. Leonard, *General Assembly Register*, 12; Hening, *Statutes*, 1:224.

32. *Proceedings of the General Assembly*, 51, 53, 63–67; Kukla, *Political Institutions*, 59–63.

33. The Council of State in its judicial capacity was known as the "Quarter Court" from 1624 to 1662 because it sat four times a year. The General Assembly changed the name to General Court in 1662 because that name more accurately described the court's jurisdiction. That distinction is maintained throughout this book.

34. Warren M. Billings, "Pleading, Procedure, and Practice: The Meaning of Due Process of Law in Seventeenth-Century Virginia," *Journal of Southern History* 47 (1981): 569–584; *Elizabeth Key v. the executors of John Mottrom*, in Billings, *Old Dominion*, 165–169.

35. Hening, *Statutes*, 1:162.

36. Edmund S. Morgan, *American Slavery, American Freedom: The Ordeal of Colonial Virginia* (New York, 1975), 412; A List of the Nomber of men women and children Inhabitinge in the severall Counties within the Colony of Virginia. Anno Domini

1634, CO 1/8, fol. 155, PRO; Jon Kukla, "Order and Chaos in Early America: Political and Social Stability in Pre-Restoration Virginia," *AHR* 90 (1985): 287.

37. Robert Paul Brenner, "Commercial Change and Political Conflict: The Merchant Community in Civil War England" (Ph.D. diss., Princeton University, 1970), 97–131; Richard Ernest Jenkins Jr., "The First Administration of Sir John Harvey, Royal Governor of Virginia, 1630–1635" (master's thesis, University of Virginia, 1967), 20–71; Kukla, *Political Institutions*, 82–92.

38. Samuel Mathews to Sir John Wolstenholme, 25 May 1635, and Sir John Harvey to the Privy Council, 1635, *VMHB* I (1894): 416–424, 425–430; Jenkins, "The First Administration of Sir John Harvey," 71–89; J. Mills Thornton, "The Thrusting Out of Governor Harvey: A Seventeenth-Century Rebellion," *VMHB* 76 (1968): 11–26.

39. John R. Pagan, "Dutch Maritime and Commercial Activity in Mid-Seventeenth Century Virginia," *VMHB* 90 (1982): 484–488; Kukla, *Political Institutions*, 98–99.

40. *Minutes of Council and General Court*, 473 (1st quotation)–474, 482 (2d quotation), 483, 494–497.

41. Ibid., 473; Billings, "Political Institutions in Virginia," 238–230; Kukla, "Order and Chaos in Early America," 285–289.

42. *Minutes of Council and General Court*, 498; Commission to Berkeley, 10 Aug. 1641, C 66/2895, PRO.

43. *Dictionary of Virginia Biography*, s.v. "Berkeley, Sir William," 1:455.

44. Articles of agreement with Sir Francis Wyatt, 4 Sept. 1641, Main Papers, 1620–1714, p. 100, HLRO.

CHAPTER 2: LITTLE PARLIAMENT

1. Warren M. Billings, "Vignettes of Jamestown," *Virginia Cavalcade* 45 (1996): 171–173.

2. *Dictionary of Virginia Biography*, s.v. "Berkeley, Sir William," 1:455; Land Patent Book No. 1, Pt. 2, 1637–1643, p. 771, LVA.

3. *Journals of the House of Burgesses, 1619–1658/59*, 66 (quotation); Craven, *Southern Colonies*, 151–153; Richard L. Morton, *Colonial Virginia* (Chapel Hill, 1960), 1:147–148; Richard Beale Davis, *George Sandys, Poet-Adventurer: A Study in Anglo-American Culture in the Seventeenth Century* (London, 1955), 257–264; Kukla, *Political Institutions*, 106–107.

4. Printed texts of the Declaration appear in Hening, *Statutes*, 1:230–236; and *Journals of the House of Burgesses, 1619–1658/59*, 66–69. The Hening rendition derives

from eighteenth-century transcripts at DLC and ViHi, and the *Journals* reprints the Hening version. References here are to the text in Randolph MSS, ViHi.

5. "Declaration against the Virginia Company," n.p., Randolph MSS. Charles I responded to the Declaration, saying that "Wee had not before the least intention to consent to the Introduction of any Company over that Our Colony." Charles I to Berkeley and the Council of State, 5 July 1642, CO 5/1354, fol. 242, PRO.

6. "Declaration against the Virginia Company," Randolph MSS.

7. *Journals of the House of Burgesses, 1619–1658/59*, 69 (quotation); Hening, *Statutes*, 1:267.

8. Hening, *Statutes*, 1:236–282; Kukla, *Political Institutions*, 108–119; Warren M. Billings, "The Growth of Political Institutions in Virginia, 1634 to 1676," *WMQ*, 3d ser., 31 (1974): 229–230; Kukla, *Speakers and Clerks*, 35–37. Stegge left the Council after its Aug. meeting, but Berkeley evidently reappointed him after his stint as Speaker because by 1647 Stegge was attending Council sessions again (LNDWO, 1637–1646, fol. 238; LNOB, 1646–1650, fols. 70, 112). Charles II named Stegge councillor when he commissioned Berkeley in 1650, but by then Stegge had returned to England to assist Parliament in bringing Virginia to heel. Commission to Berkeley, 3 June 1650, CO 5/1354, fols. 243–252, PRO.

9. William G. Stanard and Mary Newton Stanard, comps., *The Virginia Colonial Register. A List of Governors, Councillors and Other Higher Officials, and also of Members of the House of Burgesses* ... (Albany, N.Y., 1902), 24.

10. Billings, "Growth of Political Institutions," 230–245; Billings, "The Transfer of English Law to Virginia, 1606–50," in *The Westward Enterprise: English Activities in Ireland, the Atlantic, and America, 1480–1650*, ed. K. R. Andrews, N. P. Canny, and P. E. H. Hair (Liverpool, 1978), 226–242.

11. *Journals of the House of Burgesses, 1619–1658/59*, 74 (quotation); Warren M. Billings, "Sir William Berkeley and the Diversification of the Virginia Economy," *VMHB* 104 (1996): 433–454 (hereafter cited as Billings, "Berkeley and Diversification"); John R. Pagan, "Dutch Maritime and Commercial Activity in Mid-Seventeenth-Century Virginia," *VMHB* 90 (1982): 485–501; Hening, *Statutes*, 1:258; Declaration concerning the Dutch trade, 5 Apr. 1647, Acts of Assembly, 1642–1647, pp. 109–111, Acc. 21227, State Government Records Collection, LVA; An Ordinance for encouragement of Adventurers to the several Plantations of Virginia, Bermudas, Barbados, and other places of America, 23 Jan. 1646/47, *Acts and Ordinances of the Interregnum, 1642–1660*, ed. C. H. Firth and R. S. Rait (London, 1911), 1:912.

12. Act authorizing Berkeley's return to England, 1 June 1644, Acts of Assembly, 1644, LVA; commission to William Claiborne, 1 June 1644, "Acts, Orders and

Resolutions of the General Assembly of Virginia: At the Sessions of March 1643–1646," *VMHB* 22 (1915): 229–234; Robinson, "Notes," 292.

13. *Court Mercurie*, 11 Sept. 1644; Berkeley to Francis Moryson, 11 Feb. 1676/77, Coventry Papers, 77, fol. 426.

14. William L. Shea, "Virginia at War, 1644–1646," *Military Affairs* 41 (1977): 142–147; Hening, *Statutes*, 1:317–319, 323–326; Beverley, *History*, 61–62.

15. Instructions from Charles I, 10 Aug. 1641, CO 5/1354, fols. 221–242, PRO; Hening, *Statutes*, 1:240–243, 290, 309–310, 341–342; Joseph Frank, ed., "News From Virginny, 1644," *VMHB* 65 (1957): 85; Bruce, *Institutional History*, 1:253–258; John H. Latané, *The Early Relations Between Maryland and Virginia*, in *Johns Hopkins University Studies in Historical and Political Science*, ed. Herbert Baxter Adams, 13th ser., 3–4 (1895): 41–44; Edward L. Bond, *Damned Souls in a Tobacco Colony: Religion in Seventeenth-Century Virginia* (Macon, Ga., 2000), 93–176.

16. Parliamentary Council of State to Berkeley, 26 July 1649, SP 25/94, PRO; abstract of a letter from Charles II to Berkeley, ca. 23 Sept. 1649, Pepysian Library 2504, Magdalene College, Cambridge; Hening, *Statutes*, 1:359–361. No text of Berkeley's remonstrance is extant, but a reference to its content occurs in an order-in-council of 14 Dec. 1649, SP 25/3, PRO.

17. Order-in-council, 14 Dec. 1649, SP 25/3, PRO; order-in-council, 10 Aug. 1650, SP 25/8, PRO; An Act for prohibiting Trade with the Barbadoes, Virginia, Bermuda and Antego, 3 Oct. 1650, Firth and Rait, *Acts and Ordinances of the Interregnum*, 2:425–429.

18. Berkeley, *The Speech of the Honourable Sr. William Berkeley Governour and Capt. Generall of Virginea, to the Burgesses in the Grand Assembly at James Towne on the 17. of March, 1650/1 …* (The Hague, 1651). The printing of the original pamphlet was done by Samuel Browne, an English printer who lived in The Hague and whose brother Thomas was chaplain to Charles II. Only four copies of the pamphlet are extant. Three are English texts, and they reside, respectively, at the libraries of Trinity College, Dublin, and the cathedrals of Salisbury and Lincoln. A Dutch version belongs to the University of Leiden.

19. Worsley, "A Memorandum of the Virginia Plantation," ca. Feb. 1649, Worsley, "Further Animadversions about Virginia," n.d., Worsley to William Strickland, and Strickland to Sir Henry Vane, 2 Sept. [1651?], Samuel Hartlib Papers, bundle 61, pieces 5–7, University of Sheffield, Sheffield.

20. Commission and instructions to Robert Dennis et al., 26 Sept. 1651, SP 25/22, fols. 82–88, PRO; Charles M. Andrews, *The Colonial Period of American History*

(New Haven, Conn., 1934–1938), 4:34–46; An Act for increase of Shipping, and Encouragement of the Navigation of this Nation, 9 Oct. 1651, Firth and Rait, *Acts and Ordinances of the Interregnum*, 2:559–562.

21. "Report of the Commissioners," *VMHB* 11 (1903): 32–35.

22. Berkeley to Charles II, 14 May 1652, Clarendon Papers, 43, fols. 111–112; Articles for the surrendering of Virginia to the subjection of the Parliament of the Commonwealth of England agreed upon by the Honorable the Governor and Councel of State; And the Honorable the Commissioners for the Parliament, 12 Mar. 1651/52, Randolph MSS; Articles for the Surrender of the Country, 12 Mar. 1651/52, CO 1/11, fols. 129–130, PRO; Morton, *Colonial Virginia*, 1:168–173; Kukla, *Political Institutions*, 148–157. The messenger who bore Berkeley's letter to Charles II was his military attaché Col. Francis Lovelace, later governor of New York.

23. The assembly met twice in 1645, 1646, and 1648, and once in 1647 and 1651 (Leonard, *General Assembly Register*, 22–28); LNDWO, 1637–1646, fol. 161; LNDWO, 1646–1651, fols. 53, 88, 103, 154, 190; Warren M. Billings, ed., "Some Acts Not in Hening's *Statutes*: The Acts of Assembly, April 1652, November 1652, and July 1653," *VMHB* 83 (1975): 67–68, 68–69.

24. Henry Elsynge, *The Ancient Method and Manner of Holding Parliaments in England*, 4th ed. (London, 1679), 1–108; Elizabeth Read Foster, *The House of Lords, 1603–1649: Structure, Procedure, and the Nature of Its Business* (Chapel Hill, 1983), 1–203.

25. Berkeley named Richard Lee the colony's first attorney general in October 1643. Robinson, "Notes," 234.

26. *Administrators of John Clarke v. Robert Higginson*, 20 Mar. 1645/46, YDWO, No. 2, 1645–1649, 122; Beverley, *History*, 240; Bruce, *Institutional History*, 1:665–689, 2:374–376; Ira Vernon Brown, "The Governor's Council in Colonial Virginia, 1607–1689" (master's thesis, University of Virginia, 1942).

27. Kukla, *Political Institutions*, 144–148.

28. Hening, *Statutes*, 1:263 (1st quotation), 264, 267 (2d quotation), 299–300 (3d quotation).

29. *Journals of the House of Burgesses, 1619–1658/59*, 73 (1st–2d quotations), 84 (3d–4th quotations), 86, 97, 108, 117. The fact that the House ordered Burroughs to acknowledge his misdeed "likewyse in the two parish Churches, in the County of Lower Norfolk, in the tyme of divine service" suggests a sexual indiscretion of some sort. That supposition gains weight because Burroughs had been prosecuted in the county court on similar charges on earlier occasions. LNOB, 1637–1646, fols. 85, 100, 101, 113–114, 117, 122.

30. LNDWO, 1646–1656, 7.

31. Billings, "Acts Not in Hening's *Statutes*," 27–72.

32. *Journals of the House of Burgesses, 1619–1658/59*, 82 (copy of oath), 83.

33. Kukla, *Political Institutions*, 169–180.

34. Robinson, "Notes," 243; Morton, *Colonial Virginia*, 1:180.

35. Hening, *Statutes*, 1:495–505 (quotations); Morton, *Colonial Virginia*, 1:179–183; Kukla, *Political Institutions*, 192–204; Acts of Assembly, Mar. 1657/58, Sir Hans Sloane MSS 1378, fol. 231, BL.

36. Josef Redlich, *The Procedure of the House of Commons: A Study of Its History and Present Form*, trans. A. Ernest Steinthal (London, 1908), 1:6–51; William Hakewill, comp., *The Manner How Statutes are enacted in Parliament by Passing of Bills* (London, 1659), 131–178. Printers issued such works as duodecimo volumes, which made them fit conveniently in an owner's hand or pocket for ready reference. That fact adds additional credence to the arguments of Conrad Russell, *Parliaments and English Politics, 1621–1629* (Oxford, 1979), and Derek Hirst, *The Representative of the People?: Voters and Voting in England Under the Early Stuarts* (Cambridge, 1975), both of whom make the case for engaged Stuart Englishmen who were keenly aware of parliamentary procedures. Works like Hakewill's experienced heavy use. I own a copy that contains copious notes in a seventeenth-century hand, its pages are frayed from constant turning, and it has been rebound more than once. Other copies eventually wore out, which accounts for the now relative rarity of those useful little volumes.

37. Harry Clemons, ed., "Some Jefferson Manuscript Memoranda of Colonial Virginia Records," in *Minutes of Council and General Court*, 557 (quotation); Wilbur Samuel Howell, ed., *Jefferson's Parliamentary Writings: "Parliamentary Pocket-Book" and A Manual of Parliamentary Practice* in *The Papers of Thomas Jefferson*, 2d ser., ed. Julian P. Boyd et al. (Princeton, N.J., 1988), 41–46, and passim (esp. 147).

38. John Hatsell, comp., *Precedents of Proceedings in the House of Commons: With Observations* (London, 1785), 2:166–175; Hening, *Statutes*, 1:507–508 (quotation).

39. *Journals of the House of Burgesses, 1619–1658/59*, 93.

40. See, for example, Hatsell, *Precedents of Proceedings*, 1:92–95, 188–189.

41. *Journals of the House of Burgesses, 1619–1658/59*, 82–131; Warren M. Billings, ed., "*Temple v. Gerard*, 1667–1668: An Example of Appellate Practice in Colonial Virginia," *VMHB* 94 (1986): 92.

42. *Journals of the House of Burgesses, 1619–1658/59*, 95, 99, 101, 106–109, 116–117; Kukla, *Political Institutions*, 186–189; Hakewill, *Manner How Statutes are Enacted in Parliament*, 146.

43. Kukla, *Political Institutions*, 204.

44. Henry Lawrence to Samuel Mathews and the Council of State, 7 Sept. 1658, *Journals of the House of Burgesses, 1619–1658/59*, 115.

45. *Journals of the House of Burgesses, 1619–1658/59*, 116.

46. Ronald Hutton, *The Restoration: A Political and Religious History of England and Wales, 1658–1667* (Oxford, 1985), 3–123; Craven, *Southern Colonies*, 264–265; Morton, *Colonial Virginia*, 1:184–187.

47. John Frederick Dorman, "Governor Samuel Mathews, Jr.," *VMHB* 74 (1966): 429–432.

48. That warrant was included in the Crown's instructions to the governors-general. The first time the Council exercised the power was when Sir George Yeardley died and it replaced him with Francis West. *Minutes of Council and General Court*, 157.

49. Hening, *Statutes*, 1:517.

50. Warren M. Billings, "The Return of Sir William Berkeley," *Virginia Cavalcade* 47 (1998): 100–109; Hening, *Statutes*, 1:530 (quotation).

51. Billings, "Return of Sir William Berkeley," 100–109.

52. Commission from Charles II, 30 July 1660, C66/2941, PRO; proclamation of the accession of Charles II, 20 Sept. 1660, and proclamation continuing the commissions of all civil and military officers, 20 Sept. 1660, SDWI, 1652–1672, fol. 157.

53. Jon Kukla, ed., "Some Acts Not in Hening's *Statutes*: The Acts of Assembly, October 1660," *VMHB* 83 (1975): 86–87, 88, 90–91, 92–93.

54. Leonard, *General Assembly Register*, 37–40.

55. The phrase is from Thomas J. Wertenbaker, *Virginia under the Stuarts, 1607–1688* (Princeton, N.J., 1914), 136. Others have followed his argument that Berkeley had corrupted the burgesses, for example, Morton, *Colonial Virginia*, 1:220–223; Edmund S. Morgan, *American Slavery, American Freedom: The Ordeal of Colonial Virginia* (New York, 1975), 247–249; Stephen Saunders Webb, *1676: The End of American Independence* (New York, 1984), 25, 129, 136, 204.

56. Billings, "Growth of Political Institutions in Virginia," 232–240; Hening, *Statutes*, 2:17–340.

57. Authorization to return to England, 23 Mar. 1660/61, Hening, *Statutes*, 2:17 (quotation); Billings, "Berkeley and Diversification," 446–449.

58. Hening, *Statutes*, 2:21. Although county magistrates were customarily called "justices," they were statutorily designated "commissioners of the peace" until Mar. 1661/62. Hening, *Statutes*, 2:70.

59. Ibid., 2:21.

60. Ibid., 2:20 (3d–5th quotations), 21, 22–23 (2d quotation); *Journals of the House of Burgesses, 1659/60–1693*, 13 (1st quotation).

61. *Journals of the House of Burgesses, 1659/60–1693*, 11 (quotation); commission from Charles II, 30 July 1660, and commission naming Francis Moryson deputy governor of Virginia, 11 May 1661, LNDWI, 1654–1702, pp. 220–221; Kukla, *Speakers and Clerks*, 54–57, 140.

62. There are two printed versions of the revisal. One is in Hening, *Statutes*, 2:41–148; the other is Francis Moryson, comp., *The Lawes of Virginia now in Force* ... (London, 1662), the publication of which Berkeley arranged while he was in England.

63. Hening, *Statutes*, 2:41–148, esp. 108 (quotations).

64. *Journals of the House of Burgesses, 1659/60–1693*, 21–51.

65. Billings, "Berkeley and Diversification," 449–454.

66. *Dictionary of Virginia Biography*, s.v. "Berkeley, Sir William," 1:456.

67. "An act for the safeguard and defence of the country against the Indians," Hening, *Statutes*, 2:326–336.

68. Proclamation suspending Nathaniel Bacon, Jr., from all offices, 10 May 1676, CO 1/37, fol. 2, PRO; Election writ, 10 May 1676, Letters and Documents of Sir William Berkeley, 1608–1677, Mss 2596-a, ViU; Declaration and Remonstrance of Sir William Berkeley, 29 May 1676, and Berkeley to Henry Coventry, 3 June 1676, Coventry Papers, 77, fols. 103, 157–158.

69. Warren M. Billings, "'Virginias Deploured Condition,' 1660–1676: The Coming of Bacon's Rebellion" (Ph.D. diss., Northern Illinois University, 1968), Appendix II; Leonard, *General Assembly Register*, 41; Berkeley to Thomas Ludwell, 1 Apr. 1676, CO 1/36, fols. 67–68, PRO (1st quotation); *Journals of the House of Burgesses, 1659/60–1693*, 66 (2d quotation).

70. Billings, Selby, and Tate, *Colonial Virginia*, 76–96.

CHAPTER 3: NEW REALITIES

1. Charles M. Andrews, *The Colonial Period of American History*, vol. 4 (New Haven, Conn., 1934–1938); Andrews, *British Committees, Commissions, and Councils of Trade and Plantations, 1622–1675*, in *Johns Hopkins University Studies in Historical and Political Sciences*, ser. 26, nos. 1–3 (Baltimore, 1908); Wilcomb E. Washburn, *The Effects of Bacon's*

Rebellion on Government in England and Virginia, Smithsonian Institution *Bulletin* 225 (Washington, D.C., 1962); John C. Rainbolt, "A New Look at Stuart 'Tyranny': The Crown's Attack on the Virginia Assembly, 1676–1689," *VMHB* 75 (1967): 387–406; David S. Lovejoy, *The Glorious Revolution in America* (New York, 1972), 1–20; Stephen Saunders Webb, *The Governors-General: The English Army and the Definition of Empire, 1569–1681* (Chapel Hill, 1979), 57–100; J. M. Sosin, *English America and the Restoration Monarchy of Charles II: Transatlantic Politics, Commerce, and Kinship* (Lincoln, Neb., 1980), 5–91; Jack P. Greene, *Peripheries and Center: Constitutional Developments in the Extended Polities of the British Empire and the United States, 1607–1788* (Athens, Ga., 1986), 7–18.

2. Webb, *Governors-General*, 346–364; Wilcomb E. Washburn, *The Governor and the Rebel: A History of Bacon's Rebellion in Virginia* (Chapel Hill, 1957), 92–138; Berkeley to Charles II, ca. 16 June 1677, CO 1/40, fol. 244, PRO.

3. A Proclamation for the Suppressing a Rebellion lately raised within the Plantation of Virginia, 27 Oct. 1676, Coventry Papers, 77, fols. 263–265.

4. Sir John Berry, Herbert Jeffreys, and Francis Moryson to Sir William Berkeley and the General Assembly, 27 Feb. 1676/77, Samuel Wiseman Papers, Pepysian Library 2582, Magdalene College, Cambridge.

5. Some of these grievances are printed in *Journals of the House of Burgesses, 1659/60–1693*, 99–113. Contemporary file copies reside in CO 1/39, fols. 194–255, and CO 5/1371, fols. 149–169, PRO. The commissioners completed their report in July 1677, and it was presented to the Privy Council in Oct. CO 5/1371, fols. 188–205, PRO, printed in Charles M. Andrews, ed., *Narratives of the Insurrections, 1675–1690* (New York, 1915), 105–141.

6. Jeffreys to Henry Coventry, 2 Apr. 1678, Coventry Papers, 78, fols. 216–218.

7. John C. Rainbolt, "The Alteration in the Relationship Between Leadership and Constituents in Virginia, 1660 to 1720," *WMQ*, 3d ser., 27 (1970): 411–435; Edmund S. Morgan, *American Slavery, American Freedom: The Ordeal of Colonial Virginia* (New York, 1975), 316–339; cf. Kathleen M. Brown, *Good Wives, Nasty Wenches, and Anxious Patriarchs: Gender, Race, and Power in Colonial Virginia* (Chapel Hill, 1996), 167–186.

8. Warren M. Billings, *Virginia's Viceroy, Their Majesties' Governor General: Francis Howard, Baron Howard of Effingham* (Fairfax, Va., 1991), 24–32, 113–115.

9. Additional instructions from Charles II, 13 Oct. 1676, CO 5/1355, pp. 111–114, PRO.

10. Berry, Jeffreys, and Moryson to Berkeley and the General Assembly, 27 Feb. 1676/77, Wiseman Papers.

11. Berry, Jeffreys, and Moryson to Sir Joseph Williamson, 13 Apr. 1677, CO 5/1371, fol. 103, PRO.

12. Order-in-council, 30 Oct. 1678, CO 1/42, fol. 356, PRO.

13. Henry Coventry to Herbert Jeffreys, 5 Dec. 1678, Add. MSS 25120, fol. 136, BL; instructions to Culpeper, 5 Dec. 1679, CO 1/47, fols. 273–275, PRO.

14. *Journals of the House of Burgesses, 1659/60–1693*, 130 (quotation)–131, 132–136; "An act for raising a publique revenue for the better support of the government of this his majesties colony," Hening, *Statutes*, 2:466–469. Charles II subsequently disallowed both provisos.

15. Hening, *Statutes*, 2:24 (quotation), 85–86.

16. *Journals of the House of Burgesses, 1659/60–1693*, 147 (quotation), 169.

17. Spencer to the Lords of Trade, 20 Mar. 1682/83, CO 1/51, fol. 173, PRO.

18. Additional instructions to Effingham, 3 Dec. 1683, *Effingham Papers*, 43.

19. *Adventurers of Purse and Person*, 124–132; Neville Williams, "The Tribulations of John Bland, Merchant: London, Seville, Jamestown, Tangier, 1643–1680," *VMHB* 72 (1964): 19–41; affidavit of John Bland, ca. 1676, CO 1/36, fol. 140, PRO; *Dictionary of Virginia Biography*, s.v. "Bland, Anna Bennett," "Bland, Giles," 2:1–3, 7–8; *Minutes of Council and General Court*, 394, 448–449; *Executive Journals of Council*, 1:1; commission to Lord Culpeper, 6 Dec. 1679, CO 5/1355, fol. 349, PRO.

20. *Journals of the House of Burgesses, 1659/60–1693*, 122–123.

21. Ibid., 159.

22. *Legislative Journals of Council*, 1:30–33.

23. Clause 60, Instructions from Charles II, 24 Oct. 1683, and Blathwayt to Effingham, 17 Nov. 1683, *Effingham Papers*, 25, 36; minutes of Council meeting, 21 Feb. 1683/84, Monson Family Papers, DLC; Effingham to Blathwayt, 23 Apr. 1684, *Effingham Papers*, 84; *Executive Journals of Council*, 57–58.

24. *Journals of the House of Burgesses, 1659/60–1693*, 196.

25. *Legislative Journals of Council*, 1:59–60.

26. *Journals of the House of Burgesses, 1659/60–1693*, 197.

27. Ibid., 202.

28. Ibid., 202 (quotation), 228, 249; petition to Charles II, CO 5/1356, pp. 299–301, PRO; proclamation repealing five acts of assembly, 19 June 1684, *Effingham Papers*, 119–121; "Appeales how to be made," Hening, *Statutes*, 2:65.

29. *Journals of the House of Burgesses, 1659/60–1693*, 204.

30. *Records of the Virginia Company*, 3:68–69, 69–70, 93.

31. Ibid., 3:658–660, 4:18, 129–130, 167–168, 172–173, 271–273, 275–276, 283–284, 569–570; *Minutes of Council and General Court*, 5, 103, 105, 107, 141, 167; NoOB, 1640–1646, fols. 49–50; "The Church in Lower Norfolk County," *Lower Norfolk County Virginia Antiquary* 2 (1897): 14–15; Hening, *Statutes*, 1:166, 447, 2:108.

32. Robert Steele, ed., *A Bibliography of Royal Proclamations of the Tudor and Stuart Sovereigns* ..., 2 vols. (Oxford, 1910).

33. Billings, *Virginia's Viceroy*, 65–69; proclamation repealing five acts of assembly, 19 June 1684; order concerning the use of the seal of the colony, 25 Apr. 1685; proclamation repealing three acts of the General Assembly, 22 Feb. 1685/86; proclamation concerning parish registers, 8 July 1686; proclamation repealing an act of assembly, 15 Dec. 1686, all *Effingham Papers*, 119–121, 196–197, 243–244, 261–263, 274–275.

34. Sir Henry Chicheley to Sir Leoline Jenkins, 8 May 1682, Nicholas Spencer to Jenkins, 8 May 1682, Further representations of Lord Culpeper, 20 Sept. 1683, CO 1/1356, pp. 66–69, 74–79, 155–160, PRO; Hening, *Statutes*, 3:543–571; *Executive Journals of Council*, 1:55 (quotation), 498–499.

35. Billings, *Virginia's Viceroy*, 62–65; journal of the House of Burgesses, 1 Oct., 2 Nov.–13 Dec. 1685, 25, 30, 33, 41, 46, 48–49, 53, 57, Monson Family Papers, DLC. This unpublished text belonged to Effingham and was among the papers that the Monson family deposited at the Library of Congress in the 1950s. Consequently, H. R. McIlwaine believed that "the Journal of the House for this session has not been preserved." *Journals of the House of Burgesses, 1659/60–1693*, xlix.

36. Effingham to the Privy Council, 10 Feb. 1685/86; Effingham to James II, 20 Feb. 1685/86; Effingham to Robert Spencer, earl of Sunderland, 20 Feb. 1685/86; James II to Effingham, 1 Aug. 1686, all *Effingham Papers*, 237–241 (1st quotation on 239), 241–242, 263–264 (2d quotation).

37. *Journals of the House of Burgesses, 1659/60–1693*, 287; commission to Francis Page, 24 Apr. 1688, *Effingham Papers*, 371 (quotation); Billings, *Virginia's Viceroy*, 89–91.

38. Billings, *Virginia's Viceroy*, 81–88, 93–95.

39. Beverley, *History*, 97.

40. Commission from Charles II, 28 Sept. 1683, *Effingham Papers*, 11.

41. Billings, *Virginia's Viceroy*, 97–98.

42. By law, the Council sat as General Court in Apr. and Oct. (Hening, *Statutes*, 3:10). The Council met executively at the governor's call. To judge from the extant record, however, there were four regular meeting dates. Two coincided with General Court sessions, and the others usually took place in Feb. and July. *Executive Journals of Council*, 1:1–274.

43. Billings, Selby, and Tate, *Colonial Virginia*, 139–172.

44. Billings, *Virginia's Viceroy*, 96–97; Kukla, *Speakers and Clerks*, 92–94; P. Ludwell to the Council of Trade, read 30 Nov. 1689, CO 5/1305, fol. 73, PRO.

45. *Journals of the House of Burgesses, 1659/60–1693*, 133–134, 165–166, 197, 207, 228–230, 270, 304–305, 316–318; J. A. Leo Lemay, "Robert Beverley's *History and Present State of Virginia* and the Emerging American Political Ideology," in *American Letters and the Historical Consciousness: Essays in Honor of Lewis P. Simpson*, ed. J. Gerald Kennedy and Daniel Mark Fogel (Baton Rouge, La., 1987), 67–112, esp. 70, 100–102.

46. Jack P. Greene, *The Quest for Power: The Lower Houses of Assembly in the Southern Royal Colonies, 1689–1776* (Chapel Hill, 1963), 3–4.

CHAPTER 4: GOVERNORS-GENERAL

1. Beverley, *History*, 65–66, 77–85, 87–95 (3d quotation on 93), 95–97, 103–111 (4th quotation on 105), 238–240 (1st quotation on 238, 2d quotation on 239).

2. Letters patent from James I, 23 May 1609, in *The Three Charters of the Virginia Company of London, With Seven Related Documents, 1606–1621*, ed. Samuel M. Bemiss (Williamsburg, 1957), 52; Darrett B. Rutman, "The Virginia Company and Its Military Regime," in *The Old Dominion: Essays for Thomas Perkins Abernethy*, ed. Darrett B. Rutman (Charlottesville, 1964), 1–20; Kukla, *Political Institutions*, 8–17; Bruce, *Institutional History*, 2:300–309.

3. Sir Thomas Elyot, *The boke named the Governour, devised by Sr. Thomas Elyot, knight* (London, 1531), fols. 83–98, 102–106.

4. Elyot (1490–1546) modeled his work on Sir John Fortescue's treatise *A Learned Commendation of the Politique Lawes of England* (London, 1567) and also borrowed freely from Desiderius Erasmus's *Education of a Christian Prince (Institutio principis Christiani* published in London, 1515), Baldassare Castiglione's *Libro del Cortegiano* (completed in 1518 and published in Venice in 1528), and Francesco Patrizzi's *De Regno et Regis*

Institutione (Paris, 1567). If the number of editions is any measure of readership, then *The boke named the Governour* enjoyed considerable popularity with English readers, for it passed through ten editions before 1600 (*British Museum General Catalogue of Printed Books* [London, 1960], 61:338–339). Beyond that, Elyot anticipated the views of Sir Thomas Smith in his *De Republica Anglorum: The maner of Gouernement or policie of the Realme of England* ... (London, 1583), another widely read commentary on English polity. By the seventeenth century, echoes of Elyot resounded in works of popular writers such as Henry Peacham whose work *The Compleat Gentleman: Fashioning him absolute in the most necessary & commendable Qualities concerning Minde or Bodie that may be required in a Noble Gentleman* (London, 1622), and Richard Allestree whose volume *The Whole Duty of Man, Laid down In a Plain and Familiar Way for the Use of All, but especially for the meanest reader* (London, 1659, 1721) drew from Elyot. Indeed, Peacham actually acknowledged his debt to Elyot (*Compleat Gentleman*, "To my Reader"), which was rare, given the penchant of seventeenth-century authors for "borrowing" from others without attribution.

5. Elyot, *The boke named the Governour*, fol. 15.

6. Bruce, *Institutional History*, 2:316–331.

7. Contemporary file copies of the Yeardley and Wyatt documents are in the Coventry Papers, 76, fols. 1–45; those for Berkeley are in C 66/2895 and CO 5/1354, fols. 224–241, PRO.

8. Instructions to Sir William Berkeley, 13 Oct. 1676, CO 5/1355, fols. 111–114, PRO; commission and instructions to Thomas Culpeper, 2d baron Culpeper of Thoresway, 6 Dec. 1679, CO 5/1355, fols. 313–356, PRO; commission and instructions to Francis Howard, 5th baron Howard of Effingham, 28 Sept. and 24 Oct. 1683, *Effingham Papers*, 9–15, 16–31.

9. The originals of Sir Francis Wyatt's second commission (see Sandra Gioia Treadway and Edward D. C. Campbell, Jr., eds., *The Common Wealth: Treasures from the Collections of the Library of Virginia* [Richmond, 1997], 42, 43, 120) and Effingham's first commission still exist. Effingham's bears the endorsement, in the hand of Council clerk Edward Chilton, "The within Commission was then by his Excellencies order with the presence of the Council publickly read in the Court house, att the opening of the Court, and ordered to be recorded." *Effingham Papers*, 15 n. 2.

10. *Journals of the House of Burgesses, 1659/60–1693*, 279–280 (quotation); Hartwell, Blair, and Chilton, *Present State of Virginia*, 23; Jack P. Greene, *The Quest for Power: The Lower Houses of Assembly in the Southern Royal Colonies, 1689–1776* (Chapel Hill, 1963), 13–14.

11. The earliest-surviving text of the gubernatorial oath dates to Culpeper's time (Hening, *Statutes*, 2:567–568). For texts of the oaths of allegiance, supremacy, and

test, see Richard Burn, comp., *Ecclesiastical Law* (London, 1763), 2:88–100, 365–361, and Cay, *Abridgment*, 2: s.v. "recusants."

12. The quotation comes from Effingham's commission, *Effingham Papers*, 9.

13. James P. C. Southall, "Concerning George Yardley and Temperance Flowerdew: A Synopsis and Review," *VMHB* 55 (1947): 259–266; Bemiss, *Three Charters of the Virginia Company*, 1, 29, 38; *Adventurers of Purse and Person*, 374–378; Nora Miller Turman, *George Yeardley, Governor of Virginia and Organizer of the General Assembly in 1619* (Richmond, 1959); Kingsbury, *Records of the Virginia Company*, 3:220; John Pory to Sir Dudley Carleton, 28 Nov. 1618, in William S. Powell, *John Pory, 1572–1636: The Life and Letters of a Man of Many Parts, Letters and Other Minor Writings* (Chapel Hill, 1977), 74–75.

14. John Rolfe, *A True Relation of the State of Virginia lefte by Sir Thomas Dale Knight in May last 1616*, ed. John Cook Wyllie and John Melville Jennings (New Haven, Conn., 1951), 34 (1st quotation); John Chamberlain to Sir Dudley Carleton, 28 Nov. 1618, in *The Letters of John Chamberlain*, ed. Norman Egbert McClure (Philadelphia, 1939), 2:186 (2d quotation).

15. Craven, *Dissolution*, 149–175; Kingsbury, *Records of the Virginia Company*, 1:440.

16. *Dictionary of National Biography*, s.v. "Wyatt or Wyat, Sir Francis," 63:1092–1093; J. Frederick Fausz and Jon Kukla, eds., "A Letter of Advice to the Governor of Virginia, 1624," in Notes and Documents, *WMQ*, 3d ser., 34 (1977): 104–129; Kingsbury, *Records of the Virginia Company*, 1:418, 443, 444, 472, 490, 507.

17. Kingsbury, *Records of the Virginia Company*, 2:523.

18. Ibid., 2:530; letters patent from James I, 24 Aug. 1624, ibid., 2:501–504.

19. *Mecurius Aulicus*, 31 Aug. 1644, MSS 9:1 W9703:1, ViHi.

20. Lyon Gardiner Tyler, ed., *Encyclopedia of Virginia Biography* (New York, 1915), s.v. "Harvey, Sir John," 1:45; David Beers Quinn, "Sailors and the Sea: 'The Portly Sail of Ships,'" *Shakespeare Survey* 17 (1964): 21–36, 242–243.

21. Kingsbury, *Records of the Virginia Company*, 1:389, 419; Warren M. Billings, "Vignettes of Jamestown," *Virginia Cavalcade* 45 (1996): 164–179.

22. Kingsbury, *Records of the Virginia Company*, 4:459, 460–461, 461–462, 463–464, 476; *Journals of the House of Burgesses, 1619–1658/59*, 37–42; Billings, *Old Dominion*, 238 (quotation); Craven, *Dissolution*, 322–327.

23. Kevin Sharpe, *The Personal Rule of Charles I* (New Haven, Conn., 1992), 8, 13; J. Mills Thornton III, "The Thrusting Out of Governor Harvey: A Seventeenth-Century Rebellion," *VMHB* 76 (1968): 11–26.

24. Thornton, "Thrusting Out of Governor Harvey," 24–25; Hening, *Statutes,* 1:234; Billings, "Vignettes of Jamestown," 169–171; Samuel Mathews to Sir John Wolstenholme, 25 May 1635, in Billings, *Old Dominion,* 251–254; Thomas J. Wertenbaker, *Virginia under the Stuarts, 1607–1688* (Princeton, N.J., 1914), 60–84; Wilcomb E. Washburn, *Virginia under Charles I and Cromwell, 1625–1660* (Williamsburg, 1957), 10–29; Bernard Bailyn, "Politics and Social Structure in Virginia," in *Seventeenth-Century America: Essays in Colonial History,* ed. James Morton Smith (Chapel Hill, 1959), 94–98; Richard L. Morton, *Colonial Virginia* (Chapel Hill, 1960), 1:122–146.

25. *Dictionary of Virginia Biography,* s.v. "Berkeley, Sir William," 1:454–458.

26. Ibid.; Mark Charles Fissel, *The Bishops' Wars: Charles I's Campaigns Against Scotland, 1638–1640* (Cambridge, 1994), 1–62.

27. *Dictionary of Virginia Biography,* 1:454–458; warrant for a commission to Sir William Berkeley, 31 July 1641, Indexes 4214, p. 25, PRO.

28. Articles of agreement with Sir Francis Wyatt, 4 Sept. 1641, Main Papers, 1620–1714, p. 100, HLRO.

29. Warren M. Billings, "Imagining Green Spring House," *Virginia Cavalcade* 44 (1994): 84–95.

30. Wilcomb E. Washburn, *The Governor and the Rebel: A History of Bacon's Rebellion in Virginia* (Chapel Hill, 1957), 1–16; Jane Carson, *Bacon's Rebellion, 1676–1976* (Jamestown, Va., 1976), 34–60; Stephen Saunders Webb, *1676: The End of American Independence* (New York, 1984), 3–163.

31. Kingsbury, *Records of the Virginia Company,* 1:534, 4:220–222; *Dictionary of Virginia Biography,* s.v. "Bennett, Richard," 1:445–447; John Bennett Boddie, *Seventeenth Century Isle of Wight County: A History of the County of Isle of Wight, Virginia, during the Seventeenth Century, including Abstracts of the County Records* (Chicago, 1938), 34–53; *Adventurers of Purse and Person,* 111–112.

32. Mary Nicholson Browne, "Governor Richard Bennett," *Maryland Historical Magazine* 9 (1914): 307–315; *Dictionary of Virginia Biography,* s.v. "Bennett, Richard," and "Bland, Anna Bennett," 1:445–446, 2:1–3; Leonard, *General Assembly Register,* xix, 8.

33. Boddie, *Seventeenth Century Isle of Wight County,* 54–76; renewal of title to Green Spring, 9 Oct. 1652, Virginia Miscellaneous Papers, 1606–1692, DLC; deed of sale to Richard Bennett, 30 Mar. 1655, in Robinson, "Notes," 117; Berkeley to Charles Calvert, ca. 28 Apr. 1663, Proceedings of the Council of Maryland, 1636–1667, Archives of Maryland, Liber H.H., 173–175, Hall of Records, Annapolis.

34. *Adventurers of Purse and Person,* 248–253; Digges to Samuel Hartlib, 21 June 1654, in Samuel Hartlib, *The Reformed Virginia Silk-worm, Or, a Rare and New Discovery of*

A speedy way, and easie meanes, found out by a young Lady in England, she having made full proof thereof in May, Anno 1652 ... (London, 1655), 27–28; instructions to Digges, 15 Dec. 1656, *Journals of the House of Burgesses, 1619–1658/59,* 105; commission to Berkeley and others as members of the Council for Foreign Plantations, [1 Dec.] 1660, CO 1/14, fol. 112, PRO; Berkeley to Charles II, ca. June 1664, CO 1/18, fol. 202, PRO; Privy Council Minutes, 10 Aug., 5 Oct., 16 Nov., and 25 Nov. 1664, PC 2/57, fols. 181, 234, 293, 302, PRO; Berkeley to Henry Bennet, 1st earl of Arlington, 13 June 1670, CO 1/25, fols. 80–81, PRO; *Minutes of Council and General Court,* 207; Warren M. Billings, "Sir William Berkeley and the Diversification of the Virginia Economy," *VMHB* 104 (1996): 443.

35. Minnie G. Cook, "Governor Samuel Mathews, Junior," *WMQ,* 2d ser., 14 (1934): 105–113; *Adventurers of Purse and Person,* 445–447; [John Ferrar], *A Perfect Description of Virginia* ... (London, 1649), 15; Leonard, *General Assembly Register,* 30–32; LNOB, 1656–1675, fol. 40.

36. Stephen Saunders Webb, "'Brave Men and Servants to His Royal Highness': The Household of James Stuart in the Evolution of English Imperialism," *Perspectives in American History* 8 (1974): 55–80; Webb, *The Governors-General: The English Army and the Definition of the Empire, 1569–1681* (Chapel Hill, 1979), 3–56.

37. Jeffreys has no biographer, although there is a none-too-helpful entry on him in Tyler, *Encyclopedia of Virginia Biography,* 1:49–50. Webb, *Governors-General,* 122–137, provides the most detailed account of Jeffreys's career up to the time of his Virginia appointments and his tenure as lieutenant governor.

38. CO 1/41, fol. 121, PRO; [Jeffreys,] "A Narrative of Some Affairs in Virginia," ca. July 1678, address of James Bray, ca. 6 Sept. 1677, and order-in-council in reference to Bray, 6 Sept. 1677, Coventry Papers, 78, fols. 85, 134–138.

39. Jeffreys to Francis Moryson, 10 July 1678, Sherwood to Sir Joseph Williamson, 8 Aug. 1678, CO 1/42, fols. 294, 304, 345, PRO; Susanna Jeffreys letters in Coventry Papers, 78, fols. 295, 297, 329, 331.

40. *Dictionary of American Biography,* s.v. "Culpeper, Thomas, Lord," 4:590–591; Fairfax Harrison, *The Proprietors of the Northern Neck: Chapters of Culpeper Genealogy* (Richmond, 1926); L. R. A. Grove, *Hollingbourne Church Guide* (n.p., 1980); David A. H. Cleggett, *Hollingbourne and the Culpepers,* 2d ed., rev. (Maidstone, Eng., 1990); Cleggett, *History of Leeds Castle and Its Families* (Maidstone, Eng., 1990), 68–83; Webb, *Governors-General,* 101–112.

41. Hartwell, Blair, and Chilton, *Present State of Virginia,* 32.

42. Power of attorney from Sir John Berkeley, 8 Nov. 1649, Add. MSS 15857, BL.

43. Douglas Southall Freeman, *George Washington: A Biography* (New York, 1948), 1:447–482, contains perhaps the best succinct explanation, but Fairfax Harrison, *Virginia Land Grants: A Study of Conveyancing in Relation to Colonial Politics* (Richmond, 1925), and Harrison, *Landmarks of Old Prince William: A Study of Origins in Northern Virginia* ... (Richmond, 1924), are also useful.

44. Billings, Selby, and Tate, *Colonial Virginia*, 104–108; Webb, *Governors-General*, 409–410, 419, 421.

45. Warren M. Billings, *Virginia's Viceroy, Their Majesties' Governor General: Francis Howard, Baron Howard of Effingham* (Fairfax, Va., 1991).

46. Effingham to Philadelphia Pelham Howard, [23 Nov. 1683], *Effingham Papers*, 39–40.

47. Effingham to Philadelphia Pelham Howard, 19 Feb. 1683/84, ibid., 50–52 (quotation on 51).

48. Byrd to [Micajah Perry and Thomas Lane], 25 Feb. 1683/84, in *The Correspondence of the Three William Byrds of Westover, Virginia, 1684–1776*, ed. Marion Tinling (Charlottesville, 1977), 1:10.

49. Billings, *Virginia's Viceroy*, 92–98.

50. Aspects of Nicholson's varied career are developed in Bruce T. McCully, "From the North Riding to Morocco: The Early Years of Governor Francis Nicholson, 1655–1686," *WMQ*, 3d ser., 19 (1962): 534–537; and Stephen Saunders Webb, "The Strange Career of Francis Nicholson," *WMQ*, 3d ser., 23 (1966): 513–548.

51. Morton, *Colonial Virginia*, 1:334–341; Susan H. Godson et al., *The College of William & Mary: A History* (Williamsburg, 1993), 1:3–21.

52. *Dictionary of Virginia Biography*, s.v. "Andros, Sir Edmund," 1:173–174; Edith F. Carey, "Amias Andros and Sir Edmund, His Son," Guernsey Society of Natural Science and Local Research, *Transactions* 7 (1913): 38–66; Stephen Saunders Webb, "The Trials of Sir Edmund Andros," in *The Human Dimensions of Nation Making: Essays on Colonial and Revolutionary America*, ed. James Kirby Martin (Madison, Wis., 1976), 23–53; Webb, *1676: The End of American Independence*, 303–304; Jeanne Gould Bloom, "Sir Edmund Andros: A Study in Seventeenth Century Colonial Administration" (Ph.D. diss., Yale University, 1962), 159–183, 199–226.

53. Morton, *Colonial Virginia*, 1:342–350.

54. Compton, as bishop of the Diocese of London, had nominal territorial jurisdiction over Virginia. Because the colony lacked a resident diocesan, ecclesiastical matters often fell through the cracks. Until the 1680s the governors discharged certain matters normally assigned to bishops, but then Compton became bishop and attempted to remedy the situation. To that end, he appointed the Reverend John Clayton, rector of James City Parish, commissary, that is, Compton's representative who had power to do all episcopal duties short of ordaining priests (*Effingham Papers*, 219, 282, 462 n. 2). Clayton never performed as expected, but Compton could do little because he was displaced for his refusal to support King James II, and Virginia was transferred to the See of Durham (David Ogg, *England in the Reigns of James II and William III*, paperback ed. [London, 1969], 175–180; *Effingham Papers*, 274, 282). William and Mary restored Compton, who then appointed Blair commissary.

55. Godson et al., *The College of William & Mary*, 24–29; Parke Rouse Jr., *James Blair of Virginia* (Chapel Hill, 1971), Chapters 5 and 6.

56. Morton, *Colonial Virginia*, 1:356–392; Kevin R. Hardwick, "Mirrors for Their Sons: A History of Genteel Ethics in England and Virginia, 1500–1750" (Ph.D. diss., University of Maryland, 1996), 285–305; Beverley, *History*, 103–104 (quotation).

CHAPTER 5: COUNCILLORS AND BURGESSES

1. Sir Edward Coke, *The Institutes of the Laws of England* (London, 1797), 4:3.

2. Thomas J. Wertenbaker, *Patrician and Plebeian in Virginia, Or the Origin and Development of the Social Classes of the Old Dominion* (Charlottesville, 1910), 1–142; Marcus Wilson Jernegan, *Laboring and Dependent Classes in Colonial America, 1607–1783* (Chicago, 1931), 46–56; Louis B. Wright, *The First Gentlemen of Virginia: Intellectual Qualities of the Early Colonial Ruling Class* (San Marino, Calif., 1940), 38–94; John Eacott Manahan, "The Cavalier Remounted: A Study of the Origins of Virginia's Population, 1607–1700" (Ph.D. diss., University of Virginia, 1945); Bernard Bailyn, "Politics and Social Structure in Virginia," in *Seventeenth Century America: Essays in Colonial History*, ed. James Morton Smith (Chapel Hill, 1959), 90–115; Martin Herbert Quitt, "Virginia House of Burgesses, 1660–1706: The Social, Educational, & Economic Bases of Political Power" (Ph.D. diss., Washington University, 1970); Wesley Frank Craven, *White, Red, and Black: The Seventeenth-Century Virginian* (Charlottesville, 1971), 1–37; Edmund S. Morgan, *American Slavery, American Freedom: The Ordeal of Colonial Virginia* (New York, 1975), 395–432; James Horn, "Servant Immigration to the Chesapeake in the Seventeenth Century," in *The Chesapeake in the Seventeenth Century: Essays on Anglo-*

American Society, ed. Thad W. Tate and David Ammerman (Chapel Hill, 1979), 51–95; Russell R. Menard, "British Migration to the Chesapeake Colonies in the Seventeenth Century," in *Colonial Chesapeake Society*, ed. Lois Green Carr, Philip D. Morgan, and Jean B. Russo (Chapel Hill, 1988), 99–132; Martin H. Quitt, "Immigrant Origins of the Virginia Gentry: A Study of Cultural Transmission and Innovation," *WMQ*, 3d ser., 45 (1988): 629–655; James Horn, *Adapting to a New World: English Society in the Seventeenth-Century Chesapeake* (Chapel Hill, 1994), 19–77.

3. The characteristics in this composite profile derive from data that I compiled for Virginia officeholders in the period 1619–1699. The database, which was drawn from manuscript court records and various genealogical sources, includes governors-general, burgesses, councillors of state, Speakers of the House of Burgesses, clerks of the House and Council, justices of the peace, sheriffs, and clerks of court. It incorporates vital statistics, places of origin, arrival dates, kin connections, occupations, offices held, and landholdings.

4. Warren M. Billings, "The Growth of Political Institutions in Virginia, 1634 to 1676," *WMQ*, 3d ser., 31 (1974): 236–240.

5. The office was erected in 1640 (Robinson, "Notes," 24–25). How the office developed is uncertain as no records are extant. Indeed, it is a provincial post that seems to have escaped the notice of Virginia scholars.

6. If any of these offices was of statutory creation, none of the enabling legislation has come to light. More likely, Sir William Berkeley used a clause in his instructions that empowered him to "nominate and appoint all other publique Officers under the degree of the Councill" as the constitutional basis for founding the places (clause 8, Instructions from Charles I, 10 Aug. 1641, CO 5/1354, fols. 224–241, PRO). Berkeley named the first attorney general in 1643, and he appointed the first auditor and receiver general in the 1660s. The origins of the escheator general are less clear, though they probably date to the early 1660s. An act of March 1661/62 reformed the way land escheated—that is, reverted to the Crown when its owner died heirless—and could be subsequently repatented (Hening, *Statutes*, 2:136–138). Apparently, Thomas Ludwell was the first person to occupy the office.

7. The count derives from the database and Leonard, *General Assembly Register*, xix–xxi, 6–61.

8. Billings, *Old Dominion*, 42.

9. Because the deed books for all the counties do not survive, I used Nell Marion Nugent, comp., *Cavaliers and Pioneers: Abstracts of Virginia Land Patents and Grants, 1623–1732*, 3 vols. (Richmond, 1934–1979), to compute conciliar landholdings.

There is an inherent error in this method because it reveals only the land someone patented, and not the ultimate disposition of a parcel. It is also useless for determining the real estate someone acquired by purchase. The advantage, though, lies in the near completeness of the patent records, which are in the holdings of the Library of Virginia.

10. Hening, *Statutes*, 2:511–512.

11. Hartwell, Blair, and Chilton, *Present State of Virginia*, 39.

12. On at least one occasion, the Council failed to muster a quorum. *Minutes of Council and General Court*, 125.

13. Council minutes, 21 Feb. 1683/84, Monson Family Papers, DLC. The other seven councillors straggled in and took their oaths much later.

14. John Bennett Boddie, *Seventeenth Century Isle of Wight County: A History of the County of Isle of Wight, Virginia, during the Seventeenth Century, including Abstracts of the County Records* (Chicago, 1938), 54–76; *Dictionary of Virginia Biography*, s.v. "Bennett, Richard," "Bland, Anna Bennett," and "Bland, Theodorick," 1:445–447, 2:3–4, 14.

15. Nathaniel C. Hale, *Virginia Venturer: A Historical Biography of William Claiborne, 1600–1677* (Richmond, 1951); *Adventurers of Purse and Person*, 184–186; Robert Paul Brenner, "Commercial Change and Political Conflict: The Merchant Community in Civil War London" (Ph.D. diss., Princeton University, 1970), 97–104; Sarah S. Hughes, *Surveyors and Statesmen: Land Measuring in Colonial Virginia* (Richmond, 1979), 8–10; Warren M. Billings, "Vignettes of Jamestown," *Virginia Cavalcade* 45 (1996): 169; Articles condescended promised and agreed unto by mee Sir William Berkeley, Knight, 4 Sept. 1641, Main Papers, HLRO.

16. Berkeley came to regret the appointment. About 1650 he wrote to Charles II requesting that Claiborne be dismissed for his disloyalty, an action the putative king apparently took, though his order came to nothing. The letters between Berkeley and the king are lost, but Francis Moryson recalled the episode in 1677. Writing to Henry Thynne he told how an exasperated Berkeley sought to punish Claiborne. Moryson to Thynne, 2 Apr. 1677, Coventry Papers, 78, fol. 220.

17. *Journals of the House of Burgesses, 1659/60–1693*, 13.

18. Claiborne to Charles II, ca. Jan. 1677, CO 1/38, fol. 110, PRO.

19. *Adventurers of Purse and Person*, 442–445; J. E. Farnell, "The Navigation Act of 1651, the First Dutch War, and the London Merchant Community," *Economic History Review*, 2d ser., 16 (1964): 439–454; J. Frederick Fausz, "Merging and Emerging Worlds: Anglo-Indian Interest Groups and the Development of the Seventeenth-Century Chesapeake," in Carr, Morgan, and Russo, *Colonial Chesapeake Society*, 58.

20. *Minutes of Council and General Court*, 136; A Proposition concerning the winning of the Forrest, 17 May 1626, CO 1/4, fols. 28–29 (quotations on 28), PRO; Hening, *Statutes*, 1:150, 175, 177, 221.

21. Francis, baron Howard of Effingham, to William Blathwayt, 10 Apr. 1685, 29 Apr. 1686, *Effingham Papers*, 193–194, 254–255; *Adventurers of Purse and Person*, 445–446.

22. In the seventeenth century, "lawyer" and "attorney" were not synonyms, as they are today. "Attorney" was the more general term. It denoted anyone who represented the interests of another in legal proceedings. "Lawyer" signified someone who had been trained at one of the Inns of Court and called to the bar. See Cowell, *The Interpreter*, s.v. "attorney" and "lawyer."

23. *Adventurers of Purse and Person*, 447–449; *Minutes of Council and General Court*, 5–170; Leonard, *General Assembly Register*, 8.

24. Kukla, *Political Institutions*, 84–85, 237 n. 25; petition of George Menefie, ca. 17 July 1637, SP 16/323, fols. 136–138, PRO; answer of George Menefie, 4 Aug. 1637, HCA 13/112, n.p., PRO; bill of complaint, 1 Sept. 1643, C 2 Charles I M11/66, n.p, PRO; *Minutes of Council and General Court*, 477–478; LNOB, 1637–1646, fol. 43.

25. *Adventurers of Purse and Person*, 475–477; *Minutes of Council and General Court*, 9–197; Leonard, *General Assembly Register*, 5, 6; LNOB, 1637–1646, fol. 242.

26. Billings, "Vignettes of Jamestown," 170–171; plat of Rich Neck, 1642, Lee Family Papers, 1638–1867, Section 100, MssI L51 f 212–222,ViHi; *Minutes of Council and General Court*, 494–497; CO 1/10, fols. 25–26, 88, 168–173, PRO; PC 2/51, p. 191, PRO.

27. *Adventurers of Purse and Person*, 727–728.

28. John R. Pagan, "Dutch Maritime and Commercial Activity in Mid-Seventeenth-Century Virginia," *VMHB* 90 (1982): 488–490; Warren M. Billings, "Sir William Berkeley and the Diversification of the Virginia Economy," *VMHB* 104 (1996): 443.

29. This and the previous two paragraphs from Billings, *Old Dominion*, 112–115, 120–126; *Effingham Papers*, 309–310; *Dictionary of Virginia Biography*, s.v. "Allerton, Isaac," 1:102–103.

30. *Adventurers of Purse and Person*, 657–658; Leonard, *General Assembly Register*, 8, 9.

31. Robinson, "Notes," 75.

32. *Journals of the House of Burgesses, 1659/60–1693*, 4. West's descendants remained politically active until well into the eighteenth century. *Adventurers of Purse and Person*, 658–661.

33. In 1660, twenty-one men composed the Council. Ten of them were dead by 1664, and Berkeley filled four of the vacancies, for a net reduction of six.

34. *Adventurers of Purse and Person*, 695–698; [John Ferrar], *A Perfect Description of Virginia* ... (London, 1649), title page; Edward Bland, *The Discovery of New Brittaine* (London, 1651); Warren M. Billings, "Sir William Berkeley and the Carolina Proprietary," *North Carolina Historical Review* 72 (1995): 329; Alan Vance Briceland, *Westward from Virginia: The Exploration of the Virginia-Carolina Frontier, 1650–1710* (Charlottesville, 1987), 53–146.

35. Hening, *Statutes*, 1:293–294; Wesley Frank Craven, "Indian Policy in Early Virginia," *WMQ*, 3d ser., I (1944): 65–82; William L. Shea, *The Virginia Militia in the Seventeenth Century* (Baton Rouge, La., 1983), 73–78; Sir William Berkeley to Thomas Ludwell, 1 Apr. 1676, CO 1/36, fols. 67–68, PRO.

36. Kenneth B. Murdock, *The Sun at Noon: Three Biographical Sketches* (New York, 1939), 64–65; Henry Norwood, *A Voyage to Virginia. By Col. Norwood* (n.p., n.d.), in *Tracts and Other Papers, Relating Principally to the Origin, Settlement, and Progress of the Colonies in North America, from the Discovery of the Country to the Year 1776*, comp. Peter Force (Washington, D.C., 1844), 3: no. 10; Kukla, *Speakers and Clerks*, 54–57.

37. Patent to Winifred Moryson, 13 Aug. 1650, Land Patent Book No. 2 (1643–1653), 232, LVA; patent to Francis Moryson, 24 June 1653, and lease to Moryson, 6 June 1655, Land Patent Book No. 3 (1652–1655), 26, 331; lease for Rare Field, 1 Aug. 1662, Virginia Miscellaneous Papers, DLC.

38. Moryson's role in those negotiations awaits close investigation.

39. Stephen Saunders Webb, *The Governors-General: The English Army and the Definition of the Empire, 1569–1681* (Chapel Hill, 1979), 336–340, 426–430; Wilcomb E. Washburn, *The Governor and the Rebel: A History of Bacon's Rebellion in Virginia* (Chapel Hill, 1957), 92–114.

40. Berkeley to Thomas Ludwell, 1 Apr. 1676, Giles Bland to the commissioners of customs, 1675, Egerton MSS 2395, fols. 133–134, BL.

41. Douglas L. Hayward, ed., *The Registers of Bruton, Co. Somerset* (London, 1907), 1:22.

42. Thomas Jefferson Wertenbaker, *Torchbearer of the Revolution: The Story of Bacon's Rebellion and Its Leader* (Princeton, N.J., 1940), 39–59; *Dictionary of Virginia Biography*, s.v. "Bacon, Nathaniel," 1:271–274.

43. *Minutes of Council and General Court*, 401; Berkeley to Bacon, 14 Sept. 1675, Bacon to Berkeley, 18 Sept. 1675, Berkeley to Bacon, 21 Sept. 1675, Coventry Papers, 77, fols. 6, 8.

44. Billings, Selby, and Tate, *Colonial Virginia*, 77–96.

45. Quoted in Emory G. Evans's work "A 'topping people': The Rise and Decline of Virginia's Old Political Elite, 1680–1790," unpublished manuscript, 2003, Chapter 2.

46. Parke Rouse Jr., *James Blair of Virginia* (Chapel Hill, 1971), Chapters 1, 2; *Dictionary of Virginia Biography*, s.v. "Blair, James," 1:539–542.

47. Hening, *Statutes*, 2:280 (quotation); election writ, 10 May 1676, Letters and Documents of Sir William Berkeley, 1608–1677, Mss 2596-a, ViU; additional instructions from Charles II, 13 Oct. 1676, CO 5/1355, pp. 111–114, PRO.

48. Hening, *Statutes*, 2:106, 272–273, 282.

49. Ibid., 1:266, 295, 305, 464, 465, 2:145, 289, 485, 3:44, 154–162; *Journals of the House of Burgesses, 1659/60–1693*, 55; Quitt, "Virginia House of Burgesses," 194–205.

50. *Effingham Papers*, 60–64 (quotation on 63); Hartwell, Blair, and Chilton, *Present State of Virginia*, 29.

51. Leonard, *General Assembly Register*, 32–53; Quitt, "Virginia House of Burgesses," 189–192.

52. Kukla, *Political Institutions*, 186–188; Quitt, "Virginia House of Burgesses," 180–193.

53. Warren M. Billings, "'Virginias Deploured Condition,' 1660–1676: The Coming of Bacon's Rebellion" (Ph.D. diss., Northern Illinois University, 1968), 247–263; *Journals of the House of Burgesses, 1659/60–1693*, 15; Hening, *Statutes*, 2:198; *Minutes of Council and General Court*, 319; LNOB, 1666–1675, fol. 127.

54. In 1676, a full House nominally would have contained forty-one members, two per county, plus one for Jamestown, but the electors of Middlesex and Westmoreland Counties picked a single burgess each rather than the required two.

55. Billings, "'Virginias Deploured Condition,'" 264; Kukla, *Speakers and Clerks*, 65.

56. Quitt, "Virginia House of Burgesses," 68, 291–338; Leonard, *General Assembly Register*, 42–59.

57. These next nine paragraphs derive from my entries on Anthony and John Armistead in *Dictionary of Virginia Biography*, 1:201–202.

58. LNDWO, 1666–1675, fol. 41; LNOB, 1666–1675, fols. 17, 18, 22, 34, 41, 55, 84, 127.

59. Thomas Mathew, "The Beginning, Progress, and Conclusion of Bacon's Rebellion, 1675–1676," in *Narratives of the Insurrections, 1675–1690*, ed. Charles M. Andrews (New York, 1915), 33. Vividly cast, Mathew's account was written in 1705,

shortly before its author's death. There is no doubt that Mathew captured the spirit of the moment he described, but whether Carver spoke the actual words he attributed to him is another matter entirely. By his own admission, Mathew said he set things down as "Close as my Memory can Recollect." Ibid., 15.

60. Stephen Saunders Webb, *1676: The End of American Independence* (New York, 1984), 54–57.

61. Petition of Grace Grey, ca. 1 Aug. 1665, and reply to the petition of Grace Grey, 1 Aug. 1665, CCOB, 1655–1665, fols. 576–578.

62. Richard Beale Davis, ed., *William Fitzhugh and His Chesapeake World, 1676–1701: The Fitzhugh Letters and Other Documents* (Chapel Hill, 1963), 3–57.

63. Ibid., 26–35.

CHAPTER 6: CLERKS AND SPEAKERS

1. Hakewill, *Modus tenendi Parliamentum*, 15–20; John Hatsell, comp., *Precedents of Proceedings in the House of Commons: With Observations* (London, 1785), 2:183.

2. *Minutes of Council and General Court*, 14. A record copy of the oath Sharples swore is in Virginia Miscellaneous Papers, 1606–1692, DLC.

3. Clerks who followed Sharples took a modified version of the pledge he recited, a copy of which is in *Minutes of Council and General Court*, 174.

4. Hening, *Statutes*, 1:266 (1st quotation), 490 (2d quotation), 2:145–146; General Assembly accounts, 13 Dec. 1662, Clarendon Papers, 82, fols. 275–279; *Journals of the House of Burgesses, 1659/60–1693*, xl.

5. Cowell, *The Interpreter*, s.v. "clerk."

6. *Legislative Journals of Council*, 1:14; *Journals of the House of Burgesses, 1659/60–1693*, 245–246 (1st–2d quotations), 248 (3d quotation).

7. Hartwell, Blair, and Chilton styled the manuscript version of their response "An Account of the Present State & Government of Virginia." It was published in 1727 under the title *The Present State of Virginia, and the College*.

8. Ibid., 42, 55.

9. Kukla, *Speakers and Clerks*, 138.

10. William Hakewill, comp., *The Manner of Holding Parliaments in England. Collected forth of our Ancient Records . . .* (London, 1641), [C2].

11. Hatsell, *Precedents of Proceedings in the House of Commons*, 2:194–201.

12. The wording of the respective oaths in ibid., 183–184, and *Journals of the House of Burgesses, 1659/60–1693*, 292.

13. Kukla, *Speakers and Clerks*, 137; Hartwell, Blair, and Chilton, *Present State of Virginia*, 41 (quotation).

14. Kukla, *Speakers and Clerks*, 140; *Journals of the House of Burgesses, 1619–1658/59*, 100.

15. *Dictionary of Virginia Biography*, s.v. "Beverley, Robert," 1:470–471; Sir John Berry, Herbert Jeffreys, and Francis Moryson to Henry Coventry, 31 Mar. 1677, Coventry Papers, 78, fol. 214.

16. Commission of the peace for Middlesex County, 16 Apr. 1669, Middlesex, Virginia Miscellaneous Papers, 1606–1692, 98, DLC; commission to Robert Beverley, 21 June 1675, MOB, 1673–1680, p. 35; commission to Beverley as attorney general ad hoc, 10 Mar. 1675/76, *Minutes of Council and General Court*, 434; *Legislative Journals of Council*, 3:1495.

17. Commission to Robert Beverley, 13 Nov. 1676, Hening, *Statutes*, 3:567 (quotation); petition of William Howard, n.d., CO 1/41, fol. 260, PRO.

18. Address to Jeffreys, 23 Oct. 1677, address to Charles II, ca. 23 Oct. 1677, Some few observations on the insolent carriage . . . Of Robert Beverley, n.d., Coventry Papers, 78, fols. 123–127, 128–130, 329; *Legislative Journals of Council*, 3:1492–1493, 1496 (quotation)–1498.

19. *Journals of the House of Burgesses, 1659/60–1693*, 120; Sir Henry Chicheley to Sir Leoline Jenkins, 8 May 1682 and 10 Aug. 1682, CO 5/1356, pp. 66–69, and CO 1/49, fol. 100–101, PRO; Nicholas Spencer to Jenkins, 8 May 1682, CO 5/1356, pp. 69–74, PRO; warrant to John Purvis, 12 May 1682, Hening, *Statutes*, 3:543–544.

20. Surviving documents that pertain to Beverley's imprisonment and trial are in Hening, *Statutes*, 3:543–571.

21. *Minutes of Council and General Court*, 231, 250, 301, 314, 396, 398, 426, 437, 446; Sarah S. Hughes, *Surveyors and Statesmen: Land Measuring in Colonial Virginia* (Richmond, 1979), 13–19; Kukla, *Speakers and Clerks*, 86–88; *Journals of the House of Burgesses, 1659/60–1693*, 188.

22. *Journals of the House of Burgesses, 1659/60–1693*, 228–230, 250 (quotation).

23. Effingham to Blathwayt, 20 Mar. 1685/86, *Effingham Papers*, 185.

24. Effingham to the Privy Council, 10 Feb. 1685/86; Effingham to James II, 20 Feb. 1685/86; Effingham to Robert Spencer, earl of Sunderland, 20 Feb. 1685/86; James II to Effingham, 1 Aug. 1686, *Effingham Papers*, 237–241, 241–242, 242, 263–264.

25. Order-in-council, 21 Apr. 1687, *Executive Journals of Council*, 1:81. The order gives a glimpse into how Beverley stored the records between sessions. He "Safely putt" them into hampers "for the better Secure Carriage of them, [and] did usually transport them in, from his own house, to the Generall Assembly at James Town." Ibid.

26. Election writ, 17 Feb. 1687/88, *Effingham Papers*, 367.

27. *Journals of the House of Burgesses, 1659/60–1693*, 291–292.

28. Ibid., 292.

29. Ibid., 293.

30. The wording brought the new oath close to one in use in Parliament. See Hatsell, *Precedents of Proceedings in the House of Commons*, 2:183–184.

31. *Journals of the House of Burgesses, 1659/60–1693*, 391.

32. Ibid., 333 (1st quotation), 416, 417, 420, 422; Hartwell, Blair, and Chilton, *Present State of Virginia*, 42 (2d quotation).

33. Henry Elsynge, comp., *The Ancient Method and Manner of Holding Parliaments in England* (London, 1679), 147–151, 287–288.

34. Ibid., 155; Hatsell, *Precedents of Proceedings in the House of Commons*, 2:157, 160, 162–165; Kukla, *Speakers and Clerks*, 3–7.

35. Conrad Russell, *Parliaments and English Politics, 1621–1629* (Oxford, 1979), 1–70; Derek Hirst, *The Representatives of the People?: Voters and Voting in England under the Early Stuarts* (Cambridge, 1975).

36. *Journals of the House of Burgesses, 1619–1658/59*, 93.

37. Kukla, *Speakers and Clerks*, 63–64; Edmund Plowden, *Les Commentaries, ou Reportes de Edmunde Plowden vn apprentice de le Comen Ley, de dyuers cases esteantes matters en ley & de les Argumentes sur yceaux, en les temps des Raygnes, le Roye Edwarde le size, le Roigne Mary, le Roy & Roigne Phillipp & Mary, & le Roigne Elizabeth* (London, 1571, 1579). That Wynne owned Plowden's *Commentaries* is clearly established by his signature on leaf ¶ ii and various notations about the Wynne family that appear on the front and back pastedowns and flyleaves of the two volumes. Still in the original boards and leather bindings, the set is in remarkably good condition, considering its antiquity. It is now in my library.

38. *Journals of the House of Burgesses, 1659/60–1693*, 86; Kukla, *Speakers and Clerks*, 35–46.

39. *Journals of the House of Burgesses, 1619–1658/59*, 93, 114 (quotation). Fauntleroy may have opposed Hill because Hill had been suspended in 1656 from all offices for misconduct in dealing with the natives. Ibid., 99–100.

40. George Jordan to Francis Moryson, June 1676, Coventry Papers, 77, fol. 138.

41. *Journals of the House of Burgesses, 1659/60–1693,* 119; Kukla, *Speakers and Clerks,* 70–73; *Dictionary of Virginia Biography,* s.v. "Ballard, Thomas," 1:307–308.

42. *Journals of the House of Burgesses, 1659/60–1693,* 188. Ballard remained in the House through the 1686 session. Leonard, *General Assembly Register,* 48.

43. Kukla, *Speakers and Clerks,* 77–80.

44. House journal, Nov. 1685, Monson Family Papers, 1, fol. 2, DLC; Kukla, *Speakers and Clerks,* 81–84; Warren M. Billings, *Virginia's Viceroy, Their Majesties' Governor General: Francis Howard, Baron Howard of Effingham* (Fairfax, Va., 1991), 61–66.

45. *Journals of the House of Burgesses, 1659/60–1693,* 333; *Journals of the House of Burgesses, 1695–1702,* 3; Billings, *Virginia's Viceroy,* 94–97; *Executive Journals of Council,* 1:324 (quotation); Kukla, *Speakers and Clerks,* 92–94.

46. *Journals of the House of Burgesses, 1695–1702,* 58, 119–120, 132 (quotation); Kukla, *Speakers and Clerks,* 94–102.

47. *Journals of the House of Burgesses, 1619–1658/59,* 86, 127; Kukla, *Political Institutions,* 169–180.

48. Elsynge, *Ancient Method and Manner of Holding Parliaments in England,* 155.

49. Hartwell, Blair, and Chilton, *Present State of Virginia,* 41.

CHAPTER 7: LESSONS FOR LEGISLATORS

1. Portions of this chapter derive from three of my essays, "Law and Culture in the Colonial Chesapeake Area," *Southern Studies* 17 (1978): 333–348; "English Legal Literature as a Source of Law and Legal Practice for Seventeenth-Century Virginia," *VMHB* 87 (1979): 403–416; and "Justices, Books, Laws, and Courts in Seventeenth-Century Virginia," *Law Library Journal* 85 (1993): 277–296.

2. Wooley, about whom nothing is known besides this poem, wrote the verse on a flyleaf in his copy of Sir Thomas Manley, comp., *An Exact Abridgement of the Two Last Volumes of Reports of Sr. Edw. Coke, Knight* (London, 1670), which is now in my library.

3. Edward Bulstrode, comp., *The Reports of Edward Bulstrode …* (London, 1657), 1: "The Epistle Dedicatorie."

4. William Fulbeck, *A Direction, or Preparative to the Study of the Lawe* (London, 1600), Chapter 1.

5. Sir Edward Coke, *Institutes of the Laws of England* (London, 1664), I:11b.

6. H. A. Holland, "English Legal Authors Before 1700," *Cambridge Law Journal* 9 (1946–1947): 242ff; Howard Jay Graham, "The Rastells and the Printed English Law Book of the Renaissance," *Law Library Journal* 47 (1954): 6–25; Richard Beale Davis, *Intellectual Life in the Colonial South, 1585–1763* (Knoxville, Tenn., 1978), 2:500–514; Billings, "English Legal Literature," 408 n. 18; David D. Hall, "The Chesapeake in the Seventeenth Century," Chapter 2 in *The Colonial Book in the Atlantic World*, Vol. I of *A History of the Book in America*, ed. Hugh Amory and David D. Hall (Cambridge, 1999). The bibliographic data on individual titles derive from John Worrall, comp., *Bibliotheca Legum: Or, A Catalogue of the Common and Statute Law Books of this Realm, And some others relating thereto; From their First Publication, to Easter Term, 1777* (London, 1777); Joseph Henry Beale, comp., *A Bibliography of Early English Law Books and Supplement by Robert Bowie Anderson* (Buffalo, N.Y., 1966); A. W. Pollard and G. R. Redgrave, eds. *A Short-Title Catalogue of Books Printed in England, Scotland and Ireland, and of English Books Printed Abroad, 1475–1640* (London, 1926); Donald G. Wing, *Short-Title Catalogue of Books Printed in England, Scotland, Ireland, Wales, and British America, and of English Books Printed in Other Countries, 1641–1700* (New York, 1945–1951). Dates of publication refer to first editions.

7. John Wallace, *The Reporters, Chronologically Arranged: With Occasional Remarks upon Their Respective Merits*, 3d ed., rev. (Philadelphia, 1855).

8. Sir James Dyer, *Cy Ensuont Ascuns Nouel Cases* (London, 1585).

9. Edmund Plowden, *Les Commentaries, Ou Reportes de Edmunde Plowden vn Apprentice de le Comen Ley, de dyvers Cases ...* (London, 1571).

10. Sir Edward Coke, *Les Reports de Edward Coke* (London, 1600–1615).

11. See, for example, Bulstrode, *The Reports.*

12. Louis B. Wright, *The First Gentlemen of Virginia: Intellectual Qualities of the Early Colonial Ruling Class* (San Marino, Calif., 1940), 146, 202, 264; "An Inventory of the Goods Chattells and Merchandizes belonging to the Estate of Arthur Spicer ... ," 8 Feb. 1701/02, RDWI, 1699–1701, fols. 36–41; William Fitzhugh to Richard Lee, 15 May 1679, and Fitzhugh to Ralph Wormeley, 9 June 1683, in *William Fitzhugh and His Chesapeake World, 1676–1701: The Fitzhugh Letters and Other Documents*, ed. Richard Beale Davis (Chapel Hill, 1963), 65–67, 152–160.

13. Arraignment of George Talbot, 20 Nov. 1684, in *Effingham Papers*, 160–161.

14. Cay, *Abridgment*, I: Preface.

15. See, for example, [Thomas Berthelet?, comp.], *Statutes made and establisshed from the time of Kyng Henry the thirde, unto the fyrste yere of the reigne of … Kyng Henry the VIII* (London, 1543).

16. John D. Cowley, comp., *A Bibliography of Abridgments, Digests, Dictionaries and Indexes of English Law to the Year 1800* (London, 1932).

17. Purvis (fl. 1680s) was an English ship captain from Wapping, Middlesex, who took it on himself to publish the *Complete Collection* without the approval of the General Assembly, which subsequently ordered it suppressed (*Journals of the House of Burgesses, 1659/60–1693*, xlvii–xlviii, 202, 203). Despite the ban, the imperfect compilation continued to circulate for many years. Rare copies survive in the Library of Virginia, the Pennsylvania Historical Society, the Virginia Historical Society, and other repositories.

18. Fitzherbert, *La Graunde Abridgement, Collecte par le Judge tres-reverend monsieur Anthony Fitzherbert* … (London, 1565).

19. Pulton, *An abstract of all the Penall Statutes which be generall, in force and vse* … (London, 1592).

20. Rastell, *A collection of all the statutes (from the begynning of Magna Carta unto the yere of our Lorde 1557)* … (London, 1557).

21. Edmund Wingate and Thomas Manby, comps., *An Exact Abridgment of all Statutes in Force and Use. From the beginning of Magna Charta, Untill 1641* … (London, 1670).

22. Coke, *Institutes*, 4:12.

23. Among the latter procedural manuals were Hakewill, *Modus tenendi Parliamentum*; Henry Scobell, comp., *Memorials of the method and maner of proceedings in Parliament in passing bills* … (London, 1656); and Henry Elsynge, comp., *The Ancient Method and Manner of Holding Parliaments in England* (London, 1660).

24. Thorpe and Pory to Sandys, 15 and 16 May 1621, in Kingsbury, *Records of the Virginia Company*, 3:447. Thorpe's references were to the 1615 or the 1621 edition of Rastell's abridgment, to William Staunford, *Les Plees del coron* … (London, 1583), and to West, *Symboleographie*.

25. Robinson, "Notes," 176.

26. Hening, *Statutes*, 2:246. The statute required county courts to purchase these volumes as well.

CHAPTER 8: A HOUSE FOR THE GENERAL ASSEMBLY

1. Warren M. Billings, "Vignettes of Jamestown," *Virginia Cavalcade* 45 (1996): 164–179.

2. Kingsbury, *Records of the Virginia Company*, 4:93.

3. Sir John Harvey to the Privy Council, 18 Jan. 1638/39, *VMHB* 3 (1895): 30; Hening, *Statutes*, 1:226.

4. Deed of sale to Richard Bennett, 30 Mar. 1655, Robinson, "Notes," 241, 258.

5. Robinson, "Notes," 188–189. The Harvey purchase consisted of six and one-half acres of ground situated in the New Town section. Laid off by William Claiborne in 1625, it sat adjacent to a tract that belonged to George Menefie and opposite Dr. John Pott's holdings. Land Patent Book No. 1, Pt. 1, 1623–1643, p. 7, LVA.

6. Samuel H. Yonge was among the earliest students to grapple with the question of what buildings housed the General Assembly after 1619. As he put the problem, it was one of "the available information concerning the various building used for … meetings of the legislature and for holding courts [being] too incomplete, meager, and obscure to be reduced to a succinct and entirely satisfactory statement" (Yonge, *The Site of Old "James Towne," 1607–1698: A Brief Historical and Topographical Sketch of the First American Metropolis* [Richmond, 1904], 77). Yonge nevertheless concluded that "one of [Harvey's] houses, known as the courthouse" was "most probably" the first statehouse. Then he went on to note that in 1642 Sir William Berkeley received two houses and the appurtenant land from the General Assembly. There, he reasoned, the governor "erected a house adjoining on the west the first statehouse, which thus became the middlemost of three houses, all having the same dimensions in plan, viz., forty by twenty, and forming a block with a frontage on the river of sixty feet and a depth of forty feet." Part of this block, he thought, was what Berkeley sold to Bennett in 1655. Ibid., 77–78.

That interpretation became the accepted reading of the available documentary record. The subsequent discovery of the ruins of a block of buildings that appeared to coincide with Yonge's surmises lay the ground for later assumptions. In 1934, the United States Department of the Interior acquired all of Jamestown Island, save the twenty-two acres belonging to the Association for the Preservation of Virginia Antiquities. Shortly thereafter, the National Park Service undertook extensive digs of the portion of the town site that fell within its jurisdiction. Its archaeologists unearthed more of the building ruin and denominated it Structure 17.

Enter Henry Chandlee Forman. A pioneer in the field of architectural history, Forman worked as chief architect for the Park Service supervising the excavations and writing field reports. The latter formed part of the Historic American Buildings Survey, as well as the basis of Forman's *Jamestown and St. Mary's: Buried Cities of Romance* (Baltimore, 1938). His description of the "First State House" surpassed any that preceded it. Among other details, Forman included a foundation plan and a conjectural elevation of the south facade. The look, he reasoned, must have been inspired by the design of a seventeenth-century London row house. Forman also argued that Berkeley occupied the building and added to it (Forman, *Jamestown and St. Mary's*, ix, 102–116). The latter assertion had no known basis in fact, but it is an illustration of how he often allowed his imagination to run ahead of his evidence.

Forman, like Yonge, was intent on reclaiming for Jamestown and Virginia what he took as their rightful place as the source of American civilization. Consequently, he frequently fused information to fit his preconceptions, thereby misconstruing what he saw. He assumed that the General Assembly was bicameral in 1641; it was not. Then he conflated Harvey's tenement and Harvey's old house, when the record makes plain that the former governor sold two buildings, not one (Robinson, "Notes," 188). Next, although Berkeley received two houses from the General Assembly in 1642, nothing in the known record pinpoints their location, and nothing equates them with the Harvey houses (gift from the General Assembly, 2 June 1642, Hening, *Statutes*, 1:267). Moreover, if those houses were the same as Harvey's, then the Council and the assembly would have had no place to sit. Logically, one would not expect the assembly to vacate its premises just to curry favor with a new governor. Berkeley never lived in the Harvey building, and there was no reason for him to; he already owned the Kemp-Wyatt House. Finally, Berkeley built the town-house block himself. He stated as much in 1655 when he sold to Richard Bennett "the westernmost of the three brick houses which I there built" (deed of sale to Richard Bennett, 30 Mar. 1655, Robinson, "Notes," 241). Forman quoted that passage from the deed, though he failed to grasp its import. Instead, he noted "this statement undoubtedly means that Berkeley built the westernmost and not all three houses. The 'which' refers to 'westernmost'" (Forman, *Jamestown and St. Mary's*, 106, n. 15). In fact, Berkeley constructed the row house about the same time that he started work on Green Spring House, which is confirmed in a letter Secretary Kemp sent him in 1645 (Kemp to Berkeley, 27 Feb. 1644/45, Clarendon Papers, 24, fols. 48–50). The Kemp letter was unknown to Forman.

A recent reevaluation of the evidence by Carl Lounsbury, architectural historian for the Colonial Williamsburg Foundation, casts doubt on the possibility that Structure 17 ever belonged to Harvey. He made a case for another building on Park Service property, Structure 112 (Lounsbury, "The Statehouses of Jamestown," typescript in the author's possession). As Lounsbury observed, unless and until all of Jamestown is subjected to a more-intensive archaeological investigation than those of the 1930s and 1950s, questions about the precise location and employment of the Harvey houses will remain.

7. J. A. Simpson and E. S. C. Weiner, eds., *The Oxford English Dictionary*, 2d ed. (Oxford, 1989), s.v. "state-house" and "capitol."

8. Instructions from Charles I, 10 Aug. 1641, CO 5/1354, fols. 224–241, PRO; Billings, "Imagining Green Spring House," *Virginia Cavalcade* 44 (1994): 90–92; Billings, "Vignettes of Jamestown," 173.

9. *Journals of the House of Burgesses, 1619–1658/59*, 101; *Journals of the House of Burgesses, 1659/60–1693*, 8; Billings, "Vignettes of Jamestown," 173; Hening, *Statutes*, 2:245.

10. *Journals of the House of Burgesses, 1659/60–1693*, 8 (1st–2d quotations); instructions from Charles II, 12 Sept. 1660, C 66/2491 (3d quotation), PRO.

11. Billings, "Vignettes of Jamestown," 175; *Journals of the House of Burgesses, 1659/60–1693*, 24, 25, 27 (quotation).

12. Ludwell to the earl of Arlington, 10 Apr. 1665, CO 1/19, fols. 75–76 (1st quotation), PRO; *Journals of the House of Burgesses, 1659/60–1693*, 60 (2d quotation). The garret apparently sat above a porch, for it is referred to in later years as the "Porch room." *Legislative Journals of Council*, 1:92–93.

13. Samuel Yonge believed that he had identified its foundations and those of its successor, the so-called Ludwell State House group (Yonge, *Site of "Old James Towne,"* 87), but Carl Lounsbury disputed that identification. He contended that the Ludwell State House was actually Berkeley's row house block (Lounsbury, "Statehouses of Jamestown," 13–15). Lounsbury's argument is intriguing, though not ultimately persuasive.

14. *Journals of the House of Burgesses, 1659/60–1693*, 78 (quotation), 106, 110, 135.

15. Beverley, *History*, 86.

16. *Legislative Journals of Council*, 1:57.

17. Instructions from Charles II, 24 Oct. 1683, § 64, *Effingham Papers*, 26.

18. *Journals of the House of Burgesses, 1659/60–1693*, 215–216; *Legislative Journals of Council*, 1:81.

19. *Journals of the House of Burgesses, 1659/60–1693*, 114, 256; Hening, *Statutes*, 2:407.

20. *Journals of the House of Burgesses, 1659/60–1693*, 119, 174, 226, 256 (quotation), 257, 282; *Legislative Journals of Council*, 1:79, 93.

21. *Journals of the House of Burgesses, 1659/60–1693*, 220–221, 244–245 (quotation), 251.

22. *Legislative Journals of Council,* 1:93–94.

23. Ibid., 1:105; Warren M. Billings, *Virginia's Viceroy, Their Majesties' Governor General: Francis Howard, Baron Howard of Effingham* (Fairfax, Va., 1991), 60–70.

24. *Journals of the House of Burgesses, 1659/60–1693,* 282, 283 (quotation).

25. Ibid., 325; *Journals of the House of Burgesses, 1695–1702,* 8, 48, 62, 124.

26. *Executive Journals of Council,* 1:392.

CHAPTER 9: A COURT OF JUDICATURE

1. Sir William Blackstone, the foremost English legal writer of the eighteenth century, summarized the perennial view of the indivisibility of power this way: "However [governments] began, or by what right so ever they subsist there is and must be in all of them a supreme, irresistible, absolute, uncontrolled authority, in which the *jura summi imperii,* or the rights of sovereignty, reside. And this authority is placed in those hands wherein … the qualities requisite for supremacy, wisdom, goodness, and power are most likely to be found." *Commentaries on the Laws of England. In Four Books,* 5th ed. [Dublin, 1773], 1:49.

2. Sir Edward Coke, *Institutes of the Laws of England* (London, 1664, 1797), 4:20–23.

3. Treasurer and Company. An Ordinance and Constitution for Council and Assembly in Virginia, 24 July 1621, in *The Three Charters of the Virginia Company of London, With Seven Related Documents, 1606–1621,* ed. Samuel M. Bemiss (Williamsburg, 1957), 127–128.

4. *Minutes of Council and General Court,* 1–20.

5. Craven, *Southern Colonies,* 166–169; Warren M. Billings, "The Growth of Political Institutions in Virginia, 1634 to 1676," *WMQ,* 3d ser., 31 (1974): 226; Hening, *Statutes,* 1:125.

6. William Sheppard, comp., *The Court-Keepers Guide, or, A plaine and familiar Treatise, needfull and usefull for the helpe of many that are imployed in the keeping of Law Dayes, or Courts Baron,* 2d ed. (London, 1650), 1–94; Hening, *Statutes,* 1:132–133 (quotation). A few records from the monthly court on the Eastern Shore survive and are printed in *County Court Records of Accomack-Northampton, Virginia, 1632–1640,* ed. Susie M. Ames (Washington, D.C., 1954), 1–10.

7. Hening, *Statutes,* 1:303.

8. Billings, "Growth of Political Institutions," 229–232; Jon Kukla, "Counties: Historian Says It's Not Anniversary of Beginning," *Richmond Times-Dispatch,* 27 May 1984, G-2.

9. Hening, *Statutes*, 1:174, 187, 270, 461, 2:58–59 (quotations). The 1662 law also changed the opening dates from the first of the month to the twentieth and specified eighteen-day sessions, Sundays not included. An act of June 1666 moved the Mar. session to Apr. Ibid., 2:227.

10. Ibid., 3:9–10.

11. Hartwell, Blair, and Chilton, *Present State of Virginia*, 22; warrant from James, duke of York, to Sir William Berkeley, 9 Sept. 1662, HCA 1/9, pt. 1, no. 53, PRO; commission from George Villiers, 2d duke of Buckingham, and others, 25 Feb. 1664/65, Virginia Miscellaneous Papers, 1606–1692, fol. 21, DLC; commission from James, duke of York, to Francis Howard, baron Howard of Effingham, 20 Oct. 1683, *Effingham Papers*, 16; Hening, *Statutes*, 1:466–467, 537–538; Bruce, *Institutional History*, 1:702.

12. Hening, *Statutes*, 1:537–538 (quotations); *Executive Journals of Council*, 1:177, 379; Cay, *Abridgment*, 2: s.v. "Plantations"; Lawrence A. Harper, *The English Navigation Laws: A Seventeenth-Century Experiment in Social Engineering* (New York, 1939), 60–62.

13. Hening, *Statutes*, 1:227, 2:44–54; Richard Burn, comp., *Ecclesiastical Law* (London, 1763); Henry Conset, comp., *The Practice of the Spiritual or Ecclesiastical Courts* (London, 1708).

14. John Catlett and Humphrey Booth to Sir William Berkeley, 15 Apr. 1668, ORDWI, 1663–1668, pp. 484–486; petition of the Rev'd. John Waugh, ca. 6 Oct. 1674, and reply to Waugh's petition, 6 Oct. 1674, WDWI, 1665–1677, fols. 217–218; *Executive Journals of Council*, 1:310, 312–313.

15. Warren M. Billings, ed., "Some Acts Not in Hening's *Statutes*: The Acts of Assembly, April 1652, November 1652, and July 1653," *VMHB* 83 (1975): 71; Hening, *Statutes*, 1:397–398 (1st quotation), 2:63 (2d quotation)–64.

16. See, for example, commission to Sir William Berkeley, 12 Sept. 1662, C 66/2491, PRO.

17. Hening, *Statutes*, 3:102–103; Warren M. Billings, "The Law of Servants and Slaves in Seventeenth-Century Virginia," *VMHB* 99 (1991): 59–60.

18. 28 Ed. III, cap. 3, *The Statutes of the Realm* (London, 1810–1822), 1:345; Kevin Sharpe, *The Personal Rule of Charles I* (New Haven, Conn., 1992), 15–23.

19. Magna Carta, ca. 29.

20. Sir Edward Coke, *The Second Part of the Institutes of the Laws of England* (London, 1797), 45–57, esp. 50.

21. Cowell, *The Interpreter*, s.v. "process."

22. Theodore Frank Thomas Plucknett, *A Concise History of the Common Law*, 5th ed. (London, 1956), 424–505.

23. Michael Dalton, comp., *The Countrey Justice, Containing the Practice of the Justices of the Peace Out of their Sessions* (London, 1677), 382–394.

24. Ibid., 467, 539.

25. Sir James Fitzjames Stephens, *A History of the Criminal Law of England in Three Volumes* (London, 1883), 1:350.

26. Blackstone, *Commentaries*, 4: Appendix, ii.

27. Dalton, *Countrey Justice*, 326–545, esp. 539.

28. Cowell, *The Interpreter*, s.v. "tales"; SDWI, 1671–1684, fol. 69; Hening, *Statutes*, 2:63–64 (quotation).

29. Hening, *Statutes*, 2:422; Jon Kukla, "Putting Silence Beyond the Reach of Government: The Fifth Amendment and Freedom from Torture," in *The Bill of Rights: A Lively Heritage*, ed. Jon Kukla (Richmond, 1987), 99–106; Warren M. Billings, "'That All Men Are Born Equally Free and Independent': Virginians and the Origins of the Bill of Rights," in *The Bill of Rights and the States: The Colonial and Revolutionary Origins of American Liberties*, ed. Patrick T. Conley and John P. Kaminski (Madison, Wis., 1992), 335–369.

30. NoOB, 1657–1664, fols. 62–64. Records of Pannell's hearing before the General Court are lost. Nonetheless, a composite picture of what happened can be pieced together from details of similar trials, as well as information taken from Hening, *Statutes*, and Dalton, *Countrey Justice*.

31. Cowell, *The Interpreter*, s.v. "jury." The loss of many of the early records prevents a definitive determination of when grand juries first came into use in felony proceedings. Given that the Council began to follow English practices closely in the 1620s, it seems plausible that grand juries passed on indictments from that time, too. However, the first documented instance of grand jury proceedings in the General Court dates only from the year 1632 (Robinson, "Notes," 76). Grand juries were subsequently introduced at the county level in 1645. Hening, *Statutes*, 1:304.

32. Hening, *Statutes*, 2:59.

33. If Pannell had refused, she could have been forced under a judgment of *peine forte et dure* to enter her plea. The rule, as William Staunford described it, subjected one to being "laid naked upon the bare ground upon his back without any clothes or rushes under him or to cover him except his privy members, his legs and arms drawn and extended with cords to the four corners of the room, and upon his body laid as

great a weight of iron as he can bear, and more. And the first day he shall have three morsels of barly bread without drink, the second day he shall have three draughts of water, of standing water next the door of the prison, without bread, and this be his diet till he die" (quoted in Sir Matthew Hale, comp., *Historia Placitorum Coronæ: The History of the Pleas of the Crown* [London, 1736], 2:319). Hale noted, somewhat laconically, "The severity of this judgment is to bring men to put themselves upon their legal trial, and tho sometimes it hath been given and executed, yet for the most part men bethink themselves and plead" (ibid.). The terrifying prospect of such torture perhaps explains why no one in seventeenth-century Virginia underwent it.

34. The name of the attorney general is not known. It may have been Richard Lee. See Emily J. Salmon and Edward D. C. Campbell, Jr., eds., *The Hornbook of Virginia History: A Ready-Reference Guide to the Old Dominion's People, Places, and Past*, 4th ed. (Richmond, 1994), 115–116.

35. Dalton, *Countrey Justice*, 539. Dalton noted that the principle derived from an act of parliament adopted in 1303.

36. "Acts, Orders and Resolutions of the General Assembly of Virginia, at Sessions of March 1643–1646," *VMHB* 23 (1915): 226–227.

37. Hening, *Statutes*, 1:303.

38. Cowell, *The Interpreter*, s.v. "clergy." The verse reads, "Have mercy upon me, O God, according to thy loving-kindness: According unto the multitude of thy tender mercies blot out my transgressions." If the court favored the plea, then the convict was burned on the hand, albeit sometimes with a cold iron.

39. *Minutes of Council and General Court*, 183–184. In the eighteenth century, the assembly extended benefit of clergy to women and dropped the requirement that a convict actually read the neck verse (Hening, *Statutes*, 4:326, 5:546). Benefit of clergy remained an option until the nineteenth century. Benjamin Watkins Leigh, comp., *The Revised Code of the Laws of Virginia: Being A Collection of All Such Acts of the General Assembly, of a Public and Permanent Nature as Are Now in Force; With a General Index* (Richmond, 1819), 1:632–633.

40. Leigh, *Revised Code*, 1:194, 224, 252; Robinson, "Notes," 261.

41. Dalton, *Countrey Justice*, 542.

42. Pardon for Katherine Pannell, 17 Oct. 1660, and proclamation, NoOB, 1657–1664, fol. 81.

43. All of the cases recorded in the extant General Court minute books involved murder or manslaughter. *Minutes of Council and General Court*, 183–184, 190–192, 252, 259, 319, 320, 353, 380, 404, 426, 428, 429.

44. Affidavits of Thomas Collins and others, 8 Sept. 1663, Miscellaneous Virginia Papers, 1606–1692, 3–5, DLC.

45. Berkenhead had been in the colony only since 1662, when he arrived on the merchant ship *Mary & Elizabeth*. Nothing in the known record suggests that he was anything other than a run-of-the mill indentured servant. Warrant from James, duke of York, to Sir William Berkeley, 9 Sept. 1662, HCA 1/9 pt. 1, fol. 53, PRO.

46. Bill of indictment of John Gunter and others, ca. 16 Sept. 1663, Virginia Miscellaneous Papers, 1–2, DLC. Specifically, the indictment charged Gunter and his co-conspirators with breaching the statute 25 Ed. III, cap. 3. Cay, *Abridgment*, 2: s.v. "treason."

47. *Journals of the House of Burgesses, 1659/60–1693*, 28–29; Hening, *Statutes*, 2:191 (quotation), 195.

48. *Executive Journals of Council*, 1:86–87. The fate of the plotters is unclear because of the loss of the trial record. They were probably tried quickly, condemned, and executed.

49. *Minutes of Council and General Court*, 454–461; list of executed rebels, ca. Feb. 1677, CO 1/40, fols. 241–243, PRO.

50. Thomas Culpeper, 2d baron Culpeper of Thoresway, to the Committee for Trade and Foreign Plantations, 20 Sept. 1683, CO 5/1356, pp. 155–160, PRO.

51. Ibid. Culpeper based his reasoning on two English statutes, 25 Ed. III, cap. 3, and 13 Car. II, cap. 1, and Burton's Case. Cay, *Abridgment*, 2: s.v. "treason"; Edmund Wingate and Thomas Manby, comps., *An Exact Abridgment of all Statutes In Force and Use. From the beginning of Magna Charta, Untill 1641* ... (London, 1670), 550; Sir Harbottle Grimston, comp., *The First Part ... of the Reports of Sir George Croke* ... (London, 1661), 1:148.

52. *Executive Journals of Council*, 1:36.

53. Culpeper to the Committee for Trade and Foreign Plantations, 155–160 (quotations on 158–159); *Executive Journals of Council*, 1:495.

54. *Executive Journals of Council*, 1:26, 38–39 (quotation).

55. Arrest warrant, 9 July 1688, *Effingham Papers*, 392.

56. *Executive Journals of Council*, 1:107 (1st quotation); Petition of Edward Davis, John Hinson, and Lionel Delawafer, 16 Aug. 1688, *Effingham Papers*, 394–396 (2d quotation).

57. Effingham to Robert Spencer, 2d earl of Sunderland, 19 Aug. 1688; Thomas Berry to Effingham, 8 Mar. 1688/89; Effingham to Berry, 9 Mar. 1688/89; Effingham's answer to the petition of Micajah Perry, July 1689; Effingham to Francis Nicholson,

6 Nov. 1690; Effingham's answer to the petition of Edward Davis, John Hinson, and Lionel Delawafer, 3 Dec. 1690, all *Effingham Papers*, 392–395, 397, 407, 407–408, 417–419, 437–438, 439–440; *Executive Journals of Council*, 1:107–109; Susan H. Godson et al., *The College of William & Mary: A History* (Williamsburg, 1993), 1:11; Edmund Berkeley Jr., "Three Philanthropic Pirates," *VMHB* 74 (1966): 433–444.

58. Baltimore to the earl of Angelsey, 28 Apr. 1681, CO 5/723, p. 67, PRO.

59. Depositions of Thomas Allen, Edward Wade, and John Loyd, 20 Nov. 1684, CO 1/56, 98–99, fols. 100–103, PRO.

60. Maryland Council of State to Effingham, 5 Nov. 1684, *Effingham Papers*, 158–159.

61. Arraignment of George Talbot, 20 Nov. 1684, ibid., 160–161.

62. 15 Rich. II, cap. 3, Cay, *Abridgment*, 1: s.v. "admiralty"; Coke, *Institutes*, 4:134–137, 144–145, esp. 137.

63. Effingham to William Blathwayt, 25 Nov. 1684; Effingham to Sunderland, 26 Nov. 1684, both *Effingham Papers*, 163–164, 165–166.

64. Destruction of the Gloucester court records leaves the jailer's name unknown. Talbot was put in his custody because his was the nearest jail to Gloucester Hall, which served as Effingham's residence and was also the place of Talbot's arraignment.

65. Trial record in CO 1/56, fols. 104–105, 106–110, 204–205, 406–410, PRO; Spencer to Sunderland, 12 May 1686, CO 1/59, fol. 255 (quotation), PRO.

66. 2 *Henry VI*, iv. ii. ll. 78–83.

67. *Minutes of Council and General Court*, 31, 127; West, comp., *Symboleographie: Which may be termed The Art, or Description, of Instruments and Presidents* ... (London, 1647), pt. 2, pp. 311–351; Hartwell, Blair, and Chilton, *Present State of Virginia*, 47–48.

68. Hartwell, Blair, and Chilton, *Present State of Virginia*, 48.

69. Hening, *Statutes*, 1:486–487.

70. Ludwell to Henry Bennet, 1st earl of Arlington, 12 Feb. 1666/67, CO 1/21, fols. 37–38, PRO.

71. Jon Kukla, ed., "Nine Acts of the Grand Assembly of Virginia, 1641," 2, typescript in author's possession.

72. Hening, *Statutes*, 1:270–272, 273–274 (quotation), 275–276.

73. Ibid., 1:295, 303–304, 305, 461, 474, 485–486, 2:23–24, 58–63, 65–69, 71–72, 167–168, 315, 503; Ludwell to Arlington, 12 Feb. 1666/67, CO 1/21, fols. 37–38 (quotation), PRO.

74. Robinson, "Notes," 83; *Minutes of Council and General Court*, 206, 207, 210, 424; Cowell, *The Interpreter*, s.v. "non suit" (quotation).

75. John M. Murrin and A. G. Roeber, "Trial by Jury: The Virginia Paradox," in Kukla, *Bill of Rights*, 112–117.

76. Hening, *Statutes*, 1:267, 314, 2:145.

77. *Minutes of Council and General Court*, 252.

78. Jennings Cropper Wise, *Col. John Wise of England and Virginia (1617–1695): His Ancestors and Descendants* (Richmond, 1918), 36–43; *Adventurers of Purse and Person*, 541–543.

79. Privy Council to Sir William Berkeley, 11 Nov. 1668, CO 1/23, fol. 150, PRO.

80. Ibid.; Arlington to Berkeley, 23 Nov. 1668, John Grenville, 1st earl of Bath, to Berkeley, 27 Nov. 1668, CO 1/23, fols. 165, 170, PRO.

81. Ludwell to John Farvacks, 21 Feb. 1669/70, CO 1/25, fol. 16, PRO.

82. Sir Charles Scarburgh to Arlington, 19 Aug. 1670, SP 29/278, no. 15, fol. 207, PRO.

83. Ludwell to Jeffreys, 27 Apr. 1670, petition of John Farvacks to the Privy Council, 21 June 1670, CO 1/25, fols. 61, 82, PRO; Privy Council to Berkeley, 6 July 1670, PC 2/62, p. 215, PRO; Arlington to Berkeley, 21 Aug. 1670, CO 324/2, fol. 2, PRO.

84. *Minutes of Council and General Court*, 228, 239, 240–241.

85. Ibid., 256, 300.

86. The 1662 revision of the statutes in force effectively dropped the requirement that only cases involving things of monetary value above £16 could be appealed (Hening, *Statutes*, 2:65). See *Elizabeth Key* v. *Mottrom's executors*, and Fernando's case, in Billings, *Old Dominion*, 165–169; petition of John Keratan, 14 Oct. 1665, CCOB, 1655–1665, fols. 604–605; petition of Philip Gowen, 16 June 1675, Colonial Papers, LVA; *Minutes of Council and General Court*, 354. All of the appeals in the group were brought within a span of years that fell between 1656 and 1675, which roughly coincides with the period that the General Assembly began the statutory definition of slavery.

87. See, for example, *Charlton* v. *Yeardley* (1642), NoOB, 1640–1645, fol. 116.

88. Hening, *Statutes*, 1:398, 541, 2:65, 169, 265.

89. The vast majority of appellate bills went up in smoke in 1865. Scattered file copies remain among the county court records, whereas the single largest collection of original bills—survivors of the fire—is Colonial Papers, LVA.

90. *Minutes of Council and General Court,* 125–126, 144 (2d quotation), 157 (1st quotation), 234, 279, 297 (3d quotation), 336; petition of Anne Molesworth, June 1668, Colonial Papers, LVA; appointment of Berkeley as umpire in *Woolward* v. *Bacon,* 18 Oct. 1670, *Minutes of Council and General Court,* 233. It is impossible to calculate any meaningful statistical analysis of the patterns described here, given the destruction of the appellate files. The conclusions derive from impressions gleaned from the extant fragments and cases in *Minutes of Council and General Court* and elsewhere.

91. Hening, *Statutes,* 1:272.

92. Petition of William Whittacre re Thomas Bushrod, ca. 5 June 1666, *Journals of the House of Burgesses, 1659/60–1693,* 34–35; Warren M. Billings, ed., "*Temple* v. *Gerard,* 1667–1668: An Example of Appellate Practices in Colonial Virginia," *VMHB* 94 (1986): 88–107. Apart from its content, the Temple case, which concerned a land dispute, is significant for another reason. It and the Elizabeth Key case are the only two appeals to the General Assembly for which files survive largely intact. Key's contains everything but the Quarter Court ruling, whereas the Temple file records Gerard's side of the issue and the General Assembly's order.

93. *Journals of the House of Burgesses, 1619–1658/59,* 84, 92, 96, 103; *Journals of the House of Burgesses, 1659/60–1693,* 5, 12, 16–19, 27, 34; *Minutes of Council and General Court,* 276, 297, 352, 353, 354, 355, 382, 383, 433–434; Robinson, "Notes," 242; assembly judgment, 2 Dec. 1662, Ambler Family Papers, fol. 23, DLC.

CHAPTER 10: THE ART AND MYSTERY OF LEGISLATION

1. Treasurer and Company. An Ordinance and Constitution for Council and Assembly in Virginia, 24 July 1621, in *The Three Charters of the Virginia Company of London, With Seven Related Documents, 1606–1621,* ed. Samuel M. Bemiss (Williamsburg, 1957), 127–128.

2. Council minutes, 21 Feb. 1683/84, Monson Family Papers, DLC; Henry Elsynge, *The Ancient Method and Manner of Holding Parliaments in England,* 4th ed. (London, 1679), 1–77; William Hakewill, comp., *The Manner of Holding Parliaments in England. Collected forth of our Ancient Records …* (London, 1641), [G1].

3. A text of the English writ form appears in *Officium Vicecomitum. The Office and Authority of Sheriffs: Gathered out of the Statutes, and Books of the Common Laws of this Kingdom,* comp. Michael Dalton (London, 1682), 337.

4. Kingsbury, *Records of the Virginia Company,* 4:448–449 (quotation).

5. Election writ, 10 May 1676, Tracy McGregor MSS, ViU; Berkeley to Thomas Ludwell, 1 Apr. 1676, CO 1/36, fols. 67–68, PRO.

6. Submission of Nathaniel Bacon Jr., 9 June 1676, Coventry Papers, 77, fol. 116.

7. Commission from Charles II, 28 Sept. 1683, instructions from Charles II, 24 Oct. 1683, additional instructions from Charles II, 3 Dec. 1683, *Effingham Papers,* 9–15, 16–31, 42–45.

8. Election writ, 7 Mar. 1683/84, *Effingham Papers,* 66. Effingham used the same form when he called elections in 1685 and 1688. Ibid., 218, 367.

9. Sir Edward Coke, *Institutes of the Laws of England* (London, 1664, 1797), 4:7–8.

10. Pory's precise remarks went unrecorded, but then they may never have been reduced to paper because the secretary had "a long time ... bene extreame sickly" before he spoke. *Proceedings of the General Assembly,* 25.

11. Hakewill, *The Manner of Holding Parliaments in England,* [CI].

12. *The Speech of the Honorable Sr. William Berkeley Governour and Capt. Generall of Virginia ...* (The Hague, 1651); *Journals of the House of Burgesses, 1659/60–1693,* 147–149, 251–252, 262, 291–292, 336, 385; *Journals of the House of Burgesses, 1695–1702,* 4–5, 63–64, 105–106, 134, 211; *Legislative Journals of Council,* 1:227; House journal, Oct. 1685, 4–5, Monson Family Papers, DLC.

13. *Speech of the Honorable Sr. William Berkeley.*

14. To the House of Burgesses, 13 Mar. 1659/60, Virginia Miscellaneous Papers, 1606–1692, DLC.

15. Speech to the General Assembly, 19 Mar. 1659/60, ibid.

16. Berkeley also took the unusual step of addressing the Council of State in a brief speech that echoed his desire to cooperate with it. Speech to the Council of State, 21 Mar. 1659/60, ibid.

17. A reference to Richard Lawrence, one of Bacon's henchmen, who disappeared after the revolt petered out and was never seen again. *Journals of the House of Burgesses, 1659/60–1693,* 148.

18. At the time, Virginia was without an explicit naturalization statute. Consequently, the General Assembly naturalized foreign nationals by acts passed ad hoc. See James H. Kettner, *The Development of American Citizenship, 1608–1870* (Chapel Hill, 1978), 3–105.

19. *Journals of the House of Burgesses, 1659/60–1693,* 122–147, 148–149 (quotations), 157–169; *Legislative Journals of Council,* 19–61; Hening, *Statutes,* 2:458–469, 471–480, 498–501.

20. *Journals of the House of Burgesses, 1659/60–1693,* 251–252.

21. Ibid., 262, 291 (quotation)–292; House journal, Dec. 1685, 4–5, Monson Family Papers, DLC.

22. *Journals of the House of Burgesses, 1659/60–1693*, 287–329, passim.

23. *Legislative Journals of Council*, 1:176.

24. *Journals of the House of Burgesses, 1659/60–1693*, 336.

25. Raymond C. Bailey, *Popular Influence upon Public Policy: Petitioning in Eighteenth-Century Virginia* (Westport, Conn., 1979), 9–22; Hening, *Statutes*, 2:211–212, 482; AOB, 1671–1673, p. 16; *Legislative Journals of Council*, 3:1514–1515, 1517.

26. Sir William Berkeley to the Privy Council, [21 July 1662], CO 1/16, fols. 183–184, PRO.

27. Ibid.

28. Hening, *Statutes*, 2:260; Warren M. Billings, "The Cases of Fernando and Elizabeth Key: A Note on the Status of Blacks in Seventeenth-Century Virginia," *WMQ*, 3d ser., 30 (1973): 467–474.

29. *Journals of the House of Burgesses, 1659/60–1693*, 23; Hening, *Statutes*, 2:185, 189, 190–191.

30. Hening, *Statutes*, 2:341–352, 363–366.

31. Ibid., 2:356–357.

32. Ibid., 2:352–353.

33. Ibid., 2:353–355 (quotation on 354).

34. Ibid., 2:356–362. Charles II disallowed all of the June 1676 session laws, but most of the reform laws were subsequently reenacted. Proclamation against Nathaniel Bacon, Jr., 27 Oct. 1676, Coventry Paper, 77, fols. 263–265; Hening, *Statutes*, 2:393–394, 396, 397, 413–415, 418–419.

35. The route to passage is no longer clearly marked. Most of the papers that once documented the process—calendars, daily orders, draft bills, committee recommendations, conference reports, amendments, roll calls, vote tallies—burned long ago. In the case of the assembly's journals, they are skewed more toward the years after 1680 than to earlier decades. These evidentiary losses limit one's grasp of certain key features in the legislative process to the broad outlines and hide others completely.

36. See, for example, *Journals of the House of Burgesses, 1619–1658/59*, 88–89. Generally, a tithable was a free male aged sixteen years or older, male servants of any age, and any African or Indian servants or slaves of either gender. Hening, *Statutes*, 1:361, 2:84, 170, 296, 479, 492.

37. Such petitions abound in the extant assembly records. A particularly representative set of examples is in *Legislative Journals of Council*, 3:1499–1510, 1516.

38. Hening, *Statutes*, 1:143, 2:405, 421, 3:43–44, 48–49.

39. *Journals of the House of Burgesses, 1659/60–1693*.

40. *Legislative Journals of Council*, 1:5–7, 9–10, 54, 58, 111–113, 117–119, 127, 137–141, 144–145, 149–152, 167–168, 171, 172, 181–189, 201, 218–222, 235–244, 249–250.

41. From the House of Burgesses, ca. 5 June 1666, CO 1/33, fols. 239–240, PRO; Hening, *Statutes*, 2:224–226, 229–232.

42. *Journals of the House of Burgesses, 1659/60–1693*, 42–45.

43. John C. Rainbolt, "The Absence of Towns in Seventeenth-Century Virginia," *Journal of Southern History* 35 (1969): 343–360; Warren M. Billings, "Vignettes of Jamestown," *Virginia Cavalcade* 45 (1996): 164–179.

44. Hening, *Statutes*, 2:471–478.

45. Instructions from Charles II, 24 Oct. 1683, *Effingham Papers*, 26.

46. Ibid.

47. The fund was drawn from a percentage of all duties levied in Virginia.

48. House journal, 25, Monson Family Papers, DLC.

49. Ibid., 30, 33, 41.

50. Ibid., 46. Gifts of the governor, the district collectorships traditionally went to councillors of state.

51. Ibid., 48–49.

52. Ibid., 50–53.

53. Hakewill, *Modus tenendi Parliamentum*, 160–175; Thomas Manley, comp., *An Exact Abridgement of the Two Last Volumes of Reports of Sr. Edw. Coke, Knight* (London, 1670), 120.

54. House journal, 49, Monson Family Papers, DLC.

55. Ibid., 44.

56. Three copies of the bill survive. One is part of a clean draft of all the acts that Beverley produced for Effingham early in 1686, and another is a copy of the 7 Dec. version that became the subject of the dispute (both in Monson Family Papers, DLC). The second is in the hand of Council clerk Edward Chilton, and it contains the wording of the amendment written into its margin, meaning that Chilton prepared it after Effingham discovered the omission. The third is a copy Effingham sent to the Privy Council. CO 1/57, fols. 327–331, PRO.

57. Warren M. Billings, *Virginia's Viceroy, Their Majesties' Governor General: Francis Howard, Baron Howard of Effingham* (Fairfax, Va., 1991), 56–61, 64 (quotation).

58. House journal, 57, Monson Family Papers, DLC.

59. Effingham to William Blathwayt, 6–24 Feb. 1685/86; to the Privy Council, 10 Feb. 1685/86; and to James II, 20 Feb. 1685/86, all *Effingham Papers*, 234–236, 237–241(quotation on 239), 241–242.

60. From James II, 1 Aug. 1686; Effingham to Blathwayt, 15 Nov. 1686; and Effingham to the Privy Council, 22 Feb. 1687, ibid., 263–264, 273–274, 278–281.

61. Billings, *Virginia's Viceroy*, 73–76.

CHAPTER 11: ACTS OF ASSEMBLY

1. Compare *Proceedings of the General Assembly*, 39–47, 55–63, with *The Statutes at Large, from the first year of King James the First to the tenth year of the reign of King William the Third* (London, 1763), 1–123.

2. Treasurer and Company. An Ordinance and Constitution for Council and Assembly in Virginia, 24 July 1621, in *The Three Charters of the Virginia Company of London, with Seven Related Documents, 1606–1621*, ed. Samuel M. Bemiss (Williamsburg, 1957), 127–128; Sarah S. Hughes, *Surveyors and Statesmen: Land Measuring in Colonial Virginia* (Richmond, 1979), 1–71.

3. Theodore Frank Thomas Plucknett, *A Concise History of Common Law*, 5th ed. (London, 1956), 316–326.

4. Sir Thomas Smith, *De Republica Anglorum: The maner of Gouernement or policie of the Realme of England ...* (London, 1583), 34, 35.

5. Ibid., 35; Edmund Plowden, *Les Commentaries, ou Reportes de Edmunde Plowden vn apprentice de le Comen Ley, de dyuers cases esteantes matters en ley & de les Argumentes sur yceaux, en les temps des Raygnes, le Roye Edwarde le size, le Roigne Mary, le Roy & Roigne Phillipp & Mary, & le Roigne Elizabeth* (London, 1571, 1579), fol. 369; Sir Edward Coke, *The Institutes of the Laws of England* (London, 1664, 1797), 4:330.

6. Plucknett, *Concise History of the Common Law*, 324.

7. *The Statutes at Large from the first year of James the First.*

8. Hening, *Statutes*, 1:vi–vii; Warren M. Billings, ed., "Some Acts Not in Hening's *Statutes*: The Acts of Assembly, April 1652, November 1652, and July 1653," *VMHB* 83 (1975): 22.

9. Hening, *Statutes*, 1:155–177.

10. Ibid., 1:177.

11. Sir John Harvey and the Council of State to the Privy Council, Mar. 1631/32, *Journals of the House of Burgesses, 1619–1658/59*, 124.

12. The same burgesses and councillors were not at both sessions. One might therefore conclude that the newcomers mustered the strength to force a second revisal. That inference is plausible but insupportable. Although fewer of the councillors of state were at the fall meeting, the key councillors attended both. The fall election produced differences among the burgesses, but once again there was significant carryover between the old and new in the assembly. Hening, *Statutes*, 1:153, 178; Leonard, *General Assembly Register*, 10–11.

13. Hening, *Statutes*, 1:179–202, esp. 180.

14. Ibid., 1:202–229. Much of the legislation written between the two revisions has disappeared. Certain surviving statutes turned up after publication of Hening's *Statutes*. See an act of the General Assembly of Feb. 1636/37, CO 1/9, fol. 30, PRO; "Acts of the General Assembly, Jan. 6, 1639–40," *WMQ*, 2d ser., 4 (1924): 16–35, 145–162; Jon Kukla, comp., "Nine Acts of the Grand Assembly of Virginia, 1641" Acc. 28846, Personal Papers Collection, LVA; "The Virginia General Assembly of 1641: A List of Members and Some of the Acts," *VMHB* 9 (1901): 50–59.

15. Hening, *Statutes*, 1:238–282, esp. 239–240.

16. Billings, "Acts Not in Hening's *Statutes*," 22–76.

17. Hening, *Statutes*, 1:432.

18. Ibid., 1:429–494.

19. Ibid., 3:181.

20. Hartwell, Blair, and Chilton, *Present State of Virginia*, 43. See also *Journals of the House of Burgesses, 1695–1702*.

21. Hening, *Statutes*, 3:181 (quotations)–185; *Journals of the House of Burgesses, 1695–1702*, 164, 176, 182, 190, 191.

22. Parke Rouse Jr., *James Blair of Virginia* (Chapel Hill, 1971), 32–35.

23. Author's database on officeholders, 1619–1699.

24. Ibid.

25. Clerk Beverley maintained a detailed journal of the committee meetings, which is printed in *Legislative Journals of Council*, 3:1518–1533, esp. 1518–1520 (quotations).

26. *Executive Journals of Council*, 2:95, 206, 231, 278; Hening, *Statutes*, 3:229–481. The twists and turns that resulted in the Revisal of 1705 await close inquiry. I hope to publish the results of such an investigation in conjunction with a larger study of statutory revision in Virginia throughout the entire colonial era.

27. Beverley, *History*, 105.

28. Bemiss, *Three Charters of the Virginia Company*, 98.

29. Hening, *Statutes*, 1:125, 168–170.

30. Emily J. Salmon and Edward D. C. Campbell, Jr., eds., *The Hornbook of Virginia History: A Ready-Reference Guide to the Old Dominion's People, Places, and Past*, 4th ed. (Richmond, 1994), 159–171.

31. Hening, *Statutes*, 2:69–84, 87–88, 103.

32. Warren M. Billings, "The Growth of Political Institutions in Virginia, 1634 to 1676," *WMQ*, 3d ser., 31 (1974): 227–232 (1st quotation at 227 n. 5, 2d quotation on 229).

33. Hening, *Statutes*, 1:295, 303–304, 305, 357, 408, 424, 464, 465, 484, 523, 2:26, 62, 70 (quotation), 81, 145, 355, 390, 485–486, 488, 3:150, 153–164.

34. NoOB, 1632–1640, fol. 32; ADWI, 1682–1697, fol. 11; Michael Dalton, comp., *The Countrey Justice, Containing the Practice of the Justices of the Peace Out of their Sessions* (London, 1677), 64; William Lambarde, comp., *Eirenarcha: or, Of The Office of the Justices of the Peace in two Bookes . . .* (London, 1581), 294–302; *The Compleat Justice, Being an Exact and Compendious Collection out of such as have treated of the Office of Justices of the Peace . . .* (London, 1661), 69.

35. Hening, *Statutes*, 1:223–224, 2:78 (quotation).

36. Michael Dalton, comp., *Officium Vicecomitum. The Office and Authority of Sheriffs: Gathered out of the Statutes, and Books of the Common Laws of this Kingdom* (London, 1682), 1–37, 385, 385–444.

37. See, for example, *Proceedings of the General Assembly*, 57, 59; Hening, *Statutes*, 1:122–124, 180–185, 240–243, 2:44–55; Billings, "Acts Not in Hening's *Statutes*," 31–32.

38. *Effingham Papers*, 282.

39. George MacLaren Brydon, *Virginia's Mother Church and the Political Conditions under Which It Grew* (Richmond, 1947), 1:183–184.

40. Berkeley to the Council for Trade and Foreign Plantations, 20 June 1671, CO 1/26, fol. 199, PRO.

41. Hening, *Statutes*, 2:44–45.

42. Lieutenant Governor Alexander Spotswood attempted to assert his right, but the opposition of James Blair and the parish vestries defeated him. Leonidas Dodson, *Alexander Spotswood, Governor of Colonial Virginia, 1710–1722* (Philadelphia, 1932), 189–201.

43. Richard Burn, comp., *Ecclesiastical Law* (London, 1763), 2:21.

44. Hening, *Statutes*, 2:55 (quotation); *Effingham Papers*, 180–181.

45. Hening, *Statutes*, 2:25, 30–31, 56.

46. Ibid., 3:122–124; Susan H. Godson et al., *The College of William & Mary: A History* (Williamsburg, 1993), 1:7–15.

47. Patricia Seed, "Taking Possession and Reading Texts: Establishing the Authority of Overseas Empires," *WMQ*, 3d ser., 49 (1992): 183–195.

48. "Acts of General Assembly, 6 Jan. 1639–40," *WMQ*, 2d ser., 4 (1924): 153–155; Hening, *Statutes*, 1:228, 280, 316, 351, 2:31, 83, 99; Beverley W. Bond Jr., *The Quit-Rent System in the American Colonies* (New Haven, Conn., 1919), 25–34, 218–240.

49. The ensuing paragraphs rest mainly on NoOB, 1632–1640; Fairfax Harrison, *Virginia Land Grants: A Study of Conveyancing in Relation to Colonial Politics* (Richmond, 1925); W. Stitt Robinson Jr., *Mother Earth: Land Grants in Virginia, 1607–1699* (Williamsburg, 1957); John Frederick Fausz, "Patterns of Settlement in the James River Basin, 1607–1642" (master's thesis, College of William and Mary, 1971).

50. Hening, *Statutes*, 1:125.

51. Ibid., 1:227, 248–249, 417–418, 472–473, 2:98–99, 168; Billings, "Acts Not in Hening's *Statutes*," 35, 36–37.

52. Cowell, *The Interpreter*, s.v. "escheat"; Hening, *Statutes*, 1:548, 2:136–138 (quotation on 137), 3:316–318; *Effingham Papers*, 258 n. 2.

53. Darrett B. Rutman and Anita H. Rutman, "'Now-Wives and Sons-in-Law': Parental Death in a Seventeenth-Century Virginia County," in *The Chesapeake in the Seventeenth Century: Essays on Anglo-American Society*, ed. Thad W. Tate and David L. Ammerman (Chapel Hill, 1979), 153–182.

54. Hening, *Statutes*, 1:260–261 (1st–4th quotations), 416 (5th–7th quotations) –417, 2:92 (8th quotation)–95, 288, 295–296; Billings, "Acts Not in Hening's *Statutes*," 43.

55. Ralph Hamor, *A True Discourse of the Present Estate of Virginia, and the successe of the affaires there till the 18 of June. 1614* (London, 1615), 24.

56. Henry Swinburne, *A Treatise of Testaments and Last Wills* ... (London, 1677), 52; Philip L. Barbour, *The Three Worlds of Captain John Smith* (New York, 1964), 50–63.

57. Cowell, *The Interpreter*, s.v. "covenant" and "apprentice."

58. Ferdinando Pulton, comp., *An Abstract of all the Penall Statutes Which be Generall, In Force and Use* (London, 1592), fols. 178–183; Edmund Wingate and Thomas Manby, comps., *An Exact Abridgment of all Statutes in Force and Use. From the beginning of Magna Charta, Untill 1641* ... (London, 1670), 328.

59. Warren M. Billings, "The Law of Servants and Slaves in Seventeenth-Century Virginia," *VMHB* 99 (1991): 47–54.

60. See, for example, T. H. Breen and Stephen Innes, *"Myne Owne Ground": Race and Freedom on Virginia's Eastern Shore, 1640–1676* (New York, 1980).

61. Billings, "Law of Servants and Slaves," 54–62.

62. Beverley, *History*, 232.

63. Helen C. Rountree, "The Powhatans and the English: A Case of Multiple Conflicting Agendas," in *Powhatan Foreign Relations, 1500–1722*, ed. Helen C. Rountree (Charlottesville, 1993), 173–205.

64. Hening, *Statutes*, 1:127, 150, 173, 174, 175, 263, 293–294, 320, 323–326, 326–327, 525, 2:219, 326–336, 341–352; "Acts, Orders, and Resolutions of the General Assembly of Virginia: At Sessions of March 1643–1646," *VMHB* 23 (1915): 235; Wesley Frank Craven, "Indian Policy in Early Virginia," *WMQ*, 3d ser., 1 (1944): 65–82; William L. Shea, *The Virginia Militia in the Seventeenth Century* (Baton Rouge, La., 1983), 25–121.

65. Cay, *Abridgment*, 1: s.v. "arms," 2: s.v. "militia" and "soldiers."

66. Billings, *Old Dominion*, esp. Chapter 8.

67. Shea, *Virginia Militia*, 56–58; Hening, *Statutes*, 1:255.

68. William M. Kelso, Nicholas M. Luccketti, and Beverly A. Straube, "APVA Jamestown Rediscovery Field Report, 1994" (Jamestown, Va., May 1995), 24–32, esp. 31; "1995 Interim Report" (Jamestown, Va., Nov. 1996); "1996 Interim Report" (Jamestown, Va., Oct. 1997).

69. Stephen Potter, "Early English Effects on Virginia Algonquian Exchange and Tribute in the Tidewater Potomac," in *Powhatan's Mantle: Indians in the Colonial Southeast*, ed. Peter H. Wood, Gregory A. Waselkov, and M. Thomas Hatley (Lincoln, Nebr., 1989), 151–172; J. Frederick Fausz, "Merging and Emerging Worlds: Anglo-Indian Interest Groups and the Development of the Seventeenth-Century Chesapeake," in *Colonial Chesapeake Society*, ed. Lois Green Carr, Philip D. Morgan, and Jean B. Russo (Chapel Hill, 1988), 47–98.

70. Hening, *Statutes*, 1:219, 227, 255–256, 262, 521, 2:20, 124, 138, 140, 153, 215, 410–412; Billings, "Acts Not in Hening's *Statutes*," 67.

71. Hening, *Statutes*, 1:323 (quotation)–326.

72. Ibid., 1:453, 2:34, 35, 36, 138–143, 149–156, 193–194, 218–220, 280–281, 283, 316–317; Billings, "Acts Not in Hening's *Statutes*," 64–68, 69, 72.

73. Billings, *Old Dominion*, 230–235; Wilcomb E. Washburn, *The Governor and the Rebel: A History of Bacon's Rebellion in Virginia* (Chapel Hill, 1957), 40–48, 75–76; Shea, *Virginia Militia*, 109–111.

74. Martha W. McCartney, "Cockacoeske, Queen of Pamunkey: Diplomat and Suzeraine," *Powhatan's Mantle*, 179–182.

75. Sir William Blackstone, *Commentaries on the Laws of England. In Four Books*, 5th ed. (Dublin, 1773), 1:107–108.

76. Sir Thomas Ireland, comp., *An Exact Abridgment in English, Of the eleven Books of Reports of the Learned Sir Edward Coke, Knight, late Lord Chiefe Justice of England, and of the Councell of Estates to his Majesty, King James*, 2d impression (London, 1651), 271–273; George Dargo, *Roots of the Republic: A New Perspective on Early American Constitutionalism* (New York, 1974), 53–57.

77. William Fitzhugh to Ralph Wormeley II, 9 June 1683, in *William Fitzhugh and His Chesapeake World, 1676–1701: The Fitzhugh Letters and Other Documents* ed., Richard Beale Davis (Chapel Hill, 1963), 153.

78. Ibid., 152–160; Ralph T. Barton, ed., *Virginia Colonial Decisions: The Reports by Sir Randolph and by Edward Barradall of Decisions of the General Court of Virginia, 1728–1741* (Boston, 1909), 1:B1–B2.

79. Coke, *Institutes*, 4:282–288.

80. Thomas Cary Johnson Jr., ed., *A Proclamation for setling the Plantation of Virginia, 1625* (Charlottesville, 1946), [27].

81. Commission from Charles II, 3 June 1650, CO 5/1354, fols. 243 (quotation)–252, PRO; Salmon and Campbell, *Hornbook of Virginia*, 88.

82. See, for example, Instructions from Charles I, 10 Aug. 1641, CO 5/1354, fols. 224–241, PRO.

83. Hening, *Statutes*, 1:167, 172, 194, 221, 268–269, 331, 390, 483–484, 2:47, 88–89, 317; Billings, "Acts Not in Hening's *Statutes*," 32; Hartwell, Blair, and Chilton, *Present State of Virginia*, 40.

84. An Ordinance for encouragement of Adventurers to the several Plantations of Virginia, Bermudas, Barbados, and other places of America, 23 Jan. 1646/47, in *Acts and Ordinances of the Interregnum, 1642–1660*, ed. C. H. Firth and R. S. Rait (London, 1911), 1:912; declaration concerning the Dutch trade, 5 Apr. 1647, Acts of assembly, 1642–1647, pp. 109–111, Acc. 21227, State Government Records Collection, LVA.

85. Letters patent to Sir Thomas Gates and others, 10 Apr. 1606, in *The Jamestown Voyages Under the First Charter, 1606–1609*, ed. Philip L. Barbour (Cambridge, 1969), 1:31–32.

AFTERWORD

1. *Executive Journals of Council*, 2:112.

Index

Index

Dorset, Edward Sackville, fourth earl of, 15–16
Dorset Commission, 16
Dudley, William, 139
Duke, Henry, 196, 197
Dyer, Sir James, 133

E

Economic diversification, 10–11, 45–46, 75, 77, 214
Education, 203–204
Edwards, William, 116, 117, 122
Effingham, Charles Howard, fourth baron Howard of, 81
Effingham, Francis Howard, fifth baron Howard of, 81–82, 147, 161–162, 163; and clerks of assembly, 59–60, 61, 117, 121–123, 184–188; as governor, 65, 67, 83, 130, 146; and judicial power of assembly, 55, 56, 58, political influence, 179–180, 184–188
Effingham, Philadelphia Pelham, 81, 82
Elections, 18, 33, 104–107, 110; districts, 33, 34, 105; franchise, 18, 104–105; writs of, 18
Elsynge, Henry, 123, 130
Elyot, Sir Thomas, xvi, 66, 67

F

Factions; Green Spring (irreconcilables), 51, 61–62, 79, 80–81, 128; Mathews-Claiborne, 20–22, 26–27, 92–93, 94, 95, 126; moderates, 52; trimmers, 51–52
Falkland, Lucius Cary, second viscount, 73, 99
Farvacks (or Fairfax), Daniel, 167–169
Fauntleroy, Moore, 126
Ferrar, John, 16
Ferrar, Nicholas, 16
Finch, Sir Henry, *Law, Or, a Discourse Thereof*, 135
Fisher, Susannah, 146
Fitzherbert, Sir Anthony, 134
Fitzhugh, Sarah Tucker, 112
Fitzhugh, William, 112–113, 128, 134, 210
Fortescue, Sir John, *Learned Commendation of the Politique Lawes of England*, 135
Fowler, Bartholomew, 196, 197
Fox, Richard, 99
Fuller, Thomas, *History of the Worthies of England*, 135

G

Gates, Sir Thomas, 7, 68, 94
Gauler, Henry, 146
General Assembly
  annual sessions, 53
  bicameral, 27–28, 76
  calling, 7, 174–175
  clerks, 8, 39, 115–117
  committees, 10, 20
  Crown approves, 15–16
  Crown disallows bills, 179, 184, 185–186, 189
  elects governors, 35–36, 40–41, 76, 77–78
  first session (1619), xvi–xvii, 7–10, 141
  influence of increased, 34–36
    reduced, 47, 49, 170–171, 188–189
  judicial power of, 7, 19, 55–58, 149, 169–171
  legislative process, 173–189
  "Long Assembly," 43, 106, 107–108, 175–176
  members, 9–10, 87–89
  parliamentary privileges of, 17
    procedure, 59–60, 182–184, 185–188
  petitions to, 182–183
  unicameral (1619–1642), 8–9, 20
  See also Burgesses; Council; House of Burgesses
General Court, 149, 151, 152, 155–156, 166, 167–170
Gilbert, Thomas, 111
Godwin, Thomas, 47, 108, 126–127
Governors: as legislator, 173–180; governor's commissions, 12, 14, 66–67; governor's instructions, 16, 53–54, 66–67; proclamations, 58–59
Grapes, 11
Green Spring, 51, 75, 146. *See also* Factions
Grey, Francis, 112
Grey, Grace, 112
Gwynn, Humphrey, 167

H

Hakewill, William, 115
Hammond, John, 34
Hamor, Ralph, 204
Harmer, Ambrose, 126
Harrison, Benjamin, 196, 197
Hartwell, Henry, 116, 117, 148

Index

Meade, John, 116, 117–118
Menefie, George, 21, 93–94
Middle Plantation, 146, 148, 213
Milner, Thomas, 51, 120–121, 128, 188
Monthly courts, 150, 198
Moray, Alexander, 200
Moryson, Francis, 44–45, 51, 52–53, 99–100, 184, 195; *Lawes of Virginia Now in Force*, 134; royal commissioner, 49, 53, 100; Speaker, 100, 118–119

N

Native Americans, 98–99, 101–102, 207–208. *See also* Anglo-Powhatan War (1622–1632); Anglo-Powhatan War (1644–1646)
Navigation Acts (1651), 31, 35; (1696), 152
Necotowance, 29, 208
Newport, Christopher, 97
Nicholson, Francis, 65, 82–83, 102; governor, 68, 84–85, 104, 129, 180, 197, 213; lieutenant governor, 83, 123
Norfolk, Henry Howard, sixth duke of, 81
Northern Neck Proprietary, 46, 80, 98, 100
Norwood, Henry, 99

O

Opechancanough, 11, 28–29, 70, 208
Oversee, Simon, 96

P

Page, Francis, 122, 123, 196
Page, John, 77, 123
Page, Matthew, 196, 197
Pannell, Katherine, 156–159
Panton, Anthony, 94
Pate, Thomas, 109, 139, 201
Peirce, William, 94
Perry, Henry, 94
Perry, Micajah, 162
Peterborough, Henry Mordaunt, earl of, 81
Pierse, Thomas, 8
Pirates, 161–162
Plant-cutting riot, 80–81, 109, 112, 160–161
Plowden, Edmund, 133
Pory, John, 7–8, 37, 87, 115, 177
Pott, John, 20
Pountis, John, 14
Powhatan Uprising (1622), 11. *See also* Anglo-Powhatan War (1622–1632)

Powhatan Uprising (1644), 28. *See also* Anglo-Powhatan War (1644–1646)
Pulton, Ferdinando, 134
Purvis, John, *Complete Collection of All the Laws of Virginia Now in Force*, 134
Pyland, James, 34

Q

Quarter Court, 149, 150, 151

R

Randolph, Henry, 44–45, 118–119, 195
Randolph, William, 129
Rastell, John, *Terms de la Ley*, 136
Rastell, William, 134
Reade, William, 139
Religion, 29; laws relating to, 193, 200–201. *See also* Church of England
Roe, Sir Thomas, 16
Rolfe, John, 204
Roper, William, 63
Rousby, Christopher, 162–163

S

St. German, Christopher, *Dialogues in English, Between a Doctor of Divinity, and a Student of the Laws of England*, 135
Sandys, Sir Edwin, 5–6, 10–11, 65, 68, 91, 137
Sandys, George, 26
Scarburgh, Charles, 128
Scarburgh, Sir Charles, 168
Scarburgh, Edmund, 126, 167–169, 181
Secretary of the colony, 22
Sharples, Edward, 115
Sheriffs, 105–107, 199–200
Sherwood, William, 79, 121, 146–147, 148, 188–189
Silk, 11, 77
Slavery, 159–160, 204–207
Smith, John (alias Francis Dade), 36, 39, 159
Smith, Robert, 95, 100
Smith, Sir Thomas, 5, 14
Smith, Sir Thomas, *De Republica Anglorum*, 135, 137, 192
Soane, Henry, 125, 126
Speaker. *See* House of Burgesses
Spelman, Henry, 19
Spencer, Nicholas, 51, 55, 117, 147, 159–160, 164
Spicer, Arthur, 134

A Little Parliament: The Virginia General Assembly in the Seventeenth Century was designed by Calvin Smith of the Virginia Department of General Services, Office of Graphic Communications. Page layout was produced by Calvin Smith using Apple Power Macintosh G3 and QuarkXPress 5.0. Text was composed in Centaur. Printed on acid-free Phoenix C/W Tradebook paper, 55-lb. text by Phoenix Color Corp., Hagerstown, Maryland.